Spain and the Independence of Colombia
1810–1825

Spain and the Independence of Colombia 1810–1825

Rebecca A. Earle

UNIVERSITY
of
EXETER
PRESS

For David

First published in 2000 by
University of Exeter Press
Reed Hall, Streatham Drive
Exeter EX4 4QR
UK
www.ex.ac.uk/uep/

British Library Cataloguing in Publication Data
A catalogue record for this book is available from the British Library.

ISBN 0 85989 612 9

Jacket illustration: Francisco Goya, *Los Desastres de la Guerra* 'Y no hai remedio' (V&A Picture Library)

Typeset in 11/13½pt Monotype Garamond by XL Publishing Services, Tiverton

Printed in Great Britain by Short Run Press Ltd, Exeter

Contents

Table and Maps

Acknowledgements

This volume began its life as a doctoral dissertation at the University of Warwick supervised by Anthony McFarlane. I feel immense gratitude to Dr McFarlane for his friendly encouragement and I am proud to have been his student.

Christon Archer, John Fisher, Colin Jones and John Lynch very kindly read the manuscript at various stages in its life and made many useful and improving suggestions. Richard Willis, formerly of the University of Exeter Press, has also been most helpful. Several sections of this book have appeared as articles. I am grateful to *War in History* and the *Colonial Latin American Historical Review* for permission to reproduce this material.

My research in Spain was funded by the British Academy, which I would like also to thank, but it was truly made possible by my partner David Mond, without whom I might never have been in Archivo General de Indias in the first place. I dedicate this book to him.

Rebecca Earle
Leamington Spa

Abbreviations

AC	Audiencia de Caracas
ACC	Archivo Central del Cauca, Popayán, Colombia
AGI	Archivo General de Indias, Seville, Spain
AGS	Archivo General de Simancas, Simancas, Spain
AHNC	Archivo Histórico Nacional de Colombia, Santa Fe de Bogotá, Colombia
AHNM	Archivo Histórico Nacional de Madrid, Madrid, Spain
AQ	Audiencia de Quito
ASF	Audiencia de Santa Fe
BHA	*Boletín de Historia y Antigüedades*
BRAH	Biblioteca de la Real Academia de Historia, Madrid, Spain
BL	British Library, London, England
FO	Foreign Office
HAHR	*Hispanic American Historical Review*
JLAS	*Journal of Latin American Studies*
leg.	legajo
PC	Papeles de Cuba
PRO	Public Record Office, Kew, England
$	The silver *peso de a ocho reales*

A short **Glossary** of Spanish terms used in this book can be found on p. 224. A **Chronology** of political events in Europe and New Granada between 1808 and 1821 follows, on p. 226.

Introduction
'This vile rebellious rabble ...'

In 1808 the country now known as the Republic of Colombia did not exist. In its place stood the Viceroyalty of New Granada, a colony of Spain rather than an independent state. New Granada was certainly not the jewel in the Spanish crown; metropolitan officials considered it a distinctly second-rate element within the Iberian empire. From the monarchy's point of view, New Granada's importance had once lain in the gold-bearing streams of the provinces of Popayán, the Chocó and Antioquia, that in earlier centuries had generated a substantial profit for the Spanish crown in the form of taxes. By 1808, the primitive mines of these provinces had ceased to yield a revenue sufficient to cover the cost of the viceroyalty's administration. Nonetheless, colonial officials had reason to look favourably on New Granada. The viceroyalty offered Spain a strategically useful Caribbean port at Cartagena de Indias, and its population, as Viceroy Pedro de Mendinueta had explained to his successor Antonio Amar y Borbón in 1803, was 'docile'.[1] An *ancien regime* society of perhaps 1,400,000 inhabitants, New Granada did not appear to Spain a particularly problematic colony. Although in 1781 an alarmingly widespread popular rebellion had challenged the right of the crown to impose new taxes, by 1808 Spanish officials believed the majority of New Granada's population to be loyal subjects of the crown. When in February 1808 French troops acting on the orders of Napoleon invaded the Iberian Peninsula, Viceroy Amar y Borbón expected the viceroyalty's population to rally around the stricken metropolis. 'Your love of the Catholic faith, your subjection to the legitimate kings of Spain, your respect for the magistrates and established authorities is famous', he reminded New Granada's inhabitants. The public was exhorted to contribute towards Spain's defence: 'Imitate the heroines of Spain: reduce your expenses, renounce excess. Do not let a single ounce of silver or gold remain on your soil except those destined for the holy use of the Church.'[2]

Viceroy Amar was not disappointed; within months the viceroyalty had donated half a million pesos to the war against Napoleonic France. Yet less than two years later Amar was driven from New Granada by an anti-Spanish rebellion, or 'the excesses of those inhabitants who deck themselves with the name of patriot in order to overturn the legitimate authorities' as he called it. By 1817 Amar's successor Viceroy Juan Sámano would denounce his Neogranadan subjects as a 'vile rebellious rabble' bent on independence from Spain.[3]

In the decade between 1808 and 1817 Spanish officials saw New Granada's population move from being loyal subjects of the crown to a 'rebellious rabble' determined to reject peninsular authority. This transformation was repeated across Spanish America. Between 1809 and 1825 the hemisphere was engulfed in a wave of revolution that destroyed the Spanish empire in the Indies. Colony after colony rebelled, disowning peninsular rule and establishing independent governments. Spanish officials found this transformation from loyalty to sedition difficult to understand, but this did not prevent the metropolis from doing its utmost to retain control. Yet despite great effort, by 1825 Spain had lost all its colonies in mainland Latin America. This work studies the process of imperial collapse in the Viceroyalty of New Granada, the future Republic of Colombia.

The French invasion of Spain, and more particularly Napoleon's capture of the Spanish royal family in May 1808, was the spark that ignited revolt in Spanish America. But the fuse was long. The inhabitants of the Viceroyalty of New Granada at first responded to the French invasion with concern. New Granada's town councils applauded the creation in Spain of a resistance government, the Junta Central, and public outrage over Napoleon's actions ran high. Within a year, however, the surface unity had shattered. In the southern city of Quito a governing council, or junta, was established in competition with those already existing in Spain and soon other Neogranadan cities formed separate juntas intended to govern in the absence of the Spanish monarchs. Although ostensibly loyal to the imprisoned Spanish monarch Ferdinand VII, these bodies were immediately perceived as revolutionary, and by 1812 most had indeed declared independence from Spain. The unifying role played by Spain was not, however, occupied by any other entity. Efforts to create a central government in the colonial capital Santa Fe failed. New Granada instead acquired several competing governments, which soon declared war on each other. Thus, when Ferdinand VII returned to the throne after the defeat of Napoleon in 1814, there was no independent 'New Granada', but rather a disunited collection of smaller states.

The rebellions in New Granada and the other American states had attracted the concern of the anti-French resistance government in Spain itself, although only very inadequate responses had been essayed prior to the defeat of Napoleon. In 1814, however, Ferdinand VII determined to stamp out the spark of overseas revolution. A considerable military force was assembled, and the Viceroyalty of New Granada was chosen as the destination. This army, commanded by General Pablo Morillo, a veteran of the Peninsular War, arrived in the Captaincy-General of Venezuela in April 1815. Finding Venezuela already virtually restored to royal control, Morillo moved his Expeditionary Army towards Cartagena, which was in insurgent hands. After a siege of 106 days, Cartagena surrendered to the Spanish, and Morillo's army soon recaptured the remainder of the country, thus completing the 'Reconquest' of New Granada. Further south, the Audiencia of Quito itself had already been restored to Spain by an army of local royalists under the leadership of Juan Sámano and Toribio Montes. Thus, by mid-1816, the situation of the Spanish in New Granada looked promising. The interior of the country had been recaptured with only derisory resistance, and Spanish officials appeared to be well on the way to re-establishing the colonial government. By 1817, however, the state of affairs had altered considerably. A growing opposition to the royalist military was making life difficult for the Expeditionary Army, and by 1818 General Morillo was predicting catastrophe. In 1819 republican troops routed royalist forces north of the capital, and within a year Spanish control was confined to the northern and southern margins of the country. In 1822 the last Spanish troops withdrew from the viceroyalty, and New Granada, rechristened the Republic of Colombia, became truly independent.

Colombia's War of Independence has already attracted a substantial historiography. José Manuel Restrepo's great work, which remains the keystone for most subsequent research, is concerned fundamentally with the development of the Colombian state.[4] Dozens of books explore the ideas and writings of Simón Bolívar. Others study the causes underlying the move towards independence. John Lynch locates its origins in the economic and social crises confronting Bourbon Spanish America. Indalecio Liévano Aguirre attributes the initial failure of the insurgency to the unresolved social conflicts raging between Neogranadans, while Jaime Rodríguez stresses that autonomy, rather than independence, was the insurgents' primary goal.[5] Interesting recent work has explored the symbolism and ideology of the independence movements, in an effort to trace the origins of Colombian nationalism.[6] Most of this research concerns the victorious insurgents and their supporters. Yet, as Timothy Anna remarked about Mexican independence, the 'vast bibliography devoted to the process of rebel victory tells only half the story of how Spain lost political control'.[7] The war was not only won by the insurgents; it was lost by Spain. Bolívar and his allies did not defeat Morillo's Expeditionary Army solely because the former were better patriots, nor did the only battles take place in the realm of ideology, important though that domain is. Reasons for Spain's defeat must also be sought in Spain itself, and in the destructive dynamics within New Granada's royalist camp.

This book provides a new explanation of how and why Spain lost New Granada. The fall of Spanish government in New Granada will be traced to specific Spanish weaknesses. In the first place, Spain never developed a coherent strategy for responding to its revolted colonies, and attempted to pursue simultaneously a collection of often contradictory policies. Indeed Timothy Anna, whose own work has shed much light on this aspect of Spain's failure, suggests that his study of Spanish policy towards the American insurgencies might be subtitled 'Lessons in How to Lose an Empire'.[8] This institutional crisis lies at the centre of Spain's failed response.

Events in Spain must be considered together with events in New Granada. There, the reconquest suffered not only from the effects of administrative disunity in Madrid, but also from other problems that had long plagued colonial administrators. In New Granada, as elsewhere in Spanish America during the wars of independence, mutual distrust between members of established colonial structures such as the Audiencias and military officials at times overshadowed efforts to defeat the insurgents. Furthermore, colonial officials, like officials in Spain, disagreed profoundly in their proposed cures for the insurgency. Some, such as Quito's President Toribio Montes, advocated a policy of forgiveness, while others, such as New Granada's last viceroy, Juan Sámano, believed that only severe punishment would deter the rebels. Proponents of these different policies clashed openly and, on occasion, devoted more time to undermining the opposing view than to defeating the insurgents. At the highest level, General Morillo and Viceroy Francisco Montalvo came to loath each other, and each plotted the other's downfall. Further conflicts developed in 1820, after the liberal revolution in Spain. With the return of the Constitution of 1812 came a renewed outbreak of factionalism in New Granada, which led to the overthrow of Viceroy Juan Sámano.

Disagreement over policy was but one strand of the royalist crisis in New Granada. Equally serious was the chronic shortage of money suffered by both the army and the civilian administration. Spain, itself hard-pressed for cash, was unable to provide an adequate level of funding for Morillo's Expeditionary Army, which as a consequence looked to New Granada's population for sustenance. The continual demands for food, funding and supplies wore away New Granada's initial support for the reconquest, as did the arrogant and offensive behaviour of royalist troops. By 1817 irritation with the reconquerers was running high. The army's dependence on the populace might not have pressed so heavily had the administration been able to restart the colonial economy. Despite efforts to re-establish the state monopolies, and to revive trade, the reconquest economy remained stalled, able to generate only a fraction of the income routinely provided for the state two decades earlier. Perennially short of cash, the army and the administration relied on forced loans and confiscation to keep afloat. These proved an unstable base for a re-imposition of Spanish control.

Finally, the Expeditionary Army itself was scarcely secure. From the moment of its first landing in Venezuela, the army began to suffer from the ill health that would ultimately reduce it to a state of virtual nullity. British forces fighting in the Caribbean were unhappily familiar with the deadly effects of tropical disease, and Spanish troops too learned to dread service in the colonies. Dysentery, yellow fever, infection and a myriad of other ills had, within a year of its arrival in the Americas, already reduced Morillo's army by nearly a third. Despite considerable recruitment in New Granada and Venezuela itself, General Morillo was unable to restore his army to full size. Moreover, this continual and necessary recruitment proved another source of annoyance to Neogranadans, who came increasingly to view the royalist army as a parasitic oppressor. Forcing civilians to act as unpaid labourers for the army, as well as confiscating their money and possessions, could hardly have been expected to assuage local opinion. The effect of this catalogue of royalist errors was that the inhabitants of New Granada, most of whom had welcomed the expeditionaries in 1816, by 1819 gave enthusiastic support to Simón Bolívar's campaign against Morillo.

Spain, then, not only lacked a coherent policy for counter-revolution, but also failed to carry through the plans that it succeeded in putting into operation. New Granada saw the effects of this non-policy. Underfunded and disunited, royalists in New Granada did not present a convincing picture of the virtues of unity with Spain. The process by which New Granada gained independence was itself an illustration of Spain's failure as a colonial power. The 'systemic dysfunction' in Spanish government noted by Anna impeded a royalist victory, and the destructive behaviour of royalist administrators and officers in New Granada itself virtually secured republican triumph.[9] Spain lost the war as surely as the republicans won it.

The details of this failure form the subject of this work. This study, moreover, seeks not only to explain how Spain lost New Granada, but also to throw new light on a neglected portion of Colombian history. In studies of the War of Independence, the reconquest is usually dismissed with a few paragraphs.[10] This work argues that the period of the reconquest is of critical importance to a serious evaluation of Colombia's War of Independence, and to Spain's loss of its American colonies.

A few words on the term 'New Granada'. In 1808, the Viceroyalty of New Granada was an amorphous space, which included the Kingdom of New Granada, the Audiencia of Quito and the Captaincy-General of Venezuela. The Kingdom of New Granada, in turn, included present-day Colombia, as well as Panama. All these regions were under the nominal rule of the viceroy in Santa Fe de Bogotá but, in practice, the Captain General of Venezuela and the President of Quito's Audiencia functioned in virtual autonomy. I follow contemporary usage by employing the term 'New Granada' when referring to the territory now comprising modern Colombia. The term 'viceroyalty' refers to the entirety of Venezuela, New Granada, Panama and Quito. The terminology is somewhat complicated by the fact that in 1812 the Viceroyalty of New Granada was demoted to Captaincy-General, and its viceroy replaced by a captain general. (This decision was reversed in 1816, when the region was again promoted to viceroyalty.) Thus, during the years from 1812 to 1816 the correct (royalist) title for the region was the 'Captaincy General of New Granada'. The title of the country's capital city underwent similar fluctuations. During the colonial period it was referred to variously as 'Santa Fe', 'Santafé, and 'Santafé de Bogotá'. The preferred republican title was 'Bogotá, a name that was intended to emphasise the city's indigenous origins. This study is concerned with New Granada itself, and, to a lesser degree, with Panama and the Presidency of Quito, which shared jurisdiction with the Audiencia of Santa Fe over the southern portions of New Granada. Moreover, frequent mention will be made to events in Venezuela, whose history is intimately linked to that of Colombia.

PART I

CRISIS
1808–1814

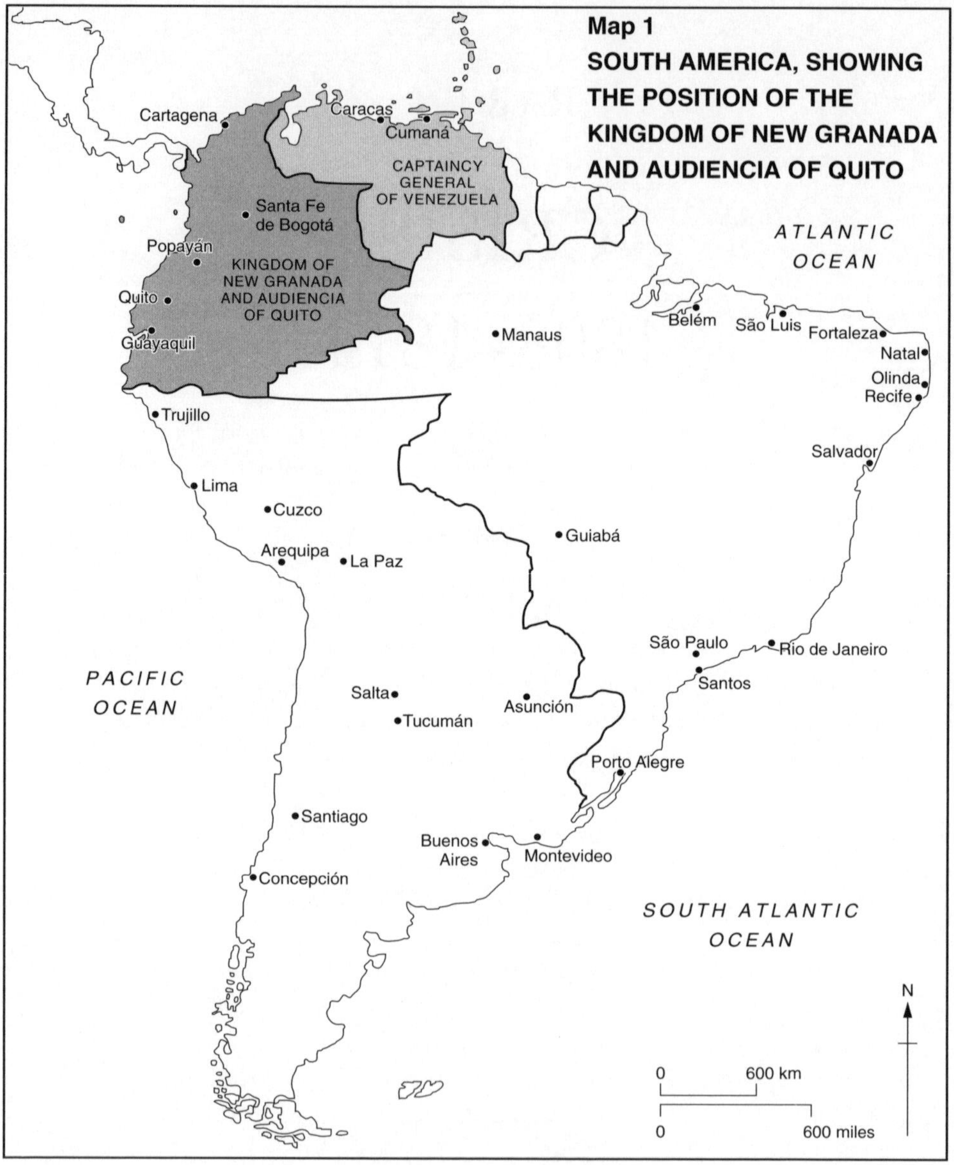

Map 1
SOUTH AMERICA, SHOWING THE POSITION OF THE KINGDOM OF NEW GRANADA AND AUDIENCIA OF QUITO

1

War in Spain and America

The Peninsular War

> The Prince of Asturias [Prince Ferdinand] is a brute, a bad lot … nothing less than a long war would induce me to recognise him as a king of Spain.
>
> Napoleon to Talleyrand, Bayonne, 1 May 1808[1]

The fall of Spain's overseas empire began in 1807, for in that year Napoleon determined to invade Portugal.[2] This decision was to have dramatic consequences not only for Europe, but also for the Americas, as it triggered the start of a decade-long struggle for independence in Spain's American colonies. In 1807, however, the striking repercussions of Napoleon's decision were not apparent, least of all to the Spanish monarchy. Manuel de Godoy, the *de facto* head of Spanish government, naively granted the French army permission to march through Spain, ostensibly in order to attack Portugal. Within a few months, French troops had occupied not only all of Portugal, but also much of Spain itself. The Spanish monarchy responded with a dramatic display of indecision. King Charles IV allowed himself and his son Ferdinand VII to be lured to a conference inside French territory, at Bayonne, where the Spanish monarchs were induced to declare Napoleon emperor of Spain and the Indies. Napoleon appointed his brother Joseph to rule in Spain, and the entire Spanish royal family was imprisoned.

Although it appeared to cement French control of the Iberian Peninsula, the detention of the Spanish monarchs ultimately proved a fatal error for Napoleon, who had failed to recognize the extraordinary enthusiasm felt across Spain for Ferdinand VII.[3] Ferdinand's mere decision to travel to

Bayonne had already caused a substantial anti-French uprising in Madrid on 2 May 1808. The cruelty with which this revolt was repressed further aroused anti-French feeling. When news of Ferdinand's imprisonment reached Asturias, the province rose in revolt. 'Asturians! … let us hasten to throw this treacherous and execrable nation out and to wipe them from the face of our peninsula', urged the newly-created 'Supreme Junta' of Asturias.[4] These sentiments were soon echoed by other 'Supreme Juntas', set up across the country to defend the rights of the imprisoned Ferdinand. When the unfortunate Joseph I entered Spanish territory in July 1808, he found a populace opposed to his rule and in revolt. Patriotic armies were quickly mobilized and, in the same month, French forces suffered their first serious defeat since 1804. Some thirty thousand irregular Spanish troops under General Francisco Xavier Castaños defeated two French divisions at Bailén.

Meanwhile, most of the regional juntas overseeing the resistance to Napoleon combined to form a single body, generally known as the Junta Central. The creation of a semi-united co-ordinating body was a step forward for the resistance forces, but the Junta Central was unable to agree on policy, and its very authority to govern was questioned, not least by colonial governments in the Americas.

Particularly contentious was the Junta Central's claim to jurisdiction over Spanish America. In January 1809 the Junta Central, by this time resident in Seville as a consequence of the French recapture of Madrid, issued an important document summoning regional delegates to attend its sessions. The summons invited not only the Spanish provinces, but also the American viceroyalties to send delegates, and declared that these latter regions would no longer be considered colonies, 'but rather essential and integral parts of the Spanish monarchy'.[5] This remarkable statement, far from inciting the unity of feeling intended by the Junta Central, merely served to engender American resentment. In particular, gross inequality governed the election of deputies. The peninsular provinces, with a population of some 10,100,000, were to elect twenty-six deputies, while the 17,000,000 inhabitants of Spanish America were initially allocated a mere nine. This inequality increased the following year, when a Cortes, or Parliament, were summoned; Spain was granted some 250 deputies, while the Americas were allowed only thirty.[6] This obvious proof of America's continued inferior status immediately became a source of complaint and resentment even among those enthusiastic about the introduction of representative government in Spain.

The war was meanwhile going exceptionally badly for Spain's patriotic resistance; by the spring of 1810 virtually all Spain lay in French hands. The Junta Central had received little support from the population of Seville, and was forced to flee the city when the French invaded Andalucía in early 1810. It set up residence on the island of Leon, off the coast of Cádiz. Confined now to a small island, the Junta Central's claims to represent the entire Hispanic world looked increasingly unconvincing. In February 1810 the Junta indeed dissolved itself and established a new governing body, the Council of Regency. The Council of Regency, based off the coast of Cádiz, soon became 'a kind of hostage' to the powerful Cádiz merchants whose wealth derived from trade with the Americas, and it was scarcely more successful than the Junta Central in convincing the American colonies of its legitimacy.[7]

Prior to its self-dissolution, the Junta Central had resolved to convoke a parliament, or Cortes, to be attended by deputies from both Spain and the Americas. This decision, already controversial because of the unequal allocation of delegates, aroused further controversy when, on 14 February 1810, the Regency proclaimed that the summoning of the Cortes would elevate Americans from degradation to 'the dignity of free men', liberating them from imperial oppression: 'From this moment, American Spaniards, ... your destinies no longer depend on ministers, viceroys or governors: your destinies are in your own hands.' This bold announcement caused 'a profound sensation' among America's active citizenry, and sent tremors of alarm among ministers, viceroys and governors.[8]

The first meeting of the Cortes was held on 24 September 1810, and was attended by 104 deputies, including thirty representing the overseas territories. The Cortes immediately declared itself the natural repository of sovereignty, an act that was to provoke the resignation of the entire membership of the Council of Regency.[9] For the next three and a half years, until the return of Ferdinand VII in 1814, Spain was governed by the Extraordinary Cortes of 1810–13 and the Ordinary Cortes of 1813–14, together with the reconstituted Council of Regency. The Cortes issued a series of decrees intended to reform government and society in both Spain and America, and, most importantly, drafted Spain's first written constitution, the Constitution of 1812.[10] The Constitution limited the role of the king and introduced a number of significant reforms. It established a constitutional monarchy; authority was to reside essentially with the Cortes.

America was declared an integral part of Spain, not a colony. The judicial system was reorganized, a single, universal tax was introduced, the military was restructured, and freedom of the press was decreed. The document was promulgated in the royalist-controlled regions of Spanish America with varying degrees of sincerity.[11]

Meanwhile, the fortunes of the French army were waning. The continued popular uprising, 'the Spanish ulcer', as Napoleon called it, proved a fatal drain on French military resources. Portugal had revolted against French rule in 1808, and with British help had forced French troops to withdraw into Spain. This provided the Duke of Wellington with a military base from which to attack the French, while Spanish irregulars whittled away at the large armies of French generals Soult and Masséna. In May 1813, French troops were forced to abandon Madrid, while allied British and Spanish troops marched through Castile. Then, on 21 June 1813, Wellington struck the fatal blow. French troops at Vitoria were defeated in a major battle that virtually ended their control of the Peninsula. Ferdinand VII was released from captivity in December 1813 and re-entered Spain on 22 March 1814. He was greeted everywhere with great popular acclaim. When Ferdinand reached Valencia, 'the joyous people yoked themselves to his carriage … From Aranjuez to Madrid Ferdinand's carriage was drawn by the people', recorded Karl Marx with disgust.[12] Although Ferdinand initially approved the establishment of the Cortes and the Regency, and appeared willing to accept their authority, he soon decided to ignore the demands of these two bodies. Immediately surrounded by the group of friends or *camarilla* that was to dominate his political life from then on, Ferdinand resolved instead to effect an absolutist coup. Leading liberal members of the Cortes and Regency were arrested; then, on 4 May 1814, Ferdinand issued a decree ordering all aspects of Spain's government to return to their status in 1808, prior to his detention at Bayonne. In particular, the Cortes were dissolved and their actions declared illegal. Absolutism was thus restored to Spain.

Meanwhile, Napoleon, the author of Spain's undoing, was experiencing difficulties on other fronts. His invasion of Russia had failed spectacularly, and nationalist sentiments in Austria and Germany aroused increasing opposition to French rule. On 6 April 1814 Napoleon accepted confinement on the island of Elba. However, despite Napoleon's defeat, war with France had already inflicted severe damage on Spain's imperial authority. While Spaniards struggled against the French in the Peninsula, the framework of imperial government had been ruptured by rebellion in the

American colonies. The first cracks appeared in 1809–10, when many of Spain's American colonies broke with the metropolitan government.

Spanish Liberals, American Juntas

Spain's grip on New Granada had weakened during the preceding two decades. Since 1793, Spain had been almost constantly at war with either France or Britain; as a result, Spanish trade with its colonies had declined precipitously.[13] Furthermore, Spain's consistent bad luck in the field of European politics did little to bolster its reputation as a powerful metropolis. Nonetheless, as Anthony McFarlane has argued, New Granada showed few signs of being a society ripe for revolution. The occasional attempts at revolutionizing the viceroyalty had been resounding failures, and increased conflict between creoles and peninsulars did not at first prevent Neogranadans from rallying to Spain's defence after Napoleon's invasion. Indeed, it was events in Spain, rather than conflicts within New Granada, which propelled the viceroyalty into revolt. Only when the breakdown of royal authority appeared complete did New Granada's provinces strike off on their own.[14]

In doing so, they mirrored the actions of the Peninsula. The dissolution of the Spanish state and the creation of rival governing juntas in Spain marked out a path soon trod by Spanish America. By 1810, Spain was not a unified entity. Sovereignty was divided unevenly between the French, who controlled most of the country, and the resistance juntas that sprang up in many cities. This division was soon replicated in New Granada. First in Quito, then in Caracas, Cartagena and Santa Fe, governing juntas were established, in competition with the Junta Central and the Regency in Spain. These American juntas at first claimed to be patriotic bodies, formed to govern New Granada only during the captivity of Ferdinand VII, but virtually all were to declare complete independence from Spain.

The breakdown of royal government within the Viceroyalty of New Granada began in the city of Quito, capital of the Presidency of Quito and seat of its Audiencia, or supreme court. Soon after learning of Ferdinand VII's imprisonment, a group of eminent Quiteño creoles overthrew the Audiencia's president and created its own junta on 10 August 1809, intended to govern the region in the absence of the king. The aristocratic revolutionaries, many of them personal friends of Xavier Eugenio de Santacruz y Espejo, Quito's greatest advocate of the Enlightenment, were veteran conspirators. Several had already been imprisoned on suspicion of plotting against the colonial government in 1808. They endowed the new junta with lordly titles, and created an elaborate administrative structure, with ministers of state and external trade. At the same time the junta affirmed its support for Ferdinand VII and declared undying opposition to the intruder Napoleon. Subsequent historiography has stressed the junta's conservative nature, but few contemporaries outside Quito were convinced by these protestations of loyalty. The creole leaders of Quito's new junta did not at this stage advocate a break with Spain, and apparently considered themselves to be loyal subjects of the king, but their action was seen as divisive and rebellious. The junta was soon labelled seditious. In southern New Granada it was denounced as a collection of 'heretical insurgents' and 'traitors'. The *cabildo* (town council) of Santa Fe described the junta as 'a hideous black shadow obscuring the glorious picture of American fidelity'.[15]

Efforts to attract support from the region's other cities were unsuccessful. Although some of the smaller towns around Quito threw in their lot with the innovators, the larger cities of Cuenca, Guayaquil and Popayán, not to mention Lima and Santa Fe, all declined to recognize the junta. The Quito junta itself became bogged down in pointless discussions concerning the type of uniform its members should wear. The junta made the further error of launching an attack the city of Pasto, to the north. Pasto, long an economic competitor of Quito, had refused to recognize the new junta. Quito's elite seized this opportunity to vanquish a rival, and sent a large but untrained army northwards. This army was entirely defeated by the Pastusos in October 1809. Quito's junta, already suffering from self-doubt, chose to dissolve itself, thus ending its brief existence.

The junta's members arranged a 'surrender' with the deposed president of the Audiencia, the Conde de Ruíz de Castilla, who promised that no reprisals would be taken. This promise was swiftly broken, and over seventy supporters of the former junta were thrown into jail in early December 1809. On 2 August 1810 an organized attempt was made to free these prisoners, still languishing in prison eight months after their arrest. The attempt failed, and in response the city's garrison went on a rampage through Quito. Many of the prisoners were massacred, along with perhaps as many as three hundred civilians.[16]

Following this attack, President Ruíz de Castilla and his supporters made a few gestures of conciliation, which in no way dispelled the growing hostility towards their government. Then, in late 1810, Quito was visited by Carlos Montúfar, special commissioner of the Council of Regency charged with informing the viceroyalty of the situation in Spain. Astonishingly, the Regency had named as commissioner the son of Juan Pío Montúfar, the Marqués de Selva Alegre, one of the principal conspirators and president of the rebel 1809 junta.[17] Carlos Montúfar's arrival in Quito gave a substantial boost to the advocates of change. He convinced Ruíz de Castilla to permit the formation of a new, quasi-official junta, headed by Ruíz de Castilla himself. The remaining posts were filled by the surviving members of the original junta. The junta recognized the Regency and organized the election of a delegate to the Cortes. This odd situation continued until October 1811, when Ruíz de Castilla resigned and was replaced as president by Quito's bishop, José de Cuero y Caicedo, who later became an outspoken advocate of independence. During this period the junta came increasingly to favour complete separation from Spain, declaring independence on 11 December 1811. Quito thus became an autonomous state, subject only to Ferdinand VII, who was still in captivity in France.

More or less simultaneously with this formation of a second junta, Joaquín Molina landed in Guayaquil, having been appointed by the Regency to replace Ruíz de Castilla as president. Molina opened negotiations with the new junta, which had once again failed to win the support of the province's other large cities. These negotiations went nowhere, and open hostilities broke out in early 1811 between the 'royalist' troops of Molina (aided by Cuenca's governor Melchor Aymerich) and the insurgent army assembled by Pedro Montúfar. Thus by 1811 there was a clear division in the Presidency of Quito between 'royalists' and 'insurgents', or, as they themselves preferred to call each other, 'reactionaries' and 'traitors'. Despite the difficulty which historians now find in determining the moment at which the advocates of autonomy began to favour outright independence, many contemporaries did not have the slightest doubt about the separatist purposes of the Quito junta and its successors.[18]

The origins of Spanish American royalism need explanation as much as the origins of republicanism. Like the revolutionaries, royalists enunciated a variety of disparate opinions on the nature and origin of the move towards independence. Nor did observers necessarily agree on whether a particular individual was in fact a royalist or a republican. The behaviour characteristic of each belief was by no means clear. A typography of royalism is thus difficult. Royalist and insurgent ideologies at times overlapped; both affirmed the central role of certain factors—for example, the Enlightenment—in the move towards independence. Nonetheless, a certain cluster of beliefs, a way of describing the 'American problem', distinguished royalist from insurgent. To focus solely on the points of agreement obscures an understanding of the revolution's dynamics. Fundamentally, royalists rejected the right of the American colonies to form their own governments, irrespective of whether such moves cloaked any revolutionary intent. Because royalists rejected republican claims to legitimacy, reconciliation ultimately proved impossible.

Central to much of Neogranadan royalism was a broad rejection of the Enlightenment. Like many insurgent commentators, royalist observers affirmed that the Enlightenment had paved the way for revolution. But while republicans such as Simón Bolívar justified independence through an appeal to reason and natural rights, many royalists viewed the entire apparatus of the Enlightenment as a noxious infection that poisoned the minds of their contemporaries. José Antonio de Torres y Peña, the Neogranadan author of a cogent antirepublican tract, denounced the 'spirit of false enlightenment that had corrupted the entire world'. Singling out Montesquieu, Voltaire and Rousseau as particular agents of contagion, Torres y Peña deplored the affected, effeminate manners of those degenerate youths hypnotized by style and elegance who later became revolutionaries.[19] The scientific expeditions that are now accorded a central place in the build-up to independence were, to royalist observers, further evidence of European, or more particularly, French, subversion. The Baron Alexander von Humboldt was often singled out as a source of infection.[20] Napoleon was similarly blamed for inciting revolt in individuals who would otherwise have remained loyal subjects of the crown; Peru's conservative Viceroy José Fernando de Abascal memorably described the revolutionary American admirers of the French emperor as 'men destined by nature to vegetate in obscurity'. Events in Europe, Abascal believed, had flung these individuals into an unnatural limelight.[21]

Many royalists likewise concurred with republicans in emphasizing the importance of creole-peninsular rivalry. They differed, however, in their explanations of why this had led to revolt. Insurgents complained of Spanish discrimination, in particular that Spaniards of the lowest classes were promoted over well-qualified locals. These complaints found their most eloquent expression in Simón Bolívar's 'Jamaica Letter', a concise justification of Spanish American independence composed while Bolívar was in temporary exile in Jamaica. In the Letter he lamented Spain's monopolization of all important positions and honours:

> We were never viceroys or governors, save in the rarest of instances; seldom archbishops and bishops; diplomats never; as military men, only subordinates; as nobles, without royal privileges. In brief, we were neither magistrates nor financiers and seldom merchants—all in flagrant contradiction to our institutions.[22]

Creoles, Bolívar explained, were condemned to an undeserved mediocrity by Spain's discriminatory policies. Rebellion was thus justified and appropriate.

Royalists viewed the situation rather differently. Repeating views that had been standard for half a century, royalists maintained that Spaniards enjoyed greater wealth and privileges simply because they worked harder. Torres y Peña, himself a creole, expressed this view clearly in his *Memorias*:

> While [the sons of wealthy creoles] live a life of ease, consuming their wealth, they see hard-working and active Spaniards arrive from across the sea, who apply themselves to the most difficult work, without shunning inconvenience, exposing themselves to danger and not disdaining those activities which are erroneously considered inappropriate for those of noble blood. [These Spaniards] acquire wealth, augment it, become respected, are offered advantageous alliances with families that attempt in this way to ensure the well-being of their daughters, and this causes no little envy in those who observe it.[23]

Where creole revolutionaries saw a conspiracy to limit their authority, royalists saw merely laziness and inaction. Where creoles saw discrimination, royalists saw equality. The incompatibility of these two mindsets is played out with particular clarity in the personal copy of Torres y Peña's memoirs owned by the republican and future vice-president of Colombia, Francisco de Paula Santander. Santander annotated the volume with outraged invective; Torres y Peña's assertion that creoles had enjoyed fair access to official posts prompted Santander to scribble 'just consider the case of Santafé and go to hell'. The complaint that republican creoles were persecuting Spaniards, rather than the reverse, drew a 'damn and blast this doctor don José Antonio Torres y Peña'. The gulf between Santander's and Torres y

Peña's positions may be seen in their vastly different etymologies of a single word: *chapetón*, a Neogranadan synonym of 'Spaniard'. To Torres y Peña, the labels of 'creole' and *chapetón* simply derived from indigenous words for native and foreigner. For Santander, *chapetón* was an Inca term for 'rascally soldier, murderer'.[24] Santander believed Spanish iniquity to be embedded in the very language of the Americas. Torres y Peña maintained that this language instead mirrored the same neutrality that governed a Spaniard's acquisition of greater wealth.

Finally, royalism, the large number of American royalists notwithstanding, was widely considered a fundamentally Spanish phenomenon, rather than a political affiliation. Spaniards were royalists; creoles were insurgents. Although Bolívar's 1813 Decree of War to the Death is often described as an attempt to impose an artificial division into Americans and Spaniards onto a conflict between insurgents and royalists, Bolívar was by no means alone in identifying Spaniards with royalists.[25] In the same year, for example, the insurgent government in Cartagena banned all Spaniards from settling inside the republic's territory, regardless of whether they were royalists.[26] Considerable republican propagandistic effort went into constructing horrific accounts of *Spanish* violence against innocent *Americans*. In describing royalist atrocities carried out almost entirely by non-Spanish troops, Bolívar nonetheless glossed the enemy as Spanish:

> The odious and cruel Spaniards have introduced desolation and death to the innocent and peaceful towns of the Colombian hemisphere … These assassins who call themselves our enemies have violated the sacred rights of man and of nations … They sacrificed our virtuous brothers in the cities of Quito and La Paz. They slit the throats of thousands of our prisoners in Mexico; they buried alive our fathers, sons and friends in the dungeons of Puerto Cabello and La Guaira in Venezuela; they immolated the president and commander of Popayán along with all his unfortunate friends, and now—Oh God!—before our very eyes they carried out in Barinas a fearful slaughter of our prisoners of war and of our peaceful compatriots.[27]

Royalists similarly coded 'American' as 'insurgent'. When Captain General Francisco Montalvo arrived in Santa Marta, a bastion of royalism, he urged the crown to send him lawyers from Spain. The local lawyers were creoles, and thus by definition unreliable. That Montalvo manifested such beliefs is all the more striking as he himself was a creole, born in Havana.[28] Observers never failed to comment on that unnatural phenomenon, the *insurgent Spaniard.* For royalists, such individuals were traitors of the worst sort, the first to be executed when the opportunity arose, while insurgents were amazed that the Spanish executed them at all. Many Americans apparently expected Spanish nationality to act as a Masonic handshake, offering protection from all punishment by fellow Spaniards. *In extremis*, marriage to a Spaniard or other equally tenuous links to Iberian culture would be produced as evidence of loyalist belief. The execution by royalists of *royalist* Spaniards was even more inexplicable to those who regarded Spaniard as a synonym for royalist. When General Pablo Morillo's troops shot a Spanish soldier for desertion, the Santa Fe diarist José María Caballero was horrified: 'if this tyrant doesn't pardon even those of his own nation, what hope is there for us?'[29] Caballero's view illustrates well the tendency to identify Spaniards with royalists. This oversimplified equation attracted adherents among all sectors of the population, much to the annoyance of creole royalist Torres y Peña, who railed against those mistaken individuals who believed that all Americans were revolutionaries.[30]

The identification of royalists with Spaniards represents an attempt to align new political divisions with an equally embryonic, but nonetheless distinct proto-nationalism. This was one interpretative schema. Other Neogranadans told different stories about the relationship between Spain and New Granada, in language that stressed not the absolute difference between the two, but rather their profound connection. Such royalists, like many insurgents, understood the developing conflict in part as a familial crisis. Both modelled the colonial relationship on the family, with monarch and colonies forming a single household. The Spanish monarch represented the parent, and the colonies, children. This is in itself unsurprising; such imagery was the long eighteenth-century's dominant metaphor for kingship. Yet it is possible to detect distinct royalist voices. Where insurgents and royalists differed was in their description of how the metaphorical family ought to function. Insurgents suggested that colonies, like children, might mature and become independent. They should then be allowed to leave home and set up their own households. Only a tyrannical parent would seek to impede this natural process, and tyrannical parents did not deserve to be obeyed. Republican discourse is thus littered with familial imagery suggesting the parental failings of the domineering Spanish. Bolívar's Jamaica Letter again provides a clear illustration. In this exposition Bolívar made repeated use of the parent-child metaphor in order to subvert Spain's claims to authority. In Bolívar's account, Spain, unwilling to allow its children to leave the family home, had forced Americans into 'a sort of permanent infancy'. Indeed. through its actions, Spain forfeited all claim to paternal authority. Thus in Bolívar's text Spain is not a parent at all, but an 'unnatural step-mother':

> We are threatened with the fear of death, dishonour, and every harm; there is nothing we have not suffered a the hands of that unnatural step-mother—Spain ... We have been harassed by a conduct which has not only deprived us of our rights but has kept us in a sort of permanent infancy with regard to public affairs ... When the French invasion ... routed the fragile government of the Peninsula, we were left orphans.[31]

The Spanish monarch, far from being a loving father, had become a hateful step-mother. Bolívar's fellow republican Antonio Nariño manipulated this language with consummate skill in his newspaper *La Bagatela.* He here dissects the term *Madre Patria*, 'so often used in our newspapers':

> This patriotic maternity, or maternal patriotism, has left me utterly bewildered, unable to understand the tangled strands of our political genealogy. If it bears any relation to natural maternity, then it does not arise from the Americas having behaved like children: rather, Spain must have taken on the role of mother ...This mother, after having supported herself at the expense of her daughter, insists on her maternal rights only when her daughter shows signs of outliving her mother ... I've enquired repeatedly about the Grandmother Patria [*Abuela Patria*], the Sister Patria [*Hermana Patria*], the Cousin Patria [*Prima Patria*], the Aunt Patria [*Tia Patria*], but the only one that I've actually met is the Stepmother Patria [*Madrastra Patria*], who treats her descendants like strangers, and her children like slaves.[32]

Royalists, while concurring with republicans on the familial nature of the colonial relationship, drew quite different conclusions. Familial relations, they explained, involved not rights and liberties, but duty and obligation. Independence represented a terrible, unnatural rejection of filial duty. It revealed the profound 'egoism' of its advocates. Spain, a kind and loving parent, had showered America with a thousand gifts, the greatest of which was the Christian religion. When French troops invaded Spain, in the *patria*'s hour of need, ungrateful creoles had spurned their father, callously ignoring his plight. Far from assisting their stricken father[land], Americans had selfishly rejected his authority. The American revolutions thus illustrated 'man's natural ingratitude'. Miguel de Lardizábel, speaking in the Cortes, reproached insurgents for their unfilial behaviour: 'Do not be ungrateful to your parents; such ingratitude is a scandalous monstrosity.'[33] Nor was royalist Spain a solely patriarchal construction. The liberal Cortes in particular preferred to present the metropolis either as a gentle mother (it was this image that Nariño ridiculed when he denounced the misdeeds of the stepmother *Patria*), or, more often, as a brother. To illustrate the deep bonds that supposedly united the two Hispanic hemispheres, the delegates of the Cortes and their supporters frequently described their revolutionary opponents as brothers, to whom they were eternally joined by blood, language and religion. As Michael Costeloe notes, during the first years of the war, 'the single word most often used [in Spain] in referring to Americans was "brothers"'.[34]

Perhaps, as Hans-Joachim König suggests, the adoption of fraternal, rather than paternal, imagery reveals the Cortes' rejection of absolutism.[35] However, unlike revolutionaries, royalists did not present the family as a site of unreasonable control and repression. To royalists, familial relations presented a model of appropriate and deferential submission. To republicans, the family might represent a site of turmoil and conflict. The eighteenth-century family, itself undergoing a process of transformation, thus came to represent the colonial conflict for both insurgents and royalists. Royalists nonetheless offered a distinctive interpretation of the familial nature of the war, as well as of its relationship to the Enlightenment, and of the nature of creole-peninsular rivalry. This constellation of ideas, together with the common, though problematic, identification of royalist with Spaniard, mapped out a loyalist terrain easily identified by the war's participants in its early phases. As the republican historian and politician Restrepo remarked, in 1811 'there were thus two very distinct parties: the patriots or independents, and the regentists, as they were then called, the supporters of the Spanish government'.[36] Not until the reconquest of 1816 did these inadequacy of these divisions become evident.

In the Presidency of Quito, fighting between royalists and revolutionaries continued during 1812, when Joaquín Molina was replaced as president by

Toribio Montes. Montes, building on earlier royalist victories, launched an attack on Quito itself, recapturing the city on 7 November 1812. After this defeat, Quito's insurgents fled north to Ibarra, where they soon surrendered to Colonel Juan Sámano. A number of insurgent officers were executed and their troops decimated: one out of every ten soldiers was shot. President Montes then took up residence in Quito and began implementing the Constitution of 1812. Popular elections were held for both the newly-created constitutional *ayuntamientos*, or local councils, and for the Spanish Cortes. The electoral process was complex and caused considerable confusion. Local officials were astonished to learn that Indians were allowed to vote, along with illiterates, as long as they were male. The implementation of the Constitution of 1812 was one element of Montes' highly controversial policy of 'reconciliation' between the warring parties, described by some as venal capitulation to former insurgents.[37] Thus, by the autumn of 1812, Quito's brush with revolution had ended. The presidency had been restored to royalist hands with little bloodshed, and no further attempts at revolutionizing the region succeeded until 1822. However, in other parts of the viceroyalty, events evolved in a substantially different way.

In the Captaincy General of Venezuela, several dissident movements had already hatched plots to overthrow Spanish authority. In 1808, after news of the capture of the Spanish monarchs reached Caracas, attempts were made to form an independent junta in the capital.[38] The move was stifled, as were similar attempts in late 1809 and early 1810. When, however, news of the virtual collapse of Spain's anti-French resistance was brought to Caracas by the Regency's special commissioner, Antonio de Villavicencio, interest in creating an independent junta revived. Ignoring the views of Captain General Vicente Emparán, a group of creoles composed mainly of members of the Caracas *cabildo* formed a 'Junta Suprema Conservadora de los Derechos de Fernando VII', ostensibly to defend the rights of the imprisoned Ferdinand. Emparán was deposed, and the junta took over government of Venezuela. Outright independence from Spain was declared on 5 July 1811. The Junta, and the elected Congress that succeeded it, represented the interests of the country's creole, landowning class. It abolished legal distinctions between whites and *pardos* (people of colour), yet preserved the social structures that permitted *de facto* discrimination against Venezuela's coloured population, who constituted over three quarters of the region's inhabitants.

This proved the downfall of Venezuela's first republic. Crypto-royalists and disgruntled *pardos* soon won a series of military victories over the precarious republic. Within six weeks of the earthquake that destroyed much of Caracas on 26 March 1812, the city surrendered to royalist commander Domingo Monteverde. Venezuela's republican leaders were swiftly imprisoned, although some, including the future *libertador* Simón Bolívar, managed to escape. The restored Audiencia of Caracas made valiant efforts to implement the Constitution of 1812, and to create a constitutional government.[39] Thus at the end of 1812, Caracas, like Quito, was again in royalist hands. Unlike Quito, which was to remain royalist for the next decade, Venezuela soon exploded into a civil war.

Spain's authority was also challenged in New Granada itself. In the port city of Cartagena, hostility between the city's conservative *cabildo*, the provincial governor Francisco Montes, and the peninsular merchants resident in Cartagena had been increasing throughout 1808 and 1809.[40] Conflict had at first centred on the desirability of legalizing trade with the Caribbean, but, by late 1809, events in Spain itself came to play a central role in the dispute. Although Cartagena's *cabildo* had already recognized the Junta Central, the junta's flight from Madrid and the depressing military reports from Spain began to have a discouraging effect.[41] Members of Cartagena's *cabildo* demanded permission to form a junta of their own, and responded angrily when Governor Montes tried to pack the cabildo with his own supporters. When the Regency's special commissioner Antonio de Villavicencio arrived in May 1810 with news of the total dissolution of the Junta Central, Montes' position became completely untenable. Bolstered by the support of Villavicencio, the cabildo of Cartagena first obliged Montes to share power with two deputies appointed by the cabildo. Then, on 14 June 1810 a ten-hour *cabildo pleno* voted to remove Montes from office altogether and replace him with the province's lieutenant governor, Colonel Blas de Soria. Shortly after this Montes and his secretary were arrested and deported to Havana.[42]

Cartagena's new junta was in some ways a conservative body. Its members were peninsular merchants and representatives of Cartagena's creole elite, and it voted immediately to recognize the Regency in Spain. Nonetheless, relations between the junta and the Regency quickly became strained. The Regency, distrustful of the new junta, ordered its dissolution, while the unequal representation of Americans in the Cortes in turn angered Cartagena's elite.[43] Elsewhere in New Granada the junta was perceived as a frankly radical installation, and Cartagena was soon described as being in a state of insurrection.[44] Moreover, the supposedly loyal junta began planning a complete restructuring of New Granada's political system. The junta designed a full-scale federal government, including a national assembly and ambassadors to foreign countries.[45] The new junta thus began a difficult balancing act between loyalty and independence.

Meanwhile, the level of social unrest in Cartagena was increasing. The junta, perched on an exceedingly narrow base consisting largely of the city's merchant elite, turned to the populace for support.[46] The mobilization of non-elites, for the junta a last resort, nonetheless gave Cartagena's move toward insurgency a broader social base. As the Spanish were later to observe, revolutionary sentiment penetrated deeply into Cartagena's population.[47] Eventually those members of the population who favoured complete independence gained the upper hand. On 11 November 1811, *pardos* from the popular neighbourhoods as well as a section of the city's garrison marched into the city and obliged the junta to swear complete independence from Spain, one month ahead of Quito's junta.[48] The city then issued a republican constitution that instituted (limited) male suffrage, expelled the Inquisition, and enacted other reforms.[49]

These actions were viewed with universal disapproval by Cartagena's neighbours. Cartagena had already gone to war with the town of Mompós the previous year after that city refused to recognize either the Regency or, more importantly, the new junta in Cartagena.[50] Cartagena's attempt to form itself into an independent constitutional republic merely aroused further hostility. None of the surrounding regions wished to become a province of the Republic of Cartagena, and the city found itself isolated. New Granada's internal provinces declined to send the traditional transfers of money needed to support Cartagena's garrison, thereby causing tremendous financial hardship for the new government.[51] Moreover, many of those Cartageneros opposed to independence had emigrated to Santa Marta, which soon became a centre for opposition to the new Republic of Cartagena.

Cartagena, unlike Quito or Caracas, maintained a precarious independence from Spain after 1811. No army of reconquering royalists overthrew Cartagena's junta during the years of the Peninsular War, and Cartagena became one of the bastions of insurgency in New Granada. The other bulwark of revolt was located in the interior of New Granada, towards which the Regency's commissioner Antonio de Villavicencio was making his way in 1810. Villavicencio, officially employed as a publicity agent expected to drum up support for the Regency, in fact played quite the opposite role. His itinerary through South America marks out a pathway of insurrection, and he himself was soon to join the revolutionaries. After witnessing the formation of the junta in Caracas, and participating in the formation of the junta in Cartagena, Villavicencio stopped briefly in Mompós, which then established an independent junta separate from Cartagena's. He journeyed on toward the capital. Meanwhile, anti-Spanish revolts broke out in several towns in the interior. In Pamplona an independent junta was formed on 4 July 1810, and on 9–10 July 1810 the town of Socorro rebelled against its *corregidor* (mayor) and established a sovereign junta independent of the viceroy in Santa Fe. Further south, the city of Cali deposed its cabildo and established a junta on 3 July 1810. All these bodies, while proclaiming loyalty to the distant Ferdinand VII, emancipated themselves from the more palpable authority in the capital, Santa Fe. The Viceroyalty of New Granada began to disintegrate.[52]

In the capital, this process of dissolution was watched with interest by members of the creole elite. Since 1809, when news of the junta in Quito had reached Santa Fe, the city had been in a state of excitement and anxiety. Tensions between creoles and peninsulars in the capital had increased over the previous decades, and several revolutionary plots had already been hatched.[53] These had all failed, but the next would prove successful. On 20 July 1810 a group of creole conspirators staged a riot in the centre of Santa Fe.[54] That evening, crowds poured onto the streets, unhindered by the militia, whose creole officers sympathized with the conspirators. Then, following this demonstration of popular anger, the city's cabildo persuaded Viceroy Antonio Amar to form and preside over a special junta. Amid popular unrest, the new junta met on 21 July 1810 and swore loyalty to the Regency. The junta further declared itself the supreme authority in New Granada, and summoned provincial representatives to participate in the formation of a provisional federal government. This call received a cold welcome from the other juntas so recently established in the provinces. On 26 July 1810, the junta revoked its recognition of the Regency, although it continued to protest its loyalty to Ferdinand VII.

The junta's authority was soon tested. Already members of the Audiencia, together with prominent peninsulars and the viceroy and vicereine themselves, had been arrested amid popular rioting. Then, on 13 August 'the dregs of society', as the patrician historian José Manuel Restrepo put it, acting independently from the junta, transferred the viceroy and his wife from house arrest to the city's public prisons.[55] This proved too much for the new junta. The individuals believed to be the intellectual authors of this act were arrested by the junta's recently formed militia, and the viceroy and vicereine were freed and sent to Cartagena.[56] After this show of strength, the now-unchallenged junta set about forming a government, and proceeded with plans to hold a congress of national deputies.

This congress met in late December 1810 but was attended by very few delegates from outside Santa Fe. Within a few months the congress had dissolved itself, to be replaced with a series of different leaders and organizations. Meanwhile, ever-greater fragmentation, rather than increased unity, was the order of the day. Mompós and Cartagena had already gone to war over Mompós' refusal to recognize Cartagena's junta, and soon Cartagena clashed with Santa Fe over the most suitable form of government for a quasi-independent New Granada. In the succeeding months separate juntas were formed in Quibdó, Neiva, Nóvita, Antioquia, Mariquita, Casanare, Girón, Santa Marta, Popayán and Tunja, and various provinces split into contending sections. Santa Fe attacked Ocaña, Socorro and, later, Tunja in an effort to incorporate these latter into the capital's system of centralized rule.[57] Santa Fe was itself besieged by forces representing a new congress in Villa de Leiva. 'There was', claimed Restrepo, 'hardly a city or town ... which didn't have ambitions of becoming an independent sovereign state.'[58] Only in the south did insurgents in Cali succeed in forming a union of regional juntas, which for the next few years alarmed royalists in Pasto.

In Spain, and indeed in New Granada itself, the dramatic events in Caracas, Cartagena, Quito and Santa Fe were regarded as frankly revolutionary. The oaths of loyalty to the imprisoned Ferdinand notwithstanding, contemporaries realized that the formation of juntas constituted a *de facto* declaration of independence. José Acevedo y Gómez, who had played a key part in the formation of the Santa Fe junta, himself acknowledged this when on 25 July 1810 he wrote to his cousin, 'from now on, Spain will be our ally, but it will no longer govern us'.[59] Indeed, within days of the creation of Santa Fe's junta, Oidor Joaquín Carrión y Moreno was referring to it as a realization of 'the old ideas of independence'.[60]

Among royalists, recriminations and finger-pointing started almost immediately. Oidor Carrión y Moreno, for his part, complained that Viceroy Amar had mishandled Santa Fe's uprising, asserting that the revolt could have been nipped in the bud by an opportune deployment of the militia. He further suggested that a military force be sent from the peninsula to defeat the insurgent juntas.[61] This suggestion was soon seconded by officials in Spain. By the end of 1811, some thousand troops had embarked for America. During the next ten years, over forty thousand Spaniards would be despatched, in an unsuccessful attempt to contain the revolutions that broke out in 1810.

Responses and Representations

New Granada was not the only colony to revolt during France's occupation of the Iberian Peninsula. By 1812, much of Spanish America was in open rebellion. From Mexico to Río de la Plata disparate groups rejected Spanish rule and proclaimed their separation from the metropolis. What was Spain's response to this continent-wide rebellion? How did the metropolis explain these revolutions, and what prescriptions were proposed to solve the 'American problem', as Spanish officials dubbed it? A number of excellent studies provide at least partial answers to these questions. Work by Edmundo Heredia, Timothy Anna, Michael Costeloe and others suggest that despite considerable efforts to do so, Spain never developed a coherent strategy for defeating the insurgents.[62] This was principally because the metropolitan governments lacked a sound understanding of the causes of the rebellion. Unable to decide why its subjects were in revolt, the crown proved incapable of designing a realistic response.

The first steps taken by the rump Spanish government to stop the war in the Indies came in July 1810. In that month the Council of the Indies first debated the causes of the newly-developing insurgencies, and proposed various half-baked plans for ending them. No decisive action was taken, and by the end of the year the Cortes in Cádiz had come to the conclusion that it was too ill-informed about the state of affairs in the Americas to be able to make reasonable decisions about how to end the war. Accordingly it established a special committee to study the matter. The committee first met in January 1811, when it discussed several proposals concerning Mexico. In the same month the Council of the Indies began work on an investigation into conditions in the Americas. It was not, however, until April 1812 that the Regency began to meet regularly with representatives from the Americas to gather information. By this time the Cortes had already drafted its great achievement, the Constitution of 1812, intended to unite both hemispheres in peace. Although regular debates were held in the Cortes on the 'American problem', American delegates grew angry with the Cortes' failure to listen to their views and the ignorance of their Spanish counterparts. Under these circumstances, it is perhaps not surprising that the Cortes proved unable to come up with an adequate response to the war. Proposals submitted by the American deputies were generally rejected, and the leisurely pace with which proposals were considered meant that the Cortes, like the colonial administration before it, were ineffective in responding to urgent crises.[63]

Little changed after the return of Ferdinand VII in May 1814. Ignorance and an inability to decide on any consistent course of action characterized Ferdinand's tenure as much as it had that of the Cortes. The ministers appointed to end the war by Ferdinand and the liberal government that succeeded him often lacked even a rudimentary grasp of American realities; as late as 1821 a deputy to the Cortes lamented that the Minister for Overseas Affairs, Ramón Pelegrín, believed the Mexican city of Valladolid, the site of the execution of some sixty Spaniards by Hidalgo's troops in 1810, was located in New Granada.[64] (The same deputy later complained that, with regard to Spanish America, 'they know more in the taverns of London than in the Spanish congress.'[65])

Ferdinand did recognize the need for sound information about Spanish America, and made regular efforts to learn more about events there, but the results of these exercises were seldom happy. One of his first actions on resuming command was to appoint several special consultants to inform him about affairs in Spanish America. The Quiteño Conde de Puñorrostro, a personal friend of Ferdinand and a delegate to the 1812 Cortes, was appointed consultant on New Granada, which by this time had rejected Spanish authority in virtually every part of its territory. The Count nonetheless reported that New Granada was largely pacified; his only suggestion for improvement was to remove corrupt officials from office. Advice of this sort was worse than useless, for it denied the seriousness of the situation facing the Spanish in New Granada.[66]

Ferdinand established various committees to formulate policy regarding what was by this time an out-and-out war: in 1815, multiple juntas were created to study the possibility of British mediation with the insurgents, and a unified Junta de Pacificaciones (Pacification Committee) was created in October 1815. Further committees, established in 1816 and 1817, considered the issuing of pardons and other war-related issues. Special colonial offices were set up within each ministry, a Junta de Generales (Council of Generals) met from July 1814, and the royal councils of war, treasury, the admiralty and the state also considered matters relating to the American war. Lobbyists from the commercial *consulados*, the associations of Spanish merchants involved in export trade, met regularly with treasury officials to discuss the financial aspect of the war. Then, in November 1818, a combined committee composed of representatives from the ministries of war, the admiralty and the Council of the Indies also began meeting. Perhaps, as Michael Costeloe has argued, the many *ad hoc* committees formed to discuss the American question show that the Spanish government cared a great deal about the war, but these separate committees contributed very little to the evolution of a unified plan of attack.[67] Not least of the problems was the tremendous number of (often conflicting) reports produced by the many different councils. Ferdinand's Minister of the Navy, José Vásquez Figueroa, complained in December 1816 that decisions were simply being lost in 'a real morass of conflicting papers'.[68] Ferdinand himself proved another obstacle to effective policy-making. Encouraged by his unofficial cabinet of friends, the *camarilla*, Ferdinand embarked on policies without discussing them with his appointed ministers, occasionally with disastrous results. A particularly notable example of the danger of this approach occurred in 1817, when, at great expense, Ferdinand arranged the purchase of several Russian warships. The navy minister was not involved in the purchase, as it had been arranged entirely through Ferdinand's personal links to the Russian ambassador. At the time the navy minister was himself engaged in negotiating the purchase of French warships. This purchase would have been made unnecessary by the king's acquisition of the Russian ships, had most of the Russian vessels not proved to be completely unseaworthy. The Spanish government was nonetheless required to pay the full sum agreed for the Russian ships, and indeed for the repatriation of their Russian crews. The incident illustrates well the danger of maintaining two parallel policies, one official and one informal.[69]

This failure of communication continued after 1820, when Ferdinand's absolutist government was for three years replaced with a liberal constitutional monarchy. Hostile towards his own government, Ferdinand was disinclined to assist in the evolution of policy. The Marqués de las Amarillas, a friend of the king and a minister during this period, described Ferdinand's manner during ministerial consultations:

> The king was … busy opening books or pamphlets which he received

> from Paris, or in tying and untying a roll of ribbon which he had on his desk, always with an affable air, but paying little or no attention to the discussion, and answering only, 'fine, whatever you like …', so that it was difficult to tell what his real opinion was, assuming he actually had an opinion at all.[70]

The many bodies established from 1810 to 1823 to study the American insurgencies failed to produce a unified recommendation. The different committees and councils proposed different solutions, all of which were applied partially, sometimes simultaneously, and never consistently. There was, however, a certain continuity in Spanish policy towards America throughout the independence period, as Michael Costeloe has documented in his careful study, *Response to Revolution*.[71] This lay in the persistence of three (sometimes contradictory) approaches to ending the war, all of which were employed by every government in power from 1810 until the mid-1820s. These were the use of military force, conciliation and negotiation, either mediated or direct.

Military force was tried most consistently. It is worth noting that it was not the absolutist Ferdinand, but rather the Cortes that sent the first troops to the Americas. In 1811, a total of 1,068 troops were sent to four different destinations, followed in 1812 by some 5,800 soldiers. By 1813 Spain was able to organize rather larger forces. In that year 9,200 soldiers were despatched to five different cities in Spanish America. In 1814, after the defeat of Napoleon, Spain was not only politically ready to throw itself frontally on the insurgents, but also had a large population of unemployed soldiers. 1814 was spent organizing a large expedition destined for the Viceroyalty of New Granada, to be headed by General Pablo Morillo. This expedition left Spain in February 1815 with over ten thousand men. Three smaller expeditions totalling about four thousand men altogether also left Spain that same year. Spain was not able to match this show of military muscle in the succeeding years, and only some 4,300 soldiers were sent annually for the next two years. By 1818, the number had fallen to about two thousand. Another great expedition was prepared for 1820, but the January revolt of Colonel Rafael Riego crippled this plan. In total, Spain sent some 41,000 peninsular soldiers to fight in the Americas. Of these approximately eleven thousand fought in New Granada.[72]

In the context of contemporary warfare these figures were small. Four decades earlier, the British had recruited 171,000 men to fight against the

North American insurgents; and even the French, hard-pressed by other military commitments, had raised over 60,000 soldiers to fight Haiti's revolted slaves.[73] In European terms, the 41,000 soldiers Spain scattered across Spanish America might have constituted a respectable force for a single encounter, but not for an entire imperial army; in comparison, Spanish forces suffered over 35,000 dead and injured in 1809 at the Battle of Ocaña alone. The 10,500 men who arrived with Morillo, while constituting the largest force ever sent by Spain to its colonies, scarcely formed an impressive army in European terms.[74]

The military solution to the war was supported by a broad coalition of interests in Spain and the Americas. First, many Spaniards, both in government and in the public, believed that the war was the result of the malicious influence of a few *hombres oscuros*, or conspirators. These malefactors, doubtless creoles, had incited the fundamentally loyal populace to revolt, perhaps by circulating false or distorted rumours about the true state of affairs in Spain.[75] This view implied that, at the very least, the revolt had no popular base, and suggested that a military force, possibly even a small military force, might easily defeat the rebels. 'Send a few troops from the peninsula and total pacification is certain', proclaimed one Spanish newspaper in 1811.[76] This was the opinion of the commercial *consulados* and of their mouthpiece, the Comisión de Reemplazos, the private agency that funded the 1815 military expedition to New Granada. The Consulado de Cádiz was one of the most persistent supporters of armed intervention, and one of the most inflexible opponents of commercial reform, which would invariably reduce its control over the Atlantic trade. The Comisión de Reemplazos thus encouraged the belief that it was only through force that Spain might retain its colonies. Reforms of the colonial system, in particular commercial reform, had no role in pacification, they intoned. The insurgencies, the Comisión delicately explained, were supported only by 'the scum of the earth' and were led solely by self-seeking traitors.[77]

Other observers, particularly those with direct experience of the American war, maintained that, on the contrary, the rebellion had deep popular roots. This view led some to advocate the same military solution advanced by those who believed the revolts had little popular base. Men such as General Pablo Morillo, the commander of the expedition sent to New Granada in 1815, came to believe that military force was the only way to defeat the rebellion. It was, he believed, impossible to convince the Americans to remain Spanish, as the populace wanted only independence.

Conciliation and reform were thus pointless. A decisive military victory was, in his view, Spain's only hope.[78]

Yet military force was not the only solution considered. Other more conciliatory approaches were also advocated. To begin with, some who believed the revolutions were the result of republican rumour-mongering and deception (the so-called 'seduction theory'), maintained that the insurgents might be defeated simply by an information campaign about events in Spain.[79] Consequently, when in 1810 the Council of the Indies made its first attempt at suffocating the revolt in Caracas, it determined to send nothing more than a special commissioner (Antonio de Villavicencio), charged with informing the public of the true state of affairs in Spain. (The government's total lack of cash also influenced this choice of response.) Similarly, in 1814 the government commissioned leading colonial officials to write pamphlets 'in a simple style' which could be distributed to the populace to explain and correct the mistaken beliefs that had caused the insurgency.[80] The consistent failure of this educational approach did not dampen the enthusiasm of its adherents, as Edmundo Heredia has observed.[81]

Others believed the war was neither the result of misinformation campaigns nor soluble only through military force. Many Spaniards, both in government and out, blamed Spain itself for the outbreak of war. Although some conservatives insisted that a decline in absolutism had cleared the way for sedition, many others, both liberals and conservatives, agreed that Spain's inept administration of the colonies was to blame. Advocates of this view suggested that the war might be ended through a combination of reform and conciliation; the colonies were to be made to feel a part of Spain, and the grossest abuses were to be ended. It should be clear that this approach would combine poorly with a military one; announcements that the Americas constituted an integral part of Spain, accompanied by the despatch of thousands of troops, would convince few that Spain did not regard America as its colony. Nonetheless, this was exactly what the Cortes attempted from 1809 to 1813. Both in 1809, with the opening of the Cortes, and in 1812, following the publication of the Constitution of 1812, equality was proclaimed between peninsulars and creoles, yet from 1811 to 1813, nearly 16,000 troops were sent to Spanish America to stamp out sedition.[82]

This example illustrates the flaw in the conciliatory approach. No Spanish government was willing to commit itself solely to conciliation, which meant that the symbolic actions intended to assure Americans of

Spain's concern for their well-being fell flat. Thus in 1820, the Cortes, while refusing to recognize the *de facto* independence of Río de la Plata, nonetheless voted to establish a university in the Argentine city of Córdoba. This university would never be built, but the vote authorizing it was intended to illustrate the Cortes' benevolent attitude towards a region that it still regarded as its colony.[83]

Proposals for genuine commercial reform were an entirely different matter, compared to the tender declarations in favour of Hispanic unity mouthed by both the Cortes and Ferdinand VII. Plans of real substance were advocated even by such absolutist bodies as Ferdinand's Junta de Pacificaciones, which was set up in late 1815 to discuss ways of ending the insurgency. In 1817, the Junta recommended that Spain offer the rebels a package of reforms, including free trade, affirming 'it is necessary and urgent to change the system'.[84] The Junta's proposal illustrates the depth of support for altering Spain's mercantilist system. Many proposals outlining such reforms as the abolition of the state monopolies and the licensing of free trade in the Americas were presented in the Cortes, and many were considered by Ferdinand's government.

The most persistent advocate of reform within Ferdinand's government was Minister of State José García de León y Pizarro. In September 1817, Pizarro proposed a grand plan for ending the insurgency.[85] This plan involved liberalizing trade with the Americas and resuming talks with Britain about diplomatic mediation of the crisis. Although it was backed by many government bodies, Pizarro's proposal was opposed by the ministers of war and justice, and in the end nothing came of it. Moreover, Pizarro himself was dismissed from office in September 1818, leaving the government in the hands of the hawks. Pizarro's plan, like all earlier proposals for commercial reform, foundered on the rock of consular opposition. The Consulado de Cádiz in particular was determined to block any change to trading legislation. As the major source of funding for the government's American war effort (via the Comisión de Reemplazos), the Consulado de Cádiz was in a good position to dictate terms. During the Cortes of 1810–14, when the delegates were actually confined to Cádiz itself, this influence naturally made itself felt most directly, but the Consulado continued to influence policy after 1814. The effect of both the *consulados* and ministerial opponents of free trade was that no real reforms of Spain's commercial policy were undertaken, although many were considered.

The third strand in Spain's response to the war explored the possibility of mediation with the insurgents via some third party, most likely Britain. Yet while foreign mediation was repeatedly considered, undermining every such proposal was the suspicion that the revolution was actually the product of cynical foreign intervention in Spain's dominions. Spain's successive governments knew that other countries were aiding the insurgents; Ferdinand in particular was much concerned that his supposed allies were assisting the rebels. All commented on the number of foreigners, especially British, fighting for the insurgents, and the persistence of the insurgency was repeatedly attributed to the aid and support given to foreign mercenaries by their perfidious governments. Many expeditions did indeed leave Great Britain to fight with the insurgents and the role of British battalions in many of Bolívar's battles has been well studied. 'It seems that the entire British army wants to move to this continent', remarked General Morillo in May 1819.[86] General Morillo was so concerned about the increasing numbers of British mercenaries that he went to the unprecedented step of issuing a proclamation in (rather fetching) English:

> To the British chiefs, officers and soldiers now serving with the insurgents … Englishmen: to you I address myself who are already acquainted with that famous personage whom you no doubt (while in England) compared to a Washington at least, but now, having seen the Hero of this despreciable republic, his troops, his Generals, and the Wiseacres who compose his government, you must be convinced of having been most shamefully imposed upon. You are serving under the command of a man in every respect insignificant, and have joined an horde of banditti who are famed for the exercise of the most barbarous cruelties, which are so averse to your national character, that you must abhor them. He who retains the least spark of honour and justice cannot remain united with such a band of ragamuffins, who are abhorred by the very country that gave them birth whose soil they have sullied with crimes of all descriptions. The people of Venezuela only wish for peace and for the extermination of those monsters …[87]

The involvement of British mercenaries and volunteers in the wars of independence, as well as Britain's obvious commercial interest in an independent Spanish America, overshadowed all attempts at ending the war through diplomacy. Britain was the only country really interested in assisting Spain in negotiating with the insurgents, but the Spanish government was too suspicious of Britain's intentions to give full support to any plan for a mediated settlement. Neither was Spain willing to grant Britain any commercial privileges in return for diplomatic assistance. In the end, Spain's well-justified doubts about the impartiality of the British undermined all attempts at a mediated settlement of the war.

The first round of British mediation, initiated by the Regency, reached a dead end by the middle of 1812, although directionless discussions continued until mid-1813. In July 1815, the newly re-established Council of the Indies advised the newly restored Ferdinand to reopen discussions with Great Britain about British mediation, which the Council believed was Spain's only hope for pacification. The Council urged Ferdinand to support a mediated settlement, even if it obliged Spain to grant Britain special trading rights. Ferdinand approved this recommendation and established several committees to investigate the matter. Plans to cede American territory in return for aid were even discussed, and other European powers were invited to assist Spain. Yet despite this no firm decisions were taken and discussions wandered aimlessly until early 1817, when Ferdinand decided to restart the discussion of British mediation. But by September 1818, mediation was again abandoned.[88] Negotiations again foundered because of Spanish distrust of the British. The British government, conscious that the presence of so many Britons in the insurgent armies discredited its offers to mediate, at various times prohibited its citizens from participating in the war, but these prohibitions did not staunch the flow of arms and men.[89]

These, then, were the interpretative schema with which Spain's governments approached the American insurgencies. Without committing itself firmly to any one approach, the metropolis attempted to implement several different policies, often simultaneously. What effect did these multiple approaches have in New Granada? How was Spanish thinking on the war translated into policy in New Granada? At first, Spanish interpretations of the war mattered little to New Granada, which was cut adrift from Peninsular rule until 1815. Royalist enclaves in New Granada functioned largely autonomously until the arrival of the General Morillo's Expeditionary Army in 1815. After Morillo's arrival the confused interpretations emanating from Spain were to have a seriously counter-productive effect on the royalist cause. To appreciate this, however, it is necessary to understand the evolution of royalist resistance to independence in New Granada from 1810 to 1815.

2

Royalist Enclaves in New Granada

By 1811, colonial government in New Granada had shattered. Into its place stepped no unified authority. Instead, Spanish rule was replaced by a disparate collection of juntas, united only in their opposition to Spain. This common enemy did not prevent New Granada's cities and provinces from pouring considerable resources into fighting each other. Provinces fought to maintain their colonial unity, and smaller towns tried to free themselves from domination by larger cities. Pre-existing regional rivalry fuelled conflict.[1] In this, New Granada mirrored the Peninsula, where the extremely regional nature of the resistance to Napoleon led at first to rivalry and dissension. But internecine struggle was not confined to New Granada's insurgent-controlled areas. Regions that recognized the Regency fought with those that had not, and different factions within royalist-controlled areas fought each other. Factional struggle crippled the royalist government-in-exile established in Panama, while Santa Marta and Pasto, the two strongly royalist provinces of New Granada, were quickly submerged in bitter conflicts with their insurgent neighbours. Despite this, Santa Marta and Pasto kept alive a semblance of imperial control in New Granada. In Panama, however, the problems facing the new viceroy, Benito Pérez, combined with the Regency's failure to provide any guidance, meant that Pérez's government contributed little to the fight against insurgency.

Liberty Trees and Bayonets

In Colombia, the years between 1810 and 1815 have traditionally been known as the *Patria Boba*, or the 'Foolish Fatherland'. This title, now discarded in favour of the more decorous 'First Republic', does have the virtue of emphazising the destructive disunity characteristic of the period. After the formation of revolutionary juntas in Antioquia, Cali, Cartagena, Casanare, El Chocó, Mariquita, Neiva, Nóvita, Quibdó, Pamplona, Santa Fe, Socorro and Tunja, New Granada badly needed a unified government capable of integrating the new juntas under a single command. This was to prove completely impossible, as the very motives which had propelled these different regions to disown the Regency and proclaim independence from Spain prohibited them from surrendering their new-found authority to a rival province. Thus the years after 1810 saw not only the formation of constitutional republics across the former viceroyalty, but also an unseemly struggle for power.[2]

There was no shortage of plans for a unified government; the difficulty lay in generating sufficient support for any one of them. The junta in Cartagena proposed the creation of a federal government with a capital in Medellín, while the Santa Fe junta advocated a centralist government, with Santa Fe as the capital. The Santa Fe junta itself was replaced by a congress, which first met in December 1810, attended by delegates from Santa Fe, Socorro, Neiva, Pamplona, Nóvita and Mariquita, but not from Cartagena or any of its satellite cities. The Congress subsequently dissolved; the capital was then governed by a series of bodies, finally establishing itself as the State of Cundinamarca under the leadership of Antonio Nariño, a veteran republican and an outspoken advocate of centralized government. Meanwhile a special congress had been convened in Santa Fe, with the purpose of composing a constitution for the new state and for any other regions which chose to affiliate. The federal constitution produced by this body—the Act of Federation of the United Provinces of New Granada—was not approved by the representatives from Cundinamarca itself. The newly-created United Provinces of New Granada thus comprised Antioquia, Cartagena, Neiva, Pamplona and Tunja. Establishing themselves in Villa de Leiva, and later Tunja, the United Provinces elected Camilo Torres president.

Thus began the struggle between federalists and centralists, between Camilo Torres and Antonio Nariño, between the United Provinces and the State of Cundinamarca. On 23 November 1812 the first military expedition left Santa Fe to attack Tunja. The Congress, the governing body of the United Provinces, sent an army commanded by Antonio Baraya to invade Santa Fe. War between the Congress and Cundinamarca persisted until January 1813, when Nariño secured a convincing victory. Two years later Simón Bolívar, acting on behalf of the congress in Tunja, again attacked

Santa Fe, conquering the city on 12 December 1814. Only then did Cundinamarca merge with the Congress, which installed itself in Santa Fe.

Meanwhile the United Provinces and Cundinamarca competed to build up their respective states. Nariño attempted to force Socorro into the State of Cundinamarca, while Socorro itself, resisting Nariño's efforts, tried to enlarge its own empire. Its eye fell particularly on the neighbouring town of San Gil, long a rival. San Gil, fleeing Socorro's unwelcome attention, sought the protection of Cundinamarca, prompted, its *cabildo* explained, by 'the shameful wrongs it had suffered' at Socorro's hands. As a result, troops from Socorro attacked San Gil, leaving its inhabitants to complain bitterly of destruction wrought by the Socorreño soldiers.[3] At the same time the town of Vélez, seeking to join the State of Cundinamarca, attacked Socorro, troops from Charalá invaded el Valle, Tunja invaded Sogamoso, while the towns of Sáchica and Chíquisa left Cundinamarca and joined the United Provinces. Further north the junta of Cartagena attacked the junta in Mompós, in a successful attempt to incorporate the city into its own orbit. Royalists in Santa Marta, however, remained at war with Cartagena until the arrival of Morillo's army. Honda conquered Ambalema, Pamplona defeated royalist Girón, and the province of Chocó split into Citará and Nóvita. Further south, the junta in Cali did succeed in uniting a number of cities into the Confederate Cities of the Cauca, which dominated the Cauca Valley until 1813. Everywhere these events were accompanied by unprecedented bloodshed and upheaval. Many thousands of refugees fled the fighting, migrating to more tranquil areas.

Yet this account of war and invasion tells only part of the story of the First Republic. The period saw not only warfare on a scale completely unprecedented in the viceroyalty, but also witnessed the creation of the first written constitutions, and the introduction of republicanism in many parts of the region. Nearly a dozen provinces composed republican constitutions, which introduced elections and the language of the French Revolution to New Granada's cities.[4] The extent to which life in New Granada was changed by these events is difficult to assess. War itself had clear and immediate consequences—death, injury, migration—but the overall legacy of these years was complex, even for a single city such as Santa Fe. On the one hand, the revolution in the capital brought obvious changes to the city's life. Men were drafted into a newly-formed army, sent to fight neighbouring cities and provinces. The arrival of war was in itself a new and terrifying development for the capital's inhabitants. Particularly alarming was the possibility that Santa Fe itself might suffer attack. With the exception of the Comunero rebels of 1781, no army had ever attempted an assault on the capital. Even the Comuneros had been halted before the reached Santa Fe. Between 1812 and 1814 Santa Fe was attacked twice by two different armies. The impact of these assaults was recalled by the historian José Manuel Groot, who was thirteen at the time of Baraya's unsuccessful attack. Rumours circulated that Baraya's army intended to sack the city and murder its inhabitants: 'What impression did this news make in Santa Fe? Oh! One had to have been there in person to understand. Even the little children were terrified.'[5] As Groot recalled, the impending invasion propelled the population of Santa Fe *en masse* into the nearest church.

Other less terrifying innovations also took place. New political institutions such as elections were introduced. The diary of José María Caballero illustrates well the transformation that overtook public life in the capital during the years of the First Republic. His memoirs, begun before 1810, move from being an account of murders, festivals and unusual occurrences, to a political narrative of congresses, wars and politics.[6] In the capital the new politics brought with it new forms of public behaviour, as the revolutionary government tried to endow itself with the solemnity of its predecessor through the use of public ritual. Traditional public events were adapted to serve new purposes. The traditional festival on 6 August celebrating the foundation of the colonial city was replaced with a festival of Religion; the Inquisition's instruments of torture were publicly destroyed in a revolutionary *Auto de Fe* in 1811.[7] These solemnities were complimented by entirely new political rituals, such as the planting of liberty trees. Several liberty trees were planted with great ceremony in 1813.[8] Yet these new festivals were accompanied by highly traditional rituals which persisted unchanged despite the new regime. When Baraya's forces threatened the capital, its residents protected themselves by attaching little cards onto their hat saying 'Jesus'.[9]

These developments brought with them some of the accoutrements of modernity, in particular, the political press. A flourishing periodical press, seen by scholars such as Jürgen Habermas and François-Xavier Guerra as an essential ingredient of modern political space, began to develop in some parts of Spanish America in the last years of colonialism. In Santa Fe the period of the First Republic saw some growth in this medium. In the capital approximately eleven new newspapers were introduced between 1808 and 1816. Newspapers such as Antonio Nariño's *La Bagatela* published sophisticated political discussions and sardonic essays. Others inserted extracts from Rousseau and Raynal, or reprinted anti-Catholic polemics penned by Protestant writers in the British Caribbean.[10] Yet this development was largely limited to Santa Fe; outside the capital only four of the regional juntas established after 1810 had access even to a printing press. Accordingly, most of New Granada experienced no great growth in printed material during the years of the First Republic. At no time between 1808 and 1816 were more than ten different newspaper titles being published in New Granada. Overall there is little evidence that these years saw the advent of a print-based 'modernity' in New Granada as a whole.[11]

The economic impact of the First Republic seems to have been negative. The many military campaigns launched by the various revolutionary governments were extremely costly; Nariño's 1813 expedition to conquer Pasto cost the capital over $200,000.[12] Most governments resorted to printing paper money, an immensely unpopular act that produced tremendous inflation. The paper currency introduced into Cartagena in 1812 suffered an immediate and substantial devaluation. One hundred paper pesos quickly came to be valued at sixteen gold pesos.[13] Government income was further reduced by the abolition decreed by many provincial juntas of many of the viceroyalty's traditional sources of funding, in particular the tobacco and *aguardiente* monopolies.

Popular support for these new governments varied substantially. In the capital committed followers of the new regime such as the diarist José María Caballero displayed a tenacious patriotism even after the collapse of the revolutionary government. Yet the signal patriotism of such individuals was to prove insufficient. When Spanish troops advanced on the capital in 1816, Santa Fe surrendered without a fight. In Cartagena, on the other hand, widespread public participation in the revolutionary government gave it unusual strength in the face of the royalist siege of 1815.[14] General Morillo would later comment on what he perceived as the extensive public support for the revolution:

> ... innumerable persons of this kingdom are caught up in the insurrection and planned independence, so that one can find hardly a single family whose members are not stained with this crime ... thus if one were to take action against them it would be necessary to imprison a considerable part of the population, [whom it would be] impossible to judge.[15]

Yet the mass of the population's failure to support the revolution was already a cause for comment in the earliest years of the war. Miguel Tacón, royalist governor of Popayán reported proudly in 1812 that 'the blacks of the coast and district of Popayán have never been in favour of their masters, whom they consider to be enemies of the king; on the contrary they have always offered to defend the government'.[16] The assertion that the majority of the population viewed the revolution with indifference, if not outright hostility would become an element of faith for both royalists and republicans. José Acevedo y Gómez, a leading member of the Santa Fe junta, recalled in his memoirs that 'the revolution was not made by the mass of the population. A tiny minority supported the sector of the upper classes of Santa Fe who favoured the revolution.'[17] Republicans later used the purported apathy of the populace to justify restrictions on access to political power, while royalists consoled themselves that independence was advocated only by a handful of perverse creole aristocrats. It is thus difficult to assess the very frequent assertion that independence was an elite affair, removed from the concerns of most Neogranadans. Such statements quickly entered the realm of dogma, separating themselves from their historical roots. Not at all removed from the concerns of many Neogranadans was the new and unwelcome experience of violence and unrest that characterized the First Republic, and this was to be the Patria Boba's most immediate legacy.

The Retreat to Panama

Although Viceroy Antonio Amar's career was ended prematurely by Santa Fe's insurgents in 1810, the Spanish Regency had already decided to replace him with Benito Pérez prior to the revolutionary events of July 1810. Pérez, who was sixty-one years old, had served in the Americas for over thirty years, and, like most of New Granada's viceroys, was a military man.[18] Pérez was appointed viceroy in August 1810, but did not take up his post until early 1812, leaving New Granada for nearly two years without even a semblance of viceregal authority. It was by 1812 impossible for the viceroy to reside in Santa Fe, as the capital, and indeed most of the country, was in the hands of the insurgents. Pérez accordingly settled in Panama, one of the few remaining royalist strongholds.

The arrival of the viceroy and establishment of a quasi-capital in Panama disturbed the existing balance of power in the isthmus. Panama's Governor

Juan Antonio de la Mata had been governing the isthmus in complete autonomy since the collapse of central government in July 1810. The arrival of Pérez and the Santa Fe Audiencia, which followed Pérez to Panama, dislodged the governor and Panama City's *cabildo* from the top of the region's hierarchy. Neither accepted this change without struggle. Bitter arguments soon broke out between the Audiencia on one hand, and the *cabildo* and governor on the other. The Audiencia complained that the *cabildo* refused to carry out its duties, while the *cabildo* alleged that the Santa Fe Audiencia, which by early 1814 was reduced to one member, was not properly constituted and therefore refused to recognize its authority.[19] Viceroy Pérez took the side of the *cabildo* and refused to release funds to pay the salaries of Audiencia officials.[20] At the heart of the conflict was the Santa Fe Audiencia's claim that the *cabildo* was a haven for smugglers, long a lucrative career for those stationed on the Caribbean coast. Viceroy Pérez allegedly aided the contraband trade, and himself profited from it.[21] The quarrel grew to include the bishop of Panama, who sided with the Audiencia, and Governor Mata, who backed the alleged smugglers. The Audiencia charged that Governor Mata too winked at smugglers and insurgents, while rumours spread that the bishop maligned Governor Mata because the governor was sheltering a renegade cleric accused of adultery.[22]

Such was the level of viceregal politics in New Granada during this critical period. Regional rivalries also surfaced, as Panama City and Portobelo struggled for supremacy. Portobelo's *cabildo* complained that the Panama City *cabildo* was trying to take over command of the entire isthmus, and alleged that the viceroy had originally intended to reside in Portobelo, but had been lured to Panama City with false promises of a healthier climate. His presence in Panama City, the Portobelo *cabildo* believed, unfairly strengthened the authority of their rival city.[23] None of these conflicts did anything to reassert royal authority in New Granada, and Panama sank into a mire of local infighting. Fortunately for royalists, Pérez was in poor health and was replaced in late 1812 by Francisco Montalvo. Montalvo, who was directed to settle in Santa Marta, rather than Panama, took up office in early 1813. Pérez's inactivity might suggest that, for royalists, the years from 1810 to 1813 were a virtual lacuna, but on the contrary, these years formed a critical period of royalist opposition to revolution, although the real action took place not in Panama, but further south and east, in the provinces of Pasto and Santa Marta. The next section examines the rivalries and dissensions that marked these two regions' involvement in the movement for independence. For Santa Marta, the city's long-standing commercial rivalry with Cartagena was at the heart of its rejection of independence. For Pasto too economic competition underlay opposition to the insurgency. Pasto's main economic rival, Quito, was leading the insurgency in the south. The elite of Pasto rejected independence as an attribute of Quito, invented to facilitate an assault on their province's territorial, political and economic integrity. These conditions placed Santa Marta and Pasto in perhaps inevitable conflict with their insurgent neighbours.

In Defence of Regionalism

> The power vacuum in the metropolitan government that led to the establishment of these governing juntas in the various provinces offered many towns and cities the possibility of a double independence: from Spain, and from the capital of their own province.[24]

Soon after the Cartagena junta's formation, its gaze fell on its neighbour Santa Marta. Santa Marta was a small provincial capital of some three thousand inhabitants, most of them free people of colour. The province itself comprised perhaps 40,000 people, a quarter the number in Cartagena Province.[25] Fearing that hostility from Santa Marta would jeopardize its own existence, Cartagena's junta invited Santa Marta to form a similar junta and ally itself with Cartagena. And indeed, on 10 August 1810, a 'security tribunal, named the "Provincial Junta"' was set up in Santa Marta.[26] However, this was no revolutionary body and, Cartagena's hopes notwithstanding, it did not align itself with anyone. The majority of the junta's members were firm opponents of republicanism, and those suspected of radical views were quickly forced to resign.[27] The junta moreover had no intention of disobeying orders from Spain. When it failed to gain the Regency's approval, it dissolved itself in 1811.[28]

The junta's failure to develop into a revolutionary body may be largely ascribed to the negative influence of Cartagena. Santa Marta was Cartagena's principal commercial rival. During the Anglo-Spanish wars of 1796–1808, Santa Marta had attracted a greatly increased share of trade with the Caribbean, and Cartagena's trading profits had declined proportionally. This commerce was by no means entirely legal. Complaints about the unrestrained smuggling encouraged by the residents of Santa Marta had long been voiced in Cartagena, although if Spain had been ineffective in its attempts to halt smuggling prior to 1810, it was now utterly impotent.[29] Santa Marta's already well developed contraband links with the British Caribbean were further strengthened when, after the establishment of Cartagena's junta, a large number of peninsular merchants left Cartagena and took up residence in Santa Marta. It is thus not surprising that the junta of Cartagena soon developed plans to attack and annex Santa Marta.[30] In the course of the next four years the inhabitants of Santa Marta were subjected to repeated attacks from Cartagena. As a result, Santa Marta's pre-existing rivalry with Cartagena and its inhabitants became yet more entrenched.

The economic assault on Santa Marta started soon after the formation of Cartagena's junta. In retaliation for Santa Marta's rampant smuggling, the new junta in Cartagena had imposed a twelve per cent tax on all goods from Santa Marta, and a $1 per *fanega* tax on salt. This was followed, in March 1811, with the threat to suspend all commercial relations between the two cities.[31] Cartagena further fomented separatist tendencies in the towns of Santa Marta Province, and gave every sign of intending to invade Santa Marta itself. By mid-1811, open war had broken out. Armed groups from both Cartagena and Santa Marta clashed along the Magdalena River. In view of Cartagena's aggressions, the government of Santa Marta wrote regularly to Spain asking to be provided with weapons, soldiers and money.[32] In 1812, the Regency responded, albeit modestly. Three hundred and eight troops were despatched to Santa Marta, followed in 1813 by a further 214, this time accompanied by a battleship.[33] Perhaps as a result, by late 1812 Santa Marta had successfully occupied much of the eastern side of the Magdalena River and had expanded its dominion into the region around Tolú. Foreshadowing later disasters, the royalist commander in San Benito Abad, Antonio Fernández Rebustillo, managed to provoke a resurgence of support for the republicans by imposing huge fines on the population and by permitting the rape of local women.[34]

Cartagena at last retaliated. On 6 January 1813, insurgent forces led by the Frenchman Pierre Labatut captured the city of Santa Marta. This victory did not require great military prowess on the part of Labatut. The *cabildo* of Santa Marta complained that the town surrendered without a fight and that the governor and military commander fled, along with most of the inhabitants and Santa Marta's military installation. The forces sent from Spain in 1812 had evidently become disaffected after the city's repeated failure to pay their salaries.[35] Republican control over Santa Marta was short-lived, largely because Labatut antagonized its inhabitants. Like Fernández Rebustillo, Labatut imposed heavy fines on the populace and, even worse, introduced a paper currency. Their combined effect was to provoke an uprising of both the region's Mamatoco Indians and Santa Marta's inhabitants, who expelled Labatut's forces on 5 March 1813. Two months later the city was again attacked by forces from Cartagena, this time unsuccessfully. Insurgent troops led by another Frenchman, Colonel Louis Bernard Chatillon, attacked Santa Marta on 10 May 1813. Although they were accompanied by several warships, the republicans were defeated. Chatillon was killed, along with some four hundred insurgent soldiers. The province's Mamatoco Indians again distinguished themselves in battle.[36]

Shortly after Chatillon's defeat, Santa Marta's role as chief royalist stronghold was strengthened by the arrival of New Granada's new captain general. In June 1813, Francisco Montalvo, the replacement of Benito Pérez, reached Santa Marta. Montalvo came not as viceroy, but as captain general, following the Regency's decision to demote New Granada from a viceroyalty to a captaincy-general. Montalvo, a wealthy landowner previously living in Cuba, arrived in Santa Marta on 1 June 1813, accompanied by only three hundred troops, to the disgust of the inhabitants. He wrote immediately to Spain, expressing the hope that they would soon send more soldiers, as 'as they couldn't possibly believe that his presence alone would be enough to pacify New Granada'.[37]

Montalvo's rule in fact extended little outside Santa Marta itself. Even in areas under royalist control his authority was openly challenged. The royalist president of Quito, Toribio Montes, initially refused to acknowledge Montalvo's authority, commenting that he had received no official order to recognize the 'Captain General of Santa Marta'.[38] Montalvo was of course Captain General of *New Granada*, but Montes' version of the title more accurately expressed the spread of Montalvo's authority. Alejandro Hore, the new governor of Panama, similarly resisted recognizing Montalvo, while in Venezuela Montalvo's command was purely nominal.[39]

Montalvo's stay in Santa Marta at first did little to improve Spain's dwindling authority in New Granada. On the contrary, he soon fell out with Santa Marta's governor, Pedro Ruíz de Porras, a hard-line absolutist who enjoyed considerable popular support.[40] The economic situation in Santa Marta was moreover miserable in the extreme. By 1814, the province's small agricultural output had been almost completely halted by the war with Cartagena, as had much of its legal trade, since its only saleable products, cotton and cocoa, were no longer grown. Food was scarce, and there were shortages of rice, maize and plantains, the region's staple diet.[41] The state of Santa Marta's army caused Montalvo great concern. Not only was it too small but, to his horror, he found upon his arrival that it was supported by a large number of Indian irregulars, who had been provided with weapons by Governor Ruíz de Porras. 'The only immediate effect of this measure', Montalvo complained, 'has been to allow the Indians to steal from the haciendas of the wealthy citizens, whom they vilify by calling "Jacobin", by which they mean "insurgent".'[42] Indeed, the possibility of an Indian uprising alarmed Montalvo almost as much as the war with Cartagena. Although he made paternalistic remarks about the dedication with which Santa Marta's Indian population fought the insurgents, Montalvo was very uncomfortable with the active role Indians were taking in the region's defence. Montalvo's discomfort contrasts sharply with the attitude of Governor Ruíz de Porras. Ruíz de Porras evidently developed an effective relationship with both the province's Indians and the many free people of colour. The basis for this relationship is suggested by documents such as those from 1814 in which Ruíz de Porras and Santa Marta's bishop José Eulalio Ziosi obtained a total exemption from tribute for the province's Indians.[43]

On arrival Montalvo made some effort to implement the Constitution of 1812. Constitutional *ayuntamientos* were created and elections were perhaps held. The impact of these reforms requires greater study. Montalvo himself, although a supporter of the Constitution, viewed it as a foreign import, poorly adapted to Santa Marta's impoverished circumstances. He reported that he had proclaimed the freedom of the press, 'despite the fact that, as far as I know, there is not a single printing press in the small area under my command'.[44] As this remark suggests, Santa Marta, although functioning as a capital city, in fact possessed very little administrative infrastructure. Its choice as Montalvo's headquarters is in itself an indication of the royalism's fragile hold on New Granada in 1813.

While Montalvo struggled to establish a royalist beachhead at Santa Marta, various towns and villages on the Caribbean coast quietly separated themselves from the jurisdiction of Santa Marta. The towns of Chiriguaná and Banco, and the whole region of Valledupar broke away from Santa Marta in 1811.[45] As has already been noted, such splits were often motivated by local politics, rather than by ideological differences, and events in the Province of Ríohacha illustrate this particularly well. A province of perhaps 4,000 inhabitants, Ríohacha separated from Santa Marta, yet both regions remained firmly royalist.[46] The local elite in Ríohacha had been in conflict with the authorities in Santa Fe since 1806, when Ríohacha's governor, Josef de Medina y Galindo, had been forced to resign by Viceroy Amar. Medina y Galindo, although out of office, waited in the wings for an opportunity to return. In 1810, during the summer outbreak of junta-formation, Ríohacha too had formed a junta, headed by the *alcalde*, or mayor, Pedro Pérez Prieto. Ríohacha's junta refused to recognize the authority of the juntas in Cartagena and Santa Fe. Then, in 1811, Medina y Galindo returned to Ríohacha, intent on regaining power. He was initially driven out by a group of Guajiro Indians led by Pérez Prieto, but he later returned, accompanied by his own group of armed men. He threatened the junta, demanding to be reinstated as governor, and succeeded in regaining control of the province. Ríohacha then separated itself from the authority of Santa Marta, whose governor Tomás de Acosta complained: 'Ríohacha is in a state of utter disorder, with its illegal governor who had refused to assist me'.[47] In 1813 Medina, still governor, was continuing his attempt to build up his regional authority at Santa Marta's expense. At his urging the town of San Juan de César placed itself under Ríohacha's protection, as did the towns of Fonseca and Barranca.[48]

All these actions were undertaken without consultation with either Santa Marta or the Regency. This was, however, no republican movement. Both Pérez Prieto and Medina were staunch defenders of the Spanish monarchy. When Cartagena attempted to invade Ríohacha, its *cabildo* made the traditional promise to 'shed our last drop of blood', before surrendering to the insurgents.[49] Rather than rebelling against Spanish rule, Ríohacha was instead freeing itself of its subordination to Santa Marta. Events in Ríohacha thus illustrate very clearly that regional friction played a decisive role in shaping the development of royalism, just as it influenced the evolution of the insurgency. The longing for regional autonomy afflicted royalists and republicans alike.

The other bastion of Neogranadan royalism lay in the south, in the Province of Pasto. The province was a mountainous region with a largely Indian population; some sixty per cent of the 30,000 inhabitants were classified as Indian in the 1778 census. The provincial capital, San Juan de Pasto, was a substantial city in colonial terms. Its population of roughly 8,000 was more than double the size of Santa Marta, the new viceregal capital.[50] In the south, Cartagena's role was filled by Quito. The two cities had long been at odds;

in 1825 the British consul in Guayaquil indeed referred to the 'rivalry and hatred which has always existed between Quito and Pasto'.[51] This rivalry was partly if not entirely economic in origin; the two regions competed for markets for their principal export, woollen cloth. Thus, the Pasto *cabildo* reacted with suspicion when in 1809 it received a letter from the newly-formed 'Supreme Junta of Quito', suggesting that Pasto recognize the junta, severing its links to the colonial authorities in Santa Fe. Instead, they correctly interpreted the letter as a threat of invasion, and prohibited all unauthorized movement in and out of Pasto.[52] On 16 October 1809, the city of Pasto was indeed attacked by about a thousand insurgent troops from Quito. An ill-equipped and rapidly assembled Pastuso army led by the patrician Tomás de Santacruz nonetheless defeated the Quiteños at Funes, south of the city of Pasto.[53]

After the battle, Pasto's *cabildo* not only sent to Spain the traditional report detailing their victory, but also enclosed an appeal for greater municipal privileges. The contents of this and subsequent appeals illustrate well the quest for autonomy so typical of New Granada's First Republic. The Pasto *cabildo*'s requests were bold. In 1809, it asked for judicial independence from Quito's Audiencia, and the erection of a college in Pasto, so that Pasto's youth would not be obliged to depend on institutions in Quito. It also called for the construction of fortifications on the frontier between Quito and Pasto and, for good measure, requested that a new Audiencia be established in Pasto.[54]

None of these requests was met; so, following further victories in 1814 the *cabildo* again wrote to Spain. No more modest than in 1809, this time it requested that Pasto be granted a bishop and better schools, as well as that certain taxes be eliminated.[55] These requests—that Pasto be the seat of a bishopric, indeed of an Audiencia—reveal the Pasto elite's longing for the emblems of colonial prestige which their rival Quito already enjoyed. Similar requests were made by Santa Marta. The *cabildo* of Santa Marta repeatedly asked for special privileges in return for their continued resistance to the republicans in Cartagena. Their petitions too suggest a deep concern with the colonial markers of status and hierarchy. On 5 March 1812, for example, Santa Marta's *cabildo* requested that the city be granted the title of *muy noble y muy leal* ('very noble and very loyal') and that a special tax be levied on aguardiente to pay for the construction of a new town hall. They also asked that members of the *cabildo* be allowed to call themselves 'excellency' and that the *cabildo* be permitted to employ two additional mace-bearers to add greater solemnity to their gatherings.[56] The new republican juntas did not need to petition anyone; the republicans in Socorro simply announced the creation of a new bishopric in their province.[57]

For the Pasto *cabildo*, the war represented an opportunity to overtake Quito. Pleas similar to those sent in 1814 were repeated throughout the war, and at one point Pasto went to the expense of appointing a special envoy to travel to Lima to present their case to the Peruvian viceroy. The envoy succeeded only in extracting a congratulatory letter praising Pasto's loyalty from the colonial authorities in Guayaquil. This being the only thing available, Pasto's *cabildo* determined that the congratulations from Guayaquil be 'printed and many copies distributed to all the cities in the Americas'.[58] Every effort was made to acquaint the world with Pasto's merit. The city's authorities hoped the outbreak of war would provide Pasto with an opportunity to increase its importance within the colonial structure. While cities such as Quito and Cali hoped republicanism would allow them to achieve a more prominent place within regional hierarchies, Pasto placed its faith in royalism. Their goals were, however, very similar.

The threat from the first junta in Quito was short-lived, as the junta collapsed by the end of 1809. However, Pasto continued to face military threats from another source. Insurgent troops from Santa Fe led by Antonio Baraya marched south, and in March 1811 defeated Pasto's royalists at Bajo Palacé, outside Popayán. This insurgent victory, the first in the war of independence, was a humiliation for Miguel Tacón, governor of Popayán and commanding royalist officer. Tacón's troops refused to obey his orders to attack, and some of his soldiers even opened fire on their own side, causing considerable damage.[59] Once Popayán was in the hands of the republicans, Governor Tacón fled down the Patía River towards Barbacoas, and eventually retreated to Pasto.[60]

These events caused great alarm in Pasto, and many believed surrender to the insurgents was the only option, particularly as they again faced attack from Quito after the establishment of Quito's second junta in April 1811. To meet this new threat, Governor Tacón, by then resident in Pasto, organized a force of some thousand men to defend the city. These troops faced an invading army roughly five times larger, which not surprisingly captured Pasto on 22 September 1811 and sacked the city. The insurgent forces from Quito remained in Pasto for some months, during which time the Pastusos 'felt heavily the miseries of war ... suffering much from the excesses of the independent troops'.[61] Prompted by the unfortunate situation in Pasto, and perhaps unsettled by the incursion of Quiteño troops into New Granada, the revolutionary Junta of the Confederate Cities of the Cauca began negotiations with the forces from Quito, whom they convinced to return to their own city. The leader of the Confederate Cities, Joaquín Caycedo y Cuero, then established a new republican government in Pasto, thus linking Pasto to the other Confederate Cities of the Cauca. This body, unlike Quito's junta, enjoyed the support of many of Pasto's prominent citizens. Indeed, on 13 October 1811, the city held a *cabildo abierto* (town meeting) presided over by Caycedo y Cuero, and attended by members of the regular *cabildo*, the clergy and other local notables, at which those attending declared that 'they recognized the Junta Suprema de Santa Fé de Bogotá; that they united themselves with the Junta of Popayán; and that the *cabildo* members, along with the secular and regular clergy and the people of the town, embraced the patriot cause and from then on would defend it'.[62] As long as the move for independence did not emanate from Quito, many of Pasto's elite were prepared to accept it.

Pasto's conversion to insurgency was short-lived. In early 1812 Caycedo y Cuero travelled to Quito. Seizing the opportunity, several prominent royalist *disafectados*, including the former mayor of Pasto, led an unsuccessful rebellion against the temporarily leaderless insurgent government. Caycedo y Cuero returned to Pasto, but was soon the victim of a more successful revolt. On 20 May 1812, royalists from the Patía Valley marched into Pasto at the invitation of the disaffected Pastusos and defeated the republicans. The Patianos, blacks from the scorchingly hot Patía Valley, formed an unlikely royalist alliance with the Pastuso elite, united in their distrust of republicanism.[63] Although it was to take several further encounters with the troops of the Confederate Cities to secure victory, the royalist alliance eventually succeeded in vanquishing its opponents. Royalists recaptured Popayán on 30 June 1813 and Cali on 6 July 1813, and successful expeditions were launched against remaining insurgents in the Cauca Valley.[64] The second Junta of Quito had already been vanquished by Toribio Montes. Republicanism was thus for a time eliminated from the south of the viceroyalty.

With the suppression of the second Junta of Quito and the defeat of Caycedo y Cuero came a lull in hostilities, but the calm was not to last. Several matters served to disrupt the re-established colonial order. To begin with, Colonel Juan Sámano was appointed commander of the royalist troops stationed in Popayán, and within a very short period he managed to irritate major sections of the Popayán citizenry. It was widely claimed that Sámano's arbitrary, abrasive and non-deferential manner drove many back into overt opposition to royal government. He allowed his troops to loot outlying haciendas, arrested a number of important citizens on suspicion of collaboration with the republicans, and detained several parish priests on the same grounds. Sámano reportedly did not get on well even with his own troops.[65]

This became a matter of importance, for in September 1813 Antonio Nariño, President of Cundinamarca, the insurgent government in Santa Fe, marched south with twelve hundred infantry soldiers and over two hundred cavalry, well supplied with ammunition and other necessities, with the intention of bringing republicanism to the south. Nariño had only recently emerged victorious from a protracted dispute with proponents of federalism over the proper form of government for an independent New Granada. After thus consolidating his position in the interior he embarked on an attack of the royalists in the South, who were the most obvious danger to the precarious republican government in Santa Fe. The pitiful forces of Captain General Montalvo in Santa Marta did not constitute a threat to anyone.

The republican offensive began well. Nariño had no problem attracting Indian guides; most of the work of transporting heavy artillery over the mountains was done by Indian porters. A number of local priests also assisted.[66] The commander of Nariño's advance guard, José María Cabal, successfully defeated Sámano on 30 December 1813 at Alto Palacé. Sámano withdrew from Popayán to Pasto, after having detonated all the gunpowder stockpiled in the city, causing thirteen deaths. Again demonstrating his poor leadership, Sámano was defeated at the hacienda of Calibío on 14 January 1814 by Nariño's army, which grew as Sámano's troops deserted. The republicans remained in Popayán until late March 1814, and then marched on Pasto.

En route they were subjected to frequent guerrilla attacks by royalist Indians. Future Colombian president José Hilario López, who participated in the campaign as a youth, claimed that the region around Pasto was infested with royalist guerrillas; throughout the campaign artificial rock slides and showers of stones rained down on the republicans, leaving them demoralized, if not dead. There was talk of returning to Popayán, and general gloom reigned in the republican camp. Matters were exacerbated, according to López, by Nariño's bad temper and inflexibility.[67] The republicans nevertheless defeated the royalists in a number of confrontations, despite the fact that Sámano had been replaced as royalist commander by the less unpopular Melchor Aymerich.[68]

In Pasto itself, preparations for the attack were underway. The *cabildo* and Nariño exchanged a series of withering letters, which served only to inflame passions on both sides. The *cabildo*'s final communication with Nariño concluded, 'In short, we place our fate in the hands of the Lord who knows how to knock down into the mud with the tiniest stone even the most colossal self-inflated big heads like you.'[69] They insisted that Nariño was the aggressor, leading an invading army intent on perturbing their customary tranquillity. Nariño had been expecting reinforcements from the north, but these failed to arrive. He nevertheless insisted, against advice, on attacking Pasto without the additional troops on 10 April 1814. Royalist commander Aymerich played little part in the conflict, which was fought by the inhabitants of Pasto and Nariño's troops. The Pastusos resisted fiercely, and thousands of men and women poured into the streets to fight. The Indians who had been summoned to defend the city also acquitted themselves well. As the Pasto *cabildo* unappreciatively put it, 'those very Indians, those degraded men so cowardly and incapable of grand enterprises, presented themselves, guns in hand, chests bared to the bullets, and were prodigal with their valour'.[70] Like Viceroy Montalvo, the elite in Pasto had difficulty in accepting the local Indians as military partners. Nevertheless, the Pasto elite, like Santa Marta's governor Ruíz de Porras, understood well the importance of good relations with their indigenous allies. The colonial authorities in Pasto made considerable effort to recruit Indians to their cause by extending favours to them. A case in point is the Indian tribute, the principal fiscal burden weighing on Indian communities in New Granada. In the years between 1808 and 1811 the *cabildo* of Pasto succeeded in reducing the level of this head tax from five pesos to one peso. The motive for this reduction was spelled out in a further attempt to reduce the tribute. In 1814 the *cabildo* wrote to Ferdinand VII to request that 'the Indians, our inseparable companions in all military efforts' be exempted entirely from the tribute, 'in this manner to stimulate them so that every day they will become more faithful and grateful to a father who so liberally rewards their service'.[71] In this regard the relationship in Pasto between elite and Indian was symbiotic, not parasitic.

The inhabitants of the city and the Indians of the *resguardos*, the land set aside by the crown for Indians, repelled Nariño's forces, and Nariño was separated from his troops during the chaotic republican withdrawal. He hid for several days in the forests, then, driven by hunger and thirst, surrendered without giving his name to a group of Indians, promising to reveal to them the location of General Nariño. On his arrival in Pasto a large and unruly crowd gathered to learn the hiding place of the wicked insurgent general. Nariño, after fortifying himself with some broth, stepped onto the balcony of the house in which he was being held to address the crowd. 'Pastusos', he cried, 'if you're looking for General Nariño, here he is!'[72] This revelation was greeted with calls for his immediate death, but Aymerich, who had been impressed with the intelligence of the previously unidentified prisoner, intervened. Despite his eloquence, Nariño was imprisoned for thirteen months in Pasto under unpleasant conditions. He later described his stay: 'Imagine for a moment, gentlemen, that you see me locked in a tiny room, lying on an uncomfortable bed, covered with a *ruana* [poncho], chains on my ulcerated feet, without a friend, without a book to distract me, and expecting every minute to [be executed].'[73] Nariño exaggerated, as he was certainly not without friends in Pasto. On the contrary, his sojourn was enlivened by the undisguised admiration shown to him by Pasto's royalist commanders. Nariño chatted openly with royalist officers about his plans for New Granada, and was on such good terms with them that rumours circulated that he was plotting a general republican uprising from his cell in Pasto.[74]

Nariño was eventually sent to Spain, where he languished for four years in prison in Cádiz before being freed in the wake of Spain's constitutional revolution in 1820. Aymerich, in disgrace after his behaviour during the battle of Pasto, did not regain President Montes' confidence, and Juan Sámano was once again appointed to command royalist troops. Even after the defeat of Nariño, some thousand insurgent troops remained in the Cauca Valley, and Popayán itself was still in republican hands.

In 1815, southern New Granada, like the Caribbean coast, was in a state of uneasy equilibrium. The two regions had been the only parts of New Granada where resistance to independence had enjoyed some success, but while Santa Marta and Pasto did not succumb to republicanism, neither succeeded in eliminating it from their domains. The royalist enclaves had served two principal purposes during New Granada's First Republic. They had blocked the expansionist ambitions of their more powerful neighbours, Cartagena and Quito, thereby weakening the movement for independence in these cities. The capture of Nariño in Pasto similarly deprived the capital of one of its ablest leaders. Secondly, the survival of two staunchly royalist centres encouraged the belief in Spain that many Neogranadans opposed independence. The absence of any such royalist focuses in the Viceroyalty of Río de la Plata was partially responsible for Spain's subsequent decision not to send military reinforcements there. The presence of reliable bases in New Granada and Venezuela, on the other hand, made the viceroyalty a much more attractive destination.[75] The royalist resistance of Santa Marta and Pasto was thus much more than a bulwark against insurgency. It helped attract the military support from Spain necessary for a royalist reconquest. The next chapters will detail the success of Spain's reconquering expedition, sent in 1815 under the command of Spanish General Pablo Morillo.

General Morillo arrived in New Granada to find a polarized society. Many regions had been in a state on continual warfare for five years. Some, like Cartagena, had tasted real autonomy for the first time and were unwilling to return to the former diet of subservience. Others had grown tired of the fighting and disorganization and were disillusioned with the advocates of independence. These rifts were not healed by the arrival of Morillo's Expeditionary Army. Centres for royalism such as Santa Marta and Pasto, which had withstood the onslaught of republicanism, expected to receive preferential treatment. Individuals who had tacitly supported independence expected to be pardoned, and the republican elite hoped to be treated with respect, rather than the disdain previously expressed by peninsulars towards creoles. All these expectations were to be dashed by General Morillo and his officers.

PART II

RECONQUEST
1815–1819

Map 2
NEW GRANADA

3

The Reconquest of New Granada

Plans to organize a substantial expedition to relieve royalist forces in the Americas were first discussed by Spain in June 1814, following Ferdinand VII's return to the throne. Ferdinand's government did not at first reveal that it intended to send such an expedition to Venezuela, and instead let it be known that its destination would be Río de la Plata. This ruse was intended to mislead the Comisión de Reemplazos, the privately-run agency that was bankrolling the expedition. The Commission was composed primarily of Cádiz-based merchants whose wealth derived from the strictly controlled trade with the American colonies. It had therefore been agitating for an army to be sent to Buenos Aires to regain control of that viceroyalty's substantial trade with Spain. The Commission had relatively little interest in protecting Spain's very limited trade to Venezuela and New Granada. The destination of the expedition was thus kept secret from both the Commission that was funding it, and from the participating officers who led it.[1]

The troops enlisted in the Expeditionary Army, although unaware of their true destination, were nonetheless extremely unhappy. Few wished to risk their lives fighting in the colonial war, be it in Buenos Aires or Venezuela. Many attempted to desert before the ships embarked, and some officers allegedly had to be bribed to remain in their posts. Rumours of barracks uprisings abounded.[2] After various delays the expedition left Cádiz on 17 February 1815 with twenty warships, fifty-nine transport vessels and 12,254 men. Two thousand, five hundred were to go to Panama. The remainder were destined for New Granada and Venezuela.[3] It was not until they had been at sea for over a week that the true destination of the expedition was revealed to the troops. The news caused general consternation.

'We all knew', recorded Rafael Sevilla, an officer in the Expeditionary Army, 'that in Buenos Aires and Montevideo the rebels were divided, and that one group was awaiting our arrival, in order to defect to our side, [while] in Costa Firme, the war was fought without quarter, with savage ferocity.'[4]

Pablo Morillo, the expedition's commander, was thirty-seven years old at the time of his appointment. Morillo had first joined the Spanish army in 1791 as an ordinary soldier at the age of thirteen. Although he had accumulated some military experience before the French invasion of Spain in 1808, it was during the Peninsular War that he rose to prominence. He was appointed field marshal in 1813 and won several notable victories against the French. In 1814, he was named to lead the expedition to the Americas and was promoted to general. A professional soldier, Morillo was widely respected for his military talents.[5] In his personal manner Morillo was described as blunt, not to say rude. Even royalists complained of his arbitrary and insulting behaviour; one official described him as 'a man without principles, with a violent nature'.[6] This negative view was not universal, but the consensus was that he was a man with little social grace and little desire to acquire any. In this regard the contrast between Morillo and the republican leader Simón Bolívar was striking. Bolívar, a privileged member of the Venezuelan elite, possessed a ready wit, a great facility with words and, by all accounts, a natural elegance. Morillo, abrasive and gauche, moreover emerged from a far humbler background than Bolívar. Although he died a marquis, Morillo remained, in the eyes of his contemporaries, fundamentally plebeian. 'He never forgot that he had been a sergeant who had mixed with the lowest classes of the army', complained the patrician José Manuel Restrepo.[7] New Granada's aristocratic revolutionaries were to find Morillo horribly unwilling to conform to the norms of their polite world.

General Morillo in Venezuela

Venezuela's First Republic had fallen in 1812, but its collapse had not restored tranquillity. Blacks who had fought with the royalists against their republican masters rebelled again, this time against the restored royalists, once it became clear that a return to Spanish rule would bring them no benefits. Within three months of the royalist commander Monteverde's triumph, an antiroyalist revolt had broken out on the coast, and pardo bands, 'half-brigands, half-revolutionaries', ranged across the country, robbing and pillaging.[8] Meanwhile, the creole revolutionaries planned a comeback. Returning from Cartagena, where he had taken refuge after the fall of Venezuela's First Republic, Simón Bolívar marched a force of some seven hundred men from New Granada into Venezuela in mid-1813, executing Spaniards as they went. He won a series of victories in his 'Campaña Admirable', capturing Caracas in August 1813. The royalists, however, were no spent force.

One individual was particularly responsible for the revival of Spain's fortunes. A Spaniard long resident in the Venezuelan Llanos, José Tomás Boves appeared on the military stage in February 1814. The Llanos, the immense flood plains that extend between Venezuela and Colombia, were home to vast herds of wild cattle and horses, and also to the Llaneros, nomadic cowboys who lived in a state of anarchic freedom described by contemporaries as shocking barbarism.[9] Leading a band of nominally royalist Llanero horsemen, Boves enjoyed victory after victory over the republicans, recapturing Caracas on 16 July 1814. Ignoring the existing royalist administrative hierarchy, he declared himself governor of Caracas, president of the Audiencia, captain-general of Venezuela and commander of the royalist army. As by this stage he commanded some twelve thousand men, few were in a position to disagree.[10]

Boves distinguished himself by the savagery of his attacks and his lack of interest in differentiating between combatants and civilians. His troops routinely sacked the cities and towns that fell to them. He was widely accused of instituting a reign of terror in Caracas after its capture; secret nocturnal executions awaited those who had not already fled.[11] Forced contributions and seizures of valuables followed. Among the republicans the name of Boves became a byword for atrocity, but the royalist commanders were often lukewarm in their condemnations. Captain General Montalvo praised his valour, and merely criticized his 'imprudence'; other royalists appear to have regarded Boves as a hero.[12]

Boves had many followers. According to Venezuela's Captain General Cajigal, this was because Boves had offered his troops

> two strong incentives [to join his forces]: the wicked were able to satisfy their depraved instincts with robbery (officially labelled 'sacking'), assassinations, rapes, and every type of depredation; while for good men, the only guarantee of personal safety was to enlist in Boves's army.[13]

There were of course other reasons for the Llaneros' anti-republicanism. Since the formation of Venezuela's First Republic, the region's creoles had been attempting to reduce the Llaneros to a 'regimented peon class'.[14] The intention was to incorporate the Llanos, once a virtually autonomous region, into the orbit of Caracas. The 'Ordenanzas de los Llanos', legislation issued by the revolutionary junta in Caracas in 1811, prohibited virtually all the activities previously carried out by the Llaneros. The plainsmen were not to travel without a passport, or they would be lashed, the rounding-up of wild cattle was outlawed, and all Llaneros were to obtain permanent employment or be forced to work on a ranch. As Miguel Izard observed, the Ordenanzas by themselves explain the ease with which Boves recruited the Llaneros to his cause.[15]

Boves' troops restored much of Venezuela to the royalists during 1814. Boves himself was killed in December 1814, but his place was taken by Francisco Tomás Morales, a man cut from the same cloth. Then, on 15 March 1815, the Expeditionary Army of General Pablo Morillo landed in Venezuela with a force of 10,500 men, equipped with thousands of guns, swords and other weapons. Morillo's brief was to re-establish Spanish control, but he soon learned that this had already been accomplished by Boves. Indeed, the only remaining military objective was the recapture of the island of Margarita, which had become the base of republicans under the leadership of Juan Bautista Arismendi. This was accomplished with great speed by Morales, who retook the island with a battalion of *zambos*, people of mixed African and Indian ancestry. Morillo pardoned Arismendi, contrary to all advice, and a military governor was placed in charge of the island.[16]

The capture of Margarita effectively completed the reconquest of Venezuela. Few committed insurgents had survived Boves' terrible slaughter of 1814, and those remaining in Venezuela were quickly captured by Morillo's troops in the months that followed. Indeed, the arrival of Morillo's army in Venezuela at first altered little the course of the conflict, as already the royalists were everywhere in military ascendancy. The army of Boves, however, was not much appreciated by Morillo. To begin with, even the most cold-blooded royalists had to admit that Boves' troops had committed some 'excesses' and were perhaps not model soldiers. More importantly, this army was composed mostly of *pardos*. Morillo, like Venezuela's republican creoles, feared he was witnessing the start of a caste war. Challenging the monarchy was deplorable, but to royalist eyes, upsetting the racial hierarchy was, if anything, worse.[17] Rather than rewarding Boves' *pardos* for their defeat of the insurgents, Morillo demoted many and retired more. These men became ready converts to Bolívar's cause.

The royalists were thus hoist on their own petard. Unable to learn from their experiences in 1812, when disgruntled *pardos* had deserted Monteverde's royalist government, the triumphant royalists again failed to acknowledge *pardo* demands. After the death of Boves in December 1814, the Llaneros' contribution to the defeat of Venezuelan insurgency went unappreciated by Spanish royalists. When Morillo dismissed and demoted Llanero leaders, what followed was a repeat of events in 1812. The Llaneros first returned to the plains of Casanare and Apure, and then raised the banner of independence. Thus republicanism, which had been virtually eliminated from Venezuela in 1814, grew in popularity after the arrival of Morillo's army.

Following Morillo's entry into Caracas, a military government was established. Morillo set up courts to try suspected insurgents and reorganized the city's bureaucracy, in particular suspending the Audiencia, an action that was to generate years of bureaucratic controversy. He also irritated virtually all of the city's existing civilian government. He demanded unreasonable quantities of food for the troops, and was gratuitously rude to government officials. Wildly exaggerated stories of Morillo's offensive behaviour circulated; Captain General Cajigal claimed one official was so badly insulted that he fell into a coma and went mad.[18] Outside Caracas, the army confiscated vast amounts of food and livestock.

By May 1815 Morillo had completed the reorganization of the Caracas administration. In July he left Venezuela for New Granada, leaving Brigadier Salvador Moxó in charge of running the Captaincy General. Moxó, whom Morillo's English language biographer Stephen Stoan regards as the true villain of the Venezuelan reconquest, was thus responsible both for the day-to-day running of the dictatorship, for that is what it had become, and for supplying the Expeditionary Army.[19]

The Siege of Cartagena[20]

> A woman with a distinguished countenance, all skin and bones and weak as a child, was competing with a vulture for the right to collect some disgusting piece of rubbish. Nearby, the bodies of an old beggar and two children were decomposing in the sun.[21]

On 22 July 1815 Morillo arrived in Santa Marta, accompanied by some eight thousand troops, of whom over three thousand were Venezuelan.[22] From Santa Marta, he began to plan the recapture of Cartagena, the most important military objective in New Granada. Given Cartagena's formidable defences, Morillo decided to besiege the city, rather than attempt a direct assault. Cartagena was at the time somewhat vulnerable, having only recently survived a siege by Simón Bolívar; disagreements between Bolívar and Manuel del Castillo y Rada, the leader of Cartagena's insurgents, had led the future liberator to blockade the city. His efforts failed, and on 9 May 1815 Bolívar had departed for Jamaica. Perfect trust had not, however, been established between Castillo and the Venezuelan troops left behind by Bolívar. This distracted the insurgent leaders from the royalist threat, which they indeed largely discounted. At the time, Cartagena contained one or two thousand insurgent troops.[23]

Many of the towns and villages surrounding Cartagena were quickly captured by the royalists and thousands of their inhabitants swore loyalty to Ferdinand VII.[24] The division of Brigadier Morales, as well as Morillo's Venezuelan vanguard, were sent ahead from Santa Marta towards Cartagena, and Brigadier Pedro Ruíz de Porras, governor of Santa Marta, marched towards Mompós with a thousand men. The royalist headquarters was established at the Hacienda de Torrecilla (now Parenquillo). The siege began on 22 August 1815, although a blockade was established some weeks earlier, and foreign governments in the Caribbean were warned against trying to trade with Cartagena.[25] Morillo did not at first attempt to negotiate with the insurgents in Cartagena, nor did he offer any conditions other than complete surrender. He did however issue numerous proclamations urging the Cartageneros to submit to Spain's gentle yoke.

The effects of the siege were soon felt. Inside the city walls, Cartagena was reduced to misery and hunger, despite the periodic shipments of flour and other foods they received from English and Haitian vessels able to evade the Spanish blockade. The Spanish repeatedly captured funds intended for the purchase of food in the Antilles, and towards the end of the siege the population was reduced to eating boiled leather.[26] Moreover, thousands of people from the surrounding countryside had swarmed into Cartagena, placing even greater strains on the food supply. The city's leaders nonetheless did not wish to surrender. Indeed, in October 1815 Castillo y Rada was removed from office in a palace coup organized by individuals who suspected him of negotiating secretly with Morillo to arrange the city's capitulation. José Francisco Bermúdez, a Venezuelan who had fled from the island of Margarita after its recapture, was then elevated to commander. Bermúdez attempted to reorganise the city's meagre food reserves, and ordered all *bocas inútiles* ('useless mouths') to leave the city.

Meanwhile, the Spanish troops were themselves in difficulties. Thousands of soldiers died from infectious diseases during the siege. In October 1815, two months into the siege, Morillo reported 'we are suffering a considerable loss of Spanish troops [because of] this perverse climate which is fatal to Europeans'.[27] By December 1815, the royalists had lost over three thousand troops to death and desertion.

Although Cartagena's insurgent leadership was expecting the arrival of help from the interior, none arrived. The misleading and unrealistic propaganda about the small size of Morillo's army and the false reports of their own strength circulated by Cartagena's republican leaders had redounded to their detriment; few in the interior realized the desperate state of Cartagena's republicans, and those who did apparently shared an unfounded confidence in Cartagena's ability to survive. No reinforcements were sent and New Granada's most important city was left to defend itself.[28] Increasingly desperate, Cartagena's leaders considered plans to place Cartagena under British protection. Moreover, over two thousand people attempted to leave the city in late November 1815. A last flotilla of escapees put to sea on 5 December 1815. The next day the city capitulated to the Spanish.

The siege had lasted 106 days. The long blockade had reduced Cartagena to a pitiful state. Morillo described the vanquished city as 'the most painful spectacle of my life'.[29] Over seven thousand people, more than a third of the city's population, had died of hunger and disease.[30] This is by far the largest death toll for a single military operation in Colombia's entire war of independence. Corpses lay unburied, while those who had survived 'were not men, but … living images of death'.[31] The Spanish immediately began a programme of fumigations, prohibited the sick from entering Cartagena and opened large communal graves into which the dead were thrown.[32] Public soup kitchens were established and, by all accounts, Spanish troops were generous in sharing their rations with the starving citizens of Cartagena.

The Army was less generous in its treatment of captured émigrés. At the time of the surrender, rumours that Morillo intended to massacre the inhabitants of Cartagena prompted hundreds of frightened families had put to sea in small, overcrowded boats, but since they had no pilots many lost their way and the passengers either died of hunger or were captured by the Spanish off the coasts of Panama and New Granada.[33] One survivor reported that he and about a hundred other people had left Cartagena in early December 1815; when he was picked up by the Spanish a few weeks later only twenty passengers remained alive.[34] Dozens of these captured émigrés were executed. In addition, over four hundred men, women and children were massacred in cold blood near Bocachica after having surrendered to Brigadier Morales.[35]

After the surrender of Cartagena the royalist blockade of the Caribbean coast was extended to the entire Atrato river region, not to be lifted until mid-August 1816.[36] From its recapture on 6 December 1815 until 1821 (with the exception of the period from mid-1818 to August 1819), Cartagena served as the administrative capital of royalist New Granada. Captain General Francisco Montalvo, who was promoted to viceroy on 28 April 1816, set up residence in the city, where he was joined by the Santa Fe Audiencia, the Tribunal de Cuentas and a variety of other colonial bureaux. Morillo established a permanent court martial to try suspected insurgents, and restored the Inquisition to its former dwellings. The rocky relationship between Morillo and Montalvo, as well as the courts martial and the other reconquest institutions, will be considered in the next chapter.

Consolidating the Conquest

The arrival of Morillo's army greatly alarmed the inhabitants of Santa Fe. In his diary the Santa Fe artisan José María Caballero recorded the increasing anxiety and sadness that enveloped the capital after the fall of Cartagena.[37] Public faith in the republican Congress had plummeted, despite a change of leader. After the resignation of Camilo Torres, José Fernández Madrid took office. Madrid, well liked and eloquent, was unable to restore confidence in the government. When in early 1816 he asked for volunteers to fight Morillo's army, no more than six individuals responded to his plea.[38] Little hope remained for the young republic.

Meanwhile, following the successful recapture of Cartagena, the Expeditionary Army began to move toward Santa Fe. (Remaining in Cartagena as a garrison were the Regimiento de León and the Battalions del Rey, Puerto Rico, Albuera (later Valencia) and Granada, as well as several smaller companies. Together these numbered some 2,500 troops.) Morillo himself left Cartagena on 16 February 1816, but already some officers who had not participated in the blockade of Cartagena had begun working their way into the interior.

These expeditions took several routes.[39] First, Santa Marta's Governor Pedro Ruíz de Porras and Vicente Sánchez Lima went directly to Mompós in September 1815. Sánchez Lima soon captured various insurgent leaders, such as Pantaleón Germán Ribón and Martín Amador. (Sánchez Lima subsequently assisted Francisco Warleta in recapturing Antioquia, where he remained as governor until removed from office by Morillo for being excessively conciliatory.) A second force led by Lieutenant Colonel Julián Bayer had left Cartagena for the Chocó, going by boat up the Atrato river in December 1815.[40] Although initially obliged to withdraw from the Chocó, Bayer subsequently succeeded in opening communications with Colonel Francisco Warleta in Antioquia.[41] Finally, Colonel Sebastián de la Calzada had been working his way into New Granada from Barinas, in Venezuela.

Sebastián de la Calzada was an uneducated and illiterate fighter, whose troops were regarded by Morillo as 'a bunch of undisciplined guerrillas'.[42] He nonetheless played an important role in the reconquest of New Granada. In late 1815, he had assembled a force of over two thousand men in Venezuela and began marching into New Granada through the Llanos de Casanare. He had suffered one defeat at the hands of Joaquín Ricaurte, but managed to arrive in Cúcuta with three-quarters of his force intact. He there defeated first Rafael Urdaneta, future president of Colombia, and then the combined insurgent force of Custodio García Rovira and Francisco de Paula Santander in a major battle at Cachirí on 21–22 February 1816 that cost the republicans over one and a half thousand men.[43] This latter victory effectively destroyed the remaining republican resistance in New Granada; henceforth no military obstacle stood between the royalists and the capital. Calzada then joined Colonel Miguel de la Torre and their two forces entered Santa Fe on 6 May 1816. They faced no resistance, as the republican reserves and indeed the republican government had fled a few days earlier. Their entry into Santa Fe prompted great anxiety and, consequently, great festivities. Determined to convince Calzada and La Torre of Santa Fe's devotion to Spain, the city's inhabitants put on a tremendous display of royalist fervour. The streets were festooned with white flags and the royalist troops were greeted by loud cheering. Caballero recorded the events:

> On this day the royalists and regentists unmasked themselves, and it was the day of the transfiguration, like on Mount Tabor, because within an hour—from 10.00a.m. to 11.00a.m.—everyone was transfigured so that all the splendour was royalist; even those distinguished patriots were transfigured in such splendour that I couldn't recognise a single one of them .... The women were a sight to see, running out into the street like madwomen with little flags and white bouquets, shouting 'Long live Ferdinand VII'. They rushed into the palace and crowded onto the balconies, and at 11.00a.m. the soldiers entered; the women on the balconies cheered enthusiastically.[44]

La Torre, in charge of the Second Division, had been proceeding via Ocaña and Girón to Santa Fe, where he was to join the Fifth Division led by Calzada. Girón distinguished itself as a centre of royalism; the city organized a ball for the troops, but all towns in this region welcomed the Spanish, including the once fervently insurgent Socorro.[45] Tunja was captured in April 1816.

Morillo himself went toward Santa Fe, via Mompós, Ocaña, Girón, San Gil, Socorro, San Benito and Zipaquirá. On 16 May 1816, he arrived in Santa Fe without a battle, amid more triumphal arches and festivities. Refusing to participate in these propitiatory celebrations, he retired immediately to his new headquarters. All efforts to convince him of the sincerity of the Bogotanos' conversion to royalism failed, and he rebuffed a collective plea for mercy delivered to him soon after his arrival by a party of elite women. He did however agree to pardon lower-ranking soldiers.[46] Simultaneously, Morillo began executing well-known revolutionaries, including many of Santa Fe's most distinguished citizens. Over one quarter of the viceroyalty's lawyers, for example, were executed in 1816.[47] This sudden execution of creole notables, a defining event in subsequent Colombian historiography, deprived the revolution of many able leaders and distinguishes the counter-revolution in Colombia from the independence processes in the remainder of Spanish America. Nowhere else was did the creole elite suffer a comparable decimation. Such executions did not occur even in Mexico, although royalists there meted out draconian punishment to suspected revolutionaries of the lower classes.[48]

Meanwhile, Colonel Francisco de Paula Warleta, who had already proceeded from Cartagena to Antioquia, was on his way up the Cauca river to Nechí and Zaragosa. On 22 March 1816, he defeated Andrés José Linares at Ceja Alta, south of Remedios. The battle lasted four days and involved over a thousand troops, although Warleta reported that the insurgents tended to flee rather than fight.[49] This important victory sealed Spanish control of the region.[50] In August 1816, he moved south to Cali, and in September was named commander of royalist forces in Popayán. Both in Antioquia and in the south he arrested and executed large numbers of people, often for the most minor offences. In this, Warleta aroused great hostility even among royalists, who accused him of undermining attempts at reconciliation.[51] Warleta remained in New Granada until 1820, when he left Cartagena in order to avoid having to swear loyalty to the Constitution of 1812.

Colonel Donato Ruíz de Santa Cruz, in turn, left Cartagena to join Brigadier Juan Sámano in Pasto, going via the Magdalena river to Honda, and thence to La Plata. He captured Nare in late April 1816.[52] Meanwhile, Juan Sámano, commander of the Third Division, marched north from Quito to destroy the remaining insurgent forces in the Cauca region. Sámano, commanding some 1,300 troops, defeated insurgent troops at the battle of the Cuchilla del Tambo, outside Popayán, on 29 June 1816. The insurgent troops, who had numbered some seven hundred, lost all their heavy artillery and most of their officers were killed.[53] This victory delivered Popayán into Spanish hands and secured the south for the royalists. The remaining republican forces, led by Pedro Monsalve, fled east to La Plata, where they were defeated by Carlos Tolrá on 10 July 1816.

By July 1816, all New Granada was again in royalist hands, with the exception of the Llanos de Casanare, to which a handful of insurgents had escaped. This 'reconquest' was completed rather rapidly. Aside from the siege of Cartagena and the two important battles of Cachirí and Ceja Alta, the recapture of New Granada did not pose major military difficulties to the Spanish. Indeed, after examining the Spanish reconquest of New Granada, the Colombian military historian Jorge Mercado acknowledged:

> The simple truth is that there was no military opposition to the realisation of [Morillo's plans]. The country was in complete anarchy and the Independent Army—if we can dignify with this name the scattered irregular forces that decorated themselves with military titles—reproduced faithfully this state of confusion and disorder.

The reconquest, he concluded, was a walkover, a mere *paseo militar*.[54] This evaluation, while perhaps exaggerated, does emphasize the relative ease with which the Spanish restored royal authority in New Granada. Unlike their Mexican cousins, New Granada's insurgents did not pose a significant military obstacle to royalist forces. Thus in 1816 Morillo's troops were not obliged to develop the sorts of innovative counter-insurgency techniques used by their royalist contemporaries in New Spain.[55] Most importantly, the inhabitants of New Granada did not oppose the Spanish invaders *en masse*. The capital itself surrendered to the royalists without a battle and welcomed the reconquerers with the traditional deputations of beautiful young women and triumphal arches. In short, in 1816 at least, Spain was still regarded by many in New Granada as a creditable agent of government. The reasons for this are not difficult to discover. By 1816, the inhabitants of New Granada were deeply disillusioned with their new republican leaders. Independence had brought civil war and conflict. Spain's General Morillo benefited from what Juan Friede has called a 'protest vote' against the insurgents.[56] Furthermore, by 1815 many of the insurgents themselves were afflicted by serious self-doubt. The defeat of Napoleon in Europe and the return of Ferdinand VII to the Spanish throne greatly disheartened republican troops. One captured insurgent officer reported in 1815 that the news of Ferdinand's return was having a terrible effect on his troops: 'he had noticed a lot of dejection, and ... every day there were resignations from officers and soldiers'.[57] General Morillo's task was an easy one. Sent to reconquer a populace ready to be reconquered, he profited from the divisions and ineptitude of the governments of the First Republic. José Manuel Restrepo indeed speculated that even had the insurgents succeeded in uniting their disparate forces under a single military command, the populace of New Granada itself would have risen up to welcome the Spanish.[58] Under such circumstances, the royalists' initial success is entirely understandable.

In the autumn of 1816, after the completion of the reconquest in New Granada, most of the royalist army returned to Venezuela. The royalist forces remaining in New Granada consisted of the Second, Third and Fifth Divisions of the Expeditionary Army. The Second Division was led by Miguel de la Torre, the Third Division by Juan Sámano and the Fifth Division by Sebastián de la Calzada.[59] Only the Third Division remained in New Granada for the duration of the war. The Second and Fifth Divisions were sent to Venezuela in 1817 and 1818. Within the divisions operating in New Granada, the most important units were the First and Second Numancia Battalions, the First Battalion of the Regimiento del Rey, the Cazadores del Tambo and the Regimiento de León, which formed the garrison in Cartagena. The Numancia Battalions and the Cazadores del Tambo were new units; only the Regimiento del Rey and the troops in Cartagena's garrison had come with Morillo from Spain.

The Expeditionary Army

Despite its initial successes, the Expeditionary Army was not an unfailing bulwark protecting the restored royal regime. On arriving in America, it had consisted mostly of veterans of the Peninsular War. This did not necessarily mean the troops were well disciplined, and in any event the stock of veterans was soon exhausted. Indeed, in 1818 Morillo was obliged to request that greater care be exercised in selecting soldiers:

> The troops sent to America should, in my opinion, consist of honourable men of good conduct, and not of the multitude of deserters and bad soldiers who are usually rounded up to be sent overseas... Here [these] men do more damage than the enemy themselves. One cannot hear without shuddering the excesses committed by the former battalion of Granada ... and the so-called Curros de Monteverde. These units, composed primarily of deserters, thieves, convicts and the most perverse soldiers in the entire army committed every sort of crime when they arrived in these provinces.[60]

'With this sort of "pacifier"', warned Morillo, 'your majesty will never reduce the revolted American provinces to their duties.'[61] Recruitment of Americans, however, produced equally undesirable troops, in the view of many officers.[62]

Numerically, Morillo's forces and those opposing him were fairly evenly matched when Morillo arrived in America, although some Colombian historians have preferred to describe the Expeditionary Army as an invincible war machine. According to Jorge Mercado, at the time of the reconquest the insurgent armies in New Granada numbered roughly six thousand. These were spread across New Granada, with the largest group concentrated in Cartagena, where about 1,600 troops were garrisoned.[63]

Many of the insurgent soldiers had previously been members of the colonial royal army and had thus received some military training, although this of course did not mean they had gained any experience of actual warfare.[64] The great difference with the royalists was that the insurgent forces were not united under a single command, and were scattered across New Granada under different political entities.

While the Expeditionary Army numbered some 10,500 troops at the time of its arrival in Venezuela, only about five thousand of these accompanied Morillo to New Granada. The remainder stayed in Venezuela under the command of Salvador de Moxó. A further three thousand-odd Venezuelan troops followed Morillo to Cartagena.[65] After the siege of Cartagena, these royalist forces were reduced by some three thousand, although new recruits from New Granada increased numbers considerably. By mid-1817, Morillo had some seven to eight thousand men in New Granada, while a further three to four thousand remained in Venezuela. Bolívar, Páez and their allies had by this time recruited an estimated fourteen thousand troops.[66]

The Expeditionary Army was rapidly creoleized, or more precisely, Americanized. Already in early 1815, 2,500 Venezuelan troops participated in the assault on the island of Margarita, and thousands of Venezuelans were recruited to accompany Morillo to New Granada.[67] Moreover, many new units were formed in both New Granada and Venezuela. Following Sámano's victory at the Cuchilla del Tambo, for example, Morillo formed a 'Batallón del Tambo', to be composed primarily of troops from Pasto.[68] The royalists also continued their earlier practice of recruiting blacks and slaves. One, and perhaps more, battalions of slaves were formed by Morillo himself in Venezuela in 1818.[69] Initially, the traditional exemptions enjoyed by married men, the very young and the very old were honoured. As the war progressed, however, the depleted royalist ranks were increasingly filled by anyone fit enough to shoulder arms. This occasioned many bitter complaints both from those recruited and from civilian officials. In 1817, for example, the president of Quito, Toribio Montes, objected that in Pasto Colonels Sámano and Warleta were recruiting indiscriminately from the married and the single, the old and the young.[70] ('Young' recruits might have been very young; it was not unknown for ten year olds to participate in fighting.[71])

While new battalions were formed, others were dissolved, either because the majority of the troops had died or deserted, or because they were guilty of misdeeds. The latter was the fate of the Third Battalion del Rey, for example.[72] Those units which remained intact often suffered dramatic reductions in size. The Second Battalion del Rey, for example, contained 750 soldiers in February 1816. By October 1821, it had been reduced to a mere three men. Overall, by 1817, there were reportedly no European troops at all in New Granada, with the exception of the Regimiento de Leon in Cartagena.[73] This implies the loss of over four thousand expeditionaries, a reduction of eighty per cent in two years.

There were two principal causes of this decline in troop numbers. The first, and most important, was the high mortality suffered by the soldiers. Death did not result only from injury during armed conflict. Thousands of royalist troops, Spanish and American, died of disease while serving in the army. The army's health will be discussed in chapter 6, although it is worth noting that disease, and not battle, was the primary cause of death during the War of Independence. The other great cause of falling troop numbers was desertion. Desertion plagued the Expeditionary Army even before it left Cádiz. There, many conscripts tried to flee, and the garrisons were constantly guarded to prevent escapes. The problem merely worsened on arrival in the Americas. Spanish soldiers did not hesitate to desert even at this great distance from their own homes.[74] In May 1816, Morillo complained that in Caracas royalist troops were 'deserting in flocks'.[75] By 1819, entire battalions were deserting.[76] Neither repeated orders that soldiers caught deserting would be shot, nor offers of generous prizes for those apprehending deserters appear to have had much effect.[77] Attempts to conscript Neogranadans never succeeded in replacing those lost to death or desertion, despite Morillo's best efforts.

Morale among Spanish troops appears to have been generally poor. Few Spanish soldiers wanted to be in the Americas in the first place. Volunteers were rare; most were conscripts: the prospect of death far from Spain had little appeal. Certainly the reports on life in the Americas that reached Spain were often alarming. Margaret Woodward records that soldiers 'brought back to Spain hair-raising descriptions of dense jungles, of deserts "like petrified seas" and tales of "putrefying corpses, impenetrable forests, man-eating reptiles", and of tigers "roaring in the night".'[78] Moreover, it soon became clear to the troops that they would see little material benefit from their hardships. Salaries were not paid, and even during the heady successes of 1816 food and supplies were in short supply.

The relationship between the members of the newly arrived Expeditionary Army and New Granada's existing military establishment did not always run smoothly. Prior to the outbreak of the war, New Granada, and indeed all of Spanish America, had been defended by the Army of the Americas. In New Granada this force consisted of garrisons in Santa Fe, Cartagena, Santa Marta, Ríohacha, the Chocó, Antioquia, Popayán and Panama. Various local militia forces also existed, although many observers had doubts about their effectiveness and loyalty. Of the regular troops, the most important were the Batallón Auxiliar de Santa Fe, The Regimiento de Infantería Fijo of Cartagena (the 'Fijo de Cartagena') and the Batallón Fijo de Panamá.[79]

Difficulties between these and Morillo's troops arose for several reasons. At one extreme were the units of the Army of the Americas that supported the movement for independence and joined the insurgents. These units, which had to be struck from the list of official Spanish forces, included some of the most important in the colonial army. The Fijo de Cartagena was heavily implicated in the outbreak of revolution in Cartagena in 1810, and ceased to exist as a royalist unit. (A later 'Fijo de Cartagena' was in fact an entirely new battalion formed by Francisco Montalvo in 1815.) The Batallón Auxiliar de Santa Fe became the backbone of the Republic of Cundinamarca's army and, after the recapture of the capital by Morillo, it was replaced by the royalist Batallón del Tambo, a new unit formed in 1816.[80] Various other colonial units were dissolved for similar reasons.[81] The shortage of royalist soldiers, however, made it necessary to recruit members of these extinguished units back into the Expeditionary Army in late 1816. This measure simply filled royalist ranks with republican supporters.[82]

Spanish troops showed little respect for their American colleagues. The widely held Spanish view that Americans were bad soldiers with no understanding of military discipline did not endear the expeditionaries to Neogranadan troops. Morillo did little to counter the prevailing prejudices when in 1815 he issued orders that Spanish troops were under no circumstances to ridicule the native troops, despite their obvious and evident backwardness.[83] The conversion of the Spanish Expeditionary Army into a largely American force alarmed Morillo, who predicted disasters would result from leaving the defence of the colony in creole hands.[84] He and other royalist officials sought consolation in history; Cortés had conquered Mexico with an army of natives, and the Romans had enjoyed their greatest military successes using foreign troops. Philosophical musings aside, however, most Spanish officers retained the greatest distrust for their

American troops. 'An ephemeral force', Morillo called them.[85] Spanish royalists never reconciled themselves to the fact that many of their allies weren't Spanish. Spanish officers particularly distrusted the blacks, mulattos and *castas* (people of mixed race) who made up a large part of the royalist army in Venezuela. These men, allegedly prone to insubordination, alarmed royalist officers who, like their republican colleagues, came to fear race war.[86] The oscillating attitude towards slave and *casta* units illustrates well this ambivalence, for royalist anxieties about arming the *castas* coexisted with pragmatic recruiting efforts. In 1817, for example, Lieutenant Colonel Simón Sicilia attempted to form a regiment of *gente de color*, or 'people of colour', in the Chocó, but then stopped, halted by the direct intervention of Viceroy Montalvo.[87] This mistrust of the section of Venezuela's population most ready to support the royalists was a grave mistake. The Venezuelan Llanero and *casta* troops increasingly joined the republican army, to devastating effect.

A further problem for the royalist forces arose over the question of who retained supreme command over troops in New Granada. Officers from the Expeditionary Army claimed authority over all other royalist commanders already in the Americas. These latter officers, who had defended the rights of the crown from 1810 to 1815, resented the expeditionaries' attempts to seize control.[88] The question of command proved particularly vexing in Venezuela. Before 1815, virtually all royalist successes had been due to José Tomás Boves, Francisco Morales, and their Llanero allies. None of these men had official posts in the royalist army and, indeed, held that institution and its commanders in the greatest contempt. With the arrival of Morillo's army came the restoration of a more professional structure, and Boves' guerrilla leaders were demoted, demobilized and dismissed. They were then replaced by Spanish officers. The guerrilla leaders, who believed with reason that the recapture of Venezuela had been their doing, were deeply offended and, as has been noted, many joined the insurgents. The conflicts between the guerrillas and the professionals were typified by Morillo's disagreements with Francisco Tomás Morales, Boves' successor. Although Morillo retained Morales as an officer, against the advice of many civilian officials, he did not immediately award Morales the authority Morales might reasonably have expected. Bitter disagreements broke out during the recapture of the island of Margarita, and their relationship never recovered fully.[89] Similar conflicts developed between Miguel de la Torre, the young commander of the Expeditionary Army's second division and eventual replacement to Morillo, and various royalist guerrilla leaders, in particular Sebastián de la Calzada and Morales. La Torre regarded both Calzada and Morales as uncultured hooligans, while these latter viewed La Torre as a rule-bound incompetent.[90] That these disagreements were serious and important should not be doubted. The disastrous royalist defeat at Carabobo in 1821, which effectively ended the war in Venezuela, has been attributed by some to the personal incompatibility of La Torre and Morales, the two participating royalist officers.[91]

Poor troops and personal divisions among the royalist officer corps were not, however, the sole problem confronting the reconquest regime. It also faced serious political challenges, not least of which was the need the deal with supporters of the independence movements of 1810–1815, and to win back loyal supporters from New Granada's population. The way in which Spanish officials confronted these tasks is the subject of the following chapter.

4

Conciliation or Confrontation?

In 1816, in the aftermath of General Morillo's reconquest, New Granada's flirtation with independence appeared to be over. Spanish officials were then confronted with the task of reconstructing colonial society. To do this, the victorious royalist government had to decide how to view the past six years of virtual independence. Most pressing was the question of what to do with people who had supported the revolution. In Spain, Ferdinand VII's government attempted simply to erase the preceding six years of liberal rule by ordering that all aspects of government should return to their pre-war condition. Colonial officials in New Granada too would have preferred to turn back the clock. In practice, this was not possible. The restored colonial government was faced with the uncomfortable fact that most Neogranadans had coexisted quietly with the insurgent governments, and that many had served, with varying degrees of political fervour, in the new institutions and organizations set up by the republicans.

Spain and the *Infidentes*

Who became an insurgent? For many Spanish officials in the Americas, the answer was clear: perverse, ambitious creoles. The *cabildo* of Pasto, for example, ascribed the insurgency to the 'bad faith' which they decided was characteristic of republicans. 'Otherwise it would never have occurred to them to become insurgents', the *cabildo* deduced.[1] Similarly, the *consulado* of Caracas explained that the revolution in Venezuela was caused by 'a handful of unnatural men from this and the surrounding provinces, who were able to pervert many of the remaining villages in order to achieve their perverse aims'.[2] Neogranadan royalists, when they articulated their views, seem often to have believed the insurgency was driven by fratricidal hatred, greed and, more generally, impious wickedness. Only rarely were the insurgents described as fighting for principles, however mistaken. Direct encounters with actual insurgents did not necessarily alter this tendency. Captured insurgents rarely defended their beliefs. Most denied hotly any accusations of republicanism and instead affirmed their support for the crown. When Juana Morales was arrested for singing the revolutionary song 'General Bolívar rides his horse to kill Spaniards, Europeans, and *Canarios* [Canary islanders]', she did not defend her revolutionary views. Rather, she insisted that she had instead been singing the innocent royalist ditty 'General Morillo rides his horse into Caracas with his vassals'.[3] Even well known leaders of the revolution tried this approach. José María García de Toledo and Manuel del Castillo y Rada, both leaders of the insurgent movement in Cartagena, claimed during their trials that they had never supported independence, and expressed 'sentiments of love, obedience, and loyalty to our King Ferdinand VII'.[4]

On those occasions where denial seemed impossible, most stressed that they had supported the insurgents only after having been threatened, or because of the financial loss entailed in emigrating to royalist-controlled areas. Tomás Vásquez of Cartagena was typical in claiming after his capture in 1816 that he had remained in Cartagena during the period of insurgent rule only because he had been harassed into staying by the republican government, and had needed to support his large family.[5] Naturally, those detained by the royalists had powerful motives for denying insurgency, since those openly admitting to supporting the revolution were generally shot. Moreover, Viceroy Montalvo had announced in 1814 that his government would not regard as traitors those who had remained in rebel territory 'because of the well-founded fear of being mistreated' if they attempted to leave, which made this line of defence particularly attractive.[6] The effect was that Spanish officers had little opportunity to hear the republican position articulated with conviction.

Royalist interpretations of the war did not originate in a philosophical quest for the origins of republicanism. The reconquerers had far more practical concerns. They wanted to decide who in New Granada was an insurgent, and then determine what ought to be done with them. Should supporters of independence be punished, or should they be pardoned? Should punishment be exemplary, with principal revolutionaries being either imprisoned or executed, or, on the other hand, should punishment be corrective, and consist mainly in fines or temporary dismissal, with the ultimate aim of reincorporating the individual back into colonial society? This proved to be a large and intractable problem.

The question of what to do with colonial officials who had held office during the years of republican rule was particularly vexing. After the recapture of Cartagena in December 1815, the royalists set about re-establishing the colonial bureaucracy. To begin with, and as a matter of course, individuals who had served under the insurgents were removed from their posts until they presented a justification of their behaviour.[7] This invariably raised the difficult question of who should then be appointed to refill the post. As an illustration of the problems thrown up by this process, consider the appointment of a postal administrator for the province of Cartagena in 1816. In the summer of 1816, various individuals petitioned the newly-restored royalist government to ask for employment as the first post-insurgent postmaster in Cartagena. After some initial vacillation, the position was awarded to Ramón de Herrera, who had held the post during the years of insurgent rule. Herrera convinced Viceroy Francisco Montalvo that he had continued to work for the republicans only because he had needed to earn his living, and that despite his having served under the republicans, he was in fact a loyal subject of the crown. Viceroy Montalvo accordingly gave him back his job. However, the viceroy's decision to reappoint someone who had actually held office under an insurgent government was strongly criticized by other royalists, not least by the person who was to succeed Montalvo as viceroy, Brigadier Juan Sámano. Brigadier Sámano regarded Herrera as an unreformed traitor who with false claims of loyalty had duped Viceroy Montalvo into reappointing him. It need hardly be said that Herrera was swiftly removed from office and imprisoned after Brigadier Sámano was appointed viceroy in 1817.[8]

This example illustrates the considerable disagreements within the royalist camp over not only the appropriate treatment of suspected insurgents, but also the best definition of insurgency. Viceroy Montalvo regarded Ramón de Herrera as a reliable subject, whose insurgent past should not be held against him, while Juan Sámano considered him a traitor. Clearly some more codified system was needed to help the royalists determine who their friends were.

One of the earliest classifications was produced in 1815 by the Caracas Junta de Secuestros (or Confiscations Committee).[9] This divided suspect insurgents into three classes. The first were the leaders of the insurgency, people so well known for their support of independence that the Junta de Secuestros did not regard it as necessary to try them. The second class consisted of people who had passively supported the revolution without taking any active role in it. The third class contained those who fled the advancing royalist army. The Junta de Secuestros considered members of the first and third classes as traitors, and decreed that their goods could be embargoed at will. Members of the second class had the right to a judicial hearing that would investigate their behaviour. This distinction between active and passive support for the revolution remained the touchstone of royalist justice, although other modifications were later introduced. In November 1817, Ferdinand VII decided that even individuals who had voluntarily served in the insurgent governments should not automatically be considered traitorous. This was complemented by a decision of the Council of the Indies, taken in May 1818, that clear distinctions ought to be made between leaders of the insurgency and those who had merely followed.[10]

After the Spanish decided which actions were treasonable, they then had to determine who had carried out such activities. The manner in which the royalists collected names of possible revolutionaries was itself open to all sorts of distortions. Juan Manuel de Cajigal, Captain General of Venezuela at the time of General Morillo's arrival, complained that he and other royalists were continually presented with anonymous denunciations of suspected insurgents.[11] It is clear that some individuals used such anonymous accusations to settle private quarrels and exact vengeance. In 1819, for example, former *corregidor* José Joaquín de la Mota complained from prison that he had been falsely accused of treason by a couple whom he had earlier prosecuted for living in concubinage. Viceroy Montalvo himself admitted that such denunciations were often based on nothing more than malice, and lamented that the war was thus being used to settle private quarrels.[12]

Repression and Punishment

One model for colonial authorities seeking to purge sedition from the body politic was provided by Spain itself. After the return of Ferdinand VII, 'juntas of purification' had been established in Spain to investigate the conduct of government officials during the French occupation. As their name suggests, the juntas were concerned to 'purify' those contaminated with treason, or *infidencia*, a favourite word of the Fernandine period. Collaborators and *afrancesados*, those sympathetic to the invading French army, were removed from their posts, while those found to be 'pure' were returned to their positions. All those investigated were subjected to a long and harassing scrutiny. The wisdom of exacerbating hostility between Spaniards by these trials was questioned by ministers such as José García de León y Pizarro, but Ferdinand VII was committed to removing all collaborators from office.[13] This was not always easy to do, and it was in any event impossible to arrest everyone who had supported either the intrusive French King Joseph I or the more extreme liberals, who also fell under suspicion. Balancing retribution, reconciliation and realism proved to be a dilemma which, together with the juntas of purification, followed the royalist armies to the Americas. Tribunals and juntas of purification were established in Venezuela and New Granada, as well as in other viceroyalties. As in Spain, they proved both controversial and difficult to operate.

The unavoidable fact was that many Neogranadans had participated in some way in the insurgency. It was obviously not possible to arrest all these people for treason, but neither was it clear to the royalists who should be excused and who should be tried. Soon after the capture of Cartagena, General Morillo attempted (as a punitive measure) to draft into the Expeditionary Army everyone who had served in Cartagena's republican army up to the grade of sergeant, but he was dissuaded from doing so by Viceroy Montalvo. Montalvo pointed out that were General Morillo to do this, the city's work-force would be decimated. Everyone, down to the shoemakers and blacksmiths, had fought for the republicans. Nonetheless, one of the first acts of the restored Spanish government in Cartagena was to suspend from their posts all colonial officials who had remained in Cartagena during the period of republican rule.[14]

The need to develop a policy for dealing with suspected insurgents was acknowledged after the trial of nine prominent Cartagenero republicans.[15] The fate of these nine individuals, regarded by republican supporters as martyrs and by the Spanish as criminals, generated a bitter debate within the royalist camp, although this debate had little effect on the fate of the nine men. All nine were shot in February 1816, even though some had surrendered under the terms of a royalist pardon, and in spite of the fact that six of the nine men roundly denied being insurgents. No real trials were held, and the technical irregularities of these executions roused alarm even within the royalist camp. The matter was referred to Spain, the first in a long line of appeals (in this case posthumous) against royalist executions.

The procedural defects of the case and the lack of any established method for trying cases of treason led General Morillo and Viceroy Montalvo to establish a Consejo de Guerra Permanente, or Permanent Court-Martial, as had been done in Caracas, which was responsible for trying cases of *infidencia*, a term that included virtually all forms of support for the various insurgent movements.[16] These Courts-Martial aroused great hostility, both among the public and among the members of the royalist civil bureaucracy. The usual complaints by members of the public were procedural. The cases were heard verbally, that is, without simultaneous written records being made, and defendants were allowed little chance to defend themselves.[17] Not surprisingly, this in itself was unpopular. When, for example, Pantaleón Gutiérrez y Quijano was sentenced by the Permanent Court-Martial to five years in the Omoa Fortress, his wife complained that the court condemned him 'without allowing him to present his defence as the law demands', and asked that his case be reopened.[18] In many cases the accused was not permitted even to present witnesses in his defence.[19]

The conditions of the trials were hardly conducive to reasoned deliberation. Juan Manuel Arrubla, a resident of Santa Fe sentenced by the Permanent Court-Martial, described his trial:

> I was tried in the midst of the most horrific confusion, [which was] in fact inevitable given the excessive number of cases considered by the Permanent Court-Martial, all of which were heard simultaneously, and the sentences were carried out immediately after being decreed.[20]

The sentences of the Permanent Court-Martial were, as Arrubla notes, usually carried out 'without delay', thus allowing no time for appeals.[21] Moreover, many civilians objected to being tried by a military council in the first place.[22] Eventually the continual complaints about the methods and jurisdiction of the Courts-Martial led to the establishment of new guidelines. These spelled out the procedure for trying political prisoners, including former republican officials.

These guidelines were issued on 28 July 1817 and specified how different types of prisoners were to be tried.[23] Eight different classes of criminal were established and the appropriate method of trial for each was listed. The most serious crimes were to be tried by court-martial, either in an officer's court-martial, or a regular court-martial, depending on whether the offender was an officer, or a soldier or civilian. If the individual wanted to appeal, the viceroy and *oidores* would rehear the case. The sentence would otherwise be carried out immediately. Less serious crimes committed by civilians would be tried by the civil authorities. The sentences would still be carried out immediately, preferably on the very spot of the supposed crime.

Trial by court-martial was thus reserved for five specific types of prisoner. The first was spies; the second was deserters from the royal army who recognized the republicans, even if they had not joined them. A third category consisted of officers in the insurgent army. A fourth type was those who had served as military leaders of the insurgent movement. Finally, all members of the colonial armed forces who served in the republican army were to be tried by court-martial. Other types of offence would be tried by civil authorities. In particular, non-military trial was permitted for those who had worked for the insurgent bureaucracy and for those who produced what the royalists deemed to be pro-insurgent propaganda. Also to be tried by civil authorities were those who had taken advantage of the 'anarchy of a revolutionary government' to commit ordinary crimes against royalists. The punishment for crimes against republicans was not specified. Government officials who had remained in their post after the revolution of 1810, 'swearing and recognizing' the republican government were also to be accorded a civil trial. Thus, following the promulgation of these guidelines, no one who had served the republican government in a non-military capacity should have been tried by court-martial, although it remained possible for the viceroy to detain individuals without trial at his discretion.

Estimates for the number of people tried by the Permanent Courts-Martial vary considerably. Viceroy Montalvo reported in his Relación de Mando of 1818 that seven thousand people 'of the most prominent families in the viceroyalty' had been sentenced to death by the councils. The execution of a substantial section of the capital's creole elite was indeed the Santa Fe Permanent Court-Martial's principal achievement. Within weeks of arriving in the capital Morillo had assembled enough information about the workings of the revolutionary government to begin executing its principal supporters. The list of those condemned includes many now considered to be Colombia's founding fathers, individuals who had distinguished themselves by their political beliefs both prior to 1810 and during the First Republic. Within two months, Antonio de Villavicencio, José María Carbonell, Crisanto Valenzuela, Miguel Pombo, Jorge Tadeo Lozano, Antonio Baraya and Pedro Lastra were dead, along with many others. Not all sources confirm Montalvo's figures, but all agree on the prevalence of execution as a characteristic feature of the reconquest. Other contemporaries offered lower estimates of those sentenced to death in the capital by the Court-Martial. Santander referred to the execution of over five hundred individuals, while royalist officer Pascual Enrile insisted in 1817 that at most ninety men had been executed by Morillo's troops. In his diary José María Caballero recorded fifty three executions and another sixty two arrests, giving a total of 115 detainees in 1816, the year of the greatest number of executions.[24]

The Courts-Martial may not have been able try everyone who had remained in republican territory during the Patria Boba, but the leaders of the royalist army were mistrustful of anyone who had been involved in any way with the insurgent authorities and forces. They were prepared to consider the merits of former republican officials only after the latter had 'purified' themselves before a Consejo de Purificación, or Council of Purification. This institution was first established in New Granada on 30 May 1816 in Santa Fe. On that day General Morillo issued a limited pardon to soldiers and some officers who had served in the republican army. Those individuals encompassed in the pardon were to be enlisted in the Expeditionary Army as common soldiers for a period of time proportional to their earlier support for the republicans. In order to determine the length of time each individual was to serve, as well as to decide whether the pardon applied to a given case, Morillo decided to establish 'un consejo de purificación', along the lines of those already operating in Spain.[25]

The Council of Purification began operating on 16 June 1816 and consisted of a committee of six men. Individuals from not only the capital, but also the cities of Tunja, Mariquita, Neiva and Socorro were expected to appear before the Council to purify themselves.[26] The Council of Purification appears to have operated in conjunction with the Permanent Court-Martial, and began to consider the cases not only of those individuals specifically mentioned in the pardon of 30 May 1816, but also of those tried by the Permanent Court-Martial for non-capital offences.[27]

The usual form of 'purification' for republicanism was either a spell in the royalist army or the payment of a large fine. Primo Groot, for example, was tried in January 1817 and was sentenced to pay a fine of $4,000. This sum was equivalent to more than the official annual salary of a member of the Audiencia, and Groot complained in 1818 that because of this fine he was unable to support his family of six children.[28] An alternative punishment was enlistment in the royalist army. Those who were found innocent of any trace of republicanism were issued with a certificate of purification.[29]

The historian Guillermo Hernández de Alba identified 449 individuals who were investigated by the Council of Purification. Of these, roughly sixty per cent were found guilty of involvement with the insurgency. Those found guilty were sentenced to serve in the royalist army or to pay a fine ranging from $25 to $2,000, or both. The majority of those undergoing purification were public officials obliged to submit to the process in order to retain their posts.[30]

Priests, who by virtue of their special *fuero* were exempt from trial in secular courts, were not arraigned in these Councils. Instead, those suspected of insurgency were tried by the army's head chaplain, an unpopular man himself accused of various misdeeds.[31] Despite the Catholic church's later reputation as a bastion of royalism, it seems that many of New Granada's priests in fact supported the insurgents; Morillo arrested dozens of clerics on charges of insurgency, and Roberto Jaramillo has documented the participation in the war of hundreds of clerics from all parts of the viceroyalty.[32] By 1818, the problem of delinquent clergy was perceived to be severe enough to warrant a special report by the Council of the Indies detailing the course of action to be taken when a priest left his post to join the republicans.[33] It seems unlikely that many republican priests were removed from office as a consequence of the Council of the Indies' recommendations, as the procedure they advocated was complicated and slow. Priests, however, did sometimes lose their seat because of their revolutionary activities. General Morillo imprisoned a number of clerics in 1816, including several prominent churchmen.[34] Other insurgent priests were not removed officially from office. Rather, they were simply hounded into exile. Domingo Belcinario Gómez, the priest of the small Cauca Valley town of El Trapiche, for example, was forced to abandon his parish after having been detained on charges of insurgency. He was absolved by President Montes of Quito but, on his return home, was unable to occupy his post. During his absence, the parish priest of Almaguer had spread such terrible rumours about Gómez's revolutionary activities that he was unable to continue in office.[35]

Conciliation and Pardon

The question of what to do with individuals of doubtful loyalty was complicated by the many pardons and *olvidos del pasado* ('forgettings of the past') that were issued between 1810 and 1820. During this period more than twenty pardons were decreed by Ferdinand VII and the royalists in New Granada.[36] Some of these were directed specifically at 'the American criminals', while others included Spain's own *afrancesados* and similar dubious types. While the pardons were supposed to clarify the circumstances in which an individual could be regarded as innocent, as often as not they muddied the waters further. The terms of the various pardons were frequently contradictory, and often failed to spell out the details of their application. Nonetheless, the promulgation of a pardon always raised hopes. Although a pardon rarely allowed officials who had served under the insurgents to return to their jobs, it might commute imprisonment or other punishment inflicted for treason. Thus there was always a flurry of interest following the promulgation of each pardon.

The precise terms of these pardons were often little understood and this in itself led to great confusion. On 9 April 1816, for example, Viceroy Montalvo issued a pardon intended specifically for the inhabitants of the Province of Cartagena.[37] Within a few months further clarifications had to be issued, as individuals not living in the province had been applying and people living in Cartagena had been applying in the name of others not resident in the province. Furthermore, it was often unclear who was supposed to determine whether the pardon applied to a given individual. Cases were on occasion referred to the Council of the Indies, and hence to the king, and sometimes people even applied directly to the Secretary of State for individual pardons tailored to their particular case.[38]

It was often believed that an *olvido del pasado* was precisely that, and that the pardoned individual would be treated as if they had never supported the republicans. Rarely was this the case. The usual sticking point was whether a pardon allowed the *indultado*, or pardonee, to return to his job. José María Castillo, for example, in 1819 asked to be allowed to resume practising as a lawyer, since his wife had obtained a pardon for him. The matter was referred to the Council of the Indies, which determined that the pardon in question simply commuted sentences and did not involve the restoration of jobs. However, an 1819 royal order affirmed that while a pardon did not guarantee the restoration of jobs, having been pardoned was not to count against an applicant either.[39]

A more fundamental problem with the pardons was that the military authorities were often unwilling to release known revolutionaries, whatever the terms of a given pardon. During the course of the war General Morillo in particular became increasingly doubtful of the expediency of issuing pardons.[40] Pardons were consequently honoured grudgingly. When General Morillo felt compelled to respect a particular pardon, he did his best to enforce it in the narrowest sense. On other occasions, Morillo felt able simply to ignore the terms of a pardon altogether.[41]

The Viceroy and the General

The reconquest government established after 1815 did not commit itself firmly to any one strategy for dealing with former and suspected revolutionaries. Pardons were issued, but not enforced. Individuals were removed from their jobs, but not prosecuted. There was no clear consensus on what constituted *infidencia*, nor was there agreement on how to stop its spread. The reason for this was that royalists disagreed profoundly about the nature of the revolution. While military policy-makers, particularly those appointed under Ferdinand VII, generally insisted that the insurrection could be ended only by a military victory, civilian authorities by and large resisted the royalist army's efforts to impose a purely military solution on the conflict. These disagreements tended to widen an already existing fissure within colonial society. Conflict between civil and military authorities was a standard feature of colonial life; disagreements about the revolution merely exacerbated this problem.[42] In a region such as New Granada actively engaged in fighting a war, these concerns took on both a particular urgency and a virulent personal element. Disagreements about the nature of the war undermined royalist unity and sowed suspicion at the highest levels. The most serious, open and immediate rift developed between General Pablo Morillo and Viceroy Francisco Montalvo, the two highest-ranking royalist officials in New Granada.

General Morillo's official instructions from Ferdinand VII had expressed the hope that the general would work in harmony with Viceroy Montalvo. Disagreements between the two nonetheless surfaced soon after their first meeting in Santa Marta in 1815.[43] These initial conflicts revolved around the question of authority. Each man believed himself to be the supreme royalist commander in New Granada, and regarded the other as a troublesome interloper. In fact, in the time-honoured Spanish tradition, the two men had indeed been given overlapping authority. General Morillo based his claims to supremacy on the secret instructions issued to him by the king. These, he claimed, granted him jurisdiction over all aspects of the reconquest.[44] Viceroy Montalvo, on the other hand, insisted that Morillo's brief did not extend beyond the purely military aspect of the reconquest, and complained regularly that Morillo acted without his approval and interfered with his own decisions. He further expressed doubt about the very existence of Morillo's instructions, commenting on:

> the mystery in which [Morillo] has tried to cloak his authority, spreading everywhere the idea that the king has given him unlimited power, and other nonsense. So far he hasn't shown me a single royal order, *cédula*, or any other document which gives him such authority, nor have I been informed of any such thing by any minister.[45]

Morillo was in fact no longer in possession of a physical copy of his instructions from the king, as it had been lost in the fire on his flagship, the San Pedro Alcántara, earlier in 1815.[46] His inability to produce any document verifying his claims about the extent of his authority did not enhance his position in Montalvo's eyes.

The question of whose authority was supreme held such urgency because Viceroy Montalvo and General Morillo differed greatly in their understanding of the insurrection. The two had conflicting interpretations of the causes and nature of the war, and this difference in approach was a major obstacle to co-operation between Morillo and Montalvo.

General Morillo insisted that the king's authority would be restored only with the bayonet and the sword. He had little time for pardons or other conciliatory gestures, and pinned his hopes on a military victory. Already in early 1816 he had written to the government in Madrid that 'it is necessary that the court face up to reality; unless we decapitate all those who have been revolutionaries, they will continue to plague us. Thus we should have no mercy for those criminals'.[47] Morillo's views are neatly encapsulated in the following letter to fellow officer Miguel de la Torre. La Torre had attracted Morillo's wrath by failing to imprison every known revolutionary after his arrival in the capital. Instead La Torre had arrested only very few people; as a result he received an outraged letter for Morillo:

> My dear La Torre,
>
> Without doubt you're either living in cloud cuckoo land, have gone crazy, or don't yet know the [true nature of] the Americans. You tell me in your letter that the few genuine insurgents have already repented … [They've said that before, we've believed them, and look at the mess

> it got us into.] Now it is necessary to follow the King's orders which are to punish the leaders or motors of the revolution no matter how many times they tell us they're sorry, and your order was to arrest them immediately after arriving in the capital ... My friend, stop deceiving yourself and open your eyes to this rabble; they're just waiting for our soldiers to die of disease so they can throw themselves on us, in which case, you might be the first person they'd hang, as a reward for being so lenient.[48]

Morillo favoured a military victory not out of optimistic militarism, but rather because he thought the royalist cause was essentially doomed. During his stay in the Americas, Morillo became convinced that the great mass of the population in Venezuela and New Granada wanted independence, not a reconciliation with Spain. This conviction deeply affected Morillo's attitude towards the revolution. If the populace wanted independence, no amount of generosity would alter their position. Clemency, in Morillo's view, was thus pointless. Indeed, it was counter-productive, as it made Spain look weak and ineffective. To Morillo, the conciliatory approach favoured by Viceroy Montalvo was practically treasonous. Pardons and the like merely tied the hands of the royalist army, without having any positive effect at all.

General Morillo moreover disliked Viceroy Montalvo intensely on a personal level. He regarded Montalvo as a whining incompetent, inept and inexperienced with both the nature of the country he headed and with warfare in general; Montalvo's sword, Morillo commented sarcastically in 1818, was 'still a virgin after its long career; it will have no other merit than that of having belonged to an owner who lived for a long time'.[49] Morillo's dislike of Viceroy Montalvo was heartily reciprocated. Viceroy Montalvo was deeply opposed to Morillo's handling of the war and favoured a far more conciliatory approach. Montalvo deluged the court in Madrid with denunciations of General Morillo's misdeeds. He condemned Morillo's harsh treatment of those suspected of supporting the insurgency, typified by Morillo's infamous execution of some hundred notable revolutionaries in the capital in 1816. He decried Morillo's confrontational and irritating manner, his failure to control the behaviour of his subordinates and his shameless requisitioning of goods and money from the populace. This behaviour had serious consequences for the restoration of royal authority, Montalvo charged. In 1817 he complained:

> [Morillo's behaviour] has caused an infinite number of ills; ills which can be corrected only by time and the exercise of a great deal of prudence by those in government … Those [in New Granada] who had remained loyal to the king … are resentful, harassed, and bitter about the [royalist army's] lack of appreciation; [and] those who had hoped to be pardoned for their errors have had their hopes dashed, and are now offended and desirous of revenge; … and the entire kingdom is destroyed.[50]

Viceroy Montalvo thus explicitly blamed General Morillo for Neogranadans' disaffection from the royalist cause, and for the continuation of the war. Morillo's policies, he charged, had alienated supporters and opponents alike. What was needed, he felt, was a policy of moderation and peace-making, which he tried to implement by urging the military to limit its demands for food and money and by issuing pardons, whose terms General Morillo did his best to ignore.

What effect did this high-level split have on the royalist administration? To begin with, it consumed time that could more profitably have been spent elsewhere. The deep distrust that developed between these two most important royalist officials in New Granada caused many of what should have been straightforward administrative decisions to develop into major power struggles between General Morillo and Viceroy Montalvo. Vast quantities of ink were split over the question of whether the Tribunal de Cuentas, the body responsible for auditing the viceroyalty's accounts, should be situated in Cartagena or Santa Fe.[51] Similarly, Morillo and Montalvo spent a substantial amount of time to urging the metropolitan government to limit the other's authority. Morillo, for example, presented the crown with spurious reports that Montalvo wanted to resign, while Montalvo's constant complaints about Morillo's behaviour ultimately resulted in Morillo (temporarily) losing much of his authority in 1818, when the crown issued a series of condemnations of the general and his second-in-command Pascual Enrile.[52] More significantly, the reconquest government in New Granada simultaneously pursued two different, indeed contradictory policies. Viceroy Montalvo devoted considerable effort to limiting the power of the army, while General Morillo did his best to side-step the viceroy on important matters. Viceroy Montalvo issued pardons; General Morillo ignored them. Morillo's troops requisitioned food and money; Montalvo complained to Spain. The result was an inconsistent policy that did not show the colonial administration at its best.

If Viceroy Montalvo was a moderate conciliator, the president of Quito, Toribio Montes, represented the extreme wing of the party of conciliation. President Montes governed the Audiencia of Quito from 1812 until 1817, and had thus been responsible for overseeing the restoration of royal order after the defeat of Quito's second independent junta in 1812. Montes adopted an exceedingly conciliatory approach and very few republicans were prosecuted during his tenure in office, with the exception of a small number of individuals intimately linked to the formation of the first Quito juntas. Montes explicitly attributed the peace that reigned in Quito from 1812 to this policy of reconciliation and forgiveness. He stressed in virtually every communication with Spain that the Audiencia de Quito was the only part of New Granada untroubled by revolution, and that this was due entirely to his non-confrontational policy of reconciliation.[53] President Montes objected strongly to the hardline militaristic approach to the reconquest, and complained regularly that it was driving Neogranadans into the arms of the insurgents.[54]

Relations between President Montes and his colleagues mirror those between Viceroy Montalvo and General Morillo, revealing identical schisms. President Montes was not without allies. Not surprisingly, he got on well with Viceroy Montalvo, and the *cabildo* of Quito indeed petitioned for Montes to be granted the significant title of Marqués de la Conciliación, or the Marquis of Conciliation, for his efforts to end the war.[55] Yet other royalists objected strongly to his approach to the reconquest. Opponents believed that, far from having wooed former insurgents back into the loyalist camp, Montes had simply capitulated to the republicans. Complaints were made regularly that he sheltered unreformed insurgents and indeed appointed them to important government posts. His own *asesor*, or legal advisor, alleged that Montes was surrounded by insurgents from dawn to dusk, complaining that 'it is they who dominate his government and enjoy all his protection'.[56] Montes' claims that through conciliation he had kept the province at peace were dismissed, and his approach was regarded by many in the royalist army as little short of treasonous. Montes' unpopularity with the royalist army was such that periodic attempts were made to engineer his removal from office, as occurred in November 1815, when hardline royalist officers launched an unsuccessful coup attempt against the president.[57]

This was an extreme step, but it indicates the depth of feeling in the Quito military. Montes' conciliatory approach was thought by the rebellious officers to threaten the very reconquest. Such splits were not confined to the top levels of royalist government, but were also reflected at the provincial level in conflicts between governors and individual royalist officers. These conflicts are particularly well documented for southern New Granada, an area that was heavily contested throughout the war. In the province of Popayán, the royalist governor and local *cabildos* complained consistently that the royalist army was driving the populace into the arms of the insurgents through its confrontational behaviour and uncontrolled violence. The army's arbitrary extractions of money, *matériel* and food incensed these civilian officials because they believed such behaviour retarded the restoration of royal control. José Solís, the royalist governor of Popayán, stated bluntly, 'if there are any towns … which are tranquil, without a resurgence of the previous revolution, it is those in which there are no royalist troops'.[58] In other words, the presence of royalist troops actually impeded a royalist victory, in the view of the governor. Governor Solís complained repeatedly to Viceroy Montalvo about the counter-productive effect of the royalist army in his province, but, although Viceroy Montalvo agreed wholeheartedly with the governor's analysis, he was powerless to intervene. Royalist officers brazenly refused to recognize any authority other than General Morillo and his second-in-command Juan Sámano.[59] The only effect of Governor Solís' complaints was that he was labelled a traitor by royalist officers.[60]

The tension implicit in the reconquest institutions was never resolved during the duration of the war, with the result that the reconquest remained an uneasy mix of conciliation and coercion. The reconquest government was able to decide neither who was an *infidente*, nor whether insurgents should be pardoned or prosecuted. The continual conflicts erupting between the army and the civilian authorities, the ongoing distrust of advocates of a different approach to the war, the constant sabotaging of the work of conciliators and the unrelenting legal attacks on the army's attempt to rule by decree all took their toll on Spain's reconquest of New Granada. The royalists did not constitute a unified force, nor could they agree on a unified plan for reconquering New Granada. The inconsistency of these different approaches was not rectified, and in the years after 1816 the reconquest unravelled.

5

The Reconquest of the Economy

The permanence of Spain's military reconquest in New Granada depended in part on the success of a fiscal reconquest. During the years of the First Republic the collection of many of the viceroyalty's prime sources of funds had been fragmented or, on occasion, abolished. After 1816, the royalists hoped to revive the state monopolies and return taxation to central control, so as to generate sufficient income to allow the colonial bureaucracy to function and to cover the costs of the military reconquest. Moreover, political motives also impelled the Spanish to restore colonial fiscal structures: on his return to the throne, Ferdinand VII had ordered that all aspects of Spanish government in both Spain and the Americas be returned to their precise condition in 1808. Thus, one of the first actions taken by Viceroy Montalvo after Morillo's arrival in New Granada was to issue an order restoring the viceregal administration and the state monopolies to their status in 1808.[1]

In the same document, Viceroy Montalvo lamented that, during the years of insurgent rule, colonial fiscal structures had been overturned. Before the outbreak of revolution, he asserted, New Granada had been governed

> by an established [fiscal] system, all its branches in the most flourishing state of health, its employees paid, and with sufficient surpluses to meet extraordinary expenses, and everything in short promising the harmony that is the consequence of the rule of law.

This happy picture was not in fact a very accurate description of late colonial state finances. While during the previous decades income from state monopolies had increased, at the cost of much civil unrest, trade with Spain had declined vertiginously since the 1790s, and subsidies from Peru and Mexico had played a vital role in viceregal finance.[2] Thus Viceroy Montalvo was confronted with a contradictory task: he was required to coax New Granada's economy into yielding sufficient income to finance the reconquest and the restoration of the colonial bureaucracy, but obliged to do this by reintroducing fiscal structures that had never been wholly adequate and which were, moreover, very often unpopular. This chapter will examine the royalists' success in reconciling these goals.

One should begin by acknowledging the difficulty in forming a complete picture of government finances during the years of the war. To begin with, it seems little fiscal documentation was actually produced during the period. Bookkeeping procedures appear to have relaxed. In royalist-controlled areas, for example, governors sometimes failed to make the customary reports on financial affairs in their province.[3] When material was recorded the records were sometimes simply destroyed by warfare.[4] Thus what information is available often lacks continuity, making longer-term analysis difficult. Unclear or downright contradictory fiscal reports abound, and the historian must tread carefully to avoid sinking into a morass of irreconcilable figures. This unsatisfactory situation led one nineteenth-century commentator to assert that 'the period from 1810 to 1821, when the Republic of Colombia was created, has no fiscal history'.[5] With these limitations in mind, we will first consider the conditions of New Granada's economy during the years of the war, and will then turn to the royalists' attempts to restore the colonial fiscal structures and generate income.

The Impact of War

There is little agreement on whether New Granada suffered an economic collapse as a consequence of the War of Independence. While not claiming to answer this question fully, this section offers a brief survey of two key areas of New Granada's economy, namely mining and agriculture, during the years of the war.

Gold was New Granada's most important export and the presence in New Granada of accessible gold had been the prime motive for Spain's interest in the region. Although by the late eighteenth century the colonial government derived relatively little income from the *quinto*, the three per cent tax levied on gold, mining itself constituted New Granada's premier economic arena; gold accounted for ninety per cent of the viceroyalty's exports.[6] Neogranadan gold mining was a low-tech activity. The majority of the gold was extracted by the most primitive methods; gold dust was separated from the surrounding mud by sifting gold-bearing sand in a wooden bowl, or by running a stream of water across an area of deposit. Neogranadan mining thus required little infrastructure or expense, aside from the gangs of slaves who performed much of the work. It was, however, a profitable sector. Although gold production is difficult to measure directly, state revenue derived from mining increased steadily throughout the eighteenth century. Placer-mining in the Chocó accounted for much of this increase, and indeed for the region's importance. Significant gold reserves were also to be found in Antioquia and the Cauca Valley. By the last years of the eighteenth century, New Granada's mines were yielding at least two million pesos worth of gold each year.[7]

During the years of the war, however, very little mining was carried out. Indeed, Hermes Tovar has estimated that from 1811 to 1820 mining activity declined by forty per cent. In the Cauca Valley in particular, the productivity of mining deteriorated precipitously, as slaves either escaped or were seized by the royalist military to work on road-building projects.[8] Thus only a small amount of gold was being mined. Little of what was extracted was registered with the state. Miners preferred to smuggle gold out of the country rather than face the very real risk its being seized by the royalist army while en route to the region's mint in Popayán.[9] As a direct consequence, very little gold was brought to the Casas de Moneda, or Minting Houses, to be minted. In the case of Popayán's Casa de Moneda, only $10,920 worth of coins were minted during the whole of 1817 and 1818. In contrast, in 1800 alone Popayán's mint had produced coins worth over $920,000.[10]

The fact that little gold was mined or minted does not of necessity indicate that the country's mining infrastructure had been demolished, particularly as placer mining requires little by way of infrastructure in the first place. Indeed, both Anthony McFarlane and Malcolm Deas have argued that mining was at most disrupted by the war, rather than destroyed.[11] However, while mines themselves were not destroyed as they were in Mexico, the effect on Neogranadan mining of the flight, or requisitioning, of slaves should not be ignored. Much of the growth in mining production in the eighteenth century had been due to an increased supply of slaves; in the Chocó in particular the use of slaves had expanded considerably.[12] Slaves were thus an essential element of the colonial mining system.

Where slaves escaped from the control of their masters, or were seized by the royalist army to assist in building roads, mining became difficult. Thus, for example, mining in the Vega de Supía, near Anserma, stopped altogether after the entire workforce fled in 1817.[13] The loss of labour prevented a rapid development of the 'industry' after independence. It was not until the middle of the nineteenth century that production levels reached those attained in the late eighteenth century.[14]

To turn now to New Granada's agricultural base, there is similar disagreement about how severely the war damaged production. McFarlane asserts that the war had relatively little impact. Miguel Izard, on the other hand, stresses the sad state of New Granada's agriculture by the 1820s, claiming that by the end of the war the country was unable to feed itself.[15] Although New Granada was not afflicted as extensively as was Venezuela, and although the extent of devastation varied considerably from region to region, the condition of New Granada's agricultural base after the war was far from vibrant.

Many sources attest to the devastating effect of military forces on the countryside in southern New Granada. Leaving aside the deliberate destruction of farmland by troops, other factors combined to disrupt the agricultural cycle. To begin with, the requisitioning of farm animals meant that agricultural labour was continually interrupted. In the area around Anserma, for example, the Third Division of the royalist army reportedly requisitioned all horses for its own use, and moreover ate all the cattle in the vicinity. This, combined with the fact that slaves were constantly being removed from their owners' farms to labour in the various road-building projects, meant that little work was accomplished on the region's haciendas.[16] Similar situations obtained elsewhere in the Cauca Valley.[17] In Popayán, agriculture was described as being at a standstill by 1817, and the region's sugar mills were said to be completely abandoned.[18] Miguel de Letamendi, a royalist military commander stationed in the Cauca Valley, summed up the situation in a report from March 1817:

> The situation of the Cauca Valley is extremely piteous and also terrible. The villages are almost deserted, the *vecinos* [city residents] are living in the hills, the fields are not cultivated ...there are no animals aside from a few thin mares, and everything, everything seems to be heading towards complete collapse.[19]

In Pasto, further south, the situation was equally serious. Many observers noted the damage to farmland wrought by the presence of troops in the heavily contested province. The British traveller John Hamilton, for example, described the Province of Pasto as 'almost a desert waste' as late as 1825.[20] Not only were farms burned by republican armies, but the troops themselves, both royalist and republican, placed a major strain on the capacities of the local economy. Bolívar noted, 'Pasto does not have the resources to support a large army … In these mountainous regions an army of two thousand men consumes in a year all the cattle of the entire population'.[21] This was, of course, a standard consequence of warfare. As John Keegan has noted, troops and their animals usually eat their way though more food than any region can support. That is why armies prefer not to remain too long in any one area.[22] The problem confronting southern New Granada was that the Expeditionary Army apparently intended to remain in the region indefinitely. The presence of troops had similarly destructive effects in the Llanos, although there damage tended to be concentrated around the region's few towns. Lieutenant Colonel Donato Ruíz de Santa Cruz, writing from Chita, commented in 1817 on 'the miserable situation of these surrounding villages exhausted of all resources by the considerable transit of troops'.[23]

Agricultural activity in other areas was also affected by the war. When the Spanish army first arrived in Antioquia in 1816, they were impressed by the region's fertility and by the abundance of food.[24] Within a few years this had changed; by 1818 officials were commenting on the 'notable decadence of agriculture'.[25] Agricultural output in Panama, on the other hand, had been in crisis long before the war broke out. Little altered with the mainland's separation from Spain.[26] In Santa Marta, decline in agricultural production was primarily a consequence of the war with Cartagena, and had been serious since 1811. When Viceroy Montalvo arrived in the city in 1813, he reported that virtually all food production had ground to a halt and that the inhabitants were able to stave off starvation only by fishing.[27] Cartagena, in addition to suffering many years of warfare up to 1815, was subjected to the added burden of serving as the royalist capital through much of the war.[28] The city's *cabildo* lamented, somewhat extravagantly, that 'nowhere in the kingdom is there a province so poor and backward'.[29]

Further problems were caused by the displacement of people that accompanied troop movements. The arrival of the royalist army often prompted entire villages to flee to the hills, leaving their houses and fields abandoned. This occurred particularly in the greater Cauca, where the royalist army's many road-building projects were the main reason for flight. However, civilian emigration was not confined to the south, and contemporaries across New Granada recorded seeing whole villages retreating into the hills.[30] In the area around Mompós, for example, the population appears by 1816 to have fallen to roughly half its size in 1780.[31] In addition to fleeing from fighting itself or from the ransacking that came in its immediate aftermath, many civilians decamped to avoid being recruited into the army. Large numbers of people reportedly fled when Colonels Francisco Warleta and Antonio Plá attempted to recruit soldiers into the royalist army in the Cauca Valley.[32] In royalist strongholds such as Pasto or Santa Marta, the situation was reversed; the inhabitants fled at the approach of the republicans. The effect was the same: the abandonment of villages and a decrease in agricultural productivity. John Hamilton noted during his visit to Pasto, 'farms once well cultivated [are] deserted, and nearly all the population is extirpated'.[33] Whatever its cause, the consequence of this displacement was, as Charles Griffin has noted, 'very disfavourable to agriculture, stock-raising and mining'.[34]

After years of war, New Granada's economy was weakened. In many areas commercial agriculture was abandoned, mining had virtually ceased and whole villages lay deserted. It was on this fragile base that the restored royalists sought to rebuild their administration. Not surprisingly, the administrators were unable to generate an adequate income for the state. The crown monopolies failed to provide the accustomed revenues, direct forms of taxation proved difficult and unpopular, and trade suffered a further decline.

Rebuilding the Colonial Economy

The first and most ready source of cash available to the royalists was the possessions of suspected or convicted insurgents. These goods could be confiscated to swell royalist coffers. Confiscation of goods was an easy punishment; the goods of royalists had been similarly confiscated by the insurgents during the First Republic.[35] As we saw in chapter 4, confiscation was imposed by the Junta of Purification in Santa Fe. Fines of considerable size were imposed. José María Caballero recorded in his diary that 'those who escape with the smallest fines have to pay $200, $300 or $500, and anyone who doesn't pay: off to the north, with the troops!'.[36]

It was simple enough to confiscate money; confiscating belongings proved to be more difficult. After goods were confiscated, the state was left with the problem of converting them into cash. This was not always easy; generally such goods were placed in a government warehouse for auction. Further problems resulted from keeping goods warehoused for long periods awaiting sale. Theft of embargoed goods was a continuing problem. New Granada's widespread and long-term shortage of specie further impeded attempts to liquefy confiscated assets. Confiscated haciendas had to be administered if they could not be sold.[37] In order to deal with these matters a Junta de Secuestros, or Confiscation Committee, was established in Santa Fe after the city was recaptured. Its primary purpose was to oversee the sale or administration of confiscated goods, although it could also order confiscations. Viceroy Montalvo felt that similar juntas ought to be established in each major town. It is not clear whether any actually were, but Montalvo evidently thought this source of income had a considerable future.[38]

While confiscation provided an easy source of money, it was not a firm base on which to rebuild government finances. The royalist administration thus made efforts to restore the institutions that had provided the bulk of New Granada's income prior to 1808. The most significant of these was the tobacco monopoly. The tobacco monopoly had been introduced into New Granada in 1764 and rapidly became the single most important contributor to the viceregal treasury, accounting for over a quarter of government revenue. Following changes introduced in the 1780s, the monopoly regularly generated between $80,000 and $100,000 each year in the Department of Cartagena alone. Nationally, it had produced an annual yield in excess of $500,000 for the crown.[39]

The war brought changes to the monopoly and its administration. The monopoly had always been unpopular and its abolition often accompanied the first outbreaks of independence; Quito's revolutionary Supreme Junta simply abolished the monopoly outright in 1809.[40] Even in royalist Panama, the monopoly was abolished by gubernatorial decree in 1813, supposedly because of the 'complete lack of tobacco'.[41] Following the reconquest, Viceroy Montalvo declared the re-establishment of the monopoly. The area around the *de facto* capital of Cartagena was the first to respond to the 20 August 1816 decree, although monopoly officials were unable to occupy Cartagena's Casa de Tabacos (the local headquarters of the tobacco monopoly), which was being used to house part of the Regimiento de León.

Local trade in tobacco slowly picked up during the remainder of 1816. That year the monopoly produced a net yield of some $7,800 in the department of Cartagena. Gross income had exceeded $15,000, but many expenses ate away profits.[42]

During 1817 and 1818 revenues improved considerably, despite the loss of over seventeen thousand pounds of tobacco from Girón which allegedly fell into a stream near Mahates. In Cartagena the monopoly generated some $45,000 net each year. Nonetheless, overall income in the department reached only half the average in the years before the war, and in some of the smaller *estanquillos* (local outlets of the monopoly), income was only about seven per cent of the average during the colonial period. Other regions were slowly re-incorporated into the monopoly's orbit.[43] One of the most important was Mompós, where the monopoly was re-established on 17 May 1817. For the next two years it produced a respectable annual income of some $50,000.[44]

In order to function, the monopoly needed a steady supply of tobacco. In some areas, especially around Ambalema, cultivation of tobacco had continued uninterrupted throughout the war. Private, illegal production of tobacco also continued in many regions, especially in Valledupar.[45] After the battle of Boyacá and the loss of Santa Fe in 1819, the tobacco monopoly generated virtually no income for the royalists, as the areas around Mompós and Ambalema, where most of the tobacco was produced, had been captured by the republicans. Tobacco then had to be imported from Cuba to supply the addictions of royalist Neogranadans.[46]

In the South, the tobacco monopoly was re-established in 1817, but does not appear to have produced much income for the state.[47] The monopoly continued, however, to attract the same unwanted attention it had suffered in the previous century. In September 1819, after the battle of Boyacá, government tobacco warehouses in the Cauca Valley were the first targets of resurgent republican guerrillas, who burned tobacco depositories and murdered an administrator.[48]

The other great arm of colonial finance was the *aguardiente* monopoly. Together with the tobacco monopoly it provided nearly sixty per cent of viceregal revenues. Always unpopular, it had been abolished by Santa Fe's insurgent Congress. Its fiscal importance, however, was such that it was re-established by the royalists even before the recapture of Cartagena.[49] Initially some slight changes were made in its administration. In particular, Francisco Montalvo decreed that individual distillers would be allowed to set up personal contracts with the government for the production of *aguardiente*.[50] (Since 1780 all distillation was intended to be carried out only by government distillers.) This liberalization was, however, only temporary. On 11 May 1816, the monopoly was reopened in all its original glory. No more individual distillation was permitted, a chief administrator was appointed, and Cartagena's Governor Gabriel de Torres ordered estate owners to begin growing sugar-cane.[51] Problems immediately became apparent. By 11 June 1816 not a single producer had presented himself to Governor Torres to state how much sugar-cane he intended to grow, and a shortage of excise guards prevented vigorous prosecution of illegal production.[52] Importation into New Granada of Peruvian *aguardiente* also reduced the sale of the Neogranadan product, and in Cartagena much of the equipment used to distil *aguardiente* had been destroyed and had to be replaced.[53]

The reconstructed *aguardiente* monopoly thus got off to a slow start. In 1816, it produced less than $600 net in the department of Cartagena. Over the next two years, income seems to have improved, but, even in 1818, the monopoly generated a net income in Cartagena of only about $8,000.[54] This was a far cry from the $40,000 to $50,000 routinely produced in the province in the years before the war.[55] Contraband and illegal production continued to be a problem as had been the case before the outbreak of war. In 1819, for example, the administrator of the *aguardiente* monopoly in Cartagena complained of the flagrant violations of monopoly law occurring in the town of Chiriguaná. There, he reported, all *aguardiente* was supplied by private clandestine distilleries, which operated with the full knowledge of the town's officials.[56]

The *aguardiente* monopoly was, if anything, more unpopular than the tobacco monopoly, and even royalist officials tried to use the war as an excuse to abolish it.[57] In Panama, the monopoly had been abolished outright by Viceroy Pérez, ostensibly to reward the province for its loyalty.[58] In Cartagena, the city's *cabildo* complained that the re-establishment of the *aguardiente* monopoly had caused 'incalculable ills' to the province, and suggested that the complete elimination of the monopoly would be the best way to revive the region's stagnant economy. Cartagena's Governor Torres added his voice to the call for deregulation. Indeed, in early 1819 Viceroy Sámano himself was considering whether the monopoly served any useful purpose, and appointed a committee of experts to consider the issue.[59] In the end, however, changes had to await the triumph of the republicans, who (temporarily) abolished the monopoly in 1821.

Other branches of the exchequer were similarly affected by the oscillating forces of the royalists and insurgents. Indian tribute, the head-tax paid by all adult male Indians, was repeatedly abolished and restored by succeeding regimes. Although it had been abolished in 1810 by both the insurgent Junta Suprema de Santa Fe and the Cortes in Spain, tribute was far from finished as a fiscal force during the remainder of the war.[60] For both the Santa Fe Junta and the Cortes, abolition had been based on philosophical principles; no advice was given on how to replace the revenue previously provided by tribute monies. This was not a serious problem in areas like Cartagena, where tribute generated a minute income, but it did pose difficulties in some regions. The authorities in Santa Marta, for example, depended on tribute to pay their clergy.[61] As a result, the abolition of Indian tribute was effectively ignored in such areas both in New Granada and elsewhere.[62] For royalists, the problem of replacing the income formerly derived from tribute was rendered academic after Ferdinand's return to the throne. The king announced tribute's re-establishment under the new and euphemistic name of *contribución* ('contribution') in March 1815, and this order was repeated in New Granada in November 1815, during the siege of Cartagena. It was not until August 1817, however, that the viceregal government in New Granada set about reassembling the lists of tribute payers for those regions where they had been lost. It is not clear how much money the royalists collected in tributes after its reinstitution.[63]

These attempts to restore the colonial sources of income were accompanied by more innovative methods of generating capital. One of the more novel ideas for raising money was considered by the Council of the Indies in 1818. In that year the Council discussed a proposal to establish a national lottery in New Granada.[64] State lotteries already existed in Mexico City and Havana, as well as in Spain itself. (The Mexico City lottery was itself relatively new and distinctive, in that the purchase of tickets was obligatory.[65]) When the proposal for a (non-obligatory) lottery in New Granada was considered, the Council of the Indies was enthusiastic, as the plan seemed a painless way of raising money. In the end, nothing came of the proposal since the Council realized it had already granted an exclusive right to establish lotteries in the Americas to Gaspar Rico y Angulo, an official from Lima. Rico had proposed extending the existing Lima-based lottery (known as the *suerte*) to all of South America. The government in Spain, completely ignorant of the existence of the Lima *suerte*, had at first been slightly suspicious of the plan, but decided to approve the plan.[66] Rico, however, did not exercise his right to set up a lottery in New Granada, and so the idea of a national lottery was abandoned until the republicans came to power.

Free Trade in Cartagena

Intimately connected to New Granada's economic viability, and hence to the royalists' survival, was the status of external trade. Government income from taxes on foreign trade was second only to that generated by the tobacco and *aguardiente* monopolies during the late colonial period.[67] Before 1810 most legal trade had passed through the Viceroyalty's principal port, Cartagena. Royalist efforts at stimulating commercial activity thus centred on that city.

Cartagena had long been in economic difficulty. The underlying problem was a steady and persistent decline in Atlantic trade. Once the mainstay of the provincial economy, commerce with Spain had in fact been shrinking since the mid-eighteenth century, while contraband steadily increased further up the coast in Santa Marta and Ríohacha.[68] Various efforts had been made at reviving the city's flagging commerce, but the most fundamental issue remained the question of free trade. Debate over whether to permit completely free trade between Spain's remaining colonies and other countries remained unresolved throughout the years of the war. While demands for freer trade had been emerging from Cartagena's merchants for two decades prior to the outbreak of war, in Spain itself there was little call to liberalize transatlantic trade. On the contrary, the merchants in Cádiz, whose wealth depended on their exclusive control of the American trade, persistently opposed any liberalization. As these merchants played the principal role in raising money for royalist troops via the Comisión de Reemplazos, their opposition to any commercial reforms counted heavily. Indeed, the very formation of the Comisión de Reemplazos had been in part motivated by the desire to block moves toward free trade with friendly countries.[69] The Cortes and the Regency consequently showed slight interest in enacting free-trade legislation, and it was not until February 1823 that Ferdinand VII belatedly sanctioned free trade in the Americas.

In the Americas, on the other hand, a considerable number of royalist officials, to say nothing of the creole elite, favoured free trade with friendly colonies.[70] In New Granada, and not only in Cartagena, merchants had been agitating for permission to trade with friendly colonies in the Caribbean for decades. In 1808 Viceroy Antonio Amar had at last granted Cartagena's traders the right to do business with foreigners, and during the First Republic Cartagena's trading links with the Caribbean and the United States were further strengthened.[71] However, after the recapture of Cartagena, Morillo imposed a total blockade on Cartagena's ports, thus ending all trade with these regions. Predictably, there were soon calls for the blockade to be lifted. In view of the catastrophic economic situation in Cartagena, exacerbated by the royalist blockade, the city's officials recommended that the ports in Cartagena, Santa Marta and Ríohacha be reopened, and that trade with friendly colonies be permitted according to the terms agreed in 1808 by Viceroy Amar. Morillo consented in August 1816 to reopen Cartagena's port; trade with the British colonies in the Caribbean was then permitted.[72] This decision to reintroduce limited free trade was made without consulting Spain, whose government would doubtless not have approved. Considerable restrictions were nonetheless placed on this trade. An import tax of twenty-one per cent was imposed on goods brought into New Granada, and duties between two and seven per cent were levied on exported goods. All trade had to be carried out via Spanish agents, and merchants who imported more goods than they exported were penalized.[73] Moreover, certain imports were still restricted; the sale of cotton cloth produced outside the Spanish colonies, for example, remained prohibited.[74] Nonetheless, this very partial liberalization seems to have had a beneficial effect on Cartagena's trade. Income from the Cartagena customs house roughly doubled between 1816 and 1817.[75]

This limited liberalization was reversed after the elevation of Juan Sámano to the office of viceroy in 1818. Sámano, a convinced opponent of free trade, did his best to reduce, rather than expand, the size of Anglo-Spanish trade.[76] Hefty import duties were levied at Cartagena and Panama City. These measures attracted the criticism of New Granada's Caribbean neighbours. In September 1819, for example, Sir Home Popham, the Admiral of Jamaica and a great advocate of free trade, wrote to Viceroy Sámano to express his worries about the incredibly high taxes being levied on British goods imported into New Granada.[77] While not referring specifically to Cartagena, Popham's remarks illustrate well the restrictions that foreign imports incurred after Sámano's appointment as viceroy. Popham pointed out that British goods imported into Lima via Panama were taxed at sixty-eight per cent. This figure increased to a staggering eighty per cent if the import tax in Panama had not been paid in advance. These sums were obviously excessive and Popham observed that, under these circumstances, contraband was inevitable. He suggested that import taxes in Panama be lowered from twenty-four per cent to seventeen per cent, which had been the level charged during Benito Pérez's tenure as viceroy. Popham's suggestions met with no support from Viceroy Sámano.

It was not until 1820 that trade with the Caribbean colonies was again permitted, and this was only because the newly-established republican siege of Cartagena made it imperative to find sources of food. In an attempt to stave off total collapse, Cartagena's Governor Gabriel de Torres decided to abolish all taxes on the importation of food and to allow food-bearing ships to import an additional amount of non-edible merchandise tax-free.[78] Although these measures were initially successful, they did not provide enough food to supply the city. In any event, by early 1821 the government was unable even to pay for food already purchased. In September 1821 the city surrendered to the republican General Montilla 'because of the lack of food'.[79] Spanish officials during the war of independence thus continued the traditional practice of loosening restrictions on trade in times of exceptional crises. By 1820 this approach succeeded neither in stimulating much commercial activity in Cartagena, nor in solving the grave alimentary problems that confronted the city after 1820. The royalists' poor success in managing Cartagena's economy was summed up by Cartagena's Governor Torres in August 1820. Governor Torres lamented that the city's treasury had been reduced to 'an absolute nothingness'. 'A nothingness', Governor Torres added:

> from which it will not be able to emerge for many years, even if these lands were totally pacified, because the state monopolies, commerce, and agriculture have disappeared almost entirely as a consequence of the bloody and destructive warfare they have suffered for ten years.[80]

Cartagena's fate illustrates the inadequacy of the royalists' efforts to restore New Granada to the flourishing prerevolutionary state lauded by Viceroy Montalvo in 1815. While attempts were made to restore the royal monopolies, and to revive trade, these efforts failed. Profits from the royal monopolies, which in the later years of the eighteenth century had been reckoned in hundreds of thousands of pesos, fell to a few thousand, or at most, tens of thousands of pesos during the years of the reconquest. Similar declines occurred in most other areas of imperial receipts. By the time of its surrender to the republicans in 1821, the quasi-capital city of Cartagena was bankrupt. The economic reconquest was a failure. It was not, however, the only failure. In the next chapters we will examine the increasing air of crisis that enveloped the reconquest, as the state of military finance, the troops' health and their relations with Neogranadans deteriorated.

6

The Cost of Reconquest

While the Spanish army won military victories in New Granada, the republicans were enjoying a comeback in Venezuela. In May 1816 Simón Bolívar returned to the mainland and Juan Bautista Arismendi recaptured the island of Margarita. This obliged General Morillo to return to Venezuela in November 1816, leaving Juan Sámano as governor of Santa Fe. Some five thousand royalist troops remained behind in New Granada, although various of these units left for Venezuela in the ensuing months.[1]

After Morillo's return to Venezuela, the royalists' military hold on New Granada began to weaken. Small republican uprisings in Purificación, Vélez, Natagaima and Prado in 1816 had been suppressed without great difficulty, but matters then took a turn for the worse. In March 1817, the insurgent Nonato Pérez, together with local Indians, killed Lieutenant Colonel Julián Bayer and captured Chire and Pore. Meanwhile, Pamplona rose in revolt and forces led by José Hilario Mora harassed royalists across the Cauca Valley. Guerrilla groups around Socorro, protected by Antonia Santos, engaged in small-scale operations until the execution of Santos in July 1819. The Almeyda brothers of Cúcuta briefly occupied Chocontá, less than eighty kilometres north of the capital Santa Fe. In the capital itself, Policarpa Salavarrieta organized an ambitious (if unsuccessful) plot to subvert royalist troops in the city's garrison. Moreover, throughout 1817 and 1818 continuing insurgency, particularly in the Llanos de Casanare, occupied the Army's attention. In the Llanos and elsewhere, small groups of guerrillas launched attacks on royalist troops and then retreated, defying capture.[2] None of these groups enjoyed any lasting success, but all succeeded in alarming the royalists and obliged them to spend months chasing small forces across large distances. Royalist officers, making little headway, lashed out at civilians, burning villages and arresting indiscriminately. The uprising in the Llanos led by the Almeyda brothers met with particularly fierce repression from Carlos Tolrá, the royalist officer in charge of the counter-insurgency campaign. Tolrá did not, however, succeed in crushing the revolt and, by early 1818, the royalists had been forced to withdraw entirely from the Llanos.[3]

From 1817 onwards, then, the populace that had once welcomed the Spanish now turned against them. The royalist Expeditionary Army was unable to retain the confidence of New Granada's population after its initial success in 1816. Why did this happen? How did Spain manage to lose the support it had earlier enjoyed? The answer lies largely with General Morillo's uncompromising approach to 'pacification'. While military force had enabled Spain to reassert its authority in the region, it was not sufficient to convince Neogranadans of the benefits of Spanish rule. On the contrary, the activities of the royalist army inflicted considerable damage on relations between the government and its colonial subjects. After receiving a generally warm reception during their triumphant campaign of 1816, the royalists were to wear out their welcome in the years of military occupation that followed, so that, when challenged by republican forces in 1819, they found scant support from New Granada's population.

The Expeditionary Army was to establish poor relations with the populace they were rescuing from republicanism. Partly because of the fiscal problems that were examined in the previous chapter, the Expeditionary Army was consistently underfunded, as we shall see. It was thus forced to live parasitically off New Granada's populace. Moreover, the royalist soldiers who arrived in New Granada with Morillo in 1815 were Spanish, not American. Spanish officers found New Granada surprisingly different from Spain. They distrusted Americans and they communicated their dislike to their peninsular troops. Until the virtually complete creolization of the Expeditionary Army in 1818, the reconquest therefore took on a quasi-nationalistic (or perhaps it would be better to say quasi-racist) quality. These facts shaped the royalist army's interactions with Neogranadans and set the sharply confrontational tone that was to characterize the entire reconquest and its aftermath.

Soldiers and Civilians

> The newly arrived officers [believe that] in this land there is no nobility, nor lineage, nor worth.[4]

The geography of South America was unlike anything the Spanish soldiers had seen before and it made a deep impression on the expeditionaries. Surprised officers commented on the unfamiliar landscapes in their official reports and private communications. The vast size of the Llanos de Casanare particularly impressed the Spanish, while the region north of Santa Fe struck many officers as attractive. The wildlife was also unfamiliar. Tigers, armadillos, snakes, and many species of birds confronted Spanish troops. Like other nineteenth-century travellers, Spanish soldiers collected souvenirs of the unusual sights; officer Rafael Sevilla brought home some alligator teeth as a memento.[5]

The expeditionaries regarded Neogranadans themselves as equally exotic. Many Spaniards were quite unprepared for the racial heterogeneity of both New Granada and Venezuela. Rafael Sevilla expressed disgust at the appearance of the first black woman he saw: 'that woman's bristly hair, her emaciated limbs, and her filth made me turn my head in disgust. She seemed the very image of heresy'.[6] Such low opinions of Venezuela's coloured population extended to the black or mulatto soldiers fighting for the crown, whom Spanish officers compared to desert Arabs, a designation that was not intended as a compliment.[7] Nor was the Spanish military necessarily prepared to view Indians with a more favourable eye. We have already noted the ambivalence, or indeed hostility, with which royalist officials regarded their Indian allies in Pasto and Santa Marta. While praising the vital support provided to the royalist army by the province's Indians, the *cabildo* of Pasto described their allies as 'those degraded men, so cowardly and incapable of great achievements'.[8] Such attitudes were neither new nor a direct consequence of the war. Since the conquest itself, the nature, and very humanity, of the American Indians had been a subject of scholarly debate, and discussion of this topic was constantly revived during the second half of the long eighteenth century. As David Brading has noted, writers on the most disparate subjects returned obsessively to the theme. While the Aztecs and Incas might have enjoyed some virtues, their benighted descendants were widely held to be indolent, deceitful and childlike. Both creole and peninsular royalists displayed these conventional views, unable to adapt their beliefs to their new circumstances.[9]

The Spanish were by and large no more impressed by New Granada's creole population. Peninsular disdain for Spanish American creoles substantially predated the outbreak of war; hostility between the two groups had increased markedly in the second half of the eighteenth century. Even before the direct onslaught on creole authority unleashed by the later Bourbon reforms of the 1770s and 1780s, creoles and peninsulars increasingly viewed each other with hostility. Jorge Juan and Antonio de Ulloa, two Spanish officials who travelled through the Americas in the 1740s, provided a classic description of this mutual hatred:

> In Peru, it is enough to be a European ... to declare oneself immediately against creoles. To be born in the Indies is sufficient for one to hate Europeans. This mutual antipathy reaches such an extreme that in some ways it exceeds the unbridled fury of two nations, completely at odds, who vituperate and insult each other.[10]

In New Granada, relations deteriorated particularly after the Comunero Rebellion of 1781. The Capitulations of Zipaquirá, a central text of the rebellion, had denounced the antipathy towards Americans displayed by Spaniards, and polarization merely worsened in the aftermath of the revolt.[11] Creole influence on the Audiencia was sharply limited and various restrictions were imposed on creole authority. The Archbishop-Viceroy Antonio de Caballero y Góngora for example insisted that only peninsulars could occupy leading positions in the colonial army. As Anthony McFarlane noted, this left creoles in no doubt that they were not considered sufficiently reliable to control the colony's defences. A decade later, a Spaniard resident in Santa Fe commented on the 'creoles' general and shared hatred of the *chapetones*'.[12] Whether creole hatred of Spaniards originated, as Spanish observers insisted, in malicious envy and vanity, or whether its roots lay rather in the prolonged peninsular attempt to stifle creole autonomy, it is European disdain for both creoles and Indians, rather than the reverse, that most concerns us here. European sources of many different types emphasized American inferiority. European dismissal of the Americas as an environmentally and climatically blighted region was freely expressed in the scientific writings of philosophers such as the Comte de Buffon, the Abbé Raynal and Cornelius de Pauw. America, Buffon explained, was too damp and too cold to produce healthy plants, animals or men:

> In this state of abandon, everything languishes, decays, stifles. The air and the earth, weighed down by the moist and poisonous vapors, cannot purify themselves nor profit from the influence of the star of life. The sun vainly pours down its liveliest rays on this cold mass, which is incapable of responding to its warmth; it will never produce anything but humid creatures, plants, reptiles, and insects; and cold men and feeble animals are all that it will ever nurture.[13]

The consequence of this climatic deficiency was clear to Raynal: 'The ruin of this world is still imprinted on the faces of its inhabitants; a race of men degraded or degenerate in their physical constitution, in their build, in their way of life, and in their minds which show so little aptitude for all the arts of civilisation.'[14] America, a large body of scholarly writing affirmed, was a backward continent, and its inhabitants, particularly the native Indians, were condemned to inferiority. (The precise mechanism ensuring creole inferiority was contested. Whether whites became degenerate because of the unwholesome environment or through a life of excess remained a topic of debate.[15]) As Antonello Gerbi has demonstrated, the works of Raynal and De Pauw were widely read and debated in both Europe and the Americas. Yet it was not necessary to study such scholarly texts to encounter European disdain for the Americas. Casual anti-Americanism permeated the Iberian world. The theories of Raynal and De Pauw find their exact echo in less scientific works. The *Libro de Moda*, a satirical analysis of Spanish fashions published in Madrid in 1795, described the difference between a *pirraca* ('a dandy') and a *currutaco* ('an ultra-fashionable dandy') in the following way: 'A pirraca is to the currutaco what the men and animals of America are to those of Europe-a weak and debased species.'[16] The elite dissections of American inferiority expressed in the writings of climatic determinists were mirrored in this sort of non-elite text. The reflexive anti-Americanism of the Spanish delegates to the first Cortes similarly demonstrates the spread of such beliefs. In a famous intervention of 16 September 1814 representatives of the Consulado de Mexico denounced Indians as lazy and stupid, *castas* as dirty drunkards and creoles as extravagant degenerates.[17] Morillo's soldiers and officers, in other words, emerged from an environment where American inferiority was taken for granted. Moreover, the common Spanish belief that the movement for independence was led solely by creoles merely confirmed pre-existing suspicions about creole loyalty. While Spanish officials considered Indians and *castas* unreliable and infantile, they consoled themselves that true sedition, genuine *infidencia*, was confined to the creoles, the wellspring of all revolt.[18] Creoleness thus became identified with insurgency, in an ironic reinforcement of Bolívar's 1813 declaration that all Americans would be considered revolutionaries, and all Spaniards as royalist enemies.[19] Even in Peru, bastion of royalism, Spanish officials smelt *infidencia* in the very creoles responsible for the defeat of Argentine insurgents in 1811.[20]

Morillo's troops thus arrived in New Granada convinced that the creole population was debauched, debased and treasonous. Military communiqués reinforced these negative views: the inhabitants of the Antioquian town of Ríonegro, a royalist briefing helpfully explained, were 'arrogant, touchy, apathetic, flighty, quarrelsome, complaining'.[21] Such beliefs manifested themselves in the haughty and contemptuous behaviour of Spanish troops, a consequence of their 'superiority complex'.[22] The deliberate humiliation of well-to-do creoles was a regular feature of the reconquest. In the Cauca Valley, the royalist military was said to be occupying private homes, leaving the owners to sleep in the street. 'We are treated worse than slaves and mules', lamented one wealthy landowner from southern New Granada, extravagantly comparing himself to the two most badly treated things he could imagine.[23] Captain General Cajigal described similar behaviour in Caracas: royalist officers installed themselves in the finest houses, expecting to be waited on hand and foot.

> They frequently invited each other to diner without giving any advanced warning other than to say to the landlord or landlady (a title the latter found offensive), with the bold disrespect usually displayed by men with enormous moustaches: 'Start getting ready; today I've invited two companions to dine with me. Treat them well, Mr. Rascally Insurgent.'

If officers behaved like this in the capital, mused Cajigal, one can only imagine how they comported themselves in the provinces.[24] Particularly obnoxious was the apparently deliberate denial of creole authority. Neither wealth, status nor office protected creoles suspected of republicanism, as the 1816 executions of aristocratic revolutionaries revealed. Royalist officers flatly rejected creole claims to respectability. Agustín de Velasco, a *regidor* in Popayán's *cabildo*, complained in 1817 that following a quarrel with a royalist officer, he was arrested and taken to the barracks. There he was insulted by the commander, who shouted 'vulgar and indecent words' and furthermore beat the offended alderman with a stick.[25] The Expeditionary Army was doing little to woo the creole elite back to the Spanish fold.

The abrasive and non-deferential manner of some members of the Spanish military upset not only the *gente decente*, or gentry, but also other sectors of society. Spaniards were widely perceived as rude and vain. 'The arrogance of that nation', commented the Santafereño diarist José María Caballero, 'rivals that of Lucifer.'[26] According to Caballero, the royalist army's arrival in Santa Fe resulted in the open and daily harassment of the capital's inhabitants. Caballero added that panic reigned in the capital, not merely because of the frequent arrests and executions of suspected insurgents, but also because of 'constant stream of the insults and robberies' directed against locals by the Expeditionary Army.[27] Officers and troops were accused of using excessively vulgar and insulting language in their day-to-day dealings with Neogranadans. Even Viceroy Montalvo was angered by the crude behaviour displayed by General Morillo and his subalterns.[28] Old age was certainly not respected; Francisco Xavier Arámbarri, an official in Caracas, commented that the youthful royalist officers made plain their conviction that, 'those of us who are older than forty are a poor, despicable, useless lot'.[29] Civilian officials in Santa Fe described the Expeditionary Army as consisting of ill-disciplined, uproarious youths milling about in the capital, not dissimilar to the royalist soldiers in Mexico whose delinquent behaviour led to their being banned from Mexico City's parks in 1814.[30]

Complaints about the behaviour of royalist troops in New Granada extended far beyond their use of offensive language when speaking to the local gentry. Unprovoked attacks on innocent civilians, public brawls, acts of drunkenness, and unspecified *desórdenes* ('disorders') were regularly denounced to the authorities.[31] Some Army units were more notorious than others. Venezuelan troops were regarded by all as troublemakers, while the Battalion of Granada was dissolved altogether as a consequence of the 'excesses' committed by its members. This particular battalion, General Morillo claimed, was composed primarily of thieves, deserters and convicts, and he was not surprised that its soldiers committed innumerable crimes. Indeed, General Morillo complained that royalist ranks were routinely filled by the dregs of Spanish society who, in his view, inevitably committed atrocities after their arrival in the Americas.[32]

The Army's behaviour certainly conformed to this gloomy prediction.

In 1818, for example, Sub-lieutenant Vicente Ruíz was disciplined for murdering six prisoners he was transporting to Cartagena from Santa Fe. Ruíz had evidently lost patience with his charges when they became too ill to travel. The six were shot or beaten to death on the roadside.[33] Such behaviour was not exceptional and the royalist army itself documented numerous cases of atrocious treatment of non-combatants. The many anti-royalist atrocity stories that circulated throughout New Granada may have further blackened Spain's reputation. Prior to the arrival of Morillo's troops the republican press had spread reports of horrifying misdeeds, which were joined by a flood of deliberately started rumours about royalist atrocities. Royalist officers, it was said, dishonoured virtuous republican widows, tortured village idiots, assaulted children.[34] Priests proclaimed the iniquity of the Spanish from the pulpit:

> They entered our territory, sacked our provinces, robbed our temples. Ah! It is with great sorrow that I view the series of atrocities committed by those barbarians! I have seen the theft of goods and the slaughter of their unhappy owners. I have seen women carrying their innocent children forced to hide themselves in the rocks and hills, hungry and afflicted … I have seen innocent maidens, afraid, miserable and weeping, fleeing the ferocious and unrestrained soldiers. I have seen the tears of a mother who hears the news that her children have died. I have heard the sad laments of a wife who learns that her husband has been torn to pieces. I have heard the sobs of a daughter told that her father has been loaded with chains and sent to the gallows … I have heard so many wives, so many girls weep over their dishonour, brought about by the brutality of soldiers who have neither honour nor religion, who have not respected even little girls only eight years old, killed to satisfy their unrestrained lust.[35]

True or not, such reports resonated with the public and verifiable behaviour Morillo's troops. Not surprisingly, these *desórdenes* and acts of violence did little to increase support for the royalists. Royalist officer José María Barreiro conceded in early 1819 that the royalists enjoyed no support whatsoever in the Llanos as a consequence of the 'excesses committed by a few officers'. 'All the inhabitants are our sworn enemies', he added.[36] Royalist officers often dismissed atrocities as the unfortunate consequence of troops disobeying orders. However, for many Neogranadans, even Morillo's official policies were entirely unacceptable. Events in Santa Fe in 1816 alone provided an ample source of horror. The execution of over one hundred prominent republicans, usually after highly arbitrary trials, the revival of the ancient and repellent custom of dismembering and displaying corpses in wire cages throughout the capital, the deliberate harassment of the female relatives of suspected republicans, and the arbitrary behaviour of royalist officers all served to fulfil the worst predictions of New Granada's revolutionaries. Bolívar's secretary Daniel Florencio O'Leary expressed this bluntly: 'The conduct of Morillo in Santa Fe did more damage to the royalist cause than the most disastrous defeat.'[37]

A particularly large body of complaint about royalist behaviour emerged from southern New Granada, an area that saw continuous fighting from 1816. The complaints centred on the Third Division of the Expeditionary Army, which was under the nominal command of Juan Sámano. The Third Division numbered some thousand men and had been stationed in various towns in the Cauca Valley from late 1816. These troops were deeply unpopular and many observers claimed that the arrival of the Third Division had jeopardized the very reconquest of New Granada. It was generally agreed that the troops were eating all the cattle, had requisitioned all the horses and had taken all the slaves to work on the Army's various road-building projects. It was thus extremely difficult to carry out any work on the numerous haciendas in the Cauca Valley, which relied on the slaves' unfree labour. It was widely alleged that the Army was engaged in wholesale robbery in the name of supporting the troops. The presence of the troops had furthermore led to an outbreak of smallpox and dysentery in the province. The *cabildo* of Anserma expressed the matter succinctly:

> [The troops'] authority derives from their guns, and everyone has been obliged to obey them. They instantly demand whatever takes their fancy; they punish people arbitrarily, and pay only the price they choose to pay … They have unjustly requisitioned all the animals [in the area], not merely because they need the animals for their own use, but also so that these animals will die, thereby inconveniencing as many people as possible.[38]

The *cabildo*'s suspicion that the Army was collecting animals not only for their own uses, but also to punish the inhabitants, was probably correct. Anserma, like the towns of Cali, Buga, Cartago and Toro, which also complained of royalist oppression, had been a member of the insurgent Confederate Cities of the Cauca during the Patria Boba and was thus regarded with suspicion by the royalist army. The Army considered willingness to provide for the troops to be a good loyalty test.[39] Forced contributions, appropriations of goods and demands for labour tended to fall heaviest on those individuals or regions most heavily implicated in the insurgency. It was for this reason that known loyalists responded with outrage when ordered to assist the troops. Indeed, many regarded such requests as tantamount to an accusation of treason. When María Manuela de Angulo of Popayán complained of the insulting manner in which she had been ordered to sew uniforms for royalist troops, she drew attention to the fact that she was a member of an illustrious family that had distinguished itself in loyalty to the crown.[40] In Angulo's view it was not for royalists such as herself to sew uniforms for the king's army. Such tasks should be left to convicted insurgents as punishment for their disloyalty.

One of the principal focuses of friction between the royalist army and the inhabitants of the Cauca Valley was the Army's ambitious road-building scheme. Various projects of military engineering were undertaken after 1816, but the road-building projects were probably the most unpopular. New roads were opened from Sonsón to Mariquita, from Zapatoca to the Magdalena, from Honda to Santa Fe, from Santa Fe to the Llanos, from Cali to Buenaventura, from the Valle de Osos to Cáceres, and from the Cauca Valley to Anchicayá. Pre-existing roads were improved as well. There is no doubt that new roads were needed; complaints about the poor quality of the roads and of transport in general were made regularly throughout the eighteenth century, and transport continued to be a problem during the war itself.[41] The royalists' plans to improve New Granada's roads were ambitious. Roads and bridges were to be several metres wide, with all surfaces covered with gravel.[42] It proved impossible to build roads to these standards but, perhaps as a consequence, most of these new roads were swallowed up by vegetation within a year of construction. Despite the failure of the royalists to make a permanent contribution to solving Colombia's transport problems, the construction of these roads placed heavy demands on local labour supplies. The royalists resorted to requisitioning slaves and labourers to work on the roads. Notable insurgents were placed in charge of overseeing the construction and heavy fines were levied on overseers who allowed labourers to escape.

The road being built from the Cauca Valley to Anchicayá, south of

Buenaventura, under the supervision of Ruperto Delgado and Francisco Warleta, was an object of particular complaint.[43] 'The name alone of [the road to Anchicayá] instils terror in the entire Cauca Valley', wrote one royalist officer.[44] The royalist military requisitioned slaves from haciendas in the Cauca Valley to work on the road, thereby bringing agricultural work to a virtual standstill. Moreover, when the requisitioned slaves began to escape into the backlands, the Army started imposing fines of $30 per escaped slave on the slave owners. The *cabildo* of Buga, for example, complained that, in the two years from 1815 to 1817, slave owners in the town had paid some $5,000 in such fines, which implies that on average a slave from Buga fled the roadworks every five days.[45] Throughout 1817, complaints about the road poured into royalist government offices. *Cabildos* across the Cauca Valley lobbied against the project and the governor of Popayán added his name to the protests. Eventually Viceroy Francisco Montalvo himself ordered construction to halt, but his command was ignored by royalist officers, who openly rejected Montalvo's authority, insisting they took orders only from General Morillo and his immediate subordinates.[46]

Paying for a War

Morillo's troops undertook the reconquest of New Granada in a financial vacuum. Spain's effort to re-impose royal authority in New Granada was consistently underfunded and this posed a further impediment to royalist victory. Spanish participation in the American wars of independence was tremendously expensive and placed enormous burdens on a system of government finance that had already been under great strain before 1808.[47] The sheer scale of the fiscal burden created by Spain's determination to rebuild its empire can be gauged from global estimates of Spain's expenditures on the American wars. Michael Costeloe has calculated that the crown alone spent over $25,000,000 on fighting the American insurgencies. Overall, each royalist soldier sent to the Americas cost his government between $150 and $400.[48]

These figures do not include the additional costs incurred by royalist governments in the Americas. After the arrival of the Expeditionary Army in Venezuela, the crown made virtually no contributions to its maintenance. The Spanish, unlike the British forty years earlier, made only minimal efforts to maintain transatlantic supply lines.[49] On the contrary, very little cash and practically no supplies were remitted from Spain to New Granada's royalist army. Funds to cover all expenses had to be found in New Granada itself. The crown's reliance on local funding to support royalist troops was predictably unpopular with Neogranadans. Indeed, the ways in which the Expeditionary Army's costs were defrayed played an important role in alienating support for the crown. We will first examine the inadequate sources of funding available to Morillo's army, and will then consider the effects of chronic underfunding on the royalist army itself.

Spain's initial response to colonial rebellion was crippled by the political and financial crises at home. The war with Napoleonic France absorbed all available funds. Only in late 1811 was the Regency in a financial position to mount any assault on the insurgents, as a result of the creation of the Comisión de Reemplazos. This body, formed in Cádiz in September 1811, provided a means of raising funds for the war.[50] Developed out of discussions between the Minister of the Navy and the Cádiz merchants, the Comisión was an essentially private organization, not directly controlled by the government, but permitted to levy taxes as if it were a governmental entity. The Cádiz merchants, who were perhaps the loudest advocates of military intervention in the Americas, were the principal contributors to Comisión funds. In 1811, they promised to raise $400,000 for a military expedition to the Indies, to be used to pay for uniforms, transport and other necessities. The Comisión also undertook to recruit soldiers. The merchants themselves promised to come up with a substantial portion of the total sum. Any remaining money would be generated by a series of special taxes. The Comisión was at first stunningly successful. In a mere twelve weeks, it had recruited, equipped and transported over a thousand soldiers, at the cost of $159,891.[51] In 1812 and 1813, twelve more expeditions were organized, two of which went to New Granada. Michael Costeloe estimates that from its creation in 1811 to 1820, the Comisión spent over $17,529,000. This considerable amount of money was generated without the direct intervention of any of Spain's governments. Spain's participation in the American wars was thus financed by an essentially private and independent institution.

With time, new measures were needed to raise money. In 1813 the Comisión was given control over the sale of mercury from the mine at Almadén, and by 1820 had generated $1,500,000 from this source. Various old taxes were revived, new ones were invented and a tax of one *real* was levied on tickets to the bullfight in Madrid. Forced loans were also extracted, primarily from Spain's merchants. None of these measures proved popular and some were hard to enforce. Moreover, the Comisión earned few friends with the snail-like pace with which it paid off its creditors. In the end, the Comisión resorted to the standard approach of previous Spanish governments: deficit financing. This method was initially very successful. The credit notes issued by the Comisión raised some $1,300,000 between 1817 and 1820. However, such practices merely postponed the day of reckoning. When the Comisión was, in practical terms, abolished in 1826, it left a debt of over $5,500,000.

In 1814, the Comisión began work on raising money for what was to become Morillo's Expeditionary Army. The Comisión provided virtually all of the funding for the army of over 12,000 men and seventy-nine ships. The Expeditionary Army and the three other, smaller expeditions sent in 1815 cost over $5,280,000, or about a third of the Comisión's total expenditure from 1811 to 1820. As a result of the Comisión de Reemplazo's activities, Morillo's Expeditionary Army left Spain well supplied and well funded. The expedition departed from Cádiz in February 1815 equipped with thousands of guns, uniforms, cash and other necessities.

Much of this money and equipment was lost before the Army even arrived in Caracas. On 24 April 1815 a fire of suspicious origins broke out at sea on board the San Pedro de Alcántara. The vessel, one of the principal transport ships, was completely destroyed, and with it over $1,000,000, thousands of guns, uniforms, and much more.[52] This loss was a terrible blow to the Army and caused it an immediate and serious shortage of food. Despite this setback, on its arrival in Venezuela the Army still retained enough equipment to impress the inhabitants. The Regent of the Caracas Audiencia commented caustically that Morillo's troops were 'completely equipped with a magnificence never seen in our own armies'.[53] But the Expeditionary Army was not to enjoy this state for long. Ferdinand's government, poised on the edge of bankruptcy throughout the years of the war, left the Expeditionary Army to fend for itself after its arrival in the Americas. Often unable to pay for basic necessities, the condition of Morillo's proud army would deteriorate to such an extent that, in the later years of the war, officers would complain that their men were marching naked, and its commander-in-chief would describe himself as rich 'only in suffering, hardship, and toil'.[54]

Prior to his departure from Spain, General Morillo was issued with secret instructions from the king which detailed the approved conduct for the war.[55] These instructions granted Morillo sweeping powers to appropriate money, but provided little guidance on how these powers were to be employed. Morillo was first of all empowered to confiscate funds from the royal monopolies in order to cover urgent war-related expenses. Although he was urged to take only what was strictly necessary, leaving the remainder for the civil government, no prescribed limit was set on the amount that could be diverted to the army. The right to appropriate unlimited treasury funds for war expenses granted to Morillo in his instructions distressed civilian officials.[56] More explosive, however, was the power granted to Morillo to 'demand loans [and] seek funds and supplies to pay the king's soldiers and employees, as well as to meet all expenses'. This power to extract forced loans was employed to the full during the Army's years in New Granada.

The imposition of a 'contribution' or forced loan, a technique the crown had often used in earlier wars, became the standard way of raising revenue following Morillo's arrival. The military authorities would determine the amount of money needed to keep the Army afloat, and then would simply demand that the sum be raised. Specific individuals might be designated to provide particular quantities of money, or a town's governing body might be required to find contributors. It has been claimed that in Mexico such forced contributions simply functioned as a form of income tax, but in the Viceroyalty of New Granada the procedure for assigning contributions was considerably less formal.[57] The Captain General of Venezuela, Juan Manuel de Cajigal, provided a lively description of the process at work. Explaining how Morillo and Pascual Enrile raised $100,000 in Caracas, he imagined Morillo in conversation with Enrile:

> '$6,000 from A; $4,000 from B; $8,000 from C; $5,000 from D, etc. Add it up: there's the $85,000.'
>
> 'No, we need $100,000. Add $3,000 from E, $2,000 from F, etc. That'll reach the total. Good! … Here comes the prior of the Consulado. My friend, look at this list and see what I've assigned each person to pay. Get them to cough up immediately.'
>
> 'Sir, this isn't right. Some people can pay much more, and some don't have any money at all.'
>
> 'All right then, divide it up however you like. The important thing is to get the $100,000.'[58]

These forced contributions, or confiscations, became the primary source of funding for the Expeditionary Army after it reached the Viceroyalty. In Santa Fe, confiscations were carried out via the Junta de Purificación and the Junta de Secuestros, as detailed in chapter 4, and the possessions of suspected republicans were routinely embargoed by the royalist army. Although the very wealthy were particularly easy targets, confiscations and forced contributions were not imposed solely on the rich.[59] All sectors of society were subject to involuntary donations to the Expeditionary Army. These extractions of money and goods were one of the chief sources of dissatisfaction with the Army, and in particular with the Third Division, stationed in southern New Granada. Complaints by *cabildos* across the Cauca Valley reveal that the Expeditionary Army relied almost entirely on the public to provide for its needs. Needing a consistent, steady income, the Army demanded monthly payments. The town of Cartago, for example, provided a regular income of $600 per month for troops stationed nearby. The city of Popayán was obliged to cover all the costs of the local garrison, including the unitemized 'expenses' of the garrison's commander (see Table 1). Even small towns like Toro were assigned regular contributions to the Army.[60]

Table 1. Daily Expenses of the Troops Stationed in Popayán in 1817

6 cows	48.0
Commander's expenses	10.0
Sheets and other supplies for the hospital	40.0
Salt	6.0
Firewood	2.4
5 *arrobas* of rice	15.0
Sugar	1.0
Soap	2.2
Wages for cooks and washerwomen	0.4
Candles	2.2
Bananas	4.4
Fodder for the horses	6.0
Salaries for 262 soldiers and 3 officers	87.0*
TOTAL	$225.0

Source: AGI, ASF, leg. 631. The amounts above are in *pesos* with the number after the decimal point in *reales* (8 *reales* = 1 *peso*).
* Salaries were paid monthly; the monthly total was $2,620.

These demands incensed local *cabildos*, which urged that some other source of funding be found. For example, in May 1817 the *cabildo* of Popayán appealed to Viceroy Montalvo to prevent large amounts of money being extracted from its citizenry through forced contributions. The city had already suffered a forced contribution of $500,000, an enormous sum more than thirty times the annual salary of the viceroy. The inhabitants of Popayán, like the inhabitants of other towns occupied by royalist troops, were particularly distressed by the completely arbitrary nature of these contributions. The *cabildo* wanted rules to be drawn up to regularize the whole procedure.[61] These complaints were supported by Viceroy Montalvo, who forwarded them to Spain. There the matter was reviewed by Ferdinand's government, and both General Morillo and his second in command Pascual Enrile were roundly condemned. The Council of the Indies further asserted that, as viceroy, Francisco Montalvo's authority was superior to Morillo's in all matters except the purely military.[62] This ruling, which was completely at variance with the position set out in Morillo's Instructions, was typical of Ferdinand VII's government. Unable to fund the Army itself, and yet unwilling to condone abuses in New Granada, the crown was caught in a difficult dilemma. The consequence was that it neither provided the Expeditionary Army with sufficient funds, nor permitted to it to seek monies elsewhere.

Minimal state backing and a haphazard system of confiscations was not a stable base on which to finance an army. Denied sufficient income, the Expeditionary Army proved unable to pay its troops. Soldiers fighting for the crown were supposed to receive a basic annual salary of about $100.[63] Beyond this, soldiers could, in theory, earn additional bonuses for exceptional feats of military prowess, and those joining Morillo's expedition in 1814 were to be paid an extra amount as an inducement to enlist.[64] The reality of the situation was quite different. For months, sometimes years on end, troops were paid nothing at all, or only a fraction of the full amount owed.[65] Occasional efforts were made to overcome the Army's complete inability to pay troops' wages by, for example, declaring that a ration of food counted as a half-*real*. Thus in the course of a year soldiers would automatically be credited about $27 towards their salary, regardless of whether they received any cash or not.[66] (This is assuming that they received their rations regularly, which was not always the case.) Moreover, officers frequently complained that their troops were obliged to march without adequate clothing or indeed naked.[67] In one unit, there were only thirty-two pairs of shoes to be shared between over three hundred recruits.[68]

Shortages of money were of course not confined to Spain's armed forces. Paying salaries to officials in New Granada's civil administration also proved difficult. Many restrictions were made. Even the highest officials were obliged to accept smaller salaries during the early years of the war. The effect of this global shortage was to increase competition for funds and to aggravate conflicts between the military and civilian wings of government. Morillo, for his part, blamed civilian officials for failing to put his Army first. Viceroy Montalvo, he complained, was more willing to pay the salaries of civilians than to 'clothe the troops which protect him from danger, thanks to whom he governs this small corner'.[69] He was equally critical of Venezuela's Captain General Salvador Moxó, whom he accused of gross negligence in failing to provide the Army with food and supplies.[70] For all his differences with Morillo, Viceroy Montalvo consistently supported Morillo's claims that the Army needed more money. He merely thought funds should come from Spain, rather than New Granada.[71]

It rapidly became clear to General Morillo that the Expeditionary Army was inadequately funded. Indeed, by January 1816, the Army's poverty had, in Morillo's view, 'become truly desperate'.[72] He complained continuously about the shortages his troops were forced to endure. His claims were authenticated by the republicans, who seized royalist documents after the capture of Santa Fe in 1819. Republican Vice-President Santander was shocked to learn of the financial hardships which had confronted Morillo and commented that, according to the royalists' own documents, 'the Third Division simply didn't get paid at all'.[73]

The effect of this chronic failure to pay and equip the troops was both predictable and disabling for the Army. Desertion, always a problem, grew worse when the troops were not paid on time. By 1820 the navy in Cartagena was owed over a year's back pay. 'There is consequently an extraordinary rate of desertion', remarked its commander.[74] When there was no prospect of ever being paid, desertion became yet more tempting. The royalist officers were well aware of this problem. They regularly begged the government to send more money and threatened civilian officials that entire regiments would desert if money were not forthcoming.[75]

What effect did such behaviour have on the stability of the reconquest regime? Did royalist abuses help swing public opinion back towards the republicans; was it indeed the critical factor in reviving the insurgency? Certainly many observers commented on the link between royalist excesses and revived support for the republicans. Viceroy Montalvo stated that the uncontrolled financial demands of junior officers were directly responsible for the continued unrest in southern New Granada.[76] The future vice-president of Colombia, Francisco de Paula Santander indeed asserted that the forced contributions imposed by the Spanish had been the principal cause of the royalists' declining support.[77] In Spain, journalists denounced the brutality of the reconquest, and even some government ministers argued that military intervention had done more harm than good.[78] Minister of State José García de León y Pizarro expressed this view succinctly: 'since the arrival of the expedition of Captain General Pablo Morillo everything has gone from bad to worse'.[79] It was widely alleged that the royalist army's excessive demands for labour and supplies led many Neogranadans to flee their homes and hide in the hills. Once outside the royalist-controlled villages, they might easily join the growing number of republican guerrillas. Further, much of New Granada's initial support for the reconquest had arisen from the widespread disillusion with the insurgents. The movement for independence had brought civil war and discord; it was hoped that with a return to royalism would come peace. When the arrival of the Spanish brought, instead, more fighting, the royalists lost their greatest advantage over the republicans. Andrés Rosillo, former insurgent and canon of the cathedral in Santa Fe, commented on this explicitly in a commissioned report to the Council of the Indies:

> The many arrests, the carelessness, hastiness, and illegality of the trials, and the extraordinary number of victims fulfilled the forecasts made in the revolutionary press, which predicted such scenes of terror, and also destroyed the [positive] image of the king's government that the royalists had built up.[80]

It is noteworthy that the areas that remained most staunchly royalist throughout the war were precisely those that experienced least harassment from royalist troops. Pasto, in the south, and to a lesser degree Santa Marta, both of which had initially supported the crown for specific local reasons, were by and large exempted from providing supplies and money for the troops, and were moreover spared many of the atrocities committed elsewhere by royalists. These two regions remained in royalist hands until the conclusion of the war. Similarly Quito, which was for some years governed by the conciliatory Toribio Montes, remained tranquilly royalist until the battle of Pichincha in 1822. The errors and abuses committed by the royalists alienated potential supporters and strengthened the resolve of committed republicans. The irony of Morillo's official title of 'Pacifier' was not lost on his contemporaries.[81]

Disease and the Royalist Army

Continual shortages of money and the consequent harassment of New Granada's population proved to be substantial obstacles to royalist success in New Granada. There were, however, others. The Expeditionary Army suffered terrible losses to disease and the resultant decline in troop strength was a constant limitation on its actions.

Prior to the twentieth century, European soldiers were much more likely to die of disease than to fall in battle. This was the case whether the troops fought in Europe itself or elsewhere. Mortality seems to have been particularly high when European troops campaigned in areas afflicted by yellow fever and other 'tropical' ailments.[82] The losses suffered by eighteenth-century British troops fighting in the Caribbean were appalling; Michael Duffy notes that during Britain's war with Revolutionary France, nearly sixty-seven per cent of the British soldiers stationed in Santo Domingo died of disease.[83] Similarly, during Cuba's war of independence in the 1890s, five times as many Spanish soldiers died from disease than were killed in battle.[84] Clearly, epidemic disease could be a formidable opponent. Spanish losses to disease during New Granada's wars of independence, while less well known, were also substantial. The military historian Julio Albi has calculated that from 1810 to 1824, Spanish troops fighting in Venezuela and New Granada suffered an overall fatality rate of between ninety and ninety-six per cent. This astonishingly high figure is attributed by Albi rather casually to 'the climate, disease, insufficient food, and primitive health care'.[85] While Albi provides little evidence, his assessment is, as we shall see, very accurate.

Morillo had arrived in Venezuela with some ten thousand troops. By 1821, when the last European troops withdrew from Venezuela, only about fifteen hundred remained alive. Within six years, nearly eight-five per cent of Morillo's original army was dead or had deserted. The majority of these troops appear to have died of disease.

Already on 5 December 1815, Morillo could report that in the six months since the Army left Puerto Cabello, nearly half of the roughly seven thousand men laying siege to Cartagena had either died or deserted.[86] As the Army's only military engagements during this period had been a handful of skirmishes outside Cartagena, it is clear that large numbers of soldiers were falling victim to the region's notorious climate. Reports of the terrifying death rate from disease in the Spanish camps spread during the siege; in March 1816 the *Royal Gazette and Bahama Advertiser* stated that an enormous number of Spanish soldiers had died, not from battle wounds, but from disease. The *Gazette* blamed 'the excessive rain, and … the excessive heat' of the coastal location.[87] Of course, Cartagena, with its tropical climate, had long been a grave for soldiers; in 1764 a full thirty per cent of the city's garrison were ill.[88] Throughout the war, the Caribbean coast was the region most afflicted by disease and it was there that Spanish troops suffered the greatest loss.

The effect on Morillo's army of the loss of so many soldiers to disease was difficult to counteract. After the capture of Cartagena, Morillo complained that the Army had been reduced to 'a very small number', because of 'the many terrible diseases' suffered by the troops during the blockade.[89] The Army grew progressively smaller despite the efforts of its commanders. As early as May 1816, Morillo noted that since he left Spain he had been unable to recruit enough new soldiers to replace those dead from disease. The Spanish never succeeded in this task. Losses were such that by November 1816 there remained only one regiment composed entirely of European soldiers.[90]

The mortality rate from disease continued to grow throughout the remainder of the war, particularly in the area of the Caribbean coast. Within months of arriving in New Granada, some fourteen per cent of the men in the Second Battalion of Albuera, an important unit stationed in Mompós, were sick.[91] In Cartagena during 1818 and 1819, nearly one in ten officers, to say nothing of the troops, appears to have been ill at any given moment.[92] By 1820, the situation was far worse. In Ríohacha, officers estimated that only one third of the troops were in even 'indifferent health'. The commanding officer, Vicente Sánchez Lima, lamented that 'nakedness, hunger and the fearful spectacle of fever now comprise the sad and melancholy lot of the soldier'.[93] By the start of the republican siege of Cartagena in 1820, over three hundred men from the Regimiento de León were in hospital. The total force of this regiment consisted in little over five hundred men; nearly two-thirds of the regiment were ill. Blame again fell on the 'very hot and damp weather'.[94]

Despite the particular risks associated with the Caribbean coast, illness afflicted troops across New Granada. A few examples will suffice. In January 1816, half the troops stationed in Zaragosa were ill and, in late 1817, outbreaks of smallpox struck troops stationed in various places. In the Llanos de Casanare, where some one thousand royalist troops were on campaign, soldiers were being sent to hospital at the rate of about one a day.[95] From Venezuela, Morillo wrote in 1817 to the Minister of War that in the two years since it had arrived in the Americas, the Expeditionary Army had lost one third of its force to disease. 'The mere bite of a mosquito', he wrote:

> often deprives a man of his life, or causes an ulcer that first incapacitates him for a long time, and then leaves him an invalid. A multitude of men in the division of Brigadier Cantarac have recently gone blind as a result of having slept outdoors [rather than in barracks]. The local diet causes every type of illness in Europeans, and very few are able to resist its fatal influence. The immense wildernesses in which the war is conducted, the lack of any sort of assistance, the contaminated water which it is often necessary to drink, and the extraordinary fatigue suffered by the soldiers, who are obliged to march over such considerable distances through such diverse climates: all this contributes to our destruction, and to the annihilation of the troops.[96]

Various diseases afflicted the Spanish troops. The most common seem to have been dysentery, smallpox and a variety of tropical fevers, particularly yellow fever. Many of these diseases typically become endemic within a population; epidemics occur with the advent of newcomers, among whom illness can spread rapidly. This is what occurred in New Granada with the arrival of the Expeditionary Army.[97] Beyond these epidemic diseases, soldiers suffered from a variety of other infirmities. Scurvy was a continual problem and troops stationed in the Llanos in 1817 were struck with some sort of haemorrhaging disease that left them spitting blood.[98] Injury also took a terrible toll, as infections were difficult to cure, particularly in hot, humid environments. Ulcerated wounds of all kinds tormented officers and troops alike. Wounds in the feet, in particular, were notoriously fatal, and amputation was often considered the only option.[99]

Soldiers tried various remedies for the diseases that attacked them. Rarely did they employ the conventional methods recommended by European doctors. One of the most common illness seems to have been *calentura*, a general term for feverish illnesses such as malaria. Rafael Sevilla, who fought with General Morillo during most of the campaign, recorded a number of different ways of treating *calentura*. These remedies give some indication of the non-institutionalized nature of the medical care available to sick soldiers. Sevilla detailed several relatively straightforward do-it-yourself cures, such as eating a particular fruit, and also listed other, more prolonged treatments. One such, invented by Sevilla himself, was to undertake a long and vigorous walk as soon as the fever began. After this he rested and drank a cup of tea. This brought on a forty-eight-hour attack of high fever, followed, he claimed, by a complete cure. Sevilla found all of these methods effective. On one occasion, however, he was given quinine (in the form of chinchona bark), which brought no positive result at all. Indeed, chinchona bark's success in treating even malaria was uneven. The amount of actual quinine in the chinchona bark-based remedies varied to such an extent that it could not be relied upon to effect a cure.[100] Sevilla also fell ill with a disease locally known as *el bicho* (possibly dengue fever), which caused nausea and fever, as well as headache and pain in the bones. He was cured of this by a reportedly very unpleasant treatment involving lemons, the details of which were not spelled out in his memoirs. Aside from his unsatisfactory encounter with quinine, Sevilla does not appear to have tried any of the standard European treatments for fever. In particular, he makes no mention of bloodletting or the use of purgatives, the two central elements of European fever management. Nor did he at any time resort to professional medical assistance.[101]

It was very common for soldiers (and indeed the public at large) to resort to folk remedies of this sort. Native medicinal products were frequently employed in ways considered deeply unorthodox by those familiar with European practices.[102] Moreover, folk healers, rather than physicians, often oversaw treatment. Throughout the eighteenth century, New Granada's trained doctors had complained about the prevalence of *curanderos*, or folk healers, whom the public consistently favoured. This was not solely due to the shortage of physicians in the viceroyalty, although this was certainly a factor. The paucity of trained doctors suggests that it was difficult to gain access to orthodox medical practitioners, even if the patient had the money and the inclination to consult one. In addition, medically-trained doctors were widely distrusted, even by members of the colonial elite. As in Europe itself, doctors might be viewed, not as educated healers, but as expensive quacks. Viceroy Montalvo, clearly of this opinion, remarked in 1815 that in Cartagena, 'medicine and surgery lie in a state of utter abandon, and the inhabitants are obliged to place themselves in the hands of local healers, whom, because of their skill and knowledge, they quite rightly prefer to Europeans doctors, who are, in fact, an ignorant lot'.[103]

Not all popular treatments involved the use of folk medicine; some were matters of simple hygiene, a concept enjoying renewed favour in Europe. In the preceding decades, European medical practitioners had laid growing emphasis on the importance of cleanliness in maintaining public health. Their concerns were echoed in New Granada, where officers repeatedly ordered their troops to keep clean and to wash as regularly as possible. To prevent the potentially fatal infections of the feet that were literally crippling the Spanish army, soldiers were advised to wash their feet daily in *aguardiente*, or, failing that, warm water. Sensibly, soldiers were frequently advised to avoid drinking water; *aguardiente* itself, or water mixed with *aguardiente*, was the preferred beverage.[104] Moreover, as the climate, or more specifically the humidity, was felt to be responsible for much of the ill health, the royalist army took measures to construct barracks that prevented the soldiers from coming into contact with the damp ground and protected them from the warm air. Soldiers were also advised to keep out of the rain, although they were provided with few means of doing so; unsurprisingly, few military manoeuvres were called off because of heavy rain.[105] In blaming New Granada's humid and unwholesome air for their troops' ill health, royalist officers reflected both the current views on the origins of fever and European prejudices about South America's climate. It was medically accepted that fevers arose from a lethal combination of dank, stagnant waters, putrid air and filth. These conditions, in particular excessive dampness, were precisely those singled out by climatic determinists such as the Abbé Raynal and the Comte de Buffon to explain South America's perceived backwardness and lack of development. These two currents of thought combined to label New Granada a singularly hostile environment for Europeans.[106] Other features of Neogranadan life were considered equally insalubrious; the local diet, regarded as unsuitable for European troops, was frequently blamed for causing illness.[107]

Other more experimental methods for preserving the soldiers' health were also tried. In late 1815 Morillo noted that few soldiers fell sick while their division was out on manoeuvres; most illness stuck while troops were confined to barracks. Deducing that the barracks themselves were insalubrious, he therefore ordered that all troops under Miguel de la Torre's command be sent out daily on a lengthy circular march with full rucksacks. Exercise, generally considered an important element in resisting tropical ailments, would thus compensate for the unwholesome environment of the barracks. This measure was intended to improve the dismal health record of La Torre's division.[108] It is worth noting that on this occasion medical policy was made, not by a doctor, but by an officer. This was far from unusual in independence-era New Granada. Even public health measures, such as the smallpox vaccination campaign of 1816–17, were initiated and run by non-medical army officers.[109]

The metropolitan government, keen to prevent the entire Expeditionary Army from dying of disease, also took an interest in the health of royalist troops. In December 1815, Ferdinand VII issued a directive to government officials urging them to provide good care for injured soldiers.[110] As a consequence, following the arrival of Morillo's Expeditionary Army in Venezuela, colonial officials in each province were requested to report on the state of health care in the region, detailing in particular the availability of hospitals. A number, but by no means all, of the Viceroyalty's governors reported the existence of hospitals run by charitable institutions, which they claimed could cope with the few soldiers who sought admission. The low demand for hospital places was, Montalvo felt, the result of the poor care provided in the hospitals, rather than an indication of the good health of the population. The hospital in Santa Marta, for example, was described by Montalvo as a place 'lacking doctors, medicine, in short, everything'.[111] The royalist army accepted the need for improved health facilities and built a number of entirely new hospitals.[112] The most important of these were built in the area around Cartagena, the quasi-capital. The principal hospital was the Hospital Militar de San Carlos. This could comfortably hold 500 patients, and in extreme cases up to 500 more could be accommodated in the hospital's corridors and hallways. There were, however, only 440 beds. Patients suffering from dysentery, which, Morillo reported 'has afflicted this army so terribly', were held in separate accommodations, indicating that hospital personnel recognized the contagious nature of this condition.[113] The hospitals were divided into various sections, with officers and enemy prisoners housed separately.

These hospitals were run in part at government expense, although food was provided by the surrounding towns and villages. Considerable amounts of both were needed; the hospital's ninety-seven non-medical staff alone consumed 126 pounds of bread, 126 pounds of meat and some twenty pounds of rice every day. The patients were fed either ordinary rations, which consisted of meat, rice and bananas or, depending on their health, on half-rations, or some other variation on the basic menu. Hospital officials thus bowed to the inevitable in permitting convalescents to consume the typical diet of the region, even though it was widely regarded as unhealthy for Europeans. The official hospital diet did create problems of public order. Complaints about its poor quality were frequent. Indeed, on 13 May 1816 an order was issued that 'any soldier who throws food at the orderlies, claiming that it is inedible, and using indecent and indecorous language inappropriate for polite society, will be punished with fifteen days in the stocks'.[114] Moreover, the food was not only unpalatable, it was also meagre. On occasion the hospital assistants actually sold to villagers the food intended for the patients.[115] Food was evidently so scarce in the hospital of Sabanalarga that patients began slaughtering their own pigs in the patio of the hospital, 'to the detriment of their health', according to hospital staff. Attempts to outlaw this behaviour met with opposition from patients, who complained of the 'despotic and arbitrary behaviour' of the hospital personnel.[116]

The ambience in these hospitals was apparently disagreeable. Hostility reigned between the patients and the staff. The '*cabos de sala*', or orderlies, complained of continual harassment.[117] The overall atmosphere of an army hospital was summed up by a hospital inspector in July 1816. He commented that in these hospitals the patient suffered from 'the pain of his ills, the loss of comfort and subsistence, ... the horrible companionship of a moribund neighbour, and the hardship of ill-treatment, ... leaving aside the shortage of clothing and bed linen, whose absence is directly disadvantageous to the patient'. Such was the lethal atmosphere of most Neogranadan hospitals that in 1818 a woman afflicted with leprosy pleaded not to be confined to one as, if she were, she would certainly die from melancholy.[118]

The level of medical care available in New Granada was in no way able to cope with the demands placed on it by the Expeditionary Army. Inadequate health care and a shortage of doctors did little to prevent deaths. There was thus little remedy to the steady decline in troop size brought about by illness. Thousands of soldiers died in the epidemics of dysentery, smallpox and other ailments, and the already small royalist army shrank irreversibly in size. Attempts at recruiting replacement troops never succeeded in filling the vacancies left by disease, nor did Spain ever send additional troops to New Granada. Those who survived the war returned to Spain with ruined health. Morillo's successor as commander-in-chief, Miguel de la Torre, left office after seven years of service with his formerly robust health 'shattered'.[119] General Morillo complained endlessly that his understaffed and undersized army stood no chance of defeating the insurgents. 'They are just waiting for us all to die of infection and disease', he lamented.[120] The severe lack of resources and the growing hostility of New Granada's population thus combined with yellow fever and dysentery to challenge the reconquest.

PART III

COLLAPSE
1819–1822

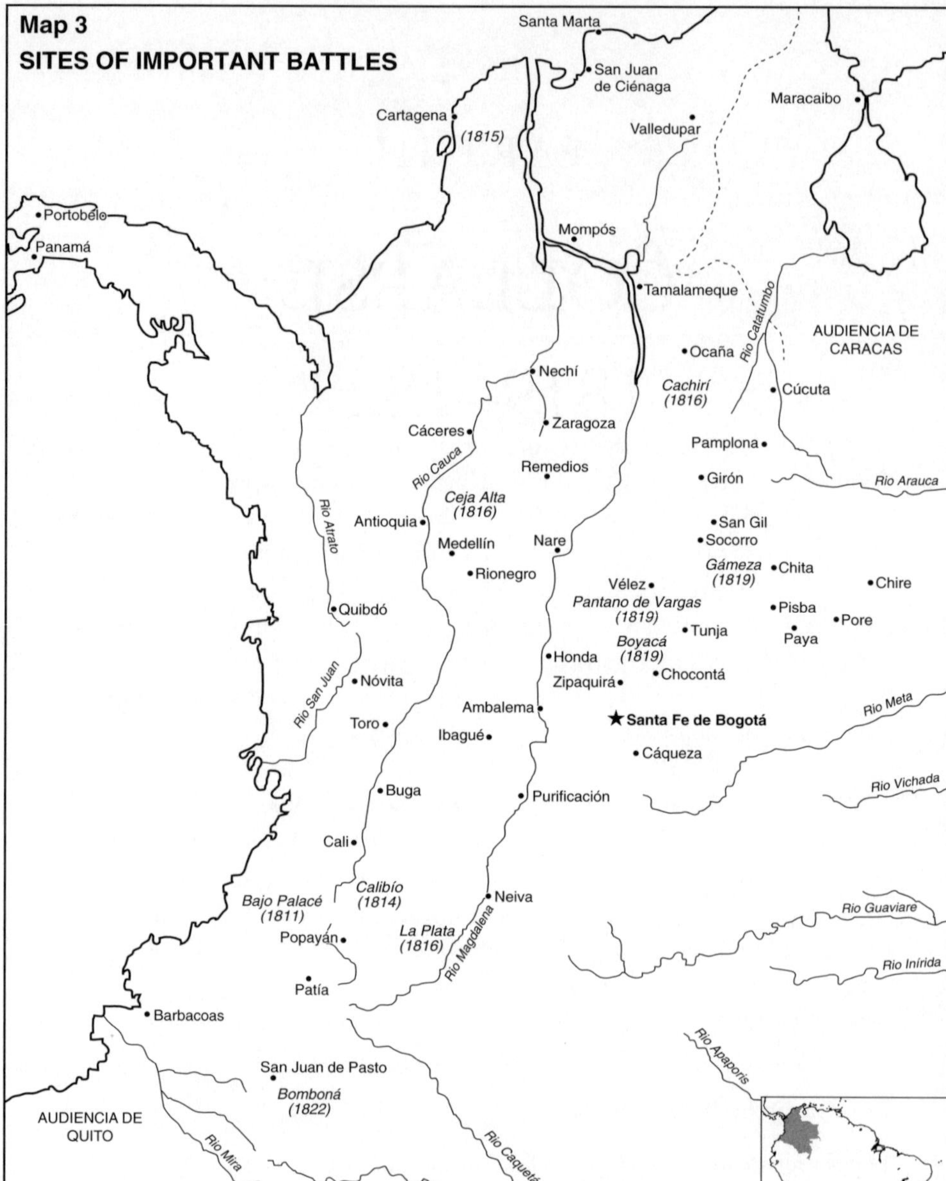
Map 3
SITES OF IMPORTANT BATTLES
Santa Marta
San Juan
de Ciénaga
Maracaibo
Cartagena
(1815)
Valledupar
Portobelo
Panamá
Mompós
Tamalameque
Río Catatumbo
AUDIENCIA DE
CARACAS
Ocaña
Nechí
Cachirí
(1816)
Cúcuta
Cáceres
Zaragoza
Pamplona
Río Cauca
Remedios
Girón
Río Arauca
Río Atrato
Ceja Alta
(1816)
Antioquia
San Gil
Socorro
Medellín
Nare
Gámeza
(1819)
Chita
Rionegro
Vélez
Chire
Pantano de Vargas
(1819)
Pisba
Quibdó
Tunja
Paya
Pore
Boyacá
(1819)
Honda
Chocontá
Zipaquirá
Río San Juan
Nóvita
Ambalema
Río Meta
Santa Fe de Bogotá
Toro
Ibagué
Cáqueza
Buga
Purificación
Río Vichada
Cali
Calibío
(1814)
Bajo Palacé
(1811)
Neiva
Río Guaviare
Popayán
La Plata
(1816)
Río Magdalena
Río Inírida
Patía
Barbacoas
Río Apaporis
San Juan de Pasto
Bomboná
(1822)
AUDIENCIA DE
QUITO
Río Mira
Río Caquetá
Río Putumayo
N
Quito

7

The Battle of Boyacá

From 1819, the royalists began to reap the fruits they had sown. New Granada's increasingly hostile population gained the opportunity to reject the royalists when Bolívar led his forces into New Granada in July 1819. Royalist troops—sick, underpaid, ill supplied and divided—proved no match for the invaders. Then, in 1820, events in Spain dealt a final blow to New Granada's royalists. After the Spanish liberal revolution of 1820, political divisions in New Granada prevented royalists from concentrating on the republican threat. By 1822, no serious royalist presence remained in New Granada. This section charts the final collapse of royal authority in what became Colombia.

We begin with events in 1819. In that year, the problems of the restored royal government stemming from financial difficulties, lack of co-ordination between civil and military powers, and the evaporation of the Expeditionary Army were compounded by a new threat. The republican army of Simón Bolívar launched a vigorous attack on royalist New Granada. The weak and divided reconquest government could neither withstand Bolívar's assaults nor regroup its forces to protect royal authority.

The Campaign of 1819

The royalist campaign that would culminate in disaster on 7 August 1819 at the Battle of Boyacá started inauspiciously in late 1818. The year had begun moderately well for the royalists. Although Bolívar defeated royalist forces at Calabozo and captured San Fernando de Apure, Morillo had won an important battle at La Puerta, and other royalist victories followed at Sombrero, Maracay and elsewhere. By November 1818, however, Morillo reported that although the troops were in good spirits, the 'utter lack of supplies in a devastated country' was crippling the entire army and impeding the start of the new campaign.[1] Morillo's primary military objective was to eliminate the many bands of republican guerrillas in the Llanos between New Granada and Venezuela, the traditional refuge from colonial justice to which republican partisans had retreated in 1816, after Morillo's reconquest.[2] Throughout 1817 and 1818, small bands of guerrillas had harassed royalist troops and occasionally penetrated the interior of New Granada. General Francisco de Paula Santander had reorganized the rather chaotic republican troops into various companies, but they continued to fight an essentially guerrilla war to which the royalists failed to adapt. A number of royalist outposts had already been established in the Llanos, yet control of the Llanos proved elusive.

From 1819, the royalist campaign in the Llanos de Casanare was led by General José María Barreiro. It seems that neither General Morillo nor Viceroy Juan Sámano knew Barreiro prior to his appointment, although Sámano displayed tremendous confidence in the new appointee.[3] Nonetheless, reality soon dawned and Barreiro was revealed to be an unimaginative officer and a disastrous general. He began to experience difficulties in the campaign in the Llanos, which began in March 1819. By early April, he was obliged to report that 'most of the Indians [had] deserted, and the remaining troops soon followed their example'.[4] The level of desertion eventually became so extreme that Barreiro was forced to withdraw completely from the Llanos into New Granada's interior.[5] The spring 1819 royalist campaign in the Llanos was, in short, a complete failure. Santander reported to Simón Bolívar on 29 April 1819 that:

> The desertion that [Barreiro's army] has suffered is extensive; our infantry battalions have been augmented notably by it; his horses have been incapacitated by the marches, counter-marches, and continual alarms; the hunger that his troops have suffered is incredible, since the soldiers receive as rations at most two ounces of meat; [and] they have been masters only of the territory they actually occupy.[6]

Moreover, in late June 1819, Barreiro, like so many soldiers before him, fell ill and was unable to undertake any work at all. Viceroy Sámano prepared to substitute Sebastián de la Calzada, but before Calzada could take command, Barreiro declared himself fully recovered and resumed control.[7]

Meanwhile, a fundamental change had occurred in the military strategy of the republicans. Rather than try to capture Caracas, they decided to concentrate on the recapture of New Granada, and in particular of Santa Fe. This decision was motivated by a desire to capitalize on Santander's organization of the Llanero plainsmen and to open a new front while Morillo was immobilized by bad weather in Venezuela. Efforts were made to co-ordinate the planned attack on the capital with invasions of the Caribbean coast, and Bolívar set about moving his Llanero troops from Venezuela into the Neogranadan interior.[8]

The royalists were aware of this change. On 17 June 1819 Colonel Antonio Tobar wrote to Barreiro from Barinas to warn him that Bolívar and Páez, accompanied by 1,400 soldiers, were marching westward.[9] This warning was followed by a virtual flood of reports about the republican advance. For example, on 5 July 1819, Sergeant Juan Figueroa y Ladrón informed Barreiro that:

> Santander and Arredondo have entered New Granada, their intention is to capture Santa Fe, their first step is to meet up with Páez, who is coming via Piedecuesta; that Bolívar, Donato Pérez and a colonel named Moreno are in Paya; that they are awaiting the arrival of two battalions which left Pisba for Socotá on Thursday 1 [July 1819].[10]

The royalists were thus well informed about the progress of the republican army across the Andes. Some of their intelligence was flawed—Barreiro was supplied with inaccurate information about the difficulty of crossing the flooded Llanos—but these errors were corrected.[11] Republican forces, in other words, did not catch royalist troops by surprise.

The republican march from the Llanos to the Andean highland stretched Bolívar's troops to the utmost limits. The Llanos were flooded, which made progress across them slow and unpleasant, but the crossing of the Andes at the Páramo de Pisba, to the north of Sogamoso, on 5 and 6 July 1819, is regarded as the most difficult feature of the march. Most of the Llanero and British soldiers had never before experienced either the cold or the thinner air of the Andean sierra. Nonetheless, Bolívar succeeded in getting some two thousand troops over the mountains into New Granada.

As Bolívar's army crossed into New Granada, news of its arrival spread to republican guerrillas throughout the provinces of Tunja, Socorro and Pamplona. Small guerrilla groups had been operating in these regions since

1816, but until 1819 succeeded only in harassing equally small royalist detachments and in intercepting communications.[12] During the spring and summer of 1819 these guerrilla groups increasingly became a real problem for Barreiro's troops. Barreiro commented frequently on their apparently growing number, complaining that the country was plagued by 'bandits, protected by the villages' or, in other words, republican guerrillas. Barreiro found it necessary to establish military outposts in Tunja, Ventaquemada, Chocontá and elsewhere. Barreiro was bitter about the behaviour of the region's inhabitants. Even the priests and officials, he complained, were crypto-insurgents and provided great help to the republicans, 'without divulging to us the slightest piece of information'. Public support for the royalists was clearly at a low ebb, and even finding couriers for official communiqués proved difficult. Overall, it is evident that Barreiro enjoyed very poor relations with the civilians in the area of conflict.[13] The Expeditionary Army was thus reaping the fruits of earlier errors. The very regions which had welcomed Morillo in 1816 during his triumphal journey to Santa Fe now rose against his army, providing invaluable support to Bolívar.

Nonetheless, as the summer progressed, Barreiro's confidence about the campaign increased. Although the royalists suffered several defeats at the hands of republican forces, they also won victories in July 1819, and Barreiro filed a series of enthusiastic reports with Viceroy Sámano.[14] Barreiro's optimism arose in part because he greatly underestimated the capacities of the republican troops. After his arrival in New Granada, Bolívar had drafted large numbers of men into the army, which came to be composed of Llanero and British soldiers, and local conscripts, in roughly equal proportions. Barreiro was dismissive of these soldiers, particularly the 'very feeble Indians', deluding himself into believing that royalist troops were far more professional.[15]

During the last week in July 1819, several encounters had taken place between the royalists and Bolívar's vanguard, but for the first six days of August no fighting occurred. Barreiro appears to have written no letters after 31 July 1819, so it is difficult to know what his intentions were during this period.[16] On 5 August he received news that Bolívar was marching on Tunja, and thus set off immediately towards that city.[17] He encountered Bolívar's army outside Tunja at the Puente de Boyacá on 7 August.

The republicans had approximately 2,800 troops.[18] These were the soldiers Bolívar had brought at such cost over the Andes. The royalist force consisted of perhaps 2,700 men.[19] Numerically, the two forces were thus quite evenly matched. This was of no avail to the royalists. When the republican cavalry charged royalist columns, the king's army simply disintegrated. Royalist Captain Manuel Martínez de Aparicio, who survived the battle, described the chaos that followed the successful republican charge: 'the infantry turned tail and ran in the most unbelievably disorganized way'.[20] The battle was fairly short, lasting some two hours.[21] Over 1,600 royalist prisoners were taken and the bulk of the Spanish officer corps was captured.[22] It was the end of Spanish control of New Granada's interior.

It remains unclear why the battle proved such a disaster for the royalists. Traditionally, the republican victory has been ascribed to Bolívar's cunning in bringing his troops over the Andes without attracting the notice of the royalist commanders. On encountering a small republican advance guard, Barreiro attacked, supposedly believing it constituted the entire republican force. When the remainder of the much larger republican force joined the battle, it was too late for the outnumbered royalists to withdraw.[23] Unfortunately, this explanation is unconvincing. The royalists were not outnumbered and Barreiro was well informed of the republican advance over the Andes. Indeed, he had set off towards Tunja in the hope of encountering Bolívar's army. It does seem that royalist troops were not immediately aware that they confronted Bolívar's entire army, but they were soon disabused of this error. Perhaps the dramatic rout can best be ascribed to the substantial difference in morale between Bolívar's and Barreiro's troops. This was certainly Bolívar's explanation: 'morale in the troops of the republic is far superior to that in the king's army which was defeated and captured at Boyacá'. Barreiro himself had been complaining for months prior to the battle that his disgruntled conscript army displayed no special loyalty to the crown, and minimal commitment to himself.[24]

After this royalist catastrophe, there was little to stop the republican advance on Santa Fe, as the capital was less than 120 kilometres from the site of the battle. It was thus essential for the royalists to warn the viceroy of the impending attack as quickly as possible. 'The terrible news that the [Third] Division had been entirely destroyed' reached Santa Fe the following day.[25] Several officers who had survived the defeat arrived in the capital in the evening of 8 August 1819 and informed the viceroy of the imminent republican occupation of Santa Fe. Sámano decided to leave the capital immediately. The night of 8 August 1819 was spent arranging for his departure: boats were to be waiting at Honda, and news of the impending invasion was circulated to other government officials.[26] At 9.00 p.m. Sámano wrote to Morillo that he intended to go to Popayán, but in fact he set off in the opposite direction, toward Cartagena. He left at 6.00 a.m. the next morning, 9 August 1819, reportedly disguised in a green *ruana* and a large hat and leaving behind virtually all of his belongings and papers.[27] The Audiencia also fled to safety in Cartagena, but the years of bad feeling between Sámano and the Audiencia were reflected in the fact that the viceroy informed them of the impending invasion only hours before his departure, leaving the *oidores* little time to prepare their own retreat.[28]

It is not evident that Sámano made the right decision in choosing to leave. Contemporary opinion was divided and some observers, in particular the governor of Cartagena, were extremely critical of the decision to abandon Santa Fe. Governor Torres commented that 'although I had foreseen the loss of New Granada, I had never imagined that a small skirmish would lead to the loss of the capital and nearly three hundred leagues of territory, but that is what has happened'.[29] Others believed the withdrawal to have been the only possible response. The capital had a garrison of some four hundred troops, insufficient to resist the entire republican army. Moreover, royalist officials had little confidence in the extent of popular support for the regime.[30] In the event, Bolívar entered Santa Fe unchallenged on the evening of 9 August 1819, some three years after Morillo's entry in May 1816.[31]

The royalist troops that survived the battle of Boyacá scattered in various directions. Governor Torres of Cartagena explained that:

> Some presented themselves to the enemy, others returned to their houses, and of the entire Third Division only about two hundred men from the infantry and cavalry managed to regroup on the banks of the Magdalena, where finding themselves without boats they saved themselves by constructing rafts which brought them to Mompós.[32]

According to Torres' calculations, over ninety per cent of the Third Division was captured, killed or deserted at Boyacá. As many of Barreiro's men were American it is not surprising that some used the defeat as an opportunity to desert. With few exceptions, the remaining survivors ended up in the republican army. It is not clear how many voluntarily joined the republicans, and how many merely surrendered to it. Following standard practice, captured royalist soldiers were immediately incorporated into the republican army; two new republican companies named 'Tunja' and 'Boyacá' were formed.[33] The royalist officers captured by the republicans were taken to Santa Fe in early September 1819. They included Barreiro himself, whom, Santander claimed, 'had the baseness to offer his services to the republic as a simple soldier'.[34] Barreiro's alleged willingness to defect notwithstanding, on 11 October 1819 Barreiro and his fellow officers were shot on Santander's orders, much to the annoyance of Bolívar, who had hoped to exchange the royalist prisoners for captured republicans.

Defeat of the Spanish reconquering army at the centre of New Granada had an immediate and profound effect on the regime it supported. As news of the disaster spread, royalist troops elsewhere took the opportunity to desert, and several provincial governments in the interior collapsed. The Governor of Antioquia, for example, fled, while the governor of the Chocó was captured and shot by the republicans.[35] Further problems were caused by the breakdown in the chain of command resulting from the rapid retreat from Santa Fe and the capture of so many officers. Uncertainty surrounded the fate of the viceroy, and it was not clear who retained supreme command of colonial government. Royalist forces were divided and old rivalries resurfaced. Particular difficulties occurred in the south, where Sebastián de la Calzada and Melchor Aymerich argued over which of them inherited Sámano's mantle of authority after the viceroy's flight.[36]

Sámano himself arrived in Cartagena in early October 1819. He was accompanied by large numbers of royalists from Santa Fe, many of whom arrived penniless at the coast.[37] The Audiencia also set itself up in Cartagena, where it was to remain until 1820 when, as a consequence of the republican siege, it retreated, bizarrely, to the British colony of Jamaica. Safe within Cartagena, Sámano claimed to be organizing the recapture of the capital, but he was never again to return to Santa Fe.[38] Indeed, from the moment of his arrival in Cartagena he ceased to play any significant role in the military campaign against the republicans. Governor Torres complained that, despite the critical state of the affairs in Cartagena, 'so far [Sámano] has done nothing beyond converting the simplest military operations into convoluted plans of action, while the enemy has advanced almost to within sight'.[39]

News of the momentous event rapidly spread throughout New Granada, but did not immediately reach Morillo in Venezuela who, weeks after the battle of Boyacá was still complaining that he had heard nothing from the luckless Barreiro. Morillo appears not to have learned of the defeat until early September 1819.[40] When Morillo did at last hear the news, he immediately determined that General Miguel de la Torre should take command of the surviving troops and replace Sámano in the event of the latter's death or capture. It was not until some days later that Morillo learned that Sámano was safe in Cartagena.[41]

Military Repercussions

Following Bolívar's victory at Boyacá, the prospects of the Expeditionary Army worsened considerably. Groups of republican guerrillas that had been lurking in the background came out into the open all at once. For some months the situation looked quite hopeless for Spain. In Socorro alone, republican guerrillas managed in just three days to assemble a force of over two thousand, which occupied the city and executed some fifteen Spaniards.[42] In Pamplona, the entire royalist garrison of El Tambo, the prisoners and the population at large rebelled.[43] Ríohacha, meanwhile, was invaded by republicans led by General MacGregor on 4 October 1819. They were driven out within a week, but not all revolts were as short-lived.[44] On 10 November 1819, royalist troops in Ocaña rebelled, killed several officers and fled from the barracks. This resulted not only in the loss of Ocaña to the republicans, but also to the temporary cessation of all communication between Sámano in Cartagena and Morillo in Venezuela.[45] In Mompós an uprising broke out on 17 November 1819.[46] From Cartagena, Sámano made a slight attempt to co-ordinate a counter-attack, but his efforts were viewed as derisory even by his own allies. Governor Torres reported that:

> With regard to military operations, the governor of Antioquia has been provided with about eighty men, with which he is supposed to reconquer a province whose population have revolted practically *en masse*; another hundred have been sent to Ocaña, where they remain without being able to do anything at all, despite the fact that the place is strategically important, because they are unable to communicate with the interior, and a small force has been assembled to recapture the Magdalena River. This is the entirety of the observable operations that have been undertaken in two months, which in my humble opinion augur very little.[47]

The Cauca Valley was thrown into immediate upheaval by the events to the north. We saw in chapter 6 that the behaviour of the Third Division had provoked widespread opposition in the Cauca Valley. The collapse of royal authority in Santa Fe provided an opportunity for the Vallecaucanos to act on their anger. The *Contador de Tabacos* in Popayán (the tobacco monopoly's accountant) reported in early September 1819 that the loss of the capital had provoked several uprisings in the region, 'which has always been in favour of the insurrection'.[48] Various tobacco *estanquillos*, or local outlets of the monopoly, were destroyed, and it was subsequently learned that Governor Pedro Domínguez, along with various officials of the tobacco monopoly and several other Spaniards had been killed. It is noteworthy that among the first targets of popular hatred were the royal monopolies. The opposition to the state-run tobacco and *aguardiente* monopolies went back decades and remained unaltered by the war.[49] According to the royalist Bishop of Popayán, the revolt was led by

> deserters and other criminals, who because of the previous revolution were hidden in the forests, [and who] on account of the enormity of their crimes and their obstinately-held mistaken beliefs, have not wanted to take advantage of the pardons that they have been offered by the most benign of monarchs.[50]

In other words, the revolt was led by individuals in the Cauca Valley who had not been reconciled to Spain during the years of royalist occupation. The bishop's remarks here and elsewhere attest to the ample evidence of popular discontent prior to the Battle of Boyacá.[51] Moreover, Sebastián de la Calzada, who had led the retreat of Santa Fe's garrison south to Popayán, was forced to abandon the city after many of his troops deserted. Popayán was then occupied by republicans.[52] Calzada's only hope lay in the Pastusos, who had up to this point been reliably royalist. Fulfilling Calzada's hopes, the Pastusos, and in particular the 'loyal Indians', assembled a sizeable army which enabled Calzada to drive the republicans from Popayán on 24 January 1820.[53] When he learned of Popayán's recapture, Bolívar was livid:

> I am going to give orders for the chief leaders, rich, noble, or plebeian, to be hanged in Pasto, and the rest of the population to be transported away to Venezuela, so that no one is left but women and children, who can do no harm to us for the present and may change their minds.[54]

Calzada, meanwhile, continued planning an attack on Santa Fe itself and had succeeded in assembling several thousand men when, in June 1820, Popayán was recaptured by the republicans. The royalists were forced to retreat once again to Pasto, never to retake Popayán.[55]

Royalist Responses

Contemporary observers did not agree about the importance of the battle of Boyacá. On the one hand, the republicans were in no doubt that the battle was of great significance. The republican *Boletín del Ejército Libertador* reported that 'the advantages which have befallen the republic with the glorious victory [at Boyacá] are incalculable', and within a few years the battlefield had become a tourist attraction.[56] Nor was the profound importance of the battle lost on General Morillo. On learning of the defeat he described himself as being in 'the most critical situation since I arrived in this continent'. Cartagena's Governor Torres likewise felt that the battle and subsequent loss of the capital were a turning point in the war.[57] Other royalist officials were more hopeful. Viceroy Sámano expressed apparently genuine confidence that with three thousand additional troops the Spanish could end the war once and for all.[58]

Although royalist opinions differed as to the importance of the battle of Boyacá, everyone agreed that it was a defeat and also that it probably could have been avoided. Almost immediately after the actual battle on 7 August 1819, royalists in New Granada began casting about for explanations of the unexpected disaster. In no way was the republican victory viewed as evidence of Bolívar's skill.[59] Responsibility was instead felt to lie with the Spanish themselves. Patterns of blame were established early; already on 8 August 1819, Viceroy Sámano was implicitly blaming the defeat on General Barreiro's incompetence, and this trend became the dominant one in the following months.[60]

Despite their initial enthusiasm about Barreiro, both Sámano and Morillo had been unhappy with his performance for some time prior to Boyacá. On 20 June 1819, Morillo had blamed the entire republican advance on 'the indolence and apathy of Señor Barreiro'.[61] Viceroy Sámano, for his part, also held Carlos Tolrá, the military commander of Antioquia, responsible for the loss of much of the Neogranadan interior. Tolrá abandoned Antioquia in late August 1819, claiming that the entire province, with the exception of Medellín and Ríonegro, supported the republicans, and that the royalist had no realistic chance of defeating them: 'I see all, *all* the towns ready to raise the cry of independence'.[62] Moreover, Tolrá pointed out that in February 1819 he had been ordered to send his entire stock of weapons to Santa Fe. He was thus completely unequipped for resistance, with a mere eighty-six troops under his command.[63]

Sámano of course had a personal motive for blaming Barreiro and Tolrá: he wished to head off criticism that he himself had behaved unwisely in fleeing to Cartagena rather than taking command of the remaining royalist troops.[64] Attacks on Sámano's behaviour came principally from Gabriel de Torres, the governor of Cartagena, who was extremely critical of the viceroy's rapid flight. Disagreements between Torres and Sámano were never resolved and Sámano's relationship with the governor deteriorated steadily during the ensuing months.[65]

Torres, indeed, had much to say about the defeat at Boyacá and his analysis provides a concise summary of the many errors of the reconquest. An astute observer, he laid the blame primarily at the door of the Expeditionary Army. In his correspondence with Spain he had already warned that the mistreatment and excessive contributions imposed on the populace by the Expeditionary Army would cause the loss of New Granada. In October 1819 he again wrote to the king, lamenting that his predictions had come true. The defeat at Boyacá was inevitable, he insisted:

> How could anything else have happened? The moral force of the villagers was destroyed ... [they were] stripped in the greatest disorder of their possessions, animals, and whatever formed their livelihood, without ever being paid a *real*, and with justice always inclined in favour of those who were responsible for their suffering. All these things combined to alter the support for your majesty, in whose name so many had been made unhappy ... The physical force of the army was moreover out of control, military discipline [was] destroyed, or at least enervated, the soldiers accustomed to being commander by leaders who, although perhaps brave, lacked almost any other military virtue. [The soldiers were] moreover impressed into the army without any control, without a fair system of selection and with no concern whatsoever for the needs of agriculture, the arts, or the families of the recruits, and were obliged to desolate their own country. How could one hope that they would be obedient soldiers, and that they would win victories and honour for your majesty's royal army?[66]

There was, however, one more blow to be struck at Spain's pretensions, which even Governor Torres had not been able to predict. This was the 1820 liberal revolution in Spain, which delivered the *coup de grâce* to the Spanish regime in New Granada.

8

Armistice and Surrender

The year 1820 was of great significance for Spaniards in both Spain and the Americas. The year opened with a revolution in Andalucía that prevented the planned despatch of troops to Río de la Plata, and moreover plunged Spain into a period of political strife. Crisis at home was succeeded by crisis in America. The year ended with virtually all of Spain's American empire in ruins. By December 1820 only Peru, Mexico City, a few Caribbean islands and a very reduced portion of New Granada remained in royalist hands; within five years all but Cuba were to become independent.

The 1820 Revolution in Spain

The roots of the 1820 crisis in Spain itself must be traced to the political polarization that came in the wake of the French invasion of 1808. The capture of the Bourbon monarchs, the coronation of Joseph Napoleon as king of Spain and the creation of the Spanish resistance juntas had led to increasing political polarization among Spaniards and the rise of *partidos*, or political parties. The different political groupings coalesced around the so-called liberals, themselves divided into subfactions, and the absolutists. The precise nature of these nascent parties need not detain us here, nor are finer dissection into *moderados*, *exaltados*, *doceañistas*, *tragalistas*, *afrancesados*, *ultramontanos* or *serviles* necessary for our purposes.[1] The division between liberals and absolutists gathered momentum during the years of Ferdinand VII's captivity in France, a period of liberal ascendancy.

After Ferdinand's return, hostility between the king and liberals of all stripes simmered ominously until 1820, when an open rupture occurred. On New Year's Day 1820 an historic uprising began in the Andalucian town of Las Cabezas de San Juan. On that day Colonel Rafael Riego, the leader of the revolt, pronounced in favour of the Constitution of 1812 and troops stationed in Las Cabezas rebelled. Over the next few days Riego marched through other towns in Andalucía, and then to Cádiz itself, where Colonel Antonio Quiroga attempted an assault on the city's military warehouses. This attack on Cádiz was unsuccessful and initially the revolt aroused little public support. The rest of the army, however, did nothing to stop the uprising, and in the ensuing months pro-constitutional revolts broke out across Spain. Three months later on 7 March 1820 the king was forced to reconvene the Cortes and reinstate the Constitution of 1812. On 9 March 1820, Ferdinand was himself obliged to swear loyalty to the very constitution that he had personally overthrown in 1814. These events ushered in a three-year period of liberal, constitutional rule in Spain.

The causes of the revolution of 1820 have been much discussed. It is clear that dissatisfaction with Ferdinand's government had increased throughout 1819 and that various anti-government plots had already been hatched.[2] Certain features, however, distinguish the revolt of 1820 from previous conspiracies. In particular, the uprising was supported by the troops not solely out of liberal sentiment, but also because of their profound disgust with the army. The first troops to rebel were new recruits about to be shipped to Buenos Aires to fight the Argentine insurgents. They joined the revolt to avoid being sent to fight in the unpopular colonial war. Antonio Alcalá Galiano indeed asserted that the revolt was entirely due to 'the repugnance of the rank and file against embarking for America'.[3] Nonetheless, their participation in the 1820 revolution was critical to events not only in Spain but also in the Americas. The impact of Riego's revolt on the American war was described clearly, if intemperately, by one absolutist officer who complained that 'the Spanish continent of America, [which was] discovered, conquered and civilised at a time when God and the Patria were respected, was lost because of [a scandalous uprising of the army in Andalucía, whose authors] later called themselves patriots'.[4] The assertion that Riego's uprising contributed to the loss of America is entirely justified. Because of the uprising, the 1819 military expedition to Río de la Plata never left Spain, thereby guaranteeing the independence of Buenos Aires. The rebellion led directly to the collapse of royalism in Mexico and the installation of Agustín de Iturbide as emperor of Mexico. The royalist enclaves in Peru, New Granada and Venezuela were also deprived of essential reinforcements. Equally importantly, the return of liberalism to Spain provoked a fatal split in New Granada's fragile royalist regime. Political division was just as virulent among royalists in Spanish America as it was in Spain. Indeed, in Peru, the political splits within the royalist camp were so great that in the evacuation that followed the royalists' defeat at Ayacucho, liberals returning to Spain would not even sit in the same section of the ship as absolutists. Constitutionalists and anti-constitutionalists remained segregated throughout the return voyage.[5]

The Constitution in Cartagena

The first colony to learn of the liberal revolt was Cuba. News of Spain's return to constitutional government reached Havana on 15 April 1820 and was greeted immediately with great enthusiasm. The Captain General of Cuba, José Manuel Cajigal, published the information without delay, and on 16 April the entire colonial government of Havana swore loyalty to the Constitution amidst general rejoicing. By the next day Havana's Royal Lottery, the Lotería Real, had changed its name to the Lotería Constitucional.[6]

Despite the appearance of order, this transfer to the constitutional system was not accomplished without discord. It appears that Captain General Cajigal had been pushed into accepting the Constitution by liberals who threatened to depose him if he did not. They intended to replace him with the liberal Francisco Montalvo, New Granada's former viceroy, who was in retirement in Cuba.[7] The rocky reception of the Constitution in Cuba presaged its welcome on the mainland. There too the change of government in Spain was used to effect changes in the colonial administration.

It took several months for news of the Riego revolution to reach Cartagena's royalists. Rumours had been circulating for some time about political divisions in Spain and there were fears that the metropolis might be enveloped in another civil war.[8] The first reports of the reinstitution of the 1812 Constitution were, however, dismissed as republican propaganda by Cartagena's Governor Gabriel de Torres.[9] Definitive news that Ferdinand had sworn loyalty to the Constitution, and of its adoption in Cuba, was brought to Cartagena from Havana in early June 1820. Viceroy Sámano, deeply opposed to the Constitution, was not willing to make the news public. Instead, he placed under house arrest one individual who had actually witnessed the oath in Cuba. This measure proved completely ineffective, as within days other ships arrived with news confirming the earlier notices.

The news caused considerable uproar in the city. Matters came to a head on 7 June 1820, almost a decade after the July 1810 riots that ended the viceregency of Antonio de Amar. Indeed, events in Cartagena, which led to the overthrow of Viceroy Sámano, neatly mirror the earlier riots; the two events bookend the war. Around half past four in the afternoon on 7 June 1820, the members of the city's Artillery Brigade and the Regimiento de León presented themselves at Cartagena's seat of government, the Palacio de Gobierno, to demand the immediate promulgation of the 1812 Constitution. The troops brought four cannons with them, and some reports state that the soldiers were accompanied by many members of the public.[10] The crowd called for Governor Torres, who informed them that, although he supported their demand for the restoration of the Constitution, he could take no action without the support of the other commanding officers and the viceroy. Viceroy Sámano had, however, already made known his opposition to the Constitution.

At this juncture, the commander of the Regimiento de León, Brigadier Antonio Cano, arrived in the plaza to declare his complete opposition to any adoption of the Constitution, his troops' behaviour notwithstanding. This, Governor Torres reported, nearly caused an armed confrontation between the members of the Artillery Brigade and Cano's own troops. It was only with great effort that Governor Torres succeeded in getting any of the troops to return to barracks. Deciding that swift action was necessary, Torres convoked a *cabildo extraordinario*, a special meeting of the city's *cabildo* also attended by the *asesor general de gobierno*, the lieutenant governor, and Torres himself. He also convened a military junta comprised of most senior officers from the garrison. (Brigadier Antonio Cano, a long-time enemy of Governor Torres, did not attend.) Both meetings agreed that Torres should send Sámano all the available documentary evidence confirming that the king had indeed embraced the Constitution, in an effort to convince the viceroy to support the new system. It was further agreed to send a deputation to the bishop of Cartagena to enlist his support. All of this was done immediately, and the *cabildo* decided to remain in session until a reply from Sámano was received, despite the fact that it was by then midnight.

While these groups were meeting, Sámano allegedly sent agents throughout Cartagena to arrest everyone who had demonstrated in favour of the Constitution that afternoon. Most liberals, suspecting something of this sort would take place, had already gone into hiding, but Sámano was able to detain two officers and an official from the city's customs house. These arrests provided Sámano with the confidence to inform Torres at 3.00 a.m. on the morning of 8 June that there was no urgent need to implement any changes to the government since Cartagena had returned to a state of complete calm. In fact, Cartagena was far from being calm; many of the city's troops were in open rebellion against their officers and one company of grenadiers had spent the entire night fully armed in the Plaza de la Merced, deaf to orders to return to barracks. The townspeople were also reported to be in a state of extreme 'effervescence'.

Another *cabildo extraordinario* was held later in the morning of 8 June and the viceroy was again urged to accept the new Constitution. Sámano, in rare alliance with the Audiencia, denounced the previous *cabildo extraordinario* as unnecessary and illegal, and deprived Torres of the authority to convoke any more meetings without written permission from Sámano himself. Meanwhile, unrest in Cartagena continued to grow and began to take on an anti-Spanish nature: American soldiers in the Company of Granaderos de León tried to expel all the Spaniards from the garrison. Violence was necessary to compel the troops to sleep in the barracks on the night of 8 June, but by the morning of 9 June order could no longer be maintained. Soldiers leaving the barracks that morning openly disobeyed their officers and seized control of the Baluarte de Santo Domingo, where they were joined by more troops who had overthrown their officers and forced open the barracks doors. Both the bishop and Brigadier Cano tried to persuade the men to return to barracks, but both were ignored.[11]

The members of the Artillery Brigade and the Regimiento de León then set off in an orderly fashion toward the Plaza de la Inquisición with the intention of proclaiming the Constitution. The soldiers also demanded the back pay owed to them. Members of the public, in an attempt to avoid further unrest, began distributing money and Viceroy Sámano, on learning of the gathering in the Plaza de la Inquisición, supplied an additional amount. The distribution of cash lasted well into the afternoon, but did not succeed in diverting the troops from their principal demand of the re-establishment of the Constitution.

The royal army was thus in revolt and Sámano had no means at his disposal to reduce them to a subordinate state. Moreover, he clearly lacked the backing of the governor and many of the city's officials. Recognizing defeat, he wrote to Governor Torres that afternoon that:; 'Finding myself gravely ill, I have resolved to retire to the town of Sabanalarga … leaving political command to the *Oidor Decano* of the Audiencia, as the law requires, and military command to you'.[12] Governor Torres, invested with this new authority, immediately convoked another *junta extraordinario*, attended by the military commanders and by civil and ecclesiastic authorities. The junta approved the adoption of the Constitution, and this resolution was put into effect immediately thereafter in front of the assembled troops, who greeted the oath with 'the greatest demonstrations of happiness'. The troops then returned to barracks in an orderly fashion.

The following day, the adoption of the Constitution was formally announced and orders to swear loyalty were sent to the remaining Spanish officials throughout the province. At 11.00 a.m. on 10 June 1820, government officials, civil and military, gathered in the cathedral to attend a Te Deum. Illuminations and public festivities were then held. Sámano did not attend these festivities and refused repeatedly to swear loyalty to the constitution. As a consequence, the junta formally removed Sámano from office, citing Article 374 of the new code, which stipulated that all office holders swear loyalty to the constitution. Sámano was thus overthrown in a constitutional coup. Over the course of the next few days *Oidor Decano* Francisco de Mosquera y Cabrera resigned from exercising the political command that he had been granted by Sámano on 9 June 1820, and Governor Torres took up political control of the province of Cartagena. Torres thus became the *de facto* viceroy, an opportunity he had been awaiting for some time.[13]

The little available evidence suggests that the initial response of the public in Cartagena to these changes was positive, but beyond the ousting of Sámano, the impact of the return to constitutional rule was slight.[14] The reintroduction of the Constitution to Cartagena resulted in some symbolic changes: Cartagena's *cabildo* began calling itself the 'Ayuntamiento Constitucional', or 'Constitutional Council', and referred to Cartagena, not as 'Cartagena de Indias', but as 'Cartagena de América'. It is not clear, however, whether the actual machinery of the Constitution was put into place. Elections for deputies to the Cortes, for example, may not have been held.[15]

No new upheavals occurred for the next week, but then, on 28 June, a ship arrived from Spain with official orders to swear loyalty to the Constitution. Now that official orders from Spain had actually arrived, Sámano immediately offered to take the oath of loyalty, but Torres was not about to surrender his new authority.[16] During the next few weeks Sámano made unsuccessful efforts to organize the anti-constitutional faction in Cartagena in order to regain command. On 5 July 1820, he set sail for Jamaica, leaving Gabriel de Torres in command of royalist forces in New Granada.

While this palace coup was occurring in Cartagena, the only important Neogranadan city remaining in Spanish hands, similarly fraught developments were taking place in Venezuela, where the royalists were in an equally dishevelled state. General Morillo was in desperate need of the reinforcements he supposed were about to depart from Spain. Unaware that these very troops had rebelled, and also that they had in any case been destined for Buenos Aires, Morillo continued to await their arrival until late March 1820, when he learned of Riego's revolution. Morillo himself swore loyalty to the Constitution in Caracas on 7 June 1820.[17] Morillo, a moderate liberal, was happy to support the Constitution of 1812. Not all officials were equally enthusiastic, and in Venezuela, as in New Granada, news of the constitutional revolution in Spain provoked high-level splits. The long-serving Francisco Tomás Morales, one of the highest-ranking royalist officers, threatened to resign after learning of the reintroduction of the Constitution.[18]

In Cartagena, too, the constitution continued to cause dissent, even after the flight of the viceroy, for there remained in Cartagena many individuals opposed to the new liberal regime. Less than a month after the coup, Governor Torres was complaining that 'persons claiming to be loyal to the king' were putting up offensive anti-constitutional lampoons.[19] The most important opponents of the new regime were two high-ranking officers, the commander of the Regimiento de León, Brigadier Antonio Cano, and Colonel Francisco Warleta. Warleta's attitude to the Constitution may be deduced from his behaviour on learning of its reintroduction:

> After he learned in the town of Barranca, where he was stationed, that the Constitution had been reinstated, he tore off all his insignias of office, burned the buttons which were embossed with the name of his regiment, opened and threw into the fire all the correspondence which dealt with this matter, and under the pretext of illness, withdrew to the town of Soledad, abandoning his post.[20]

The effect of this high-level opposition was serious. The public breach between the governor and the viceroy led to a further breakdown in discipline in the army and, reportedly, a general decline in respect for royalist authorities. Mariano Sixto, Governor Torres' representative to General Morillo, reported in early December 1820 that 'The garrison of Cartagena ... because of the extremely bad example set by the Brigadier Antonio Cano and the Colonel Francisco Warleta when the Constitution was reinstated, is now entirely undisciplined'.[21] The breakdown in control facilitated increasing desertion from the royalist army in the months after the rift.[22] Moreover, Colonel Warleta's refusal to accept the constitutional regime was directly responsible for the loss of the town of Barranca, which was captured by republicans within days of the colonel's decamping. Most importantly, the struggle between the viceroy and the governor distracted the royalists from the real threat to the Spanish presence in New Granada: the republican army. While Sámano and Torres argued over politics, the republicans were preparing to lay siege to Cartagena. Four days after the defeated Sámano left the city, republican General Mariano Montilla began the blockade that resulted in Cartagena's surrender. During the preceding weeks, Cartagena's royalist government had focused little attention on preparing for this siege. Royalist energies had instead centred on the struggle between Governor Torres and Viceroy Sámano, and on containing the army's pro-constitutional agitations.

The 1820 liberal revolution thus had several consequences for royalists in New Granada. To begin with, the restoration of the 1812 Constitution was directly responsible for the overthrow of Viceroy Sámano. Secondly, Spain's new liberal regime resolved to open direct talks with the insurgents, the results of which dialogue will be considered in the next section. Finally, it remains to make one general point. This concerns the broader effect of the politicization of the Spanish bureaucracy. Timothy Anna has persuasively argued that the division within the royalist camp greatly discredited the Spanish cause in America.[23] Spanish authority, already wounded by the long sequence of events in Spain starting in 1808, was finally shown to be not only enfeebled, but indeed irrelevant to the Americas. Bolívar's aide-de-camp Daniel Florencio O'Leary put it concisely: 'the bond uniting the people of Colombia to the Spanish nation was at last broken'.[24] This remark might indeed be generalized to much of Spanish America. The Constitution had questioned the very basis of traditional Spanish government and the dispute within the royalist camp over its implementation accentuated this.

It was simply not possible to present Spain as a unified entity. This situation was clear to the republican leadership in New Granada; Simón Bolívar wrote to Governor Torres in August 1820, 'it is the height of madness, and moreover of idiocy, to suggest that the Republic of Colombia submit itself to Spain … Do you still imagine that decrepit and corrupt Spain could govern this modern world?'[25] The inhabitants of New Granada could see that while the myth of imperial unity dissolved, the republican forces marched ever closer to victory. It was clear the royalists, with or without the Constitution, had little to offer.

However, this was not at all clear to Spain's new liberal government. In Madrid, many officials remained convinced that the defeat of absolutism and the return of the Constitution of 1812 provided an ideal format for reconciliation with Spain. One of the immediate consequences of the 1820 revolution was a renewed commitment on the part of Spain's government to end the American war by diplomatic means. In early April 1820, the new liberal government announced a unilateral cease-fire in the overseas territories and prepared to send commissioners to negotiate with rebel leaders. The task of the commissioners was to convince the insurgents to accept the Constitution of 1812, as a first step towards re-incorporation into the Spanish empire. Only if the insurgents failed to accept the Constitution was the war to continue. This decision to negotiate was, as Timothy Anna notes, 'the first important policy breakthrough since 1814. Yet at its core was an idea that was not only not revolutionary but not even original.'[26] In 1812, officials in both Spain and the Americas had clung to the hope that the promulgation of the Constitution would in itself end the war, as it was felt that the Constitution corrected any errors in the administration of the colonies, and thus eliminated the need for independence.[27] In the face of considerable evidence, the liberals of 1820 again placed their faith in the Constitution. 'The insurrection in America will probably be calmed if the Constitution is made general', proclaimed the liberal newspaper *El Universal*.[28]

Evidently, no lessons had been learned from the past. The government's official line, echoing the failed hopes of 1812, was that the insurgents no longer had any reason to continue fighting, as the Constitution provided an ideal format for reconciliation. This view was advanced publicly by Ferdinand in his May 1820 declaration to the Americans, in which he announced the readoption of the Constitution.[29] In fact, Ferdinand was privately convinced the 1820 liberal revolution was intended specifically to cause the loss of America, notwithstanding his official pronouncements to the contrary. He summed up his views in a letter to fellow absolutist Tsar Alexander I of Russia: 'The Constitution formed in Cádiz, and the revolution made in Spain, were the work of the machinations of those who desired to separate the Americas from the metropolis. Thus it has happened. Now they are lost, and only with difficulty can they be recovered.'[30]

Ferdinand's private scepticism was shared by many royalist officials. Doubts about the unifying effects of the Constitution transcended political divisions between liberals and absolutists. General Morillo himself put the matter succinctly:

> It is madness, in my view, to allow oneself to believe that this part of America wants to unite with [Spain], adopting the Constitution … They don't want to be Spanish; they've made this perfectly clear from the moment they declared independence, and they've stuck to this position regardless of events in the Peninsula. They continue to repeat this, without laying down their weapons, they'll go on repeating this, and no matter what we do, or what government we have, complete independence or war is the only choice they're offering us.[31]

Nonetheless, the plans to send peace commissioners to the Americas progressed. Unfortunately for Spain, the commissioners proved to be too little, too late.

Peace Commissions

> They repeat that they will accept nothing but independence or death.
>
> Pablo Morillo to the Minister of War, 6 August 1820[32]

In April 1820 the Spanish Council of State drew up a set of instructions for the special commissioners.[33] These stipulated that, on arriving in the Americas, the commissioners were to form juntas of reliable royalists to discuss the situation in each region and were to then open negotiations with the insurgent leaders. The commissioners were to offer a cease-fire and an *olvido eterno de lo pasado* (an 'eternal forgetting of the past'). They were also to obtain oaths of loyalty to the Constitution from insurgent leaders. The commissioners were instructed then to begin negotiations over trade restrictions; Spain was prepared to permit direct trade with other countries, provided certain tariff differentials were maintained. This concession, which would have been welcomed in 1808, was to be entirely ignored during the actual negotiations. Neither the commissioners nor the insurgents took seriously the proposed relaxation of Spanish trading legislation over a region almost entirely liberated from Spanish control. The proposal in itself indicates the hopelessly slow pace with which Spain's governments assimilated new ideas.

The commissioners had been named by early June 1820. Nine were appointed in total; Brigadier José Sartorio and Captain Francisco Espeluis were to go to Venezuela, while Captains Juan Barry and Tomás de Urrechea were to go to New Granada.[34] Arrangements for their support were finalized, and a code for communicating secret reports was devised. Within weeks of being named, however, the commissioners began expressing doubts and several, including Barry and Urrechea, tried to resign.[35] Barry and Urrechea pointed out that everything they had read about the situation in the Americas suggested that the Americans were committed to independence, yet their instructions made no mention of this.[36] Moreover, in a foretaste of events to come, prior to departure they were already owed months of back-salary. They were eventually persuaded to leave Cádiz, and set sail on 11 November 1820.

By the time the commissioners arrived in Caracas, events had left them behind. Morillo had already opened negotiations with Bolívar and had arranged an armistice. The commissioners nonetheless soldiered on, although they still had not been paid.[37] The commissioners destined for New Granada decided to remain in Venezuela, and Barry and Urrechea wrote to Bolívar to explain their mission. No answer was forthcoming. Urrechea meanwhile fell ill and returned to Seville. Barry, Sartorio and another officer were eventually granted an audience with two Colombian officials, who politely rejected all of the Spaniards' proposals. Barry and Sartorio, disillusioned, informed the government that their commission was entirely pointless and requested permission to return to Spain.[38]

Far from being permitted to return to Spain, the government decided to keep the commissioners in the Americas, as part of a new commission established in 1821.[39] It was admitted that Spain had not been kind to its agents. The Cortes acknowledged that the 1820 commissioners had still received no pay, and 'survive in Puerto Cabello on soldier's rations, without a penny'.[40] The Cortes nonetheless insisted that the commissioners had a purpose and drew up new orders for negotiations in 1821, 1822 and 1823.

The commissioners themselves were not so sure. When Sartorio heard a rumour that another large military expedition was being organized in 1821 to reconquer Mexico, under the command of the Conde de Abisbal, the disillusioned commissioner suggested 'the best thing would be to leave the 11,500 men at peace in Cádiz, or wherever they are, and the count in Madrid, or wherever he is'.[41] Barry and Sartorio were kept in the Americas, lamenting their fate and accomplishing nothing, until the restoration of absolutism in 1824, when Ferdinand cancelled the credentials of all 'so-called commissioners' who asserted that Spain was about to recognize the independence of America and recalled them to Spain.[42]

The peregrinations of the special commissioners might be taken as a metaphor for Spain's futile efforts to restore peace in the Viceroyalty of New Granada. They came too late, had too little authority and were unsure about the merits of their own mission. Moreover, they moved at the margins. While the commissioners were still in Cádiz, serious negotiations were already underway in Venezuela. At the same time as the special commission was being dreamed up, Ferdinand ordered Morillo to open direct negotiations with the insurgents and, by June 1820, a special Conciliation Committee, or Junta de Conciliación, had been established in Caracas. Morillo, responding to Ferdinand's order, informed the republican commanders that he was instituting a unilateral cease-fire for the period of one month.[43] He also appointed his own commissioners to negotiate with Bolívar and the republican Congress established in Guayana. Tomás de Cires and José Domingo Duarte were to negotiate with the Congress, while Francisco González de Linares and Ramón Correa were named to talk with Bolívar himself. Miguel de la Torre and Gabriel de Torres also began direct negotiations with Bolívar. Morillo was from the start sceptical about the likelihood of success, confiding to La Torre his belief that the republicans would accept nothing short of full independence.[44]

Preliminary contacts began in July 1820. Approaches were made to Simón Bolívar, José Antonio Páez, Mariano Montilla and the Congress of Angostura in Guayana. In their initial approach, the commissioners suggested that an armistice be arranged and asked that the republicans accept the Constitution of 1812. One prominent Neogranadan republican did believe that reunion with Spain under the constitutional system was possible. The great *prócer* ('founding father') Antonio Nariño allegedly told the Spanish ambassador to England that 'if it were up to him alone, he would that very moment sign his country's surrender to the king of Spain under the constitutional system'. He added, however, that most people in America did not share his views, and that 'the insurgents would rather subjugate themselves to the kingdom of the Moors, than to the Spanish'.[45] Nariño's prediction of republican aloofness was correct. All republican officials in New Granada flatly refused to accept the Spanish Constitution of 1812. Bolívar moreover observed that, as Colombian forces were poised to recapture all of Venezuela and Quito, an armistice was not to their advantage. The Congress in Guayana and José Antonio Páez refused to open negotiations or even meet the royalist envoys, as the latter had failed to acknowledge the independence of Colombia.[46] Bolívar, however, agreed to discuss a cease-fire, and appointed Antonio José Sucre, Pedro Briceño Méndez and José Gabriel Pérez to negotiate for the republicans.[47]

Despite expressing an interest in negotiating an armistice, Bolívar continued to manoeuvre his troops and, in the autumn of 1820, attacked the royalist Third Division at Bailadores.[48] The royalists were forced to withdraw towards Cúcuta, and Bolívar gained control of most of Maracaibo and Barinas Provinces. Furthermore, Bolívar failed to abide by an arrangement to meet the royalist negotiators in San Fernando de Apure. This behaviour enraged royalist negotiators, who had journeyed needlessly to San Fernando, and further convinced Morillo of the 'perfidy of those enemies of Spain'.[49] Negotiations nonetheless continued and by November 1820 discussions about the armistice began in earnest. The negotiators at last met face to face in Trujillo in late November.[50] There was some difficulty in agreeing to the length of the proposed armistice, but the real sticking point of the negotiations proved to be the demarcation of boundaries between the two forces. Discussions occupied several days of intense negotiation. Finally, on 25 November 1820, an accord was reached.[51]

The accord granted many of the republican demands. Bolívar was referred to as the president of Colombia, not as the president of the Congress in Angostura, which had been the preferred (and inaccurate) Spanish formula.[52] The length of the armistice was to be six months, not the year proposed by the Spanish. The terms for the exchange of prisoners classified spies as prisoners of war, contrary to Morillo's wishes.[53] However, a compromise was reached on the demarcation of limits. On the eastern border a slight variation of the royalist proposal was used, while on the western border the republican option was followed. Royalist territory thus included Caracas and the surrounding region bordered by the Unare, Guanape, Orinoco, Apure and Santo Domingo rivers. At the same time, both sides agreed to a regularization of the war, which stipulated that prisoners were to be exchanged, rather than killed and that the war would be conducted according to the norms of 'civilized peoples'.[54] Bolívar privately described the armistice as highly advantageous to the republic and added, somewhat mendaciously, that the treaty 'honours us greatly, for we proposed it'.[55]

Despite the concessions made by Spain, Morillo was moderately pleased with the result and even expressed the wish to meet Bolívar in person. This was arranged, and on 27 November 1820 Morillo and Bolívar met in the town of Santa Ana. The meeting was surprisingly cordial, and both participants left written records. Morillo recorded that

> It is not possible to give an idea of the different emotions, sensitivity, frankness, sincerity and nobility with which their excellencies manifested in a thousand different ways the profound satisfaction they enjoyed at that moment in which … those who had previously been destined to mutual extermination for the first time saw themselves not merely as men, but also as friends.[56]

Bolívar too was enthusiastic about the meeting. In a letter to Santander he described both Morillo and La Torre as likeable and honest men, adding that the royalist negotiator Ramón Correa was 'without question the best man who treads this earth'. Bolívar further announced that:

> A report is being drawn up of what passed at our interview, which is certain to amaze and astonish even our friends. From Morillo down, the Spaniards vied with each other in the courtesies that they showed up and in their protestations of friendship … There were many courteous and clever toasts, but I was most pleased with those of Colonel [Juan] Tello and General La Torre. The former drank 'to the victories of Boyacá, that brought freedom for Colombia'; and the latter 'to the Colombians and the Spaniards, who side by side will march through Hell itself, if necessary, against despots and tyrants'. Morillo, among many other exuberant and liberal sentiments, toasted 'the heroes who died fighting for their country and their country's freedom.' Indeed, it would take a volume to record the toasts that were offered, for,

as I have indicated, each Spaniard contended for the honour of eulogizing us.[57]

This account, and there are others like it, paints a striking picture of royalist sentiment.[58] According to Bolívar, Spanish officers drank a toast to Colombian independence. It is hard to imagine a clearer illustration of royalist disaffection from the colonial war. Sympathy for the insurgent cause had penetrated the royalist army at the highest levels. Lower-ranking royalist troops had for years been referring to the republicans as 'patriots', rather than the officially-sanctioned 'insurgents', 'rebels' or *facciosos* ('armed troublemakers').[59] Now even Spanish officers implicitly affirmed the legitimacy of the Republic of Colombia, equating its leaders with Spain's own liberals. The many toasts to liberty and freedom further indicate the spread of liberalism within the royalist camp.

Shortly after this happy event, Morillo received his much longed-for permission to retire to Spain. The post of commander-in-chief of the royalist army then passed to Miguel de la Torre. In Spain, Morillo developed an amicable friendship with his erstwhile opponents, describing the republican Generals Soublette and O'Leary as 'good friends and comrades'.[60]

News of the armistice was greeted with joy in much of Venezuela.[61] Nonetheless, disagreements between the two sides continued to arise. A particular source of difficulty concerned the question of whether particular cities could change sides under the terms of the armistice. Maracaibo, for example, was included in royalist territory under the armistice but in February 1821 a republican uprising occurred in the city. The royalists demanded that the city remain in Spanish hands, and hinted that the republican leadership had fomented the unrest. Bolívar, for his part, insisted that the uprising had been spontaneous and maintained that there was no reason to return the city to the Spanish if its inhabitants had chosen to join the Republic of Colombia.[62] In contrast, the residents of the town of Trujillo, which fell on the republican side of the border, were allegedly heartbroken to be consigned to the Republic of Colombia. Antonio Van Halen, a royalist officer who was escorted by the republicans through Trujillo in early 1821, reported that during his visit there:

> various vecinos including some alcaldes told me ... [of] their desire that we should reoccupy the country, freeing them from 'those rogues' (as

> they put it) and more than once they asked me with tears in their eyes, 'will Spain be so cruel as to abandon us?'[63]

This was exactly the sort of thing officials in Spain wanted to hear. The fact that the occasional village expressed the desire to remain Spanish fuelled the belief that independence was fundamentally unpopular. This idea, plausible in 1814, in 1821 merely postponed recognition of Spain's defeat.

Bolívar, meanwhile, arranged to send his own commissioners (José Revenga and José Echeverría) to Spain, a confident move requiring *de facto* recognition from Madrid. In early 1821 he also began discussing his conditions for extending the armistice beyond the initial six months. Miguel de la Torre, now leading the royalist forces, rejected Bolívar's demand that the Spanish surrender much of the territory granted to them under the 1820 armistice and, in April 1821, discussions were suspended.[64] Armed confrontations resumed and, on 14 May 1821, Caracas fell to the republicans. Then, on 24 June 1821, Bolívar defeated royalist forces at the second battle of Carabobo, virtually eliminating the royalists from the military scene in Venezuela. Survivors fled to Puerto Cabello, which held out for a further four and a half months.

Meanwhile, Spain attempted various last minute bureaucratic reshuffles of colonial officials. In particular, a new viceroy was appointed for New Granada. On 9 September 1820, following Sámano's resignation, the commander general of Panama, Alejandro Hore, had been named viceroy; however, he never held office, as he had in fact died two months prior to his appointment.[65] It might be argued that the inadvertent appointment of a corpse to head New Granada's royalists was highly symbolic. Juan de la Cruz Mourgeon was then assigned to replace him.[66] Cruz Mourgeon arrived in the midst of disaster. The entire royalist army in Venezuela was by this time reduced to three thousand men, trapped in Puerto Cabello with Miguel de la Torre as a result of Bolívar's victory at Carabobo. Like the peace commissioners Barry and Sartorio, who were also trapped in Puerto Cabello, the new viceroy insisted that his presence in the besieged city was entirely pointless, and took the first opportunity to retreat to Jamaica, from where he tried unsuccessfully to assemble an army.[67] Then, in August 1822, General La Torre surrendered command of the remaining royalist troops to Francisco Tomás Morales. La Torre moved to Puerto Rico to take up the post of captain general of the island. Soon after arriving, he wrote a passionate denunciation of Morales, whom he condemned as a bloodthirsty tyrant. All chance of reconquering Venezuela was destroyed, he asserted, with the appointment of Morales as commander-in-chief.[68] Of course, there was by this stage little hope of reconquering Venezuela, with or without Morales.

The Surrender of Cartagena

¿No es cosa bien resalada,	Here's a bit of spicy gossip
y que a todos desatina	sure to annoy everyone:
ver virgen nuestra *Marina*	Our Navy is still a virgin
y la plaza bloqueada?	and the city's under blockade.
Ella piensa no hacer nada	The Navy has no plans at all
según demuestra y yo infiero	as far as I can tell,
por poner un guerrero	because in place of a warrior
para manegar la armada	to command the Armada
hicieron la gran *Cagada*	they've fucked up
de ponernos un Cordero.	and given us a Lamb.

1820 lampoon from Cartagena
[Cartagena's navy was led by Manuel Cordero, whose surname means 'lamb'][69]

As the lampoon suggests, Cartagena was under blockade while the armistice negotiations were going on. Ríohacha had already surrendered to republican Luis Brion in March 1820 and throughout May, June and July fighting had occurred in the villages surrounding Cartagena and in its bay.[70] By 7 July 1820, the last Spanish outposts in the towns of Santa Rosa, Ternera and Turbaco returned to the city, defeated by the insurgents. Then, on 9–10 July 1820, naval forces led by Luis Brion and republican infantry under Mariano Montilla surrounded Cartagena and began a slow but effective strangulation of the city.[71]

Even before the official start of the siege, lack of food had obliged Governor Torres to order all 'useless mouths' to leave the city.[72] The Audiencia chose to leave as well and its remaining members established themselves in Jamaica.[73] Cartagena's government was in a continual state of crisis throughout the siege, and constant efforts at increasing the city's supply of food were necessary.[74] Lack of food, poor weather and exhaustion soon reduced the royalist garrison to a mere 630 men fit for active service, plus an additional 550–man 'volunteer' militia. The remaining five hundred members of the garrison were incapacitated by ill health. Governor Torres was unable to determine precisely how large the republican force was, since his spies inevitably deserted or were captured, but he estimated that the troops on land numbered perhaps 1,700. These numbers increased steadily as republican victories elsewhere freed men to join the blockade. Torres calculated that, by September 1821, republican forces had grown to over four thousand. By this time the total royalist force consisted of only 732 men, many of whom were ill and unfit for service.[75]

Meanwhile, Santa Marta fell to the republicans. It was captured by Luis Brion after a simultaneous naval and terrestrial attack on 11 November 1820. Governor Pedro Ruíz de Porras fled and the surviving royalists regathered in Ríohacha, virtually the only remaining royalist holdout in northern New Granada, with the exception of Cartagena.[76]

The signing of the armistice in Venezuela, news of which reached Cartagena in late 1820, did not much alter the situation. Governor Torres had already been engaged in unsatisfying negotiations with the besieging insurgents since August 1820.[77] Torres was extremely unenthusiastic about the discussions, informing Morillo that he had entered into negotiations solely 'out of pure obedience'.[78] As had been the case in Venezuela, in New Granada the major difficulty lay in establishing demarcation lines between the two camps. From December 1820, considerable effort was devoted to negotiating this point. The Spanish in Cartagena were unhappy about surrendering to the republicans any of the small amount of territory remaining in their hands, but they were not in a strong negotiating position.[79] There was little royalist negotiator Manuel de Landa could do, aside from express disgust over 'the absurd and ambitious proposals, offensive to the dignity of the monarchy' made by the republican negotiator Justo Briceño about the demarcation.[80] By February 1821, Landa had given up and Governor Torres resumed the post of royalist negotiator, much to his own regret.[81] Despite the ongoing hostilities, efforts were made by both sides to conduct the war within the bounds described by the treaty regularizing the war. That is, both sides complained energetically when they felt the other was violating the spirit of the accords. Thus, in May 1821, General Montilla protested vigorously that in a recent proclamation Governor Torres had referred to the republicans as 'a lawless horde of men without country, ruler, or religion'. Such language was entirely opposed to the spirit of the treaty regularizing the war, Montilla observed.[82] Torres' response to this complaint merely enraged the republican further, and communication between the two camps was temporarily suspended.

Meanwhile, republican military advances continued. By May 1821 republican troops controlled all of the bay of Cartagena. In early July 1821 the Castle of Bocachica fell to the republicans.[83] Morale among the royalist troops declined alarmingly and, by the end of August 1821, the prospects for royalist victory were remote. Governor Torres proposed a month-long suspension of hostilities, supposedly to facilitate negotiations. This suggestion was rejected out of hand by the republican leadership, who correctly sensed imminent victory. Then, in early September 1821, Governor Torres began negotiating the capitulation of the only important city in New Granada remaining in royalist hands. By the end of September, the negotiations had been completed and a generous surrender was arranged.[84] The town was not to be sacked, an amnesty was offered to everyone who wanted to remain in the city; those who did not wish to remain were permitted to leave. Cartagena was evacuated by the royalists on 10 October 1821. Over 1,300 people, nearly a tenth of the city's population, chose to sail to Havana with the royalist troops.

Royalist Guerrillas in Pasto

Following the surrender to Cartagena, the only part of New Granada remaining in royalist hands was the province of Pasto. The Bolívar-Morillo armistice had not been received warmly in the region. In 1821 the Bishop of Popayán had attempted in vain to win support for it, and the republican commissioners charged with explaining the armistice had no success in selling its virtues. Indeed, the commissioners had been forced to flee Pasto under armed escort following a hostile reception.[85] The region thus remained entirely anti-republican, and in consequence Bolívar turned his attention to it.

He attempted to win the supposedly influential Bishop of Popayán (then in residence in Pasto) to the republican cause, but, this at first failing, he prepared to lead a campaign against Pasto in person.[86] Reports of the imminent arrival of the dreaded Bolívar sent Pasto into a flurry of frantic preparations. The army began holding exercises and the city organized a reasonable military force, under the command of Basilio García. García was widely regarded as both cruel and politically inept, but the morale of his troops was reportedly excellent.[87] In April 1822, at Bomboná, these southern royalists were attacked by the republicans, who enjoyed a pyrrhic victory. Nonetheless, the royalists were obliged to sue for surrender to Bolívar.[88]

While negotiations were underway, the fate of Pasto's royalists was being decided two hundred kilometres to the south. On 22 May 1822, José Antonio de Sucre scored a decisive victory over Melchor Aymerich at the Battle of Pichincha, above Quito. The royalists, however, controlled the roads, and hence the mail, from Quito, and so prevented reports of Sucre's tremendous victory from reaching Bolívar. Pasto's commander García was thus able to negotiate a surrender considerably more favourable than could have been obtained had Bolívar known of the royalists' defeat at Pichincha.[89] The surrender was, however, viewed with hostility by many Pastusos, who were adverse to negotiations, and some of whom regarded the purported cause of the surrender, the Battle of Bomboná, as a royalist victory. The surrender appears to have exacerbated existing splits in Pasto's population. The city's elite, recognizing the inevitable and disillusioned by the failure of their bid for regional power, embraced republicanism, while the province's Indians maintained a dogged loyalty to Spain.[90] Indeed, from this point on, royalism became a primarily lower-class cause in Pasto. A series of royalist guerrillas attempted to rally support for the king, but these were invariably suppressed by the *gente decente* of Pasto itself.

The most important such uprising began in July 1822, when Benito Boves, a would-be imitator of the erstwhile terror of Venezuela, attempted to lead a royalist revolt in Pasto. Benito Boves (who was in fact a relative of José Tomás Boves) was joined by Agustín Agualongo, a low-ranking Indian royalist officer, and together they led a lengthy but doomed resistance to republicanism. Boves and Agualongo, backed by a few wealthy Pastusos, for a time enjoyed considerable success. For several months Boves and Agualongo, commanding some thousand men (mostly royalist soldiers, Indians and labourers), controlled much of the province of Los Pastos, collecting weapons in small raids and interfering with the republicans' communications.[91] In December 1822, however, Field Marshall Sucre marched toward Pasto and, after suffering an initial defeat in the hands of the Pastusos, recaptured the city after a major battle.[92]

Following the fall of Pasto to the republicans, Boves fled, Agualongo went into hiding and support for the royalists tailed off dramatically. Agualongo, however, rallied and led another uprising in June 1823.[93] Accompanied by some six hundred Indian troops armed with sticks and machetes, he captured Pasto, prompting Bolívar to issue a proclamation announcing: 'The infamous Pasto has again raised its odious head of sedition, but this head will be severed forever … Pasto will disappear from the catalogue of cities if its vile inhabitants do not surrender to Colombia before firing a single shot.'[94] Francisco de Paula Santander, by then vice-president of the Republic of Colombia, offered to send a delegation to Pasto to negotiate a peaceful return to republicanism. Santander met with no success in his attempt at negotiation, but the royalist rebels were nonetheless expelled from Pasto.[95] Agualongo enjoyed a few more victories, and even succeeded in reoccupying Pasto for a third time, but in mid-1824 he was captured, taken to Popayán and shot, reportedly crying 'long live the king' as he died.[96]

After Sucre's victory over the royalists at Ayacucho on 8 December 1824, Spain's war in South America effectively ended. In New Granada, the royalist war effort was reduced entirely to bands of Indians and *castas* who roamed southern New Granada, ambushing groups of republican soldiers and committing acts of political banditry.[97] In Pasto, in particular, a number of royalist *facciosos* continued the attempt to drive the republicans out of the province. In 1824 there were reportedly over two thousand such guerrilla fighters, none of them Spanish.[98] Many guerrilla bands consisted of little more than a handful of men armed with a few muskets, but some of their members did have considerable military experience. In 1825, for example, a royalist guerrilla from the Patía named Pedro Galíndez was captured by the republicans.[99] Galíndez, who was twenty-two years old, was found to have served under five different royalist guerrilla leaders, including the famous Agualongo. Few of these *desafectados*, however, achieved anything approaching Agualongo's success. Royalism was acknowledged to be a lost cause by all but a small minority of Indians and *castas*. The British Consul H.M. Wood commented on this fact, remarking in 1825 that '[They] who so late as 1822 were zealous supporters of the government of Spain, are now seen voluntarily bearing arms in support of Colombia, and gratuitously devoting their time to her service'.[100] Spain's view of the war had been inverted. It was not independence that was supported only by the quixotic and the marginalized; it was royalism.

Epilogue

Spain and the Loss of Colombia

Spain's surrender of Cartagena in October 1821 was followed by a pro-republican uprising in Panama in November 1821, which forced the royalists to withdraw from the isthmus. Then, in May 1822, Sucre's victory at the Battle of Pichincha ended Spanish control of southern New Granada. Bolívar and Páez's defeat of royalist forces at Carabobo in June 1821 had already cleared Venezuela of any meaningful Spanish presence. Thus the war with Spain was in practical terms over by the end of 1821. The war at home, however, continued. As we saw in the previous chapter, the republicans faced a series of revolts and continued guerrilla warfare in various parts of the former viceroyalty, particularly in the south. Annoying guerrilla war was not the only problem faced by the new republic. Creating a functional alternative to Spanish rule was perhaps the most pressing challenge to Colombia's republican leaders.

Much thought had already gone into the question of constructing an independent state. Some members of the viceroyalty's creole elite had perhaps been considering the most appropriate form of government for a hypothetically independent New Granada even before the outbreak of war in 1810, and the experiences of the First Republic had provided clear illustrations of the dangers to be avoided.[1] Thus the outlines of Colombia's new government sketched at the Congress of Angostura in 1819 cannot be called a preliminary draft. They were the outcome of over a decade of thought and discussion.[2] The proposals were, however, extremely cursory. The Congress of Angostura proclaimed the unity of Venezuela, Colombia and Quito, and proposed a presidential system, with separate vice-presidents governing Colombia and Venezuela. Much was left unspecified. In 1821, another constitutional congress was held in Cúcuta, and it was there that the details were filled in. The Constitution of Cúcuta confirmed the basic form given to the new government at Angostura. A centralized government was accepted, although in practice the division between the three units of the former colony was not eliminated. A number of other alterations were also introduced. Most importantly, the Constitution enshrined a law of free birth, liberating all slaves born in the future once they had reached a specified age. Indian *resguardos* were also abolished and various changes were made to the fiscal system. As the Spanish liberals had done in 1812, the delegates in 1821 abolished the Indian tribute, although they, like the Spanish, would choose to reinstate it when confronted with the monetary consequences of abolition. No attempt was made to eliminate the tobacco monopoly, but the *alcabala* sales tax was ended, freedom of the press was proclaimed and the role of the church was somewhat limited. The man elected to oversee these policies in Colombia was Francisco de Paula Santander, the country's first vice-president.

Santander was presented with a number of challenges during his years in office. Among the more substantial were the difficulties that arose in maintaining the unity of Gran Colombia. This was in the end to prove impossible. In Venezuela, hostility towards Colombia in general, and Santander in particular, led to increasing demands for separation from Bogotá, which culminated in revolt. When Venezuelan General José Antonio Páez was summoned to Bogotá to stand trial for abuse of power, he instead rose in rebellion.[3] This initial move towards separation was quelled, but only temporarily. In 1829, Páez again rebelled; by 1830, Venezuela was a separate country. Meanwhile, in Pasto, local *caudillo* José María Obando began patiently to build up support for an insurrection against the dictatorship of Bolívar, which began in October 1828. This rebellion ended in Obando's surrender in December 1828, but proved to be only the first in a series of revolts in the south.[4]

Further confounding unity was the attempt by Juan José Flores to separate the old Presidency of Quito from Colombia. His proposed new state of Ecuador was to include the provinces of Pasto and Popayán as well. The ensuing war was ended in 1831 with the creation of the Republic of Ecuador, but the question of Colombia's southern border was far from resolved.[5] There were almost immediate complaints that Ecuador was not respecting the agreed boundary, and border conflicts with Ecuador arose both in the 1840s during the Guerra de los Supremos, and in 1860, in an uprising engineered by Tomás Cipriano de Mosquera.

The Republic of Colombia, then, faced serious challenges from the moment of its birth. Moreover, in many ways life in the Republic of Colombia was little different from life in the old viceroyalty. Several historians have observed that the transformative power of the war of independence was extremely limited.[6] The war did not bring any great reordering of society, nor did its leaders intend it to do so. Furthermore, it was some decades before the economic possibilities of independence were acted upon. Yet, while many aspects of Colombian society remained unaltered, one fundamental political change had occurred: Colombia was no longer a Spanish colony. It had triumphed, as the English traveller Charles Stuart Cochrane put it in 1825, over the 'mean and mistaken policy' of Spain.[7] Perhaps, as David Bushnell claims, Colombia was not yet a nation, but it was undoubtedly not a colony of Spain. This change, however, was not at all visible from Madrid. Indeed, while Colombia was launching itself into the difficult arena of nationhood, a very different process was discernible from Spain's vantage point. Far from acknowledging the loss of its former colony, Spain's governments refused even to recognize that Colombia was independent, much less that it had a moderately successful government and was not in a state of utter anarchy.

No great outcry from the Spanish public greeted the fall of royalist New Granada. On the contrary, the wars of independence in the Americas had never aroused an overwhelming level of interest among Spaniards, nor did attention to the former colonies revive substantially after their loss. When the final defeat came at the battle of Ayacucho in December 1824, the reaction in Spain was muted. Contemporary newspapers scarcely mentioned the event.[8] This lack of attention has by some accounts continued well into the twentieth century. The historian Melchor Fernández Almagro asserted in the 1940s that most of his contemporaries would claim Spain lost its colonies in 1898 after the war with the United States, not in the 1820s.[9] Overall, he stated, the loss of the Americas made but a faint impression on Spanish consciousness. However, while the loss of their colonies did not propel Spaniards into deep, collective soul searching of the sort that occurred after the loss of Cuba in 1898, there were some repercussions in Spain. Newspapers continued to insist on the importance of the American question, even if they did not recognize that it had already been settled, and a number of participants in the war published memoirs of their experiences.[10]

The most immediate reactions to the royalist defeats occurred, as might have been expected, within the military itself. While many officers had long believed the war in New Granada was unwinnable, others were unprepared to accept the end when it came. The 1821 surrender of Cartagena to the republican Mariano Montilla became the focus of discontent. The circumstances surrounding the surrender had attracted attention and criticism was soon directed at Governor Torres for his handling of it. Principally, critics objected that Torres had begun negotiations with the republicans prematurely, and that the city had surrendered earlier than was necessary. In particular, attention was drawn to the allegation that, at the time of the surrender, the city's food supplies had been sufficient for two more months. The real motive for this criticism, however, lay elsewhere. The surrender of Cartagena had been a body blow to royalist hopes for New Granada, and there were those who could not accept that Spain had lost the war. In blaming Governor Torres for the surrender of Cartagena, critics were denying that the loss was inevitable. If the surrender had been premature or unnecessary, then perhaps royalism was not a dead letter in New Granada.

In order to refute these charges of poor leadership, Torres himself demanded that the case be tried by court-martial. This was agreed, and the trial began in September 1824, some three years after Cartagena's surrender.[11] The investigations lasted over two years. On 13 November 1826 a final verdict was at last given. The nine members of the tribunal concluded that Torres was innocent of wrongdoing. Three judges censured some of Torres' actions, but all save one agreed that the surrender had been necessary and correct. As Brigadier Rafael Arze noted, the impossibility of surviving the blockade entirely justified the evacuation.[12] The court-martial had thus been a trial not merely of Torres' behaviour, but also of the viability of royalist resistance in New Granada. The verdict of not guilty was a concession of defeat, an implicit acceptance that royalism had been vanquished, and not merely surrendered by venal officers. The trial, however, did not lay to rest the ghosts of a betrayed royalist victory. While Torres' trial was underway, the Spanish Council of State considered court-martialling the officers involved in the defeat at Ayacucho.[13]

Although the Council of State suspected royalist officers, especially liberal officers, of selling out to the republicans, many officers were themselves unwilling to accept the finality of the loss of America. Miguel de la Torre, for example, who had been appointed Captain General of Puerto Rico after his resignation as commander of the Expeditionary Army in

1822, remained ready to launch a reconquest of the mainland throughout most of the fifteen years he spent in Puerto Rico. He allegedly believed that he and the royalists émigrés who surrounded him would return in triumph to Venezuela.[14]

Miguel de la Torre was far from alone in his belief that the Spain would eventually reconquer the Americas. The Spanish government itself took many years to admit that the colonies were irretrievably lost. While a few deputies to the Cortes insisted that Spain face reality, throughout the 1820s the government continued to act as though a royalist victory were possible. Indeed, Spain was unwilling even to acknowledge those compromises it had already made. Although the armistice signed by Morillo and Bolívar in 1820 had referred to the latter as the President of Colombia, in 1821 the Spanish government was still instructing its commissioners to refer to the republicans only as 'dissidents', and not as *de facto* heads of state.[15] With no apparent irony, the decisive republican victory at Ayacucho was referred to in the *Gaceta de Madrid* as a 'momentary reverse'.[16] A particularly intractable obstacle was Ferdinand's profound belief that the majority of Americans really wanted to remain Spanish. Ferdinand maintained to the end of his days that the Americans would themselves demand a reunion with Spain, once the republican experiment revealed itself to be a failure. Convinced of America's continued loyalty, the king wept publicly during a reading of an ode affirming the undying Spanish heritage of the Americas.[17] This attitude exasperated Spain's European allies. British diplomats complained about Spain's obstinate belief that there was 'still great attachment on the part of the inhabitants [of the Americas] to the Mother Country'.[18] This mistaken view led the Spanish to contemplate every type of scheme to recapture the Americas. Throughout the 1820s Spain's governments discussed the launching of military expeditions to Venezuela and elsewhere.[19] Various other unlikely plans were also considered. The idea of installing Spanish princes as independent American monarchs was one of the more plausible. An official in Buenos Aires suggested that a reconquest of that region could be effected by a private commercial company composed of merchants from across Europe, while attempts were made to interest the Rothschilds in funding an expedition.[20] These plots found their last expression in the 1829 expedition commanded by Isidro Barradas that attempted unsuccessfully to invade Mexico. Although Ferdinand continued to believe that the failure of this expedition was due to mismanagement, not flawed aims, no further attacks on Spain's former colonies took place.

It was not until the reign of Ferdinand's daughter Isabel II that Spain made formal steps towards recognizing American independence. The first former colony to be recognized diplomatically was Mexico, whose independence was acknowledged in 1836.[21] Ecuador was recognized in 1840 and Venezuela in 1845, while Colombia had to wait until 1881. The independence of Honduras was not acknowledged until 1895.[22]

It is one thing to lose a colony; it is another thing to grieve over its loss. During the 1820s it became increasingly popular to claim that the American colonies had in fact been a burden to Spain. The debate over the value of the colonies had already been in full swing in the eighteenth century. The often-repeated prediction that Spanish America's independence was only a matter of time, combined with Spain's obvious economic prostration, meant the topic was not merely an academic exercise.[23] The American war proved an additional stimulus to debate. Pessimists declared that the loss of the colonies would be fatal to Spain's flagging economy. Gabriel de Torres, for example, maintained that while the original discovery of the colonies had perhaps hindered Spain, 'today their loss would be a mortal blow to commerce, agriculture, the arts and industry'. The Spanish ambassador to the United States put it bluntly: 'the loss of America will spell the destruction of Spain'.[24] While the ambassador exaggerated, it is now clear that the loss of the Americas was a severe blow to Spain's commerce.[25] Yet for many observers, Spain was well rid of its troublesome overseas colonies. The colonies, it was alleged, had stifled industry and enterprise in the peninsula. They had sapped Spain of its population. They had diverted the crown's attention away from the needs of the peninsula itself. Even some merchants asserted that Spain had little to gain from retaining its colonies. The attractions of this thesis to Spaniards who had just lost the majority of their overseas possessions should be obvious. 'When all was said and done,' one writer commented in 1821, 'what we received from America was venereal disease, yellow fever and the vomit'.[26]

Notes

Introduction: 'This vile rebellious rabble ...'

1. Relación de Mando de Pedro de Mendinueta, December 1803, in Eduardo Posada and P.M. Ibáñez (eds), *Relaciones de Mando. Memorias presentadas por los gobernantes del Nuevo Reino de Granada*, Imprenta Nacional (Bogotá, 1910), p. 482. The parlous state of the colonial fisc is discussed in Anthony McFarlane, *Colombia before Independence: Economy, Society and Politics under Bourbon Rule*, Cambridge University Press (Cambridge, 1993), chapters 8, 11.
2. Proclama de Antonio Amar y Borbón a los generosos leales habitantes del Nuevo Reino de Granada, Santafé, 15 September 1808, reprinted in Mario Herrán Baquero, *El Virrey Don Antonio Amar y Borbón. La crisis del régimen colonial en la Nueva Granada*, Banco de la República (Bogotá, 1988), pp. 293–96. For the population of New Granada in 1808, see José Manuel Restrepo, *Historia de la revolución de Colombia*, Ediciones Bedout (Bogotá, 1969), vol. 1, p. 401. If one includes the Presidency of Quito, the population reached some two million.
3. Antonio Amar y Borbón to the Council of Regency, La Coruña, 13 January 1811, reprinted in Herrán Baquero, *Antonio Amar*, pp. 305–10.
4. See Germán Colmenares, '*La historia de la revolución* por José Manuel Restrepo: una prisión historiográfica', in Germán Colmenares *et al.*, *La independencia: ensayos de historia social*, Instituto Colombiano de Cultura (Bogotá, 1986), pp. 9–23; and Restrepo, *Historia de la revolución.*
5. John Lynch, *The Spanish American Revolutions*, 1808–1826, W.W. Norton (New York, 1986); 'The Origins of Spanish American Independence', in Leslie Bethell (ed.), *The Independence of Latin America*, Cambridge University Press (Cambridge, 1987); Indalecio Liévano Aguirre, *Los grandes conflictos sociales y económicas de nuestra historia*, 2 vols, Editorial Tercer Mundo (Bogotá, 1985); and Jaime E. Rodríguez O., *The Independence of Spanish America*, Cambridge University Press (Cambridge, 1998).
6. See, for example, Inge Buisson, Günter Kahle, Hans-Joachim König and Horst Pietschmann (eds), *Problemas de la formación del estado y de la nación en hispanoamérica*, Lateinamerikanische Forschung 13, Böhlau Verlag (Cologne, 1984); Georges Lomné, 'Las ciudades de la Nueva Granada: teatros y objetos de los conflictos de la memoria política (1810–1830)', Coloquio Internacional: Les Enjeux de la Mémoire (Paris, 1992); Margarita Garrido, *Reclamos y representaciones. Variaciones sobre la política en el Nuevo Reino de Granada, 1750–1815*, Banco de la República (Santafé de Bogotá, 1993); *Caravelle*, Special Issue on 'L'éxpression des identités américaines

a partir de 1492', vol. 62 (1994); François-Xavier Guerra and Mónica Quijada (eds), *Imaginar la Nación*, AHILA (Hamburg, 1994); Hans-Joachim König, *En el Camino hacia la Nación: Nacionalismo en el proceso de formación del Estado y de la Nación de la Nueva Granada, 1750 a 1856*, Banco de la República (Santafé de Bogotá, 1994); and Anthony McFarlane, 'Identity, Enlightenment and Political Dissent in Late Colonial Spanish America', *Transactions of the Royal Historical Society*, sixth series, vol. 8 (1998).

7. Timothy Anna, *The Fall of the Royal Government in Mexico City*, University of Nebraska Press (Lincoln, 1978), p. ix.
8 Timothy Anna, *Spain and the Loss of America*, University of Nebraska Press (Lincoln, 1983), p. xv.
9. Anna, *Spain and the Loss of America*, p. xv.
10. For a recent work on Colombian independence which virtually ignores the years from 1816 to 1819, see Rafael Gómez Hoyos, *La independencia de Colombia*, MAPFRE (Madrid, 1992).

1: War in Spain and America

1. J.M. Thompson (ed.), *Napoleon's Letters*, Everyman (London, 1964), pp. 198–9.
2. For a thorough account of the Peninsular War, see Gabriel Lovett, *Napoleon and the Birth of Modern Spain*, 2 vols, New York University Press (New York, 1965).
3. Ferdinand's remarkable popularity extended to Spanish America. A suggestive discussion of the cult of Ferdinand in Mexico is provided in Eric Van Young, 'The Messiah and the Masked Man: Popular Ideology in Mexico, 1810–1821', in Steven Kaplan (ed.), *Indigenous Responses to Western Christianity*, New York University Press (New York, 1995); and Eric Van Young, 'Quetzalcóatl, King Ferdinand, and Ignacio Allende Go to the Seashore; or Messianism and Mystical kingship in Mexico, 1800–1821', in Jaime E. Rodríguez O. (ed.), *The Independence of Mexico and the Creation of the New Nation*, University of New Mexico Press (Los Angeles, 1989).
4. Proclamation of the General Council of the Principality of Asturias, Oviedo, 24 May 1808, W.N. Hargreaves-Mawdsley (ed.), *Spain under the Bourbons, 1700–1833: A Collection of Documents*, University of South Carolina Press (Columbia, 1973), pp. 211–12.
5. For a useful discussion of this event, see François-Xavier Guerra, 'La independencia de México y las revoluciones hispánicas', *Cuadernos de Historia Latinoamericana: El liberalismo en Mexico*, no. 1, (1993), pp. 31–32.
6. The figure for Spain's population is drawn from the 1788 census. See J.R. Aymes, *La guerra de la independencia en España (1808–1814)*, Siglo Veintiuno (Madrid, 1990), p. 127. The approximate population of Spanish America is given in Lynch, *The Spanish American Revolutions*, p. 1.
7. Anna, *Spain and the Loss of America*, p. 60. See also pp. 60–62, 80–84. For contemporary Neogranadan comments on the Junta Central and the Regency, see, for example, *Aviso al Público*, no. 7, 10 November 1810, reprinted in Luis Martínez Delgado and Sergio Elias Ortiz (eds), *El periodismo en la Nueva Granada, 1810–1811*, Biblioteca Eduardo Santos, vol. 22, Editorial Kelly (Bogotá, 1960).
8. Restrepo, *Historia de la revolución*, vol. 1, p. 117. Very many contemporary accounts

mention the impact of this announcement. See, for example, José Antonio de Torres y Peña, *Memorias sobre la Revolución y sucesos de Santafe de Bogotá en el Transtorno de la Nueva Granada y Venezuela* (1814), reprinted in Guillermo Hernández de Alba (ed.), *Memorias del Presbítero José Antonio de Torres y Peña*, Biblioteca de Historia Nacional, vol. 92, Editorial Kelly (Bogotá, 1960), p. 86.

9. See Anna, *Spain and the Loss of America*, pp. 66–67.
10. For a clear summary of the provisions of the 1812 Constitution, see Mario Rodríguez, *The Cádiz Experiment in Central America, 1808 to 1826*, University of California Press (Berkeley, 1978), pp. 75–100.
11. There is a considerable literature on the application of the Constitution of 1812 in Mexico. Jaime Rodríguez reviews the historiography in a lucid discussion of the constitution in Mexico and Quito in *The Independence of Spanish America*, chapter 3.
12. Karl Marx and Frederick Engels, Despatches for the *New York Daily Tribune* (1854), reprinted in *Revolution in Spain*, Greenwood Press (Westport, 1975), p. 71.
13. See McFarlane, *Colombia before Independence*, pp. 297–324.
14. McFarlane, *Colombia before Independence*. The hesitancy with which Americans approached independence from Spain has been heavily stressed by Jaime Rodríguez in *The Independence of Spanish America*.
15. The coup is discussed in Restrepo, *Historia de la revolución*, vol. 1, pp. 109–12; Marie-Danielle Demélas and Yves Saint-Geours, *Jerúsalen y Babilonia: Religión y política en el Ecuador, 1780–1880*, Biblioteca de Ciencias Sociales, vol. 21, Corporación Editora Nacional (Quito, 1988), chapters 5–6; Scarlett O'Phelan Godoy, 'Por el rey, religión y la patria: Las juntas de gobierno de 1809 en La Paz y Quito', *Bulletin de l'Institut Français d'Etùdes Andines*, vol. 17 (1988); and Martin Minchom, *The People of Quito, 1690–1810: Change and Unrest in the Underclass*, Westview Press (Boulder, 1994), pp. 241–56. For a detailed list of all those involved in the revolution in Quito, see Report by Ramón Núñez del Arco, Quito, 22 May 1813, AGI, AQ, leg. 257.

    Pastuso responses to the revolt in Quito are discussed in Ignacio Rodríguez Guerrero, 'Repercusiones de la revolución quiteña de 10 de agosto de 1809, en la Nueva Granada', *Revista de Historia*, vol. 7 (Pasto, 1967), p. 10; and Gerardo León Guerrero, '¿Por qué vinieron los quiteños? Dos invasiones al distrito de Pasto, 1809–1811', *Raices Historicas*, Academia Nariñense de Historia, (Pasto, 1987), pp. 106–7. For the *cabildo* of Santa Fe's reaction, see Torres y Peña, *Memorias*, p. 93.
16. See Restrepo, *Historia de la revolución*, vol. 1, p. 110–21; Pedro Pérez Múñez, Historia de la revolución de América en 35 cartas, Quito, 31 December 1815, carta 16, AGI, Diversos, leg. 42; and Minchom, *The People of Quito*, p. 249.
17. Costeloe suggests that Montúfar's appointment was facilitated by General Xavier Castaños, President of the Council of Regency and Montúfar's patron. See Michael Costeloe, *Response to Revolution: Imperial Spain and the Spanish American Revolutions, 1810–1840*, Cambridge University Press (Cambridge, 1986), p. 15.
18. The fact that observers labelled these movements insurgent does not mean that the 'insurgents' necessarily considered their behaviour treasonous; Jaime Rodríguez argues that most juntas wanted *autonomy*, rather than *independence*. (See Rodríguez, *The Independence of Spanish America*, pp. 144–50, for comments on the junta in Quito.) Yet this useful observation should not obscure the clarity with

which contemporaries viewed the situation. As the insurgent Joaquín de Caycedo y Cuero admitted in September 1811, 'we have been branded with the infamous labels of insurgent and revolutionary'. (Joaquín de Caycedo y Cuero to Tomás de Santacruz, Pueblo de La Cruz, 13 September 1811, quoted in Ortiz, *Agustín Agualongo y su tiempo*, p. 173). For concise examples of the immediacy with which these movements were accorded insurgent status, see Costeloe, *Response to Revolution*, pp. 29–31.

19. Torres y Peña, *Memorias.* Revolutionary sentiment was frequently understood in terms of infectious contagion; insurgents had been infected with the germ of revolt. Even those with insurgent sympathies employed this language. For examples, see Christon Archer, '"La Causa Buena": The Counterinsurgency Army of New Spain and the Ten Years' War', in *The Independence of Mexico and the Creation of the New Nation*, p. 85; Joseph Domingo Diaz, *Recuerdos sobre la Rebelión de Caracas*, Leon Amarita (Madrid, 1827); or J.J. Dauxion Lavaysse, *Viaje a las Islas de Trinidad, Tobago, Margarita y a Diversos partes de Venezuela en la América Meridional* (1813), Universidad Central de Venezuela (Caracas, 1967), p. 213. The influence of the Enlightenment on Bolívar's thought is clearly revealed in the Jamaica Letter. See Simón Bolívar to a Gentleman of this Isle ('Jamaica Letter'), Kingston, 6 September 1815, Vicente Lecuna (ed.), *Selected Writings of Bolívar*, The Colonial Press (New York, 1951), vol. 1, pp. 103–22.

20. Humboldt is explicitly attacked in Historia de la rebelión de América en 35 cartas, by Pedro Pérez Múñoz, Quito, 6 May 1816, AGI, Diversos, leg. 42; and in Torres y Peña, *Memorias*, pp. 75–77. The importance of the scientific enlightenment is stressed in Groupe Interdisciplinaire de Recherche et de Documentation sur L'Amérique Latin, *L'Amérique Espagnole a L'Epoque des Lumieres: Tradition-Innovation-Representations*, Maison des Pays Iberiques (Paris, 1987, also published in Spanish under the same title by the Instituto de Cooperación Iberoamericana); Thomas Glick, 'Science and Independence in Latin America (with special reference to New Granada)', *HAHR*, vol. 71 (1991); and Diana Soto Arango, Miguel Angel Puig-Samper and Luis Carlos Arboleda (eds), *La Ilustración en América Colonial*, Consejo Superior de Investigaciones Científicas (Paracuellos de Jarama, 1995).

21. Proclama by José Fernando de Abascal y Sousa, Lima, 13 July 1810, AGI, Audiencia de Panama, leg. 262.

22. Simón Bolívar, 'Jamaica Letter', in Lecuna (ed.), *Selected Letters of Bolívar*, vol. 1, p. 112.

23. Torres y Peña, *Memorias*, p. 51. Compare this with Jorge Juan and Antonio de Ulloa, *Noticias Secretas de America*, Historia 16 (Madrid, 1991), pp. 427–29.

24. Torres y Peña, *Memorias*, pp. 39–40, 43, 133.

25. The Decree of War to the Death declared that republican troops would kill all Spaniards who did not explicitly embrace American freedom. Americans would be spared, even if they fought for the royalists. See Decreto de Guerra a Muerte, Trujillo, 15 June 1813, in Simón Bolívar, *Escritos del Libertador*, Sociedad Bolivariana de Venezuela (Caracas, 1968), vol. 4, pp. 305–6.

26. Report by the Bishop of Cartagena, Havana, 30 March 1813, in Roberto Arrazola (ed.), *Documentos para la Historia de Cartagena, 1813–1820*, Edición Oficial (Cartagena, 1963), vol. 2, pp. 41–42.

27. Proclama de Bolívar a los valerosos meridanos, 8 June 1813, in Luis Horacio López (ed.), *A los colombianos: Proclamas y discursos 1812–1840*, Biblioteca de la Presidencia de la República (Bogotá, 1988), pp. 23–24.
28. Francisco Montalvo to Minister of Grace and Justice, Santa Marta, 22 August 1813, AGI, ASF, leg. 746.
29. José María Caballero, *Diario*, Biblioteca de Bogotá, Editores Villegas (Bogotá, 1990), pp. 217–18.
30. Torres y Peña, *Memorias*, p. 116.
31. See Simón Bolívar, 'Jamaica Letter', in Lecuna (ed.), vol. 1, pp. 103–22. For an excellent discussion of the use of the family metaphor by New Granada's revolutionaries, see König, *En el Camino hacia la Nación*, pp. 205–34. Mary Lowenthal Felstiner, 'Family Metaphors: the Language of an Independence Revolution', *Comparative Studies in Society and History*, vol. 25 (1983) discusses the use of identical language by Chilean revolutionaries, while Jay Fliegelman, *Prodigals and Pilgrims: the American Revolution against Patriarchal Authority, 1750–1800*, Cambridge University Press (Cambridge, 1982); and Lynn Hunt, *The Family Romance of the French Revolution*, University of California Press (Berkeley, 1993) illustrate that such metaphors were not confined to Spanish America. For comments on the broader phenomenon, see Rebecca Earle, 'Rape and the Anxious Republic: Revolutionary Colombia, 1810–1830', in Elizabeth Dore and Maxine Molyneux (eds), *Hidden Histories of Gender and the State in Latin America*, Duke University Press (Chapel Hill, 2000).
32. Antonio Nariño, *La Bagatela*, no. 8, 1 September 1811, in *Nariño Periodista*. Or consider *La Bagatela*, no. 10, 15 September 1811, in *ibid.*
33. Costeloe, *Response to Revolution*, p. 21; for 'natural ingratitude', see Jaime Delgado, *La independencia de América en la prensa española*, Seminario de Problemas Hispanoamericanos (Madrid, 1949), pp. 231–32. For another clear example, see Juan Manuel de Cajigal, *Memorias del Mariscal de Campo Don Juan Manuel de Cajigal sobre la revolución de Venezuela*, Biblioteca Venezolana de Historia (Caracas, 1960), p. 19.
34. Costeloe, *Response to Revolution*, p. 21.
35. König, *En el Camino hacia la Nación*, p. 215.
36. Restrepo, *Historia de la revolución*, vol. 1, p. 155.
37. See Toribio Montes to Juan Sámano, Quito, 22 November 1812, AGI, AQ, leg. 257; and Toribio Montes to Minister of Overseas, Quito, 7 October 1814, AGI, AQ, leg. 260. For the introduction of the Constitution of 1812, see Rodríguez, *Independence of Spanish America*, pp. 97–103.
38. See Lynch, *The Spanish American Revolutions*, pp. 193–99; and Antonio de Villavicencio to Cortes, Cartagena, 29 May 1810, AGI, ASF, leg. 747.
39. For the Constitution of 1812, see Rodríguez, *Independence of Spanish America*, p. 119.
40. A clear account is provided by McFarlane, *Colombia before Independence*, pp. 338–44.
41. See, for example, Observaciones sobre el estado presente de la España, sobre los males que amenazen a la América, y sobre las medios de precaverlos (written by José María García de Toledo?) Cartagena, 28 April 1810, AGI, ASF, leg. 1011.
42. Restrepo, *Historia de la revolución*, vol. 1, pp. 128–29; Antonio de Narváez y la Torre to Antonio Amar, Cartagena, 19 June 1810, AGI, ASF, leg. 1011; and Bando de Francisco de Montes *et al.*, Cartagena, 23 May 1810, AGI, ASF, leg. 747.

43. See Junta de Cartagena to Regency, Cartagena, 20 November 1810, AGI, ASF, leg. 747.
44. Juan Antonio de la Mata to Cortes, Panama, 1 September 1810, AGI, Audiencia de Panama, leg. 262.
45. See La Provincia de Cartagena de las Indias a las demás de éste nuevo Reyno de Granada, Cartagena, 19 August 1810, AGI, ASF, leg. 745; and also Gabriel Jiménez Molinares, *Los mártires de Cartagena de 1816 ante el consejo de guerra y ante la historia*, vol. 1, Edición Oficial (1948), pp. 164–73.
46. See Restrepo, *Historia de la revolución*, vol. 1, pp. 189–91, 203–4; and Liévano, *Los grandes conflictos*, vol. 2, pp. 559–61.
47. See, for example, Francisco Montalvo to Ministry of Grace and Justice, Cartagena, 13 December 1815, 6 February 1816, both in AGI, PC, leg. 707.
48. The text of the Acta de independencia is printed in Jiménez Molinares, *Los mártires de Cartagena*, vol. 1, pp. 249–57.
49. See Manuel Antonio Pombo and José Joaquín Guerra (eds), *Constituciones de Colombia*, Biblioteca Popular de Cultura Colombiana (Bogotá, 1951), pp. 93–176.
50. See Liévano Aguirre, *Los grandes conflictos*, vol. 2, pp. 560, 649–50; and Jiménez Molinares, *Los mártires de Cartagena*, pp. 136–46.
51. See Restrepo, *Historia de la revolución*, vol. 1, pp. 192–94, 201–2.
52. For the formation of juntas see Sergio Elias Ortiz, *Génesis de la revolución del 20 de julio de 1810*, Biblioteca Eduardo Santos, vol. 19, Editorial Kelly (Bogotá, 1960), pp. 136–39; and Restrepo, *Historia de la revolución*, vol. 1, pp. 130–31.
53. These conspiracies are described in McFarlane, *Colombia before independence*, pp. 272–338. For a contemporary account, see Caballero, *Diario*, pp. 63–75. Santa Fe had a population of approximately 16,000, and was thus roughly the same size as Cartagena. See McFarlane, *Colombia before independence*, Appendix A, Tables 1–6.
54. For a blow-by-blow description of the July 1810 revolution see Ortiz, *Génesis de la revolución*. A summary may be found in McFarlane, *Colombia before Independence*, pp. 341–346.
55. Restrepo, *Historia de la revolución*, vol. 1, p. 140.
56. For Viceroy Amar's version of events, see Antonio Amar to Regency, La Coruña, 13 January 1811, Herrán Baquero, *Antonio Amar*, pp. 305–10.
57. See Caballero, *Diario*, pp. 83–110; Restrepo, *Historia de la revolución*, vol. 1, p. 142–50; Junta provisional de ...Santa Marta to the Regency, Santa Marta, 22 September 1810, AGI, ASF, leg. 746; Bando on formation of junta in Antioquia, 11 October 1810, AGI, ASF, leg. 747; Tomás de Acosta to Council of the Indies, Santa Marta, 29 November 1811, AGI, ASF, leg. 746; and Caballero, *Diario*, pp. 95, 109.
58. Restrepo, *Historia de la revolución*, vol. 1, p. 149.
59. Ortiz, *Génesis de la revolución*, p. 147. See also Rodríguez, 'Repercusiones de la revolución', pp. 14–15.
60. Extract of letter by Joaquín Carrión y Moreno to Regency, Cartagena, 28 August 1810, AGI, ASF, leg. 746.
61. Joaquín Carrión y Moreno to Regency, Havana, 10 March 1811, AGI, ASF, leg. 747.
62. See Anna, *Spain and the Loss of America*; Costeloe, *Response to Revolution*; Edmundo

Heredia, *Planes españoles para reconquistar hispanoamérica, 1810/1818*, Editorial Universitaria de Buenos Aires (Buenos Aires, 1974); Melchor Fernández Almagro, *La emancipación de América u su reflejo en la conciencia española*, Insatiate de Estudios Políticos (Madrid, 1954); José Luis Comellas García Llera, *Los primeros pronunciamientos en España, 1814–1820*, Consejo Superior de Investigaciones Científicas (Madrid, 1958).

63. A careful examination of the American deputies to the Cortes is provided by Marie Laure Rieu-Millan, *Los diputados americanos en las Cortes de Cádiz (igualdad o independencia)*, Consejo Superior de Investigaciones Científicas (Madrid, 1990); and Marie Laure Rieu-Millan, 'Les Cortès de Cadix face à la dissidence américaine: les raisons d'un échec (1810–1814)', *Caravelle*, no. 68 (1997).
64. Manifiesto a la Nación Española by José Moreno de García, Cádiz, 16 February 1822, quoted in Iris Zavala, *Masones, comuneros y carbonarios*, Siglo XXI (Madrid, 1971), p. 261. For other striking examples of ignorance, see Heredia, *Planes españoles*, pp. 45, 348.
65. Demetrio Ramos, 'Las Cortes de Cádiz y América', *Revista de Estudios Políticos*, vol. 126 (1962), p. 434. See also Instructions to the royalist commissioners, Junta de Conciliación de Venezuela, Caracas, 18 January 1821, AHNM, Estado, leg. 8733, doc. 24.
66. See Heredia, *Planes españoles*, pp. 124, 137–38.
67. See Costeloe, *Response to Revolution*, pp. 10–13, for descriptions of these various groupings.
68. Michael Costeloe, 'Spain and the Spanish American Wars of Independence: *The Comisión de Reemplazos*, 1811–1820', *JLAS*, vol. 13 (1981) p. 223.
69. See Costeloe, *Response to Revolution*, pp. 110–15 for details of the Russian ship purchase.
70. Pedro Voltes, *Fernando VII vida y reinado*, Editorial Juventud (Barcelona, 1985), pp. 182–83.
71. Costeloe, *Response to Revolution.*
72. See Costeloe, *Response to Revolution*, p. 89 and Lúcas Alamán, *Historia de Mejico* (1849), Editorial Jus (Mexico City, 1969), vol. 5, p. 14n. (Note the discrepancy in the figures given by Costeloe and Alamán.) The Comisión de Reemplazos estimated that 47,000 troops in total had been sent. See Anna, *Spain and the Loss of America*, p. 101. For modern estimates of troop numbers, see Heredia, *Planes españoles*, pp. 79, 94, 252–53; Margaret Woodward, 'The Spanish Army and the Loss of America, 1810–1824', *HAHR*, vol. 48 (1968), pp. 587–89 (with lower figures for the 1813 expedition); and also Julio Albi, *Banderas olvidadas: el ejército realista en América*, Ediciones de Cultura Hispánica (Madrid, 1990), pp. 401–5.
73. Piers Mackesy, *The War for America, 1775–1783*, Longmans (London, 1964), p. 176; and C.L.R. James, *The Black Jacobins. Toussaint L'Overture and the San Domingo Revolution*, Alison & Busby (London, 1984), p. 369.
74. Anna, *Spain and the Loss of America*, p. 60. For representative examples of the size of European armies, see Christopher Duffy, *The Military Experience in the Age of Reason*, Routledge (London, 1987), pp. 17–18; and George Rudé, *Revolutionary Europe, 1783–1815*, Fontana (London, 1964), pp. 267–69.
75. For a discussion of this point, see Costeloe, *Response to Revolution*, pp. 28–41.

76. *El Redactor General*, 7, 19 September 1811, quoted in Costeloe, *Response to Revolution*, p. 53.
77. See La Comisión de Reemplazos representa a la Regencia ... el estado de insurrección en que se hallan algunas provincias de ultramar, Cádiz, 1 March 1814, AGI, I.A. 5/20.
78. For a concise statement of this view, see Pablo Morillo to the Ministry of Overseas, Valencia, 26 July 1820, AGI, Indiferente General, leg. 1568.
79. See Woodward, 'The Spanish Army and the Loss of America'. See also Anna, *Spain and the Loss of America*, p. 47; and Delgado, *La independencia de América*, pp. 223–25. Royalist and insurgent rumour-mongering are discussed in Rebecca Earle, 'Information and Disinformation in Late Colonial New Granada', *The Americas*, vol. 54:2 (1997).
80. Francisco Montalvo to Ministry of War, 22 November 1816, AGI, ASF, leg. 631.
81. See Heredia, *Planes españoles*, p. 19.
82. Costeloe discusses this point well; see *Response to Revolution*, particularly pp. 7–8, 42–44.
83. See Manifiesto a la Nación Española by José Moreno de García, Cádiz, 16 February 1822, Zavala, *Masones, comuneros y carbonarios*, p. 259.
84. Anna, *Spain and the Loss of America*, pp. 166–68. See also Costeloe, *Response to Revolution*, pp. 73–82, 140–41.
85. Pizarro's plan is discussed in Fernández Almagro, *La emancipación de América*, pp. 83–87.
86. Luis Miguel Enciso Recio, *La opinión pública española y la independencia hispanoamericana, 1819–1820*, Universidad de Valladolid (Valladolid, 1967), p . 55. For details of the British volunteers, see Eric Lambert, *Voluntarios británicos e irlandeses en la gesta bolivariana*, vol. 1, Edición de la Corporación Venezolana de Guayana (Caracas, 1981).
87. Proclama de Morillo a los Jefes ... Ingleses, Achaguas, 26 March 1819, Antonio Rodríguez Villa, *El Teniente General Don Pablo Morillo, Primer Conde de Cartagena, Marqués de la Puerta (1778–1837)*, Real Academia de Historia (Madrid, 1908–1910), vol. 4, pp. 108–9 (the original is in English).
88. See Heredia, *Planes españoles*, p. 193–206, 377; and AGI, Estado, leg. 88, Document 10, which contains much information on the British mediation. For the British side of the negotiations, see C.K. Webster (ed.), *Britain and the Independence of Latin America, 1812–1830*, Octagon Books (New York, 1970), vol. 2, pp. 309–442.
89. Prohibitions were issued in 1814, 1817 and 1819. See Enciso Recio, *La opinión pública española*, pp. 37–38; Act by George III, 3 July 1819, AGI, PC, leg. 742; and the Duke of San Carlos to Pablo Morillo, London, 23 July 1819, Rodríguez Villa, *Pablo Morillo*, vol. 4, pp. 111–12. See also D.A.G. Waddell, 'British Neutrality and Spanish-American Independence: the Problem of Foreign Enlistment', *JLAS*, vol. 19 (1987); and D.A.G. Waddell, 'Anglo-Spanish Relations and the "Pacification of America" during the "Constitutional triennium" 1820–1823', *Anuario de Estudios Americanos*, vol. 44 (1989). For details of the negotiations, see Anna, *Spain and the Loss of America*, pp. 104–10, Heredia, *Planes españoles*, pp. 74, 83, 193–225; and John Rydjord, 'British Mediation between Spain and her Colonies, 1811–1813', *HAHR*, vol. 21 (1941). An insurgent view on negotiation is provided by Report by José

María del Real, London, 7 December 1814, AGI, Estado, leg. 57, Doc. 34A, letter 2 (also in AGS, Estado, leg. 8287).

2: Royalist Enclaves in New Granada

1. For a classic discussion of regional rivalry, see Hermes Tovar, 'Guerras de opinión y represión en Colombia durante la independencia (1810–1820)', *Anuario Colombiano de Historia Social y de la Cultura*, no. 11 (1983). See also Brian Hamnett, 'Popular Insurrection and Royalist Reaction: Colombian Regions, 1810–1823', in John Fisher, Allan J. Kuethe and Anthony McFarlane (eds), *Reform and Insurrection in Bourbon New Granada and Peru*, Louisiana State Press (Baton Rouge, 1990); and, for a useful comparison with Peru, see John Fisher, 'Royalism, Regionalism and Rebellion in Colonial Peru, 1808–1815', *HAHR*, vol. 59 (1979).
2. A thorough modern history of the First Republic has yet to be written; Restrepo, *Historia de la revolución*, vols 1–2, is still the best account I have read. See also José Manuel Groot, *Historia eclesiástica y civil de Nueva Granada*, vol. 3, Editorial M. Rivas (Bogotá, 1889–1893); and Tovar, 'Guerras de opinión'.
3. *Cabildo* of San Gil applies to join the Province of Cundinamarca, in Guillermo Hernández de Alba (ed.), *Archivo Nariño 1812–1815*, vol. 5, Biblioteca de la Presidencia de la República (Bogotá, 1990), pp. 75–77, 86.
4. Manuel Antonio Pombo and José Joaquín Guerra (eds), *Constituciones de Colombia*, 2 vols, Biblioteca Popular de Cultura Colombiana, Bogotá, 1951; and Glen Dealy, 'Prolegomena on the Spanish American Political Tradition', *HAHR*, vol. 48 (1968).
5. Groot, *Historia eclesiástica*, vol. 3, p. 192.
6. Caballero, *Diario.*
7. Lomné, 'Las cuidades de la Nueva Granada'. There is a growing literature on civic rituals in colonial and independence-era Mexico. See the special issue on Spectacle in Colonial Mexico edited by Linda A. Curcio-Nagy in *The Americas*, vol. 52 (1996); and Mariano E. Torres Bautista, 'De la fiesta monárquica a la fiesta cívica: El tránsito del poder en Puebla, 1821–1822', *Historia Mexicana*, vol. 45:2 (1995).
8. See Groot, *Historia eclesiástica*, vol. 3; Caballero, *Diario*, p. 201; and Descripción de a Ceremonía que antecedió a la plantación de l "Arbol de la Libertad" en la Plazuela de San Victorino, Santafé, 29 April 1813, in *Archivo Nariño, 1812–1814*, pp. 271–72.
9. Groot, *Historia eclesiástica*, vol. 3, p. 218.
10. For Nariño's paper, see Carlos Restrepo Canal (ed.), *Nariño Periodista*, Academia Colombiana de Historia, vol. 20, Editorial Kelly (Bogotá, 1960). See also Renan Silva, *Prensa y revolución a finales del siglo XVIII. Contribución a un análisis de la formación de la ideología de independencia nacional*, Banco de la República (Bogotá, 1989). Jürgen Habermas, *The Structural Transformation of the Public Sphere: An Enquiry into a Category of Bourgeois Society*, MIT Press (Cambridge, 1991) and François-Xavier Guerra, *Modernidad e Independencias. Ensayos sobre las Revoluciones Hispánicas*, MAPFRE (Madrid, 1992) both comment incisively on the role of the press in the formation of modern public space.
11. See Earle, 'Information and Disinformation'.
12. Groot, *Historia eclesiástica*, vol. 3, p. 151.

13. Restrepo, *Historia de la revolución*, vol. 1, pp. 202–3, 221–22; and Demonstración del demérito que tenía el papel moneda, enclosed in Ramón de Herrera to Corregidor Intendente de la Plaza, Cartagena, 15 December 1815, AGI, PC, leg. 889B.
14. Spanish officials commented on the broad popular participation in the revolution. See Francisco Montalvo to Gabriel de Torres, Cartagena, 6 February 1816, AGI, PC, leg. 707.
15. Pablo Morillo to Ministry of War, Santa Fe, 31 May 1816, Rodríguez Villa, *Pablo Morillo*, vol. 3, p. 159.
16. Victor M. Uribe Uran, 'Rebellion of the Mandarins: Lawyers, Political Parties and the State in Colombia, 1780–1850', Doctoral Dissertation, University of Pittsburgh (Pittsburgh, 1993), p. 124.
17. Uribe, 'Rebellion of the Mandarins', p. 169.
18. See Herrán Baquero, *Antonio Amar*, pp. 72–73. The Regency's original plan had been to replace Amar with Francisco Xavier Venegas, who was subsequently named viceroy of Mexico. A biography of Pérez may be found in José María Restrepo Sáenz, *Biografías de los mandatarios y ministros de la Real Audiencia (1671 a 1819)*, Biblioteca de Historia Nacional, vol. 84, Editorial Cromos (Bogotá, 1952), pp. 245–49.
19. Benito Pérez to the Regency, Panama, 17 September 1812, AGI, ASF, leg. 746; Joaquín Carrión y Moreno to Minister of Grace and Justice, Panama, 25 August 1814, AGI, ASF, leg. 580; and Act of the Audiencia de Santa Fe, Panama, 14 November 1812, AGI, ASF, leg. 746.
20. Benito Pérez to Minister of Grace and Justice, Panama, 1813, AGI, ASF, leg. 580. See also the many other documents in AGI, ASF, leg. 580 (ramo 3) and leg. 665.
21. Joaquín Carrión y Moreno to Minister of Grace and Justice(?), Panama, 19 July 1813, 22 June 1814, and 31 October 1814, all in AGI, ASF, leg. 665. The history of smuggling on the Caribbean coast is discussed in Lance Grahn, *The Political Economy of Smuggling: Regional Informal Economies in Early Bourbon New Granada*, Westview Press (Boulder, 1997).
22. See Declaration of Tomás de Bajo, Panama, 18 November 1812, AGI, ASF, leg. 746; Juan Antonio de la Mata to Cortes, Panama, 20 June 1810; Manuel Bishop of Panama to Juan Antonio de la Mata, Panama, 17 September 1810; all in AGI, Audiencia de Panama, leg. 262. Also see Joaquín Carrión y Moreno and Manuel García to Minister of Grace and Justice, Panama, 10 June 1812, AGI, ASF, leg. 665.
23. Report by Council of the Indies, 7 February 1811, AGI, ASF, leg. 747.
24. Tovar, 'Guerras de opinión', p. 189.
25. McFarlane, *Colombia before Independence*, Appendix A, Tables 1–5.
26. Junta provisional … de Santa Marta to the Regency, Santa Marta, 22 September 1810, AGI, ASF, leg. 746.
27. Junta Provisional de Santa Marta to Council of the Indies, Santa Marta, 20 March 1811, AGI, ASF, leg. 746; and Jiménez Molinares, *Los mártires de Cartagena*, vol. 1, p. 185–86. See also Ernesto Restrepo Tirado, *Historia de la Provincia de Santa Marta*, vol. 2, Ministerio de Educación Nacional, (Bogotá, 1953), pp. 310–42.
28. Acta del Ayuntamiento de Santa Marta, Santa Marta, 5 July 1811, AGI, ASF, leg. 745.

29. See Report by Martín de Pando, Cartagena, 29 July 1819, AGI, PC, leg. 750; McFarlane, *Colombia before Independence*, pp. 126–84 *passim*, 297–307; and Grahn, *Political Economy of Smuggling*.
30. See Jiménez Molinares, *Los mártires de Cartagena*, pp. 184–86; and Donaldo Bossa Herazo, *Cartagena independiente: tradición y desarrollo*, Ediciones Tercer Mundo (Bogotá, 1967), p. 13.
31. Report by Junta de Santa Marta, Santa Marta, 4 June 1811, AGI, ASF, leg. 745; and Jiménez Molinares, *Los mártires de Cartagena*, vol. 1, pp. 202–4, 208–9. Santa Marta responded by imposing trading restrictions of its own; see Acta capitular de la ciudad de Santa Marta, Santa Marta, 22 August 1811, AGI, ASF, leg. 745.
32. See Jiménez Molinares, *Los mártires de Cartagena*, vol. 1, pp. 214–35; José María Martínez de Aparicio to Regency, Santa Marta, 25 November 1810, AGI, ASF, leg. 746; Junta of Santa Marta to Regency, Santa Marta, 4 June 1811; Francisco Pérez Dávila to Regency, Santa Marta, 3 July 1811; and Tomás de Acosta to Council of the Indies, Santa Marta, 29 November 1811; all in AGI, ASF, leg. 745.
33. See Heredia, *Planes españoles*, pp. 79, 94.
34. See Jiménez Molinares, *Los mártires de Cartagena*, vol. 1, pp. 306–8; and Miguel de Bustillo y Colina to Cortes, Kingston, 12 March 1813, Jiménez Molinares, *Los mártires de Cartagena*, vol. 1, pp. 312–19.
35. See Miguel de Bustillo y Colina to Cortes, Kingston, 12 March 1813, Jiménez Molinares, *Los mártires de Cartagena*, vol. 1, pp. 312–19.
36. Biographies of both Labatut and Chatillon may be found in Sergio Elías Ortiz, *Franceses en la independencia de la Gran Colombia*, Biblioteca Eduardo Santos, vol. 1, Editorial ABC (Bogotá, 1971).
37. Francisco Montalvo to Minister of State, Santa Marta, 25 February 1815, AGI, ASF, leg. 580.
38. Toribio Montes to Minister of Overseas, Quito, 7 October 1814, AGI, AQ, leg. 260; and also Toribio Montes to Manuel Bernardo Alvarez, Quito, 27 September 1814, *Archivo Nariño 1812–1815*, vol. 5, pp. 379–80.
39. Francisco Montalvo to Juan Sámano, Cartagena, 30 January 1818, *Los últimos virreyes de Nueva Granada, Relación de Mando del Virrey don Francisco Montalvo y noticias del Virrey Sámano sobre la pérdida del Reino (1813–1819)*, Eduardo Posada and P.M. Ibáñez (eds), Biblioteca de la Juventud Hispano-Americana, Editorial América (Madrid, n.d.), pp. 101–2; and José Francisco Heredia, *Memorias del Regente Heredia (de las Reales Audiencias de Caracas y México)*, Editorial América (Madrid, n.d.), pp. 291–93.
40. Francisco Montalvo to Minister of Grace and Justice, Santa Marta, 4 March 1814, and Rafael de Zúñiga to Francisco Montalvo, Santa Marta, 12 January 1814, both in AGI, ASF, leg. 631; Reflections on the Loss of Santa Marta, 10 November 1820, AHNM, estado, leg. 8733, fol. 26; Pedro Ruíz de Porras to Minister of Grace and Justice, Santa Marta, 7 January 1814, AGI, ASF, leg. 746; and also Restrepo Tirado, *Historia de Santa Marta*, vol. 2, pp. 370–71.
41. Francisco Montalvo to Minister of Hacienda, Santa Marta, 23 June 1814, AGI, ASF, leg. 631.
42. Francisco Montalvo to Minister of Overseas, Santa Marta, 21 August 1813, AGI, ASF, leg. 631.
43. Report by Council of the Indies, 25 June 1816, AGI, ASF, leg. 549. Also see

Cabildo de Santa Marta to Ferdinand, Santa Marta, 28 July 1814, AGI, ASF, leg. 580.

44. Francisco de Montalvo to the Secretary of Ultramar, Santa Marta, 16 December 1813, in Arrazola, *Documentos*, vol. 2, p. 46. (On printing presses, see also Francisco Montalvo to Minister of Grace and Justice, Santa Marta, 22 August 1813, AGI, ASF, leg. 746.) Some information about the introduction of the Constitution of 1812 is contained in Arrazola, *Documentos*, vols 1, 2.
45. See Jiménez Molinares, *Los mártires de Cartagena*, vol. 1, pp. 215–17.
46. For Ríohacha's population in the late eighteenth century see McFarlane, *Colombia before Independence*, Appendix A, Table 2.
47. Tomás de Acosta was replaced as governor by Pedro Ruíz de Porras in 1812. Tomás de Acosta to Council of the Indies, Santa Marta, 29 November 1811, AGI, ASF, leg. 746. See also Restrepo Tirado, *Historia de Santa Marta*, vol. 2, pp. 330–32, 352–56.
48. Representación de los vecinos del sitio de San Juan de César, San Juan de César, 13 March 1813; Ayuntamiento de Ríohacha to the Council of the Indies, Ríohacha, 6 May 1813; and Francisco Montalvo to Minister of Overseas, Santa Marta, 4 November 1813; all in AGI, ASF, leg. 746.
49. Ayuntamiento de Ríohacha to Council of the Indies, Ríohacha, 6 May 1813, AGI, ASF, leg. 746; and Restrepo Tirado, *Historia de Santa Marta*, vol. 2, p. 355.
50. See McFarlane, *Colombia before Independence*, Appendix A, Tables 2–4, and Manuel Sobrevida, Descripción histórico-geográfica, política, eclesiástica y militar de la América Meridional, Lima, 1796, BL, Gayangos 15,740.
51. H.M. Wood to George Canning, Popayán, 30 June 1825, PRO, F.O. 18/21, ff. 86–91.
52. Sergio Elias Ortiz, *Agustín Agualongo y su tiempo*, Editorial ABC (Bogotá, 1958), p. 82.
53. Cabildo de Pasto to Ferdinand, Pasto, 13 June 1814, BL, Egerton, 1809. (Also in AGI, AQ, leg. 276.) See also Cabildo of Pasto to Pablo Morillo, Pasto, 13 October 1816, printed in Gustavo Guerrero, *Documentos históricos para los hechos ocurridos en Pasto en la guerra de la independencia*, Imprenta del Departamento, (1912), pp. 136–42.
54. Ortiz, *Agustín Agualongo*, p. 99.
55. Cabildo of Pasto to Ferdinand, Pasto, 13 June 1814, BL, Egerton, 1809, f. 442.
56. Petition by Sala Capitular de Santa Marta, Santa Marta, 5 March 1812, and Minister of Overseas to Minister of Grace and Justice, Cádiz, 23 September 1812, both in AGI, ASF. leg. 746. See also Report by Council of the Indies, 1 December 1817; and Report by Council of the Indies, 5 May 1819, both in AGI, ASF, leg. 549.
57. Garrido, *Reclamos y representaciones*, p. 320; and Informe a la Corte sobre los sucesos de la Nueva Granada, Havana, 10 March 1811, in Arrazola, *Documentos*, vol. 1, p. 128.
58. Ortiz, *Agustín Agualongo*, p. 339.
59. Miguel Tacón to Joaquín Molina, Pasto, 14 May 1811, AGI, AQ, leg. 235.
60. Remaining in republican Popayán was Ana María Polonia García de Tacón, the governor's wife. Following her husband's defeat at Bajo Palacé she was detained by the insurgents, who sent threatening letters to Governor Tacón warning that if he did not return to Spain immediately he would never see his family alive again.

She was later released unharmed and became something of an advocate of her former captors. See Manuel Santiago Vallecilla *et al.* to Miguel Tacón, Popayán, 11 April 1811; Antonio Baraya to Miguel Tacón, Popayán, 11 April 1811; and Miguel Tacón to Manuel Santiago Vallecilla, Pasto, 28 April 1811; all in AGI, AQ, leg. 235.

61. H.M. Wood to George Canning, Popayán, 30 June 1825, PRO, F.O. 18/21.
62. Ortiz, *Agustín Agualongo*, p. 181.
63. Cabildo of Pasto to Ferdinand, Pasto, 13 June 1814, BL, Egerton, 1809. The Patianos were to remain royalist until the last days of the war. Most were escaped slaves who lived from banditry. The clientelistic networks developing out of their system of brigandage led easily to the formation of guerrilla bands following the outbreak of the War of Independence. The Patianos' royalism is traditionally attributed to the provocative behaviour of the republican troops that marched through the Patía in 1811. The republican troops sacked houses, confiscated cattle, and burnt the church of the small town of Patía. (See Francisco Zuluaga, 'Clientelismo y guerrillas en el Valle del Patía, 1536–1811', in Germán Colmenares (ed.) *La independencia, ensayos de historia social*, Instituto Colombiano de Cultura, (Bogotá, 1986), p. 114; and José María Obando, *Apuntamientos para la historia*, vol. 1, Editorial ABC (Bogotá, 1945), p. 19.)
64. Cabildo de Pasto to Pablo Morillo, Pasto, 13 October 1816, Guerrero, *Documentos históricos*, pp. 138–39. See also Cabildo de Pasto to Ferdinand, Pasto, 13 June 1814, BL, Egerton 1809; and H.M. Wood to George Canning, Popayán, 30 June 1825, PRO, F.O. 18/21.
65. Hamnett, 'Popular Insurrection and Royalist Reaction'; Cabildo de Pasto to Ferdinand, Pasto, 13 June 1814, BL, Egerton, 1809, f. 439; and Toribio Montes to Francisco Montalvo, Quito, 21 June 1817, AGI, ASF, leg. 631.
66. Antonio Nariño, *Escritos políticos*, El Ancora, (Bogotá, 1982), pp. 77, 80.
67. José Hilario López, *Memorias*, vol. 1, Editorial ABC (Bogotá, 1942), pp. 46–58.
68. Cabildo de Pasto to Ferdinand, Pasto, 13 June 1814, BL, Egerton 1809; and Toribio Montes to Ministers of State and War, Quito, 7 July 1814, AGI, AQ, leg. 260.
69. Cabildo de Pasto to Antonio Nariño, Pasto, 8 April 1814, *Archivo Nariño*, vol. 5, pp. 319–20. Translation from Thomas Blossom, *Nariño, Hero of Colombian Independence*, University of Arizona Press (Tucson, 1967), p. 123.
70. Cabildo de Pasto to Ferdinand, Pasto, 13 June 1814, BL, Egerton 1809, fol. 441; López, *Memorias*, p. 59; and Testimonio sobre la campaña del General Nariño en Pasto, 21 April 1814, *Archivo Nariño*, vol. 5, pp. 321–24.
71. Cabildo de Pasto to Ferdinand, Pasto, 13 June 1814, BL, Egerton 1809, fol. 442; and Ortiz, *Agustín Agualongo*, p. 125.
72. Liévano, *Los grandes conflictos*, vol. 2, pp. 830–32, Nariño, *Escritos políticos*, pp. 139–140, and Cabildo de Pasto to Ferdinand, Pasto, 13 June 1814, BL, Egerton 1809, fol. 442.
73. Nariño, *Escritos políticos*, p. 145.
74. See Blossom, *Nariño*, p. 127; Declaration by Francisco Arteta, Palmira, 19 May 1815, BRAH, sig. 9/7648 (leg. 52), fols 147–51; Declaration by José Brandenberg, Quito, 29 June 1815; and Declaration of Juan Guerra, Quito, 4 July 1815, both in

AGI, AQ, leg. 275.
75. See Edmundo Heredia, 'El destino de la expedición de Morillo', *Anuario de Estudios Americanos*, vol. 29 (1972), p. 326.

3: The Reconquest of New Granada

1. See Heredia, 'El destino de la expedición de Morillo', pp. 315–40, and Costeloe, 'Spain and the Spanish American Wars of Independence', pp. 223–37.
2. Costeloe, *Response to Revolution*, p. 114; and Comellas García Llera, *Los primeros pronunciamientos*, p. 307.
3. Costeloe, 'Spain and the Spanish American Wars of Independence', p. 229, and Antonio Rodríguez Villa, *El Teniente General Don Pablo Morillo, Primer Conde de Cartagena, Marqués de la Puerta (1778–1837)*, 2 vols, Editorial América (Madrid, 1920) (henceforth Rodríguez Villa, *Pablo Morillo* (1920)), vol. 1, p. 120. Rafael Sevilla, *Memorias de un oficial del ejército español, campañas contra Bolívar y los separatistas de América, Editorial América*, (Madrid, 1916), p. 23, gives slightly different figures for the number of ships.
4. Sevilla, *Memorias*, p. 24.
5. See Stephen Stoan, *Pablo Morillo and Venezuela*, Ohio State University Press (Columbia, 1974), pp. 64–65; and Daniel Florencio O'Leary, *Bolívar and the War of Independence*, University of Texas Press (Austin, 1970), pp. 186–87.
6. Francisco Xavier Arámbarri, *Hechos del General Pablo Morillo en América*, Ediciones de la Embajada de Venezuela en España (Madrid, 1971), p. 20.
7. Restrepo, *Historia de la revolución*, vol. 2, pp. 137, 139.
8. Lynch, *The Spanish American Revolutions*, p. 200. For a description of the war in Venezuela, see Lynch, pp. 190–207.
9. Jane Rausch has written several definitive books on the Llanos. See particularly *A Tropical Plains Frontier: The Llanos of Colombia, 1531–1831*, University of New Mexico Press (Albuquerque, 1984).
10. Boves' force was the largest to fight in Venezuela's war of independence. See German Carrera Damas, *Boves, aspectos socio-económicos*, Colección Vigilia (Caracas, 1968), p. 35.
11. See Heredia, *Memorias*, pp. 278–85.
12. Francisco Montalvo to the Regency, Santa Marta, 27 June 1814, *Los últimos virreyes*, pp. 47–48. For the views of a royalist civilian, see Josef González Llorente to Juan Bautista Sacristan, Kingston, 14 April 1815, AGI, ASF, leg. 549.
13. Cajigal, *Memorias*, p. 13.
14. David Bushnell, 'The Independence of Spanish South America', in Leslie Bethell (ed.), *The Independence of Latin America*, Cambridge University Press (Cambridge, 1987), p. 109.
15. See Miguel Izard, *El miedo a la revolución: la lucha por la libertad en Venezuela (1777–1830)*, Editorial Tecnos (Madrid, 1979), pp. 132–33.
16. The pardon is dramatically recounted in Sevilla, *Memorias*. Also see Rodríguez Villa, *Pablo Morillo*, vol. 1 (1920), p. 123.
17. Attitudes towards slavery reveal clearly the ambivalence with which both royalist and republican leaders viewed their coloured allies. With rare exceptions, both

sides freed slaves only when they intended to recruit them into their respective armies. In 1812 Francisco de Miranda offered to free slaves who fought with him for ten years; in the same year Quiteño revolutionaries freed slaves who joined their army; Bolívar did the same in 1816 and 1818; as did royalists in Pasto during the early years of the war. See Izard, *El Miedo a la Revolución*, pp. 55–65; Eduardo Pérez, *Guerra irregular en la independencia de la Nueva Granada y Venezuela, 1810–1830*, Publicaciones de la Universidad Pedagógica y Tecnológica de Colombia (Tunja, 1982), p. 271; Historia de la rebelión de América en 35 cartas, by Pedro Pérez Múñoz, Quito, 31 December 1815, AGI, Diversos, leg. 42. The situation was similar in Peru. See Peter Blanchard, *Slavery and Abolition in Early Republican Peru*, SR Books (Wilmington, 1992), chapter 1.

18. Cajigal, *Memorias*, p. 153 and Arámbarri, *Hechos del General Morillo*, p. 19. Stoan, *Pablo Morillo*; and Cajigal, *Memorias*, provides details about the establishment of the military government in Venezuela.
19. Serious disagreements were soon to develop between Moxó and Morillo over the latter aspect of Moxó's duties. See Stoan, *Pablo Morillo*, esp. pp. 88–89, 111–15.
20. The following section is drawn, where not otherwise indicated, from the following sources: Restrepo, *Historia de la revolución*, vol. 2; Jiménez Molinares, *Los mártires de Cartagena*, vol. 2; and Liévano, *Los grandes conflictos*, vol. 2.
21. An English account of the entrance of the Expeditionary Army into Cartagena, quoted in Arrazola (ed.), *Documentos*, vol. 2, pp. 160–61.
22. Restrepo, *Historia de la revolución*, vol. 2, pp. 51–52.
23. Restrepo, *Historia de la revolución*, vol. 2, p. 61.
24. See Oath of Loyalty and Lists of those swearing loyalty, August–September 1815, AGI, PC, leg. 717.
25. See Pablo Morillo to Admiral Douglas, the Captain General of the Antilles, Santa Marta, 30 July 1815, Rodríguez Villa, *Pablo Morillo*, vol. 2, pp. 573–74.
26. See Testimonios contra los insurgentes en Cartagena, December 1815–January 1816, AGI, PC, leg. 891A.
27. Pablo Morillo to José de Abascal, Torrecillas, 21 October 1815, AGI, Diversos, leg. 4, ramo 1.
28. See Restrepo, *Historia de la revolución*, vol. 2, p. 65–66.
29. Rodríguez Villa, *Pablo Morillo*, vol. 1, p. 447.
30. See Restrepo, *Historia de la revolución*, vol. 2, p. 86; Bossa Herazo, *Cartagena independiente*, pp. 24–29 (for estimates of Cartagena's population); and Francisco Montalvo to Juan Sámano, Cartagena, 30 January 1818, *Los últimos virreyes*, p. 88. Pascual Enrile estimated that about two thousand people died of hunger (Rodríguez Villa, *Pablo Morillo*, vol. 1 (1920), p. 177); while the Bishop of Cartagena claimed that over three thousand died (Juan José Oderiz to Minister Universal de Indias, Cartagena, 28 December 1815, AGI, ASF, leg. 747, ramo 2).
31. Sevilla, *Memorias*, p. 68. See also Gabriel de Torres to Ferdinand, Cartagena, 15 July 1819, Bossa Herazo, *Cartagena independiente*, pp. 69–76); and Juan José Oderiz to Minister Universal de Indias, Cartagena, 28 December 1815, AGI, ASF, leg. 747, ramo 2.
32. Various Bandos of Gabriel de Torres, Cartagena, December 1815, AGI, PC, leg. 717; and Ruling by Ferdinand, Madrid, 16 April 1819, AGI, PC, leg. 742.

33. Gabriel Porras Troconis, *La magna epopeya de Cartagena: el sitio del año 1815*, Editorial Temis (Bogotá, 1965), p. 60, 68, lists many of the émigrés.
34. Testimonios contra los insurgentes en Cartagena, December 1815–January 1816, AGI, PC, leg. 891A.
35. See Pablo Morillo to Ministry of War, Cartagena, 16 February 1816, Rodríguez Villa, *Pablo Morillo*, vol. 3, pp, 131–32, for a partial list of those shot; the Siege of Cartagena as described by Juan García del Río, quoted in Arrazola (ed.), *Documentos*, vol. 2, p. 157; and Restrepo, *Historia de la revolución*, vol. 2, p. 86.
36. Pablo Morillo to Luis de Onis, Santa Fe, 1 July and 17 August 1816, Rodríguez Villa, *Pablo Morillo*, vol. 3, pp. 24–26.
37. See Caballero, *Diario.*
38. See Restrepo, *Historia de la revolución*, vol. 2, p. 101.
39. There are several secondary sources which describe the military campaigns of 1816–1818. See, for example, Albi, *Banderas olvidadas*; and Jorge Mercado, *Campaña de invasión del Teniente General Don Pablo Morillo, 1815–1816*, Ejército de Colombia, Estado Mayor General (Bogotá, 1919). José Cervera Pery, *La marina española en la emancipación de hispanoamérica*, MAPFRE (Madrid, 1992), gives an account of the naval actions in the Caribbean. Biographies of many of the most important officers may be found in José María Restrepo Saenz, *Gobernadores de Antioquia, 1571–1819*, vol. 1, Imprenta Nacional (Bogotá, 1932).
40. For information about the capture of Cartagenero insurgents, see Expedición del Río Atrato en diciembre de 1815 por el Teniente Coronel Don Julián Bayer, In AGI, Mapas y Planes: Panama, ff. 313–18.
41. Borrador de Ystoria del Cuartel General, desde 30 de Mayo de 1816 a 18 de agosto del mismo, entry for 8 June 1816, AGI, PC, leg. 759A.
42. Pablo Morillo to Miguel de la Torre, Ocaña, 25 March 1816, AHNM, Estado, leg. 8717, doc. 48. See also Restrepo, *Historia de la revolución*, vol. 2, p. 77.
43. For reports on the battle of Cachirí, see Sebastián de la Calzada to Pablo Morillo, Suratá, 23 February 1816, Rodríguez Villa, *Pablo Morillo*, vol. 3, p. 30; and Pablo Morillo to Francisco Montalvo, Mompós, 9 March 1816, AGI, PC, leg. 717.
44. Caballero, *Memorias*, pp. 212–13. Similar scenes are described in the anonymous account from 1817 published by Carlos Cortes Vargas in 'De la época del Terror', *BHA*, vol. 29:327 (1942), p. 86.
45. Rodríguez Villa, *Pablo Morillo*, vol. 1 (1920), p. 210, and Restrepo, *Historia de la revolución*, vol. 2, p. 99.
46. The delegation of Bogotanas is described in Sevilla, *Memorias*, p. 95, and Caballero, *Diario*, pp. 214–15.
47. See Victor Uribe, 'Kill all the Lawyers!: Lawyers and the Independence Movement in New Granada, 1809–1820', *The Americas*, vol. 52:2 (1995). New Granada did not have a large population of lawyers; significance lies in the decimation of the educated elite, rather than in the absolute number of victims.
48. For concise remarks about the counter-revolution in Mexico, see Archer, 'La Causa Buena'. Royalist policy in Mexico is discussed Anna, *The Fall of the Royal Government in Mexico City*. For a partial list of those executed in New Granada, including the reasons for their execution, see Relación de las Principales Cabezas de la Rebelión de este Nuevo Reino de Granada …, Santa Fe, 4 September 1816,

AGI, PC, 1901.

49. For official reports of the battle of Ceja Alta, see the two letters of Francisco Warleta to Pablo Morillo, Cancan, 23 March 1816, AGI, PC, leg. 707 (also in leg. 717).
50. See José Manuel Restrepo, *Autobiographia, con apuntamientos sobre la emigración que hice en 1816 de la provincia de Antioquia a la de Popayán*, Biblioteca de la Presidencia de Colombia, vol. 30 (Bogotá, 1957), pp. 17, 65–69.
51. See Restrepo Saenz, *Gobernadores de Antioquia*, vol. 1, pp. 289–304; Francisco Warleta to Juan Sámano, Cali, 22 August 1816, BRAH, sig. 9/7665 (leg. 22), fols. 60–61; and Pablo Morillo to Miguel de la Torre, Barquisimeto, 17 December 1819, AHNM, Estado, leg. 8717, Doc. 281.
52. Pablo Morillo to Ministry of War, Bucaramanga, 13 May 1816, Rodríguez Villa, *Pablo Morillo*, vol. 3, pp. 156–57.
53. Borrador de Ystoria del Cuartel General, desde 30 de Mayo de 1816 a 18 de Agosto del mismo, entry for 27 July 1816, AGI, PC, leg. 759A; and Juan Sámano to Toribio Montes, Cuchilla de Tambo, 30 June 1816, BRAH, sig. 9/7665 (leg. 22), fols 18–19.
54. Mercado, *Campaña de invasión*, p. 201.
55. For the use of counter-insurgency techniques in Mexico, see Brian Hamnett, 'Royalist Counterinsurgency and the Continuity of Rebellion: Guanajuato and Michoacán, 1813–1820', *HAHR*, vol. 62 (1982); and Archer, 'La Causa Buena'.
56. Juan Friede, *La otra verdad: la independencia americana vista por los españoles*, Tercer Mundo (Bogotá, 1972), pp. 14–15.
57. Declaration of Vicente Vanegas, Pasto, 25 Oct. 1815, AGI, AQ, leg. 275. See also Oswaldo Díaz Díaz, *La reconquista española*, vol. 1, Historia Extensa de Colombia, vol. 6 (Bogotá, 1964), p. 64.
58. Restrepo, *Historia de la revolución*, vol. 2, p. 132.
59. See Orden General del 28 de Noviembre de 1816, del 13 de Febrero de 1817, and del 21 de Junio de 1818, AGI, PC, leg. 759B.
60. Pablo Morillo to Ministry of War, Valencia, 22 April 1818, Rodríguez Villa, *Pablo Morillo*, vol. 3, pp. 563–67. Cf. Pablo Morillo to Ministry of War, Barquisimeto, 22 July 1818, Rodríguez Villa, *Pablo Morillo*, vol. 3, pp. 596–600. Cf. Christon Archer, *The Army in Bourbon Mexico, 1760–1810*, University of New Mexico Press (Albuquerque, 1977), pp. 254–55.
61. Pablo Morillo to Minister of War, Caño de Atamayca, 28 February 1819, Rodríguez Villa, *Pablo Morillo*, vol. 4, pp. 10–14.
62. See, for example, Valentín Capmany to Gabriel de Torres, Mompós, 4 April 1816, AGI, PC, leg. 712.
63. Mercado, *Campaña de invasión*, p. 26.
64. Francisco Montalvo to Juan Sámano, Cartagena, 30 January 1818, *Los últimos virreyes*, p. 21.
65. Laura Ullrick, 'Morillo's Attempt to Pacify Venezuela', *HAHR*, vol. 3 (1920), pp. 541–42; and Pablo Morillo to Ministry of War, Santa Fe, 31 May 1816, Rodríguez Villa, *Pablo Morillo*, vol. 3, p. 162.
66. Ministry of State to Ministry of War, Madrid, 15 March 1817, Rodríguez Villa, *Pablo Morillo*, vol. 3, pp. 646–48; and Ejército Expedicionario, Resumen histórico de las operaciones y movimientos de las columnas y tropas … desde el mes de noviembre

de 1816, AGI, PC, leg. 759B.

67. See Sebastián González García, 'El aniquilamiento del ejército expedicionario de Costa Firme (1815–1823)', *Revista de Indias*, vol. 22, p. 138.
68. Pablo Morillo to Ministry of War, Santa Fe, 17 September 1816, Rodríguez Villa, *Pablo Morillo*, vol. 3, pp. 216–17.
69. Pablo Morillo to Ministry of War, Valencia, 25 January 1818, Rodríguez Villa, *Pablo Morillo*, vol. 3, pp, 493–98.
70. Toribio Montes to Francisco Montalvo, Quito, 21 June 1817, AGI, ASF, leg. 631. See also Juan Sámano to Pablo Morillo, Popayán, 19 August 1816, BRAH, sig. 9/7665 (leg. 22), fols 55–58; Manuel Ficillo to Agirra, Sitio Nuevo, 17 February 1820, AGI, PC, leg. 747; and, for efforts at drafting students, see José Más and Santiago de Lecuna to Gabriel de Torres, Cartagena, 16 March 1818, AGI, PC, leg. 716. See also Vicente Sánchez Lima to Francisco Montalvo, Medellín, 4 August 1817, AGI, ASF, leg. 631. For many complaints about recruitment of soldiers in Buga in 1817, see the numerous letters from the Cabildo de Buga to the military commander of Buga, Buga, 1817, AGI, Estado, leg. 57, doc. 35–D (1b). For comparisons with the royalist military in Mexico, see Anna, *The Fall of Royal Government in Mexico City*, pp. 84–86, 89–90.
71. See Ayuntamiento de Ríohacha to Council of the Indies, Ríohacha, 6 May 1813, AGI, ASF, leg. 746; Cayetano Sarmiento to José Solís, Llanogrande, 12 August 1817 and Cayetano Sarmiento to José Solís, Llanogrande, 19 August 1817; both in AGI, Estado, leg. 57, doc. 35–D (1b); and Pérez, *Guerra irregular*, p. 364.
72. Pascual Enrile to Pablo Morillo, Madrid, 15 July 1817, Rodríguez Villa, *Pablo Morillo*, vol. 3, pp. 331–32. See also Pablo Morillo to Ministry of War, Valencia, 22 April 1818, Rodríguez Villa, *Pablo Morillo*, vol. 3, pp. 563–67.
73. Francisco Montalvo to Minister of Grace and Justice, Cartagena, 24 September 1817, AGI, ASF, leg. 631.
74. During the war against their own revolted American colonies, the British had lost nearly thirty per cent of their soldiers to desertion. See Mackesy, *The War for America*, p. 176.
75. Woodward, 'The Spanish Army and the Loss of America', p. 590.
76. Woodward, 'Spain and the Loss of America', p. 591. See also Toribio Montes to Ministers of State and Overseas, Quito, 22 July 1815, AGI, AQ, leg. 275; Valentín Capmany to Gabriel de Torres, Mompós, 17 October 1816, AGI, PC, leg. 712; list of individuals who have deserted the Battalion de Infantería de Tambo, 1817, AHNC, Archivo Anexo, Guerra y Marina, tomo 152, ff. 218–19; Minister of State to Minister of War, Madrid, 15 March 1818, Rodríguez Villa, *Pablo Morillo*, vol. 3, pp. 646–48; Pablo Morillo to Minister of Overseas, Barquisimeto, 31 October 1820, AGI, Indiferente General, leg. 1568; list of deserters from 27 August 1821 to 8 October 1821, AGI, PC, leg. 717. For comparative figures for the insurgent armies in Río de la Plata, see Hans Vogel, 'The Wars of Independence in Northwest Argentina, 1810–1814', unpublished conference paper, Fourth Spanish-Dutch Historical Colloquium (Avila, 1991).
77. Bando de Pablo Morillo, Cumaná, 2 May 1815, BRAH, Sig. 9/7651 (leg. 8); Circular of Francisco Montalvo, Torrecillas, 20 September 1815, AGI, PC, leg. 707; Circular de Gabriel de Torres, Cartagena, 19 March 1816, AGI, PC, leg. 717;

Orden General del Día, 5 February 1817, BRAH, Sig. 9/7651 (leg. 8); Pablo Morillo to Miguel de la Torre, Parapara, 23 January 1819, BRAH, Colección Morillo, sig. 9/7664 (leg. 21), ff. 76–77; and Bando de Pablo Morillo, Calabozo, 30 June 1819, Alberto Lee López (ed.), *Los ejércitos del Rey, 1819*, vol. 2, Biblioteca de la Presidencia de la República (Bogotá, 1989), pp. 188–90.

78. Woodward, 'The Spanish Army and the Loss of America', pp. 587, 593. See also Enciso Recio, *La opinión pública española*, p. 54n; Costeloe, 'Spain and the Spanish American Wars of Independence', p. 230, and Fernández Almagro, *La emancipación de América*, pp. 92, 97–98.
79. See Camilo Riaño, *Historia Militar: La independencia (1810–1815)*, Historia Extensa de Colombia, vol. 18, Ediciones Lerner (Bogotá, 1971), pp. 19–28. For the militias, see Allan J. Kuethe, *Military Reform and Society in New Granada, 1773–1808*, University of Florida Press (Gainsville, 1978).
80. See Albi, *Banderas olvidadas*, p. 52.
81. Francisco Montalvo to Juan Sámano, Cartagena, 30 January 1818, *Los últimos virreyes*, pp, 94–100.
82. Bando de Gabriel de Torres, Cartagena, 22 November 1816, AGI, PC, leg. 717.
83. Instrucciones particulares a los jefes del ejército, by Pablo Morillo, aboard the San Pedro, 1 April 1815, AHNM, Estado, leg. 8717, doc. 16.
84. Rodríguez Villa, *Pablo Morillo*, vol. 1 (1920), pp. 240, 300.
85. See Juan Sámano to Pablo Morillo, Santa Fe, 29 August 1818, BRAH, sig. 9/7665 (leg. 22), fols 607–9; and González García, 'El aniquilamiento del ejército expedicionario', pp. 138–39.
86. For a clear example, see Instructions to Francisco González de Linares and Pedro José Mijares, Caracas, 18 January 1821, AHNM, Estado, leg. 8733, doc. 24.
87. Pablo Morillo to Ministry of War, Caracas, 5 October 1817, Rodríguez Villa, *Pablo Morillo*, vol. 3, pp, 448–50. See also Ruperto Delgado to José Solís, Popayán, 14 July 1817, AGI, ASF, leg. 631.
88. Pablo Morillo to José de Abascal, Torrecillas, 21 October 1815, AGI, Diversos, leg. 4.
89. Liévano, *Los grandes conflictos*, vol. 1, pp. 894–95; and Cajigal, *Memorias*, p. 148. Morillo did, however, retain considerable respect for Morales, as his correspondence with him shows.
90. See letters of Pablo Morillo to Miguel de la Torre, February–March 1816, AHNM, Estado, leg. 8717, docs 42, 45, 48.
91. See González García, 'El aniquilamineto del ejército expedicionario', p. 140.

4: Conciliation or Confrontation?

1. Cabildo of Pasto to Ferdinand, Pasto, 13 June 1814, BL, Egerton, vol. 1809.
2. Consulado de Caracas, 20 December 1816, Ildefonso Leal (ed.), *Documentos del Real Consulado de Caracas*, Universidad Central de Venezuela (Caracas, 1964), p. 187.
3. Hector García Chuecos (ed.), *Causas de Infidencia: Documentos inéditos relativos a la Revolución de la Independencia*, vol. 2, Imprenta Nacional (Caracas, 1952), pp. 231, 241.
4. See Roberto Arrazola, *Los Mártires responden ...*, Ediciones Hernández (Cartagena,

1973), pp. 9–35, for transcripts of the trials.

5. See Interrogation of Tomás Vásquez, Havana, 15 February 1816, AGI, PC, leg. 891A. For another nice example, see the various documents relating to the priest Juan Marcelo Laguna in AGI, Audiencia de Caracas, leg. 386. Father Laguna attributed his former insurgency to 'weakness, fear, and a poor understanding of politics'.
6. Bando de Francisco Montalvo, Santa Marta, 26 August 1814, AGI, Audiencia de Caracas, leg. 109.
7. Bando de Gabriel de Torres, Cartagena, 28 December 1815, AGI, PC, leg. 717.
8. Juan Sámano to Ministry of State, Santa Fe, 29 May 1818, AGI, Estado, leg. 53, Doc. 44.
9. Plan de Gobierno de la Junta Superior … de Secuestros de Caracas, Caracas, 2 June 1815, AGI, Audiencia de Caracas, legs 109, 386.
10. Report by the Council of the Indies, Madrid, 18 May 1818, AGI, ASF, leg. 549.
11. Cajigal, *Memorias*, pp. 142, 163.
12. Report by the Council of the Indies, 14 February 1819, AGI, ASF, leg. 551; and Bando de Francisco Montalvo, Santa Marta, 26 August 1814, AGI, Audiencia de Caracas, leg. 109.
13. The Spanish Juntas de Purificación are discussed in Anna, *Spain and the Loss of America.* See also Royal Order of 13 April 1815, AGI, PC, leg. 718.
14. Francisco Montalvo to Gabriel de Torres, Cartagena, 6 February 1816; and Francisco Montalvo to Gabriel de Torres, Cartagena, 13 December 1815; both in AGI, PC, leg. 707.
15. The documents related to the trial are reproduced in Jiménez Molinares, *Los mártires de Cartagena.*
16. Leaflet by the Ministry of War, Madrid, 28 July 1817, AGI, ASF, leg. 665 (also in AGI, ASF, leg. 748). The Venezuelan Courts-Martial are discussed in Stoan, *Pablo Morillo.*
17. See Carlos Cortés Vargas, 'De la época del terror', *BHA*, vol. 29 (1942), p. 89. It appears that a brief written record summarizing the trial was made at the end of the hearing when the accused was a royalist soldier. See Proclama de Pablo Morillo, Santa Fe, 5 August 1816, Rodríguez Villa, *Pablo Morillo*, vol. 3, pp. 98–101.
18. Representation by Doña Francisca Morena e Isabella, Santa Fe, 19 October 1817, AGI, ASF, leg. 549. Also see Caballero, *Diario*, p. 219.
19. Restrepo Saenz, *Gobernadores de Antioquia*, vol. 1, p. 350. See also Report on the case of Jorge Tadeo Lozano, 1818, AGI, ASF, leg. 551; Caballero, *Diario*, p. 218; and Report by the Minister of War, Palace, 1 October 1818, AGI, ASF, leg. 580.
20. Petition by Juan Manuel Arrubla, Valencia, 4 October 1817, AGI, ASF, leg. 549.
21. Report by the Fiscal de Perú, Madrid, 7 April 1818, AGI, ASF, leg. 665.
22. See, for example, Report by the Council of the Indies, 17 January 1818, AGI, ASF, leg. 551; Arámbarri, *Hechos del General Pablo Morillo*, p, 90; and Pablo Morillo to the Duke of Manchester, Mompós, 15 March 1816, Rodríguez Villa, *Pablo Morillo*, vol. 3, p. 4.
23. Leaflet by the Ministry of War, Madrid, 28 July 1817, AGI, ASF, legs 665, 748.
24. Francisco Montalvo, Relación de Mando, 30 January 1818, *Los últimos virreyes*, p. 158; Francisco de Paula Santander to Simón Bolívar, Santa Fe, 10 October 1819,

in *Cartas Santander-Bolívar*, vol. 1, Biblioteca de la Presidencia de la República (Bogotá, 1988) vol. 1: 1813–1820, pp. 133–35; Exposition by Pascual Enrile, Madrid, 19 June 1817, AGI, Estado, leg. 57, Doc 35–c (2a) (also in AGI, ASF, leg. 748); Stoan, *Pablo Morillo*, p. 141; and Caballero, *Diario*, pp. 210–28. For other reports on executions, see Díaz, *La reconquista española*, vol. 1, pp. 119–25; Francisco Xavier Arámbarri, *Hechos del General Pablo Morillo* en América (1821), Ediciones de la Embajada de Venezuela en España (Murcia, 1971), Introduction by Carlos Capriles Ayala, p. 15. Restrepo reported 125 executions. See Restrepo, *Historia de la revolución*, vol. 2, p. 142.

25. Pardon by Pablo Morillo, Santa Fe, 30 May 1816, AGI, ASF, leg. 551.
26. Borrador de Ystoria del Cuartel General, desde 30 de Mayo de 1816 a 18 de Agosto del mismo, AGI, PC, leg. 759A, and Report by ASF, Cartagena, 17 December 1816, AGI, ASF, leg. 631.
27. Some individuals were allegedly purified first in the Council of Purification, and then charged with other offences in the Permanent Court-Martial.
28. Representation by Primo Groot, 9 August 1818, AGI, ASF, leg. 748.
29. See Certification of the Purification of Martín Urdaneta, Santa Fe, 27 June 1816, AGI, ASF, leg. 631.
30. See Guillermo Hernández de Alba, 'Recuerdos de la reconquista: el Consejo de Purificación', *BHA*, vol. 22 (1935).
31. Rodríguez Villa, *Pablo Morillo*, (1920), vol. 1, pp. 234–35.
32. See Roberto Jaramillo, *El clero en la independencia*, Universidad de Antioquia (Medellín, 1946); Brian Hamnett, 'The Counter Revolution of Morillo and the Insurgent Clerics of New Granada, 1815–1820', *The Americas*, vol. 32 (1976); and Leslie Bethell, 'A Note on the Church and the Independence of Latin America', Leslie Bethell (ed.), *Independence of Latin America*, Cambridge University Press (Cambridge, 1987).
33. Report by Council of the Indies, 31 May 1818, AGI, Estado, leg. 57, doc. 37.
34. See Morillo's list of insurgent clerics from New Granada, Santa Fe, 23 October 1816, Hamnett, 'Morillo and the Insurgent Clerics', pp. 615–17.
35. Report by Council of the Indies, 22 August 1819, AGI, ASF, leg. 551. See also Hamnett, 'Popular Insurrection and Royalist Reaction', p. 306.
36. Pardons were issued as follows: 15 October 1810 by the Cortes, 25 May 1812 by President Toribio Montes (for Quito), 24 May 1814 by Ferdinand, 14 October 1814 by Ferdinand, 23 September 1815 by General Pablo Morillo (for Cartagena), 9 April 1816 by Viceroy Francisco Montalvo (for Cartagena), 24 April 1816 by General Morillo (for Ocaña), 17 April 1816 by Ferdinand (this pardon was approved by the Council of the Indies on 3 October 1816 and its scope extended on 10 December 1816), 31 May 1816 by General Morillo (for Santa Fe), 24 January 1817 by Ferdinand, 7 May 1817 by Governor Vicente Sánchez Lima (for Antioquia), 12 June 1817 by General Morillo (for Cariaco), 8 November 1817 by Ferdinand (for those under military *fuero*), 1 March 1818 by General Morillo, 24 April 1818 by General Morillo (for Valencia), 18 and 22 September 1818 by General Morillo (for Caracas), 9 November 1819 by Ferdinand, 20 December 1819 by Ferdinand, 15 January 1820 by Ferdinand, 9 March 1820 by Ferdinand, 19 July 1820 by Ferdinand, 27 September 1820 and 10 October 1820 by the Cortes.

37. Indulto de Francisco Montalvo, Cartagena, 9 April 1816, AGI, PC, leg. 747 (also in AGI, ASF, leg. 747). See also Francisco Montalvo to Gabriel de Torres, Cartagena, 7 June 1816, AGI, PC, leg. 707.
38. See, for example, Report by the Secretary of State, the Palace, 6 September 1818, AGI, ASF, leg. 549; Pedro Groot to the Council of the Indies, Santa Fe, 19 March 1818, AGI, ASF, leg. 549; and Representation by Primo Groot, 9 August 1818, AGI, ASF, leg. 748.
39. Report by the Council of the Indies, 22 August 1819, AGI, ASF, leg. 551; and Francisco Xavier de Manzanos y Castillo to Minister Universal, Quito, 22 April 1820, AGI, AQ, leg. 236. See also Report on Francisco Xavier de Torres y Roxas, 1819, AGI, PC leg. 888.
40. Rodríguez Villa, *Pablo Morillo*, vol. 3, pp. 239–41. See also Valentín Capmany to Gabriel de Torres, Mompós, 16 July 1816, AGI, PC, leg. 712; and Ignacio Romero to Gabriel de Torres, Cartagena, 30 April 1816, AGI, PC, leg. 710A, for examples of military unwillingness to regard *indultados* as innocent.
41. See for example, Pablo Morillo to the Council of the Indies, Barquisimeto, 16 July 1818, AGI, ASF, leg. 551; Juan Sámano to Ministry of War, Santa Fe, 19 December 1819, AGI, PC, leg. 720A; José María de Alos to Ministry of War, 9 October 1819, AGI, Estado, leg. 57, Doc. 40; Report of the Royal Pardon of 24 January 1817, Caracas, 21 September 1817, AGI, Audiencia de Caracas, leg. 386; Report by the Council of the Indies, 20 June 1818, AGI, ASF, leg. 549; and Pablo Morillo to the Council of the Indies, Calabozo, 10 July 1819, AGI, ASF, leg. 549.
42. For comments on this point, see Juan Friede, *La otra verdad*, p. 39.
43. Pablo Morillo to Ministry of War, Santa Fe, 17 September 1816, Rodríguez Villa, *Pablo Morillo*, vol. 3, pp. 218–23. Such disagreements were at first covered up. See Pablo Morillo to Francisco de Abascal, Torrecilla, 21 October 1815, AGI, Diversos, leg. 4.
44. See Pablo Morillo to Ministry of War, Santa Fe, 17 September 1816 and Calabazo, 22 December 1817, Rodríguez Villa, *Pablo Morillo*, vol. 3, pp. 218–23, 469–74; and Pablo Morillo to Juan Sámano, Santa Fe, 6 September 1816, BRAH, Sig. 9/7665 (leg. 22), fol. 76. The Instructions are printed in Rodríguez Villa, *Pablo Morillo*, vol. 2, pp. 437–48.
45. Francisco Montalvo to Ministry of Grace and Justice, Cartagena, 24 September 1817, AGI, ASF, leg. 631. See also Francisco Montalvo to Pablo Morillo, Cartagena, 19 August 1816, AHNM, Estado, leg. 8739, Doc. 139; and Report by the Council of the Indies, 14 February 1817, AGI, ASF, leg. 549.
46. Stoan, *Pablo Morillo*, p. 74.
47. Liévano, *Los Grandes conflictos*, vol. 2, p. 909. Also see Arámbarri, *Hechos del General Pablo Morillo*, p. 14; Pablo Morillo to the Duke of Manchester, Mompós, 15 March 1816 and Pablo Morillo to Luís de Onís, Santa Fe, 23 June 1816, both in Rodríguez Villa, *Pablo Morillo*, vol. 3, pp. 4–5, 22–23; and Proclama de Pablo Morillo a los hombres leales de Cartagena, Torrecilla, 23 September 1815, AGI, ASF, leg. 747.
48. See two letters of Pablo Morillo to Miguel de La Torre, Guadalupe, 19 May 1816, AHNM, Estado, leg. 8717, Docs 68, 69 (doc. 69, quoted here, is also printed in full in Díaz, *La reconquista española*, vol. 1, pp. 76–77). Also see Pablo Morillo to Salvador de Moxó, Santa Fe, 24 June 1816, AGI, Audiencia de Caracas, leg. 386;

and Report on letter by Andrés Rosillo, AGI, ASF, leg. 1017. La Torre's pardon is reproduced in Tovar, 'Guerras de opinión', p. 218.

49. Restrepo Saenz, *Biografías de los mandatarios y ministros*, p. 258. See also Pablo Morillo to Ministry of War, Santa Fe, 31 May 1816, and Calabozo, 22 December 1817, Rodríguez Villa, *Pablo Morillo*, vol. 3, pp. 164–69, 469–74; and Report by Pascual Enrile, Madrid, 18 May 1819, AHNM, Estado, leg. 8739, doc. 139.
50. Francisco Montalvo to Ministry of Grace and Justice, Cartagena, 24 September 1817, AGI, ASF, leg. 631.
51. Report by Council of the Indies, 14 February 1817, AGI, ASF, leg. 549.
52. See, for example, Francisco Montalvo to the Ministry of Grace and Justice, Cartagena, 20 August 1816, AGI, ASF, leg. 747; and Pablo Morillo to Minister of War, Santa Fe, 16 August 1816, Rodríguez Villa, *Pablo Morillo*, vol. 3, pp. 190–91.
53. Report by Toribio Montes, Quito, 7 April 1813, AGI, AQ, leg. 257; Proclama de Montes, Quito, 1 July 1817, BRAH, Sig. 9/7665 (leg. 22), fol. 470; Toribio Montes to Ministry of State, Quito, 26 July 1817, AGI, AQ, leg. 259; and Juan Ramírez to Ministry of Hacienda, Quito, 21 November 1818, AGI, AQ, leg. 260.
54. José de Abascal to Toribio Montes, Lima, 7 December 1813, AGI, AQ, leg. 258; Toribio Montes to Ministers of State and War, Quito, 7 July 1814, AGI, AQ, leg. 260; Toribio Montes to Ministry of Overseas, Quito, 7 October 1814, AGI, AQ, leg. 260; Toribio Montes to Ministry of State, Quito, 22 May 1815, AGI, AQ, leg. 258; Toribio Montes to Francisco Montalvo, Quito, 21 June 1817, AGI, ASF, leg. 631; and Report by Ministry of War, 29 January 1818, AGI, Estado, leg. 57, doc 35C.
55. Joaquín Miguel de Araujo to Juan Sámano, Quito, 21 November 1816, BRAH, Sig. 9/7665 (leg. 22), fol. 146; and Suplica particular del Ayuntamiento de Quito, n.d., AGI, AQ, leg. 275. For Montalvo's relations with Montes, see Francisco Montalvo to Ministry of Grace and Justice, Cartagena, 24 September 1817, AGI, ASF, leg. 631.
56. León Pereda de Sarabia to Pedro Macanas, Quito, 7 December 1814 and León Pereda de Sarabia to Cristóbal de Góngora, Quito, 20 December 1814, AGI, AQ, leg. 275. Also see Juan Ramírez to Ministry of Hacienda, Quito, 21 December 1818, AGI, AQ, leg. 260; Andrés, Bishop of Cuenca to Toribio Acebal, Cuenca, 14 January 1813, AGI, Diversos, leg. 3. Recent accounts inaccurately describe Montes as an implacable hardliner opposed to pardons. See Jorge Salvador Lara, *Quito*, MAPFRE (Madrid, 1992), p. 184.
57. Extensive (and conflicting) details of the attempted coup may be found in AGI, AQ, leg. 275.
58. Report to Ministry of War, 29 January 1818, AGI, Estado 57, Doc 35C; and José Solís to Francisco Montalvo, Popayán, 20 June 1817, AGI, ASF, leg. 631.
59. For good examples, see Vicente Romero to José Solís, Anserma, 22 May 1817; Ruperto Delgado to José Solís, Popayán, 13 July 1817; and Francisco Montalvo to José Solís, Cartagena, 18 August 1817, AGI, ASF, leg. 631.
60. Ruperto Delgado to Juan Sámano, Popayán, 20 July 1817, AGI, ASF, leg. 631. Also see José María Barreiro to Juan Sámano, Molinos, 10 July 1819, AGI, PC, leg. 747.

5: The Reconquest of the Economy

1. Circular by Francisco Montalvo, Torrecilla, 30 November 1815, AGI, PC, leg. 707.
2. See McFarlane, *Colombia before Independence*, esp. pp. 297–307; and also Malcolm Deas, 'The Fiscal Problems of Nineteenth-Century Colombia', *JLAS*, vol. 14 (1982).
3. José María Ramírez to Francisco Montalvo, Cartagena, 30 August 1817, AGI, ASF, leg. 631. See also Manuel Alonso Velasco to Juan Sámano, Popayán, 20 May 1819, AHNC, Visitas del Cauca, tomo 4, ff. 741–45.
4. For example, Juan Ramírez to Minister of Hacienda, Quito, 6 February 1819, AGI, AQ, leg. 261.
5. Aníbal Galindo, quoted in Jaime Jaramillo U., Adolfo Meisal R., and Miguel Urrutia M., 'Continuities and Discontinuities in the Fiscal and Monetary Institutions of New Granada, 1783–1850', unpublished conference paper delivered at the Buenos Aires pre-conference of the Twelfth International Economic History Congress (Seville, 1998).
6. See Jaramillo, Meisal and Urrutia, 'Continuities and Discontinuities'.
7. See McFarlane, *Colombia before Independence*, pp. 71–95, for information about mining in New Granada. Ann Twinam discusses mining in Antioquia; see Ann Twinam, *Miners, Merchants, and Farmers in Colonial Colombia*, University of Texas Press (Austin, 1982).
8. Hermes Tovar Pinzón, 'La lenta ruptura con el pasado colonial (1810–1850)', José Antonio Ocampo (ed.), *Historia económica de Colombia*, Siglo Veintiuno (Bogotá, 1987), pp. 103–4; and Toribio Montes to Francisco Montalvo, Quito, 21 June 1817, AGI, ASF, leg. 631.
9. See Francisco Gregorio de Angulo to José Solís, Popayán, 16(?) July 1817, AGI, ASF, leg. 631. See also Report on the state of the real hacienda, Mompós, 24 July 1816, AGI, PC, leg. 712.
10. Restrepo, *Historia de la revolución*, vol. 1, p. 25; and McFarlane, *Colombia before Independence*, p. 365.
11. See Anthony McFarlane, 'The Transition from Colonialism in Colombia, 1819–1875', in Christopher Abel and Colin Lewis (eds), *Latin America: Economic Imperialism and the State: The Political Economy of the External Connection from Independence to the Present*, The Athlone Press (London, 1985), p. 102; Malcolm Deas, 'Venezuela, Colombia and Ecuador', in Leslie Bethell (ed.), *Spanish America After Independence, c.1820–c.1870*, Cambridge University Press (Cambridge, 1987), p. 210. Cf. David Bushnell, *The Making of Modern Colombia*, University of California Press (Berkeley, 1993), pp. 48–49.
12. McFarlane, *Colombia before Independence*, pp. 75–79.
13. Vicente Romero to José Solís, Anserma, 22 May 1817, AGI, ASF, leg. 631; and Brian Hamnett, 'Popular Insurrection and Royalist Reaction', pp. 297–98. See also Tulio Halperín Donghi, 'Economy and Society', in Leslie Bethell (ed.), *Spanish America after Independence, c. 1820–1870*, Cambridge University Press (Cambridge, 1987), pp. 9–11.
14. Bushnell, *The Making of Modern Colombia*, p. 80.
15. McFarlane, 'The Transition from Colonialism in Colombia', pp. 102–3; and Izard, *El miedo a la revolución*, p. 40.

16. See, for example, Vicente Romero to José Solís, Anserma, 22 May 1817, AGI, ASF, leg. 631; and also David Bushnell, *The Santander Regime in Gran Colombia*, Greenwood Press (Westport, 1970), pp. 127–28.
17. Zamira Díaz de Zuluaga, 'La fuerza de trabajo en el Cauca Grande: 1810–1830', in Germán Colmenares *et al.*, *La independencia: ensayos de historia social*, Instituto Colombiano de Cultura (Bogotá, 1986), p. 57.
18. Asesor Carvajal to José Solís, Popayán, 8 July 1817; Cabildo of Buga to José Solís, Buga, 30 June 1817, both in AGI, ASF, leg. 631; and also Zamira Díaz de Zuluaga, 'El Cauca Grande en la independencia; estructura económico-social (1800–1830), *Raices Históricas*, Academia Nariñense de Historia (Pasto, 1987), pp. 99–100.
19. Diary of the Primer Batallón del Regimiento de Infantería de Numancia, March 1817, AGI, PC, leg. 759A. See also anonymous *hacendado* to Vicente Sánchez Lima, Vicente Sánchez Lima to Francisco Montalvo, Medellín, 4 August 1817, AGI, ASF, leg. 631.
20. J.P. Hamilton, *Travels through the Interior Provinces of Colombia*, John Murray (London, 1827), vol. 2, p. 44. See also López, *Memorias*, vol. 1, p. 58.
21. Pérez, *Guerra irregular*, p. 392.
22. See John Keegan, *A History of Warfare*, Hutchinson (London, 1993), pp. 301–15.
23. Diario de operaciones de la Colunma Volante del Primer Batallón del Regimiento de Infantería del Rey, 17 August 1817, AGI, PC, leg. 759A.
24. Plano de observaciones topográficas de la provincia de Antioquia, 12 May 1816, AGI, PC, leg. 897.
25. Report by Council of the Indies on a letter from Antioquia, 22 January 1818, AGI, ASF, leg. 551.
26. Report on letter of Benito Pérez to Minister of Hacienda, Panama, 30 March 1812, AGI, ASF, leg. 579.
27. Francisco Montalvo to Minister of State, Santa Marta, 25 February 1815, AGI, ASF, leg. 580; and Francisco Montalvo to Minister of Hacienda, Santa Marta, 23 June 1815, Santa Fe, leg. 631.
28. Gabriel de Torres to (?), Cartagena, 15 July 1819, AHNM, Estado, leg. 8725, doc. 9.
29. Report by Martín de Pando, Cartagena, 29 July 1819, AGI, PC, leg. 750.
30. See, for example, Restrepo, *Autobiografía*, p. 65; Sevilla, *Memorias*, p. 87; Eusebio Pirón to Gabriel de Torres, Turbaco, 19 January 1816, AGI, PC, leg. 712; Francisco Warleta to Juan Sámano, Cali, 22 August 1816, BRAH, sig. 9/7665 (leg. 22), fols 60–61; Diary of the Primer Batallón del Regimiento de Infantería de Numancia, April 1817, AGI, PC, leg. 759A; Toribio Montes to Francisco Montalvo, Quito, 21 June 1817; AGI, ASF, leg. 631; José María Ramírez to Ferdinand, Cartagena, 30 August 1817, AGI, ASF, leg. 631; and Manuel Fiallo to Juan Sámano, Sitio Nuevo, 19 February 1820, AGI, PC, leg. 747.
31. Compare Estado que manifiesta la población y recursos de esta jurisdicción, Mompós, 16 September 1816, AGI, PC, leg. 712; with McFarlane, *Colombia before Independence*, pp. 357–78. See also Hamnett, 'Popular Insurrection and Royalist Reaction', p. 301.
32. See, for example, Diary of the Primer Batallón del Regimiento de Infantería de Numancia, March 1817, AGI, PC, leg. 759A.

33. Hamilton, *Travels through Colombia*, p. 90. See also López, *Memorias*, vol. 1, p. 58.
34. Charles Griffin, *Los temas sociales y económicos en la época de la independencia*, Fundaciones John Boulton y Eugenio Mendoza (Caracas, 1962), p. 16. Also see Tovar Pinzón, 'La lenta ruptura con el pasado', p. 90–94; and for the comments of the Swedish traveller Severin Lorich, see Carlos Vidales, 'El agente diplomático sueco Severin Lorich y su misión en la Gran Colombia (1823)', Informes de Investigación, Instituto de Estudios Latinoamericanos (Stockholm, 1991), pp. 9–10.
35. See Tovar Pinzón, 'La lenta ruptura con el pasado', pp. 92–93.
36. Caballero, *Diario*, p. 233. Cf. Hernández de Alba, 'Recuerdos de la reconquista'.
37. Francisco Montalvo to Gabriel de Torres, Cartagena, 29 February 1816, AGI, PC, leg. 707. Comparable problems occurred after the expulsion of the Jesuit Order in 1767. The colonial government was then left with the problem of converting confiscated Jesuit estates into cash. See Germán Colmenares, *Haciendas de los Jesuítas en el Nuevo Reino de Granada*, siglo XVIII, Tercer Mundo (Bogotá, 1983).
38. Francisco Montalvo to Pablo Morillo, Cartagena, 13 July 1816, AGI, PC, leg. 707.
39. Jaramillo, Meisal and Urrutia, 'Continuities and Discontinuities'; McFarlane, *Colombia before Independence*, pp. 222–23; Allan J. Kuethe, 'The Early Reforms of Charles III in the Viceroyalty of New Granada, 1759–1776', in *Reform and Insurrection in Bourbon New Granada and Peru*, p. 31; Report on the Tobacco Monopoly by Ramón de Herrera, Cartagena, 12 February 1816, AGI, PC, leg. 717; and Report on the Rentas Reales by Ventura Ferrer, Cartagena, 1 September 1817, AGI, PC, leg. 715. Restrepo gives an annual figure of $470,000. See Restrepo, *Historia de la revolución*, vol. 1, pp. 28–29.
40. Restrepo, *Historia de la revolución*, vol. 1, pp. 112, 150.
41. Carlos Meyner to (?), Panama, 29 November 1813, AGI, Audiencia de Panama, leg. 262. The monopoly was, moreover, abolished by the Cortes in March 1814, although this decree was overturned after the return of Ferdinand. (See José María Ots y Capdequi, *Las instituciones del Nuevo Reino de Granada al tiempo de la independencia*, Consejo Superior de Investigaciones Científicas (Madrid, 1958), pp. 354–55).
42. Francisco Montalvo to Gabriel de Torres, Cartagena, 22 June 1816, AGI, PC, leg. 707. See also Report on the Tobacco Monopoly by Ramón de Herrera, Cartagena, 12 February 1816, AGI, PC, leg. 717. See also Josef María de la Verga to Gabriel de Torres, Cartagena, 21 March 1816, AGI, PC, leg. 717; Estado general … [de] la real renta de tabacos del Departamento de Cartagena desde el día 20 de agosto de 1816 … hasta del día 31 de diciembre del año pasado de 1818, Cartagena, 22 April 1819, AGI, PC, leg. 715; and Various documents related to tobacco monopoly in AGI, PC, leg. 707.
43. Estado general … [de] la real renta de tavacos del Departamento de Cartagena desde el día 20 de agosto de 1816 … hasta del día 31 de diciembre del año pasado de 1818, Cartagena, 22 April 1819, AGI, PC, leg. 715. Cf. Izard, *El miedo a la revolución*, p. 117; in Venezuela, income declined by more than eighty per cent.
44. See Monthly and annual reports from cajas reales de Mompós, 1817–1818, AGI, PC, leg. 715.
45. See Griffin, *Los temas sociales*, p. 34; and Report on Tobacco in Valledupar, Cartagena, 15 October 1819, AGI, PC, leg. 742.
46. Gabriel de Torres to Alejandro Ramírez, Cartagena, 5 June 1820, AGI, PC, leg.

714; Report by administrador de tabacos, Cartagena, 24 September 1819, AGI, PC, leg. 742; and Report by administrador de tabacos, Cartagena, 24 September 1819, AGI, PC, leg. 742. Excess tobacco from other royalist regions was also sent to Cartagena to augment the city's supply; see Report by contador general de tabacos, Cartagena, 18 November 1819, AGI, PC, leg. 742.

47. Isidro Villareal to Contador general de tabacos, Popayán, 21 September 1819, AGI, PC, leg. 742; and José Solís to Simón Sicilia, Popayán, 16 July 1817, AGI, ASF, leg. 631.
48. Isidro Villareal to José Rodríguez, Popayán, 8 September 1819, AGI, PC, leg. 742. See also Isidro Villareal to contador general de tabacos, Popayán, 21 September 1819, AGI, PC, leg. 742. For information on eighteenth-century opposition to the tobacco monopoly, see McFarlane, *Colombia before Independence*, pp. 214–15.
49. Griffin, *Los temas sociales*, p. 44; and Circular by Francisco Montalvo, Torrecilla, 30 November 1815, AGI, PC, leg. 707. For the fiscal importance of the *aguardiente* monopoly, see Jaramillo, Meisal and Urrutia, 'Continuities and Discontinuities'.
50. Circular de Francisco Montalvo, Torrecilla, 30 November 1815, AGI, PC, leg. 717.
51. Circular de Gabriel de Torres, Cartagena, 11 May 1816, AGI, PC, leg. 717; and Orders relating to the re-establishment of the *aguardiente* monopoly, Cartagena, May 1816, AGI, PC, leg. 707.
52. Bando de Gabriel de Torres, Cartagena, 11 June 1816, AGI, PC, leg. 717. Sugar producers had opposed the monopoly for some decades. See Kuethe, *Military Reform and Society*, p. 64; Anthony McFarlane, '"The Rebellion of the Barrios": Urban Insurrection in Bourbon Quito', in *Reform and Insurrection in Bourbon New Granada and Peru*, p. 287; and Rebecca Earle, 'Indian Rebellion and Bourbon Reform in New Granada: Riots in Pasto, 1780–1800', *HAHR*, vol. 73 (1993), p. 104.
53. Francisco Montalvo to Juan Sámano, Cartagena, 30 January 1818, *Los últimos virreyes*, p. 191; and Report by Council of the Indies, 14 February 1817, AGI, ASF, leg. 549.
54. See Report by Ventura Ferrer, Cartagena, 1 September 1817, and various reports on the cajas reales de Cartagena; all in AGI, PC, leg. 715.
55. See Report by Ventura Ferrer, Cartagena, 1 September 1817, AGI, PC, leg. 715; and Report on income in Cartagena in 1809, AGI, PC, leg. 717.
56. Report by contador general de aguardiente, Cartagena, 29 October 1819, AGI, PC, leg. 742. See also Estado que manifiesta el consumo de caudales, Cartagena, 20, April 1819, nota 1, AGI, PC, leg. 715.
57. For eighteenth-century opposition to the *aguardiente* monopoly, see Gilma Lucía Mora de Tovar, *Aguardiente y conflictos sociales en la Nueva Granada durante el siglo XVIII*, Universidad Nacional de Colombia (Bogotá, 1988).
58. Costeloe, *Response to Revolution*, p. 122.
59. Report by Martín de Pando, Cartagena, 29 July 1819, AGI, PC, leg. 750; Juan Sámano to Gabriel de Torres, Santa Fe, 29 March 1819, AGI, PC, leg. 708; and Gabriel de Torres to Ferdinand, Cartagena, 15 July 1819, Bossa Herazo, *Cartagena independiente*, pp. 69–76.
60. Bando de la Suprema Junta de Santa Fe, Santa Fe, 24 September 1810, AGI, ASF, leg. 668; and Ots y Capdequi, *Las instituciones del Nuevo Reino de Granada*, p. 364. See

also Mark van Allen, 'The Lingering Death of the Indian Tribute in Ecuador', *HAHR*, vol. 61 (1981).

61. Tomás de Acosta to Regency, Santa Marta, 23 August 1811, AGI, ASF, leg. 745; and Restrepo Tirado, *Historia de la Provincia de Santa Marta*, vol. 2, p. 336.
62. Heredia, *Planes españoles*, p. 120; and Anna, *Spain and the Loss of America*, p. 94.
63. Circular de Francisco Montalvo, Torrecilla, 30 November 1815, AGI, PC, leg. 717; and Francisco Montalvo to Gabriel de Torres, Cartagena, 30 August 1817, AGI, PC, leg. 708. See also Ots y Capdequi, *Las instituciones del Nuevo Reino de Granada*, p. 383.
64. See Report by the Council of the Indies, 21 August 1818, AGI, ASF, leg. 549. Similar plans to establish a monthly lottery in Caracas had already been examined; see Martín de Garay to (?), Palacio, 13 March 1817, AGI, Audiencia de Caracas, leg. 386.
65. See Timothy Anna, 'The Last Viceroys of New Spain and Peru: An appraisal', *American Historical Review*, vol. 81 (1976), p. 54; and Anna, *The Fall of the Royal Government in Mexico City*, p. 156.
66. See Martín de Garay to José Manuel de Aparici, Palacio, 30 December 1816, AGI, Audiencia de Lima, leg. 1618; and also Juan Sámano to Comandante of Mompós, Santa Fe, 28 February 1819, AGI, PC, leg. 708.
67. Jaramillo, Meisal and Urrutia, 'Continuities and Discontinuities' (in 1808 income from *alcabalas* and tribute overtook the *almojarifazgo*).
68. See McFarlane, *Colombia before Independence*, pp. 126–84 *passim*, 297–307; Grahn, *The Political Economy of Smuggling;* and John Fisher, *Trade, War and Revolution: Exports from Spain to Spanish America, 1797–1820*, Institute of Latin American Studies (University of Liverpool, 1992), pp. 25, 91. See also Report by Martín de Pando, Cartagena, 29 July 1819, AGI, PC, leg. 750; Estado que manifiesta el consumo de caudales, Cartagena, 20, April 1819, nota 3; and Report on expenses in Cartagena before the war, n.d.; both in AGI, PC, leg. 715.
69. For comments about the attitude to free trade of Spain's governments during the war, see Costeloe, *Response to Revolution*, pp, 119–48.
70. See McFarlane, *Colombia before Independence*, pp. 311–23; and for general comments, Anna, *Spain and the Loss of America*, pp. 229–31.
71. For Viceroy Amar's introduction of free trade in 1808, see McFarlane, *Colombia before Independence*, pp. 338–39.
72. Bando de Gabriel de Torres, Cartagena, 3 September 1816, AGI, PC, leg. 717; and Pablo Morillo to Luis de Onís, Santa Fe, 17 August 1816, Rodríguez Villa, *Pablo Morillo*, vol. 3, p. 26.
73. Gabriel de Torres, Cartagena, 3 September 1816, AGI, PC, leg. 717.
74. Bando de Gabriel de Torres, Cartagena, 16 February 1816, AGI, PC, leg. 717.
75. See Various reports on the Aduana in Cartagena, 1816–1817, in AGI, PC, leg. 715.
76. Juan Sámano to Gabriel de Torres, Santa Fe, 29 March 1819, AGI, PC, leg. 708. Sámano was appointed viceroy in August 1817, but did not take up the post until the following year.
77. Home Popham to Juan Sámano, Jamaica, 21 September 1819, AGI, PC, leg. 741B.
78. Merchants could import up to 1/3 the value of the food in other merchandise. See Proclama de Gabriel de Torres, Cartagena, 13 September 1820, AGI, PC, leg. 714.

79. Declarations of Ramón Pérez and Francisco Pérez Dávila, Havana, 11 November 1824, AGI, PC, leg. 2136A.
80. Gabriel de Torres to Minister of Hacienda, Cartagena, 18 August 1820, AGI, ASF, leg. 1017. See also Gabriel de Torres to Juan Sámano, Cartagena, 20 March 1819, Alberto Lee López (ed.), *Los ejércitos del Rey*, 1819, vol. 2, pp. 18–21; and Ventura Ferrer and Vicente Colorete to (?), Cartagena, 9 September 1819, AGI, PC, leg. 747.

6: The Cost of Reconquest

1. See Proyecto de marcha para la vanguardia de la division de los Llanos para su movimiento desde Pore a Guasdualito, December, 1816, AGI, PC, leg. 897.
2. See Díaz, *La reconquista española*, vol. 1, pp. 149–78, 335–95, vol. 2, pp. 230–56. See also Pablo Morillo to Minister of War, Chaguarama, 8 May 1817 and Cumaná, 28 August 1817, Rodríguez Villa, *Pablo Morillo*, vol. 3, pp. 379–85, 430–39; Sevilla, *Memorias*, pp. 86–87; and Noticias sobre José Ylario Mora, Cartagena, 21 July 1817, AGI, PC, leg. 717.
3. For information about the guerrilla war in the Llanos, see Díaz, *La reconquista española*, vol. 2, pp. 29–112; and Rausch, *A Tropical Plains Frontier*, chapter 7.
4. The Ayuntamiento of Mexico City to the Crown, 1766, quoted in David Brading, *The First America, the Spanish Monarchy, Creole Patriots, and the Liberal State 1492–1867*, Cambridge University Press (Cambridge, 1991), p. 467. As this quotation suggests, the subsequent behaviour of royalist troops in New Granada was consonant with the anti-creole ethos of the early Bourbon reforms.
5. Sevilla, *Memorias*, pp. 84, 138; Francisco Ximénez to Juan Sámano, Apiay, 6 January 1817, BRAH, sig. 9/7665 (leg. 22), fols 199–200; Ejército Expedicionario, Resumen histórico de las operaciones y movimientos de las columnas y tropas … desde el mes de Noviembre de 1816, AGI, PC, leg. 759B; Description of route past Mogotes, AGI, PC, leg. 897; and Woodward, 'The Spanish Army and the Loss of America', p. 593. For a discussion of European travellers in Spanish America, Mary Louise Pratt, *Imperial Eyes: Travel Writing and Transculturation*, Routledge (London, 1992), and Jean Franco, 'Un viaje poco romántico: Viajeros británicos hacia Sudamérica, 1818–28', *Escritura*, vol. 7 (Caracas, 1979), pp. 129–42.
6. Sevilla, *Memorias*, p. 38.
7. Instructions to Francisco González de Linares and Pedro José Mijares, Caracas, 18 Jan. 1821, AHNM, Estado, leg. 8733, doc. 24.
8. Sala Capitular de Pasto to the King, Pasto, 13 June 1814, AGI, AQ, leg. 276.
9. Brading, *The First America*, splendidly illustrates the centrality of this theme to virtually all discussions of American identity.
10. Juan and Ulloa, *Noticias Secretas*, p. 427. See also McFarlane, 'Identity, Enlightenment and Political Dissent', which provides a good overview of the debate about creole identity.
11. See the text of the Capitulations in Pablo E. Cárdenas Acosta, *El movimiento comunal de 1781 en el Nuevo Reino de Granada (Reivindicaciones Históricos)*, Tercer Mundo (Bogotá, 1980), vol. 2, pp. 18–29. (European antipathy to Americans is discussed on p. 26.)

12. Thomas Gómez, 'La république des cuñados: Familles, pouvior et société à Santa Fé de Bogotá (XVIIIe siècle)', *Caravelle*, vol. 62 (1994); and McFarlane, *Colombia before Independence*, pp. 272–86.
13. Georges Louis Leclerc, Comte de Buffon quoted in Antonello Gerbi, *The Dispute of the New World: The History of a Polemic, 1750–1900*, University of Pittsburgh Press (Pittsburgh, 1973), p. 8.
14. Guillaume Thomas François Raynal, quoted in Gerbi, *The Dispute of the New World*, p. 49. Gerbi provides an admirable discussion of this topic.
15. Creole degeneracy is discussed in Brading, *The First America*, particularly chapter 19.
16. Charles Kany, *Life and Manners in Madrid, 1750–1800*, AMS Press (New York, 1932), p. 184.
17. 'Informe del Real Tribunal del Consulado de México sobre la incapacidad de los habitantes de N.E. para nombrar representantes a las Cortes, Mexico City, 27 May 1811', in J.E. Hernández y Dávalos (ed.), *Colección de documentos para la Historia de la Guerra de Independencia de México de 1808 a 1821* (1878), vol. 2, Kraus Reprints (Nedeln, 1968), pp. 450–66. See also Costeloe, *Response to Revolution*, pp. 23–27; and Rodríguez, *Independence of Spanish America*, pp. 84–85.
18. For a clear statement of this view, see Gabriel de Torres to Ministry of Overseas, Cartagena, 22 September 1820, AGI, ASF, leg. 1017. Or consider Cajigal, *Memorias*, pp. 24–25.
19. Decreto de Guerra a Muerte, Trujillo, 15 June 1813, *Escritos del Libertador*, vol. 4 (1968), pp. 305–6.
20. Brading, *The First America*, p. 554.
21. Plano de observación topográfica de la Provincia de Antioquia, 12 May 1816, AGI, PC, leg. 897.
22. The phrase is from Albi, *Banderas olvidadas*.
23. See Vicente Sánchez Lima to Francisco Montalvo, Medellín, 4 Aug. 1817; and Sala Capitular de Buga to José Solís, Buga, 30 June 1817; both in AGI, ASF, leg. 631, doc. 64.
24. Cajigal, *Memorias*, p. 157.
25. Sala Capitular de Popayán to Francisco Montalvo, Popayán, 5 July 1817, AGI, ASF, leg. 631. See also Cabildo of Buga to José Solís, Buga, 9 Aug. 1817; Cabildo of Buga to José Solís, Buga, 11 Aug. 1817; and Cayetano Sarmiento to José Solís, Llanogrande, 19 Aug. 1817; all in AGI, Estado, leg. 57, doc. 35–D (1b); and Horacio Rodríguez Plata, *La antigua provincia del Socorro y la independencia*, Biblioteca de Historia Nacional, vol. 98 (Bogotá, 1963), p. 411.
26. Caballero, *Diario*, p. 192. The French traveller J.J. Dauxion Lavaysse made the same point with regard to Venezuela: 'The Spaniards display a certain air of superiority towards the colonials'. (Dauxion Lavaysse, *Viaje*, p. xxxvi.). Or see Restrepo, *Historia de la revolución*, vol. 1, p. 101.
27. Caballero, *Diario*, p. 213.
28. Francisco Montalvo to Minister of Grace and Justice, Cartagena, 24 Sept. 1817, AGI, ASF, leg. 631.
29. Arámbarri, *Hechos del General Morillo*, p. 31.
30. For the royalist army in Mexico, see Anna, *The Fall of the Royal Government in Mexico*

City, pp. 90–91. See also Archer, *The Army in Bourbon Mexico*, pp. 255–58.

31. See, for example, Miguel de la Torre to Sebastián de la Calzada, Mompós, 14 March 1816, AHNM, Estado, leg. 8721, doc. 86; Pablo Morillo to Miguel de la Torre, Ocaña, 25 March 1816, AHNM, Estado, leg. 8717, doc. 48; Two letters of Pablo Morillo to Gabriel de Torres, Ocaña, 22 April 1816, AGI, PC, leg. 709; Lorenzo Josef Noriega to Gabriel de Torres, Fragata Atocha, 4 April 1816; AGI, PC, leg. 707; Pablo Morillo to Miguel de la Torre, Bucaramanga, 13 May 1816, AHNM, Estado, leg. 8717, doc. 64; Pablo Morillo to Francisco Montalvo, 29 July 1816, AGI, PC, leg. 707; Investigation into Lieutenant Juan José Guevara, Cartagena, 1 Dec. 1816, AGI, PC, leg. 739; the various complaints from the Cauca Valley in 1817 in AHNC, Archivo Anexo, Guerra y Marina, tomo 152, fols 226–41; Orden General del Día, 5 February 1817, BRAH, sig. 9/7651 (leg. 8); and Pablo Morillo to Miguel de la Torres, Calabozo, 8 Nov. 1817, AHNM, Estado 8171, doc. 147.
32. Pablo Morillo to Ministry of War, Valencia, 22 April 1818, Rodríguez Villa, *Pablo Morillo*, vol. 3, pp. 563–67, and Stoan, *Pablo Morillo*, p. 206. Cf. Archer, *The Army in Bourbon Mexico*, p. 254–55.
33. Investigation into deaths of 6 prisoners, Cartagena, 1819, AGI, PC, leg. 719B. See also Summary of letter by Pablo Morillo, Calabozo, 28 July 1819, AGI, PC, leg. 742; Orden General, 9–10 September 1816, BRAH, sig. 9/7658 (leg. 15); José María Barreiro to Juan Sámano, Molinos, 10 July 1819, AGI, PC, leg. 747; Francisco Warleta to Pablo Morillo, Cancan, 23 March 1816, BRAH, sig. 9/7658 (leg. 15), fols 49–50; Cortés Vargas, 'De la época del terror', p. 92; and Restrepo, *Historia de la revolución*, vol. 2, p. 147.
34. Atrocity stories and republican propaganda are discussed in Earle, 'Information and Disinformation'; and Earle, 'Rape and the Anxious Republic'. For murder and torture, see, for example, Restrepo, *Historia de la revolución*, vol. 2, pp. 86–87, 146–50. A good illustration of the destabilizing effect of rumoured atrocities in 1810 is provided in Torres y Peña, *Memorias*, pp. 105–6.
35. Tovar, 'Guerras de opinión', pp. 225–26.
36. Díaz, *La reconquista española*, vol. 2, p. 326. (This particular quote was recorded in early 1820.)
37. O'Leary, *Bolívar and the War of Independence*, pp. 93–94.
38. Sala capitular de Anserma to José Solís(?), Anserma, 7 July 1817; AGI, ASF, leg. 631; and Tomás de Heres to Ruperto Delgado, Cali, 20 May 1817, AGI, ASF, leg. 631.
39. See Pablo Morillo to Minister of War, Santa Fe, 9 November 1816, Rodríguez Villa, *Pablo Morillo*, vol. 3, p. 227. See also Hamnett, 'Royalist Counterinsurgency and the Continuity of Rebellion', p. 34, for similar attitudes among royalist officers in Mexico.
40. Testimony of María Manuela de Angulo to Sala capitular de Popayán, Popayán, 19 June 1817, AGI, ASF, leg. 631.
41. McFarlane, *Colombia before Independence*, pp. 137–38, 162, 261, 312, 317–20; and Francisco Warleta to Pablo Morillo, Remedios, 17 March 1816, BRAH, sig. 9/7658 (leg. 15), fols 38–39.
42. Restrepo, *Autobiografía*, p. 20. See also Pablo Morillo to Miguel de la Torre, San Gil, 16 May 1816, AHNM, Estado, leg. 8717.

43. Much information about the opposition to the road to Anchicayá, including reports by local *cabildos*, army officers, and private citizens, may be found in AGI, ASF, leg. 631, ramo 64.
44. Diary of the First Battalion of the Regimiento de Infantería de Numancia (Third Division), March 1817, AGI, PC, leg. 759A.
45. Vicente Romero to José Solís, Anserma, 22 May 1817; Sala Capitular to Buga to José Solís, Buga, 30 March 1817 and 30 June 1817, all in AGI, ASF, leg. 631.
46. Ruperto Delgado to José Solís, Popayán, 13 July 1817; Ruperto Delgado to Juan Sámano, Popayán, 20 July 1817; both in AGI, ASF, leg. 631. See also Report by Pascual Enrile, Madrid, 18 May 1819, AHNM, Estado, leg. 8739, doc. 139.
47. Jacques Barbier, 'Peninsular Finance and Colonial Trade: the Dilemma of Charles IV's Spain', *JLAS*, vol. 12 (1980), p. 23 (table 2).
48. Costeloe, *Response to Revolution*, pp. 102, 104 (Note the inconsistency between the figures in Costeloe, *Response to Revolution*, p. 102 and in Michael Costeloe, 'Spain and the Spanish American Wars of Independence', p. 236); Heredia, *Planes españoles*, p. 254; and also Alamán, *Historia de Mejico*, vol. 5, p. 14n for comments on other estimates.
49. For comments about British military funding during the American Revolution, see Mackesy, *The War for America*, pp. 65–69, 118–20, 222–24.
50. Michael Costeloe has made a careful study of the Comisión, and the following remarks about its role are based on his work. For details about the Comisión de Reemplazos, see Costeloe, 'Spain and the Spanish American Wars of Independence'; and Costeloe, *Response to Revolution*, pp. 101–16. Also see 'La Comisión de Reemplazos representa a la Regencia del Reyno el estado de insurrección en que se hallan algunas provincias de ultramar', AGI, I.A. 5/20.
51. Costeloe, 'Spain and the Spanish American Wars of Independence', p. 228.
52. Sevilla, *Memorias*, p. 44; and Pablo Morillo to José de Abascal, Torrecillas, 21 October 1815, AGI, Diversos, leg. 4. Jorge Mercado disagrees with Sevilla's figures, and estimates that at most $250,000 and some 1,000 weapons were destroyed. See Mercado, *Campaña de invasión*, p. 82. See Historia de la rebelión de América en 35 cartas, by Pedro Pérez Múñoz, Quito, 31 December 1815, letter 33, AGI, Diversos, leg. 42, for report that the fire was the result of an accident with a cask of *aguardiente*.
53. Heredia, *Planes españoles*, p. 299.
54. Pablo Morillo to Miguel de la Torre, Guanaparo, (1819?), AHNM, Estado, leg. 8717, docs 205–6.
55. Instrucciones dadas a Morillo para su expedición a Costafirme, Madrid, 18 November 1814, Rodríguez Villa, *Pablo Morillo*, vol. 2, pp. 437–48.
56. See for example Report by Council of the Indies on various letters of Montalvo, 30 November 1817, AGI, ASF, leg. 549.
57. Anna, *The Fall of the Royal Government in Mexico City*, p. 155.
58. Carrera Damas, *Boves*, pp. 58–59.
59. For some very large confiscations, see Caballero, *Diario*, pp. 222–23; and Sevilla, *Memorias*, p. 98ff.
60. See Request enclosed in José Solís to Francisco Montalvo, Popayán, 17 June 1817, AGI, ASF, leg. 631; See List of monthly expenses of the troops in Popayán in José

Solís to Francisco Montalvo, Popayán, 17 June 1817; and Daily expenses of troops in Popayán enclosed in Vicente Romero to José Solís, Anserma, 22 May 1817; both in AGI, ASF, leg. 631; Cabildo de Toro to José Solís, Toro, 27 June 1817; and Tomás de Heres to Ruperto Delgado, Cali, 20 May 1817; both in AGI, ASF, leg. 631. See also Cabildo de Anserma to José Solís(?), Anserma, 7 July 1817; Cabildo de Anserma to Francisco Montalvo, Anserma, 27 June 1817; and Ruperto Delgado to José Solís, Popayán, 14 July 1817; all in AGI, ASF, leg. 631.

61. See Cabildo of Popayán to José Solís and Francisco Montalvo, Popayán, 3 May 1817; Dictamen of Anselmo de Bierna y Mazo, Cartagena, 29 August 1817, José Solís to Francisco Montalvo, Popayán, 17 June 1817; and also Cabildo of Buga to José Solís, Buga, 30 June 1817; all in AGI, ASF, leg. 631.

62. Council of the Indies to Pablo Morillo, Madrid, 13 January 1818; and Council of the Indies to Pascual Enrile, Madrid, 13 January 1818; both in AGI, ASF, leg. 549.

63. See Noticia de los sueldos que disfrutan en esta plaza las tropas de la guarnición, Cartagena, 26 August 1816, AGI, PC, leg. 715; and List of daily expenses of troops in Popayán, enclosed in Vicente Romero to José Solís, Anserma, 22 May 1817, AGI, ASF, leg. 631.

64. Costeloe, *Response to Revolution*, pp. 114, 245.

65. See various soldiers' wills in AGI, PC, leg. 759B. See also Pablo Morillo to Francisco Montalvo, Cartagena, 22 January 1816, AGI, PC, leg. 707; Francisco Montalvo to Gabriel de Torres, Cartagena, 6 August 1817, AGI, PC, leg. 708; Francisco Igrica to Minister of War, 6 June 1818, AGI, Estado, leg. 57, doc. 35E; José María Barreiro to Juan Sámano, Sogamoso, 23 March 1819, *Los ejércitos del Rey*, 1819, vol. 2, pp. 31–33; Francisco Gascón, Juan Otalora and others to Manuel Cordero, Cartagena, 23 November 1819; and Antonio Cano to Juan Sámano, Cartagena, 22 September 1819, both in AGI, PC, leg. 747; Pablo Morillo to Minister of Overseas, Valencia, 26 July 1820, AGI, Indiferente General, leg. 1568; Gabriel de Torres to Minister of Hacienda, Cartagena, 18 August 1820, AGI, ASF, leg. 1017.

66. Francisco Montalvo to Juan Sámano, Cartagena, 30 January 1818, *Los últimos virreyes*, p. 104.

67. See, for example, Pablo Morillo to Minister of War, Santa Fe, 9 November 1816, in Rodríguez Villa, *Pablo Morillo*, vol. 3, pp. 223–34; Simón Sicilia to José Solís, Popayán, 16 July 1817, AGI, ASF, leg. 631; and José María Barreiro to Juan Sámano, Tunja, 3 July 1819 and 7 July 1819, in *Los ejércitos del Rey*, vol. 2, pp. 216–17, 238–42, respectively; and Andrés Delgado to Juan Sámano, Magangue, 23 April 1820, AGI, PC, leg. 747.

68. Relación de la prendas que se hallan, Mompós, 26 November 1816, AGI, PC, leg. 712.

69. Pablo Morillo to Minister of War, Santa Fe, 9 November 1816, Rodríguez Villa, *Pablo Morillo*, vol. 3, pp. 223–34. See also Report by Council of the Indies, 30 November 1817, AGI, ASF, leg. 549; and also Francisco Montalvo to Juan Sámano, Cartagena, 30 January 1818, *Los últimos virreyes*, p. 153.

70. See Pablo Morillo to Salvador de Moxó, Chaparro, 27 May 1817, AGI, Audiencia de Caracas, leg. 386. See also other letters of Pablo Morillo to Salvador de Moxó, 1817, in AGI, Audiencia de Caracas, legs 110 and 386; Pablo Morillo to Duke of

San Carlos, Caracas, 16 November 1818, AGS, Estado, leg. 8223; Rodríguez Villa, *Pablo Morillo* (1920), vol. 1, p. 303; and Pablo Morillo to Salvador de Moxó, el campo del paso del Frío, en el Río Apure, 2 February 1817, Rodríguez Villa, *Pablo Morillo*, vol. 3, p. 265.

71. See Francisco Montalvo to Minister of Grace and Justice, Cartagena, 2 August 1816, AGI, ASF, leg. 631; and Francisco Montalvo to José de Abascal, Torrecilla, 21 October 1815, AGI, Diversos 4. See also Juan Sámano to Joaquín de la Pezuela, Cartagena, 5 March 1820, AGI, PC, leg. 709.
72. Pablo Morillo to Francisco Montalvo, Cartagena, 22 January 1816, AGI, PC, leg. 707. See also Pablo Morillo to Minister of War, Santa Fe, 17 September 1816, Rodríguez Villa, *Pablo Morillo*, vol. 3, pp. 218–23; Pablo Morillo to Gabriel de Torres, Barquisimeto, 20 November 1819, AGI, PC, leg. 709; and Pablo Morillo to Minister of Overseas, Barquisimeto, 31 October 1820, AGI, Indiferente General, leg. 1568.
73. Francisco de Paula Santander to Simón Bolívar, Santa Fe, 7 January 1820, *Cartas Santander-Bolívar*, vol. 1, pp. 263–65.
74. See Manuel Cordero to Juan Sámano, Cartagena, 1 February 1820, AGI, PC, leg. 747. See also Miguel de Bustillo y Colina to Cortes, Kingston, 12 March 1813, Jiménez Molinares, *Los mártires de Cartagena*, vol. 1, pp. 312–19, esp. p. 316.
75. See Simón Sicilia to José Solís, Popayán, 16 July 1817, AGI, ASF, leg. 631; Pablo Morillo to Minister of War, Santa Fe, 31 August 1816, Rodríguez Villa, *Pablo Morillo*, vol. 3, pp. 195–207; and José María Barreiro to Juan Sámano, Sogamoso, 23 March 1819, *Los ejércitos del Rey*, pp. 31–33.
76. For expressions of this view from Montalvo and other high-ranking royalist officials, see Francisco Montalvo to Minister of Grace and Justice, Cartagena, 2 August 1816; José Solís to Francisco Montalvo, Popayán, 20 June 1817; Toribio Montes to Francisco Montalvo, Quito, 21 June 1817; Order by Francisco Montalvo, Cartagena, 18 August 1817, Francisco Montalvo to Minister of Grace and Justice, Cartagena, 24 September 1817; all in AGI, ASF, leg. 631.
77. Francisco de Paula Santander to Simón Bolívar, Santa Fe, 10 October 1819,and 17 October 1819, in *Cartas Santander-Bolívar*, vol. 1, pp. 133–35, 154–56. See also Francisco de Paula Santander to Simón Bolívar, Santa Fe, 17 October 1819, *Cartas Santander-Bolívar*, vol. 1, pp. 154–56.
78. Delgado, *La Independencia de América*, discusses the opinions advanced by newspapers of the period.
79. Anna, *Spain and the Loss of America*, pp. 184–85.
80. Report on letter by Andrés Rosillo, AGI, ASF, leg. 1017; and Report on letter of Andrés María Rosillo to Ministry of Grace and Justice of 13 July 1818, AGI, Estado, leg. 57, Doc. 36. Also see Celestino Bruguera, Paris, 12 July 1820, AGI, Indiferente General, leg. 1568; and Reports of the Tercera División del Primer Batallón del Regimiento de Infantería de Numancia, January to October 1817, AGI, PC, leg. 759A.
81. For contemporary comments about Morillo's title of 'Pacifier', see Arámbarri, *Hechos del General Pablo Morillo*, p. 86; and Groot, *Historia eclesiástica*, vol. 4, p. 111.
82. For a clear statement of this fact, see Keegan, *A History of Warfare*, p. 361; or Roger Cooter, 'War and Modern Medicine', in W.F. Bynum and Roy Porter (eds),

Companion Encyclopedia of the History of Medicine, Routledge (London, 1993), Vol. 2, Table 1.

83. See Michael Duffy, *Soldiers, Sugar and Seapower: The British Expedition to the West Indies and the War against Revolutionary France*, Oxford University Press (Oxford, 1987), pp. 326–67); Richard Harding, *Amphibious Warfare in the Eighteenth Century: The British Expedition to the West Indies, 1740–1742*, The Royal Historical Society (Irthlingborough, 1991), pp. 3, 83–84, 149; and Mackesy, *The War for America*, pp. 6, 336, 526.
84. See Hugh Thomas, *Cuba or the Pursuit of Freedom*, Eyre and Spottiswoode (London, 1971), p. 414. For disease in the colonial army, see Juan Marchena Fernández, *Oficiales y soldados en el Ejército de America*, Escuela de Estudios Hispano-Americanos (Sevilla, 1983), pp. 195–237, esp. p. 234; and Archer, *The Army in Bourbon Mexico*, pp. 38–61, esp. 55, 61.
85. Albi, *Banderas olvidadas*, pp. 403–5.
86. Rodríguez Villa, *Pablo Morillo*, vol. 1 (1920), p. 181.
87. Translated article from the *Royal Gazette and Bahama Advertizer*, 27 March 1816, AGI, Estado, leg. 57, doc. 32. See also Pablo Morillo to José de Abascal, Torrecillas, 21 October 1815, AGI, Diversos, leg. 4, ramo 1.
88. Marchena Fernández, *Oficiales y soldados*, pp. 210, 213, 214.
89. Pablo Morillo to Francisco de Montalvo, Cartagena, 5 February 1816, AGI, PC, leg. 707. Also see Francisco Montalvo to Juan Sámano, Cartagena, 30 January 1818, *Los últimos virreyes*, pp. 94–95.
90. Pablo Morillo to Minister of War, Santa Fe, 31 May 1816; and Pablo Morillo to Minister of War, Santa Fe, 9 November 1816, both in Rodríguez Villa, *Pablo Morillo*, vol. 3, pp. 164–69, 229, respectively.
91. Reports on the Second Battalion of Albuera, Mompós, 1816, AGI, PC, leg. 738.
92. See Vicente Villete to Subinspector General, Cartagena, 31 December 1819; and also Report by Ignacio de La Ruz, Cartagena, 3 February 1819, for comments about troop mortality in Santa Marta, both in AGI, PC, leg. 738.
93. Vicente Sánchez Lima to Comandantes Militares de la Hacha, Moreno, 26 November 1820, AGI, Indiferente General, leg. 1568.
94. First Declaration of Gabriel de Torres, Havana, 2 November 1824, AGI, PC, leg. 2136A. The local diet, regarded as unsuitable for European troops, was frequently blamed for causing illness. See Francisco Montalvo to Juan Sámano, Cartagena, 30 January 1818, *Los últimos virreyes*, p. 40.
95. See, for example, Vicente Sánchez Lima to Pedro Ruíz de Porras, Zaragosa, 8 January 1816, AHNM, Estado, leg. 8745; Antonio Meléndez to Gabriel de Torres, Mompós, 5 April 1817, AGI, PC, leg. 712; Cabildo de Anserma to Francisco Montalvo, Anserma, 27 June 1817, AGI, Santa Fe, leg. 631; Diary of the Primer Batallón del Regimiento Infantería de Numancia, 15 December 1817, AGI, PC leg. 759A; Rodríguez Villa, *Pablo Morillo*, (1920), vol. 2, p. 31; Caballero, *Diario*, p. 217; and Pablo Morillo, Description of the 1816 attack on the interior of New Granada, BRAH, sig. 9/7651 (leg. 8).
96. Pablo Morillo to Minister of War, La Guaira, 10 September 1817, Rodríguez Villa, *Pablo Morillo*, vol. 3, p. 442–43. Also see Miguel de la Torre to Pablo Morillo, Guayana, 4 May 1817, AHNM, Estado, leg. 8718, docs 51–52; and Pablo Morillo

to Minister of War, Caño de Atamayca, 28 February 1819, Rodríguez Villa, *Pablo Morillo*, vol. 4, pp. 10–14.

97. See Pablo Morillo to Minister of War, Maracay, 1 April 1817, Rodríguez Villa, *Pablo Morillo*, vol. 3, p. 369; Tomás de Heres to Ruperto Delgado, Cali, 20 May 1817, AGI, Santa Fe, leg. 631; Diary of the Primer Batallón del Regimiento Infantería de Numancia, 13 November, 15 December 1817, AGI, PC, leg. 759A; Lists of sick officers in Venezuelan hospitals, 1820, AHNM, Estado, leg. 8728, docs 379–408; Miguel de la Torre to Minister of Overseas, Caracas, 22 March 1821, AGI, Audiencia de Caracas, leg. 55; Juan de la Cruz Mourgeon to Minister of Overseas, Panama, 28 August 1821, AGI, Santa Fe, leg. 668; and Sevilla, *Memorias*, p. 124. Information on yellow fever, dengue, malaria, amoebic and bachillary dysentery, smallpox and scurvy may be found in Kenneth Kiple (ed.), *The Cambridge World History of Human Diseases, Cambridge University Press*, (Cambridge, 1993).

98. Reports of Carlos Tolrá, Chocontá, November 1817, BRAH, sig. 7665 (leg. 22), fol. 512. See also Juan Sámano to Pablo Morillo, Santa Fe, 29 August 1818, BRAH, sig. 7665 (leg. 22), fols 607–9; and Cabildo de Anserma to Francisco Montalvo, Anserma, 27 June 1817, AGI, Santa Fe, leg. 631.

99. Colin Jones has noted that in France, military surgeons often favoured amputation for both humanitarian and economic reasons: amputation was effective and it required a shorter, and therefore cheaper, convalescence. The same may well have been true in New Granada. See Cooter, 'War and Modern Medicine', p. 1557; Marchena Fernández, *Oficiales y soldados*, pp. 219–20; List of invalids in Puerto Cabello, 20 November 1815, AGI, PC, leg. 897; Francisco Warleta to Pablo Morillo, Remedios, 17 March 1816, BRAH, sig. 9/7658 (leg. 15), fols 38–39; Pablo Morillo to Miguel de la Torre, Santa Fe, 23 June 1816, AHNM, Estado, leg. 8717; Diary of the Primer Batallón del Regimiento Infantería de Numancia, 15 December 1817, AGI, PC, leg. 759A; Pablo Morillo to Minister of War, Barquisimeto, 22 July 1818, Rodríguez Villa, *Pablo Morillo*, vol. 3, p. 598; and Antonio Van Halen to Miguel de la Torre, Caracas, March 1821, AGI, Audiencia de Caracas, leg. 55.

100. Sevilla discusses his medical experiences in *Memorias*, pp. 45, 144, 166, 198. Compare the treatment of yellow fever and soroche (altitude sickness) in Archer, *The Army in Bourbon Mexico*, pp. 42–44; and Albi, *Banderas olvidadas*, p. 162. On quinine, see Duffy, *Soldiers, Sugar and Seapower*, p. 359.

101. See, for example, William Bynum, 'Cullen and the Study of Fevers in Britain, 1760–1820', in W.F. Bynum and V. Nutton (eds), *Theories of Fever from Antiquity to the Enlightenment, Medical History*, Supplement 1 (London, 1981); and Peter Mathias, 'Swords and Ploughshares: the Armed Forces, Medicine and Public Health in the Late Eighteenth Century', in J.M. Winter (ed.), *War and Economic Development*, Cambridge University Press (Cambridge, 1975), pp. 78–79.

102. For an example, see Francis Hall, *Colombia: su estado actual* (1824), reprinted in David Sowell (ed.), *Santander y la opinión angloamericana*, Biblioteca de la Presidencia de la República (Santafé de Bogotá, 1991), pp. 61–71.

103. Francisco Montalvo to Juan Sámano, Cartagena, 30 January 1818, *Los últimos virreyes*, pp. 136–37. Also see Memorial de Francisco Flórez Moreno, Cádiz, 10 January 1811, AGI, Ultramar, leg. 811, for highly critical remarks by a Spanish

physician about that state of health care in the Americas in 1789; Relaciones de Mando de José de Ezpeleta (1796) and Pedro de Mendinueta (1803), in Posada and Ibáñez (eds), *Relaciones de Mando*; and Marcelo Frías Núñez, 'Enfermedad y sociedad en la crisis colonial del antiguo regimen: Nueva Granada en el tránsito del siglo XVIII al XIX. Las epidemias de viruelas', Tesina de Licenciatura, Centro de Estudios Históricos (Madrid, 1991), p. 66. Compare this with the British sailors' use of 'folk-medicine' (i.e. rum) in the West Indies in Duffy, *Soldiers, Sugar and Seapower*, p. 374. For concise comments about the contemporary status of doctors in England, see Roy Porter, *Disease, Medicine and Society in England, 1550–1860*, The Economic History Society (London, 1993).

104. Oscar Beaujón, 'La medicina en la Campaña del Sur', *Boletín de la Academia Nacional de la Historia*, vol. 57 (Caracas, 1974), pp. 720–21; Pascual Enrile to Miguel de la Torre, Santa Fe, 10 August 1816, AHNM, Estado, leg. 8724, doc. 55; and Morillo's Instrucciones para la marcha de los cuerpos, Caracas, 30 May 1815, AHNM, Estado, leg. 8717, doc. 17.

105. See Pablo Morillo to Miguel de la Torre, Santa Fe, 23 June 1816, AHNM, Estado, leg. 8717, Doc. 78; Orden General del 19 de agosto 1818, AGI, PC, leg. 759B; and Ejército Expedicionario, Resúmen histórico de las operaciones y movimientos de las columnas y tropas ... desde el mes de noviembre de 1816, entry for 30 December 1816, AGI, PC, leg. 759B.

106. For the climate debate, see Gerbi's magisterial work, *The Dispute of the New World*; and also Glick, 'Science and Independence'; and Anthony Pagden, *European Encounters with the New World*, Yale University Press (New Haven, 1993). Fever is discussed in Bynum and Porter, *Companion Encyclopedia*, especially the chapters on humoralism, environment and miasmata, fevers and tropical medicine.

107. See, for example, Francisco Montalvo to Juan Sámano, Cartagena, 30 January 1818, in *Los últimos virreyes*, p. 40.

108. Pablo Morillo to Miguel de la Torre, Torrecilla, 4 October 1815, AHNM, Estado, leg. 8717, doc. 33. The importance of exercise is stressed, for example, in Hall, *Colombia*, pp. 61–71; and Bynum and Porter, *Companion Encyclopedia*, chapters on tropical medicine, and medicine and colonization.

109. Interesting material on the reintroduction of the smallpox vaccine to New Granada may be found in AGI, PC, leg. 712; Juan Sámano to Pablo Morillo, Popayán, 19 August 1816, and Jaime Serra to Juan Sámano, Popayán, 31 August 1816, both in BRAH, sig. 7665 (leg. 22), fols 52–53, 75. (Francisco Tamariz, who spearheaded the drive to reintroduce the vaccine, may have had some medical training.)

110. Francisco Montalvo to Juan Sámano, Cartagena, 30 January 1818, *Los últimos virreyes*, p. 114.

111. Francisco Montalvo to Juan Sámano, Cartagena, 30 January 1818, *Los últimos virreyes*, p. 114.

112. See, for example, Antonio Meléndez to Gabriel de Torres, Mompós, 26 May 1817, AGI, PC, leg. 712; Miguel de la Torres to Pascual Enrile, Mompós, 2 January 1816, AHNM, Estado, leg. 8724, doc. 4; Resúmen histórico de las operaciones y movimientos de las columnas y tropas, AGI, PC, leg. 759B; Caballero, *Diario*, p. 217; Díaz, *La reconquista española*, vol. 2, p. 285; José María Barreiro to Juan Sámano, Tunja, 16 October 1818, and Juan Sámano to José María Barreiro, Santa Fe, 19

November 1818, both in *Los ejércitos del rey*, vol. 1, pp. 68–70, 97–98.

113. Pablo Morillo to Minister of War, Santa Fe, 9 June 1816, Rodríguez Villa, *Pablo Morillo*, vol. 3, p. 174; and Pablo Morillo to Miguel de la Torre, Torrecillas, 4 October 1815, AHNM, Estado, leg. 8717. By the end of March 1816 there were already over 500 patients in the two hospitals. See Estado de enfermos en el hospital de San Carlos, Cartagena, 31 March 1816, AGI, PC, leg. 715.
114. Orden no. 1 for Hospital in Sabanalarga, 13 May 1816, AGI, PC, leg. 714.
115. Orden no. 1 for Hospital in Sabanalarga, 13 May 1816, AGI, PC, leg. 714; Dictamen de Anselmo de Bierna y Maza, Cartagena, 24 April 1816, AGI, PC, leg. 707; and Estado de enfermos en el hospital de San Carlos, Cartagena, 31 March 1816, AGI, PC, leg. 715.
116. Antonio María Díaz to Gabriel de Torres, Sabanalarga, 17 May 1816, AGI, PC, leg. 714.
117. Orden no. 1 for Hospital in Sabanalarga, 13 May 1816, AGI, PC, leg. 714.
118. Informe sobre hospitales militares de la Plaza de Cartagena de Indias, Cartagena, 29 July 1816, AGI, PC, leg. 714; and Josef Alvarez to Gabriel de Torres, Mompós, 13 May 1818, AGI, PC, leg. 712. For military hospitals in Mexico, see Archer, *The Army in Bourbon Mexico*, pp. 261–67.
119. Hoja de Servicio of Miguel de la Torre, AHNM, Estado, leg. 8718, doc. 100.
120. Pablo Morillo to Miguel de la Torre, Guadelupe, 19 May 1816, AHNM, Estado, leg. 8717, doc. 69.

7: The Battle of Boyacá

1. Pablo Morillo to Duque de San Carlos, Caracas, 16 November 1818, AGS, Estado, leg. 8223.
2. For details of the republican guerrillas in the Llanos, see Díaz, *La reconquista española*, vol. 2, pp 279ff; and Rausch, *A Tropical Plains Frontier*, chapter 7. Bolívar's letters from 1818 provide a good picture of the royalist collapse in the Llanos. See Lecuna, *Selected Writings of Bolívar*, vol. 1, pp. 153ff; and also *Los Ejércitos del Rey*, vol. 2.
3. Juan Sámano to Pablo Morillo, Santa Fe, 7 April 1818, BRAH, sig. 9/7665 (leg. 22), fols 567–69.
4. Camilo Riaño, *La campaña libertadora de 1819*, Editorial Andes (Bogotá, 1969), p. 52. See also Díaz, *La reconquista española*, vol. 2, p. 287–88, for problems with the weather; and José María Barreiro to Juan Sámano, Sogamoso, 23 March 1819, *Los ejércitos del Rey*, 1819, vol. 2, pp. 31–33.
5. Juan Sámano to Minister of War, Cartagena, 26 September 1819, in Juan Friede (ed.), *La Batalla de Boyacá, 7 de agosto de 1819, a través de los archivos españoles*, Banco de la República (Bogotá, 1969), pp. 284–88. See also Díaz, *La reconquista española*, vol. 2, p. 299.
6. Francisco de Paula Santander to Simón Bolívar, La Palma, 29 April 1819, *Cartas Santander-Bolívar*, vol. 1, pp. 83–85.
7. José María Barreiro to Juan Sámano, Tunja, 28 June 1819, *La Batalla de Boyacá*, pp. 25–26; Juan Sámano to José María Barreiro, Santa Fe, 6 July 1819 and the exchange of letters between Calzada, Barreiro and Sámano, *Los ejércitos del Rey*, vol. 2, pp. 231, 244–46; Juan Sámano to Minister of War, Cartagena, 26 September 1819, *La*

Batalla de Boyacá, pp. 284–88; and Díaz, *La reconquista española*, vol. 2, p. 361.

8. Riaño, *La campaña libertadora*, pp. 71,78, 108. See also Díaz, *La reconquista española*, vol. 2, pp. 309–10.
9. Antonio Tobar to José María Barreiro, Barinas, 17 June 1819, *La Batalla de Boyacá*, pp. 53–54.
10. Juan Figueroa y Ladrón to José María Barreiro, Labranzagrande, 5 July 1819, *Los ejércitos del Rey*, p. 229. See also José María Barreiro to Juan Sámano, Tunja, 25 June 1819, *La Batalla de Boyacá*, pp. 22–24, and *Los ejércitos del Rey*, vol. 2, pp. 162–63; Juan Figueroa y Ladrón to José María Barreiro, Labranzagrande, 2 July 1819, *Los ejércitos del Rey*, vol. 2, p. 204; 2 letters of Juan Sámano to José María Barreiro, Santa Fe, 3 July 1819, *Los ejércitos del Rey*, vol. 2, pp. 205–6, 207; José María Barreiro to Juan Sámano, Tunja, 3 July 1819, *Los ejércitos del Rey*, vol. 2, p. 217; Pablo Morillo to Juan Sámano, Calabozo, 12 July 1819, *Los ejércitos del Rey*, vol. 2, pp. 267–68; and Antonio Plá to Juan Sámano, Sesquilé, 24 July 1819, AGI, PC, leg. 742.
11. José María Barreiro to Juan Sámano, Tunja, 3 July 1819; and José María Barreiro to Juan Sámano, Tunja, 5 July 1819, *Los ejércitos del Rey*, vol. 2, pp. 218–19, 225–26, respectively.
12. See Díaz, *La reconquista española*, vol. 2, pp. 259–76, esp. p. 273.
13. José María Barreiro to Juan Sámano, Tunja, 3 July 1819; and José María Barreiro to Juan Sámano, Molinos, 10 July 1819, *La Batalla de Boyacá*, pp. 33–34, 63–65. See also La Batalla de Bogotá, pp. lii–lv; José María Barreiro to Juan Sámano, Paipa, 19 July 1819; and Juan Sámano to José María Barreiro, Santa Fe, 14 July 1819, all in *Los ejércitos del Rey*, vol. 2, pp. 290, 321–22; and Díaz, *La reconquista española*, vol. 2, p. 327.
14. See, for example, José María Barreiro to Juan Sámano, Molinos, 10 July 1819, *Los ejércitos del Rey*, vol. 2, pp. 261–62.
15. See José María Barreiro to Juan Sámano, Paipa, 31 July 1819, *La Batalla de Boyacá*, pp. 100–4. See also Francisco de Paula Santander to Simón Bolívar, La Trinidad, 19 January 1819, *Cartas Santander-Bolívar*, vol. 1, pp. 44–46; José María Barreiro to Juan Sámano, Molinos, 10 July 1819, *La Batalla de Boyacá*, pp. 63–65; and *La Batalla de Boyacá*, pp. liv–lv.
16. Juan Sámano to Minister of War, Cartagena, 26 September 1819, *La Batalla de Boyacá*, pp. 284–88. Friede reports that Barreiro did write a report on 6 August 1819, but that it has been lost (*La Batalla de Boyacá*, p. lvii).
17. Declaration of Manuel Martínez de Aparicio, Santa Fe, 8 August 1819, AGI, PC, leg. 747.
18. Riaño, *La campaña libertadora*, pp. 226–28, 270. The royalists estimated 4,000. See Gabriel García Vallecillos to Ferdinand, Cartagena, 10 October 1819, *La Batalla de Boyacá*, pp. 289–91. See also Rodríguez Villa, *Pablo Morillo*, vol. 4, p. 80.
19. Riaño, *La campaña libertadora*, pp. 226–28, 270. Bolívar reported that the royalists had 4,000 to 5,000 troops. See Simón Bolívar to Francisco Antonio Zea, Bogotá, 14 August 1819, *Selected Writings of Bolívar*, pp. 205–6.
20. Declaration of Manuel Martínez de Aparicio, Santa Fe, 8 August 1819, *Los ejércitos del Rey*, vol. 2, pp. 432–34. Also see declarations of Juan Loño and Sebastián Díaz, Turbaco, 9 October 1819, *La Batalla de Boyacá*, pp 124–40.
21. Gabriel García Vallecillos to Ferdinand, Cartagena, 10 October 1819, *La Batalla*

de Boyacá, pp. 289–91.

22. Declaration of Manuel Martínez de Aparicio, Santa Fe, 8 August 1819, AGI, PC, leg. 747.
23. See, for example, Gómez, *Independencia de Colombia*, pp. 228–29; or Rodríguez, *Independence of Spanish America*, p. 191.
24. Simón Bolívar to Luis Brion, Angostura, 14 December 1819, *Selected Writings of Bolívar*, vol. 1, pp. 209–10; Riaño, *La Campaña Libertadora*; and José María Barreiro to Juan Sámano, Sogamoso, *Los Ejércitos del Rey*, vol. 2, pp. 31–33.
25. Juan Sámano to Pablo Morillo, Santa Fe, 8 August 1819, Díaz, *La reconquista española*, pp. 375–76.
26. Juan Sámano to Minister of War, Cartagena, 26 September 1819, *La Batalla de Boyacá*, pp. 284–88.
27. Juan Sámano to Pablo Morillo, Santa Fe, 8 August 1819, Díaz, *La reconquista española*, pp. 375–76; Melchor Aymerich to Minister of War, Quito, 6 September 1819, *La Batalla de Boyacá*, pp. 257–60; Riaño, *La campaña libertadora*, p. 28; Juan Sámano to Gabriel de Torres, Cartagena, 13 September 1819, AGI, PC, leg. 708; and Gabriel de Torres to Ferdinand, Cartagena, 18 October 1819, *La Batalla de Boyacá*, pp. 296–303.
28. Riaño, *La campaña libertadora*, p. 287.
29. Gabriel de Torres to Ferdinand, Cartagena, 18 October 1819, *La Batalla de Boyacá*, pp. 296–303; and Díaz, *La reconquista española*, vol. 2, p. 378.
30. Gabriel García Vallecillos to Ferdinand, Cartagena, 10 October 1819, *La Batalla de Boyacá*, pp. 289–91; and Secretary of Juan Sámano to José Caparrós, Santa Fe, 18 July 1819, *Los Ejércitos del Rey*, vol. 2, p. 310.
31. Juan Sámano to Minister of War, Cartagena, 26 September 1819, *La Batalla de Boyacá*, pp. 284–88.
32. Gabriel de Torres to Ferdinand, Cartagena, 18 October 1819, *La Batalla de Boyacá*, pp. 296–303. See also Donato Ruíz de Santa Cruz to Juan Sámano, Mompós, 26 August 1819, AHNM, Estado, leg. 8719, doc. 276. This (or a very similar) document may also be found in *La Batalla de Boyacá*, pp. 115–22.
33. See, for example, Miguel de la Torre to Juan Sámano, San Antonio de Cúcuta, 29 October 1819, AGI, PC, leg. 742. See also Pablo Morillo to Miguel de la Torre, Barquisimeto and Sarare, 13–31 December 1819, AHNM, Estado, leg. 8717, docs 281–88.
34. Francisco de Paula Santander to Simón Bolívar, Santa Fe, 17 October 1819, *Cartas Santander-Bolívar*, vol. 1, pp. 154–56. An account of the execution is provided in Francisco de Paula Santander to Simón Bolívar, Santa Fe, 17 October 1819, *Cartas Santander-Bolívar*, vol. 1, pp. 157–58.
35. See Francisco de Paula Santander to Simón Bolívar, Santa Fe, 3 December 1819, *Cartas Santander-Bolívar*, vol. 1, pp. 249–52; Gabriel García to Faustino Martínez, Antioquia, 29 August 1819, *La Batalla de Boyacá*, pp. 319–20; and Juan Sámano to Miguel de La Torre, Cartagena, 18 November 1819, AGI, PC, leg. 742.
36. Melchor Aymerich to Minister of War, Quito, 6 September 1819; and Melchor Aymerich to Sebastián de la Calzada, Quito, 6 September 1819; *La Batalla de Boyacá*, pp. 257–60, 240–42.
37. Riaño, *La campaña libertadora*, p. 289; and Gabriel de Torres to Ferdinand,

Cartagena, 18 October 1819, *La Batalla de Boyacá*, pp. 296–303.

38. Juan Sámano to Minister of War, Cartagena, 26 September 1819, *La Batalla de Boyacá*, pp. 284–88.
39. Gabriel de Torres to Ferdinand, Cartagena, 18 October 1819, *La Batalla de Boyacá*, pp. 296–303. See also Gabriel de Torres to Pablo Morillo. Cartagena, 8 July 1820, AGI, PC, leg. 714.
40. Pablo Morillo to Miguel de la Torre, Valencia, 16 August 1819, AHNM, Estado, leg. 8717, doc. 256; and Pablo Morillo to Miguel de la Torre, Valencia, 6 September 1819, AHNM, Estado, leg. 8717, doc. 261.
41. Pablo Morillo to Miguel de la Torre, Valencia, 7 September 1819, AHNM, Estado, leg. 8717, doc. 261.
42. List of Spaniards executed in Socorro, Ocaña, 12 October 1819, AGI, PC, leg. 749.
43. Juan Sámano to Miguel de la Torre, Turbaco, 15 September 1819, AHNM, Estado, leg. 8719, doc. 267.
44. See the extensive documentation of the republican invasion of Ríohacha in AGI, PC, leg. 745.
45. Juan Sámano to Miguel de la Torre, Cartagena, 17 November 1819, AHNM, Estado, leg. 8719, doc. 272; and Sumario contra Geronimo Caro, Camilo Almansa, y Julián Carbello, AGI, PC, leg. 743.
46. See Proceso criminal contra [various], Mompós, 17 November 1819, AGI, PC, leg. 741A.
47. Gabriel de Torres to Ferdinand, Cartagena, 18 October 1819, *La Batalla de Boyacá*, pp. 296–303.
48. Isidro Villareal to José Rodríguez, Popayán, 8 September 1819, AGI, PC, leg. 742. See also Hamnett, 'Popular Insurrection and Royalist Reaction'.
49. There is a substantial literature on late colonial opposition to royal monopolies. See, for example, Gilma Lucía Mora de Tovar, *Aguardiente y Conflictos Sociales en el Nuevo Granada durante el Siglo XVIII*, Universidad Nacional de Colombia (Bogotá, 1988); Anthony McFarlane, 'Civil Disorders and Popular Protests in Late Colonial New Granada', *HAHR*, vol. 30 (1984); and McFarlane, 'The Rebellion of the Barrios'.
50. Salvador de Enciso to Juan Sámano, Popayán, 8 September 1819, AGI, PC, leg. 743.
51. See also Salvador de Enciso to Juan Sámano, Popayán, 14 September 1819, AGI, PC, leg. 743; Salvador de Enciso to Minister of State, Popayán, 8 September 1819, AGI, Ultramar, leg. 811; and Sebastián de la Calzada to Juan Sámano, Popayán, 8 September 1819, AGI, PC, leg. 747.
52. Ramón Zambrano to Melchor Aymerich, Sapuyes, 31 August 1819, AGI, ASF, leg. 748.
53. Sebastián de la Calzada to Melchor Aymerich, Popayán, 24 January 1820, AGI, PC, leg. 1945.
54. Salvador de Madariaga, *Bolívar*, Hollis and Carter (London, 1952), p. 417.
55. Sebastián de la Calzada to Juan Sámano, Popayán, 8 September 1819, AGI, PC, leg. 747; and Melchor Aymerich to Minister of State, Quito, 6 September 1819, *La Batalla de Boyacá*, pp. 257–60.
56. See the anonymous *Cartas escritas desde Colombia durante un Viaje de Caracas a Bogotá*

y desde allí a Santa Marta en 1823, Archivo de la Economía Nacional, Banco de la República (Bogotá, 1975), pp. 86–87.

57. Declaration of Manuel Martínez de Aparicio, Santa Fe, l8 August 1819, AGI, PC, leg. 747; Pablo Morillo to Juan Sámano, San Carlos, 10 October 1819, AGI, PC, leg. 742; and Gabriel de Torres to Ferdinand, Cartagena, 18 October 1819, *La Batalla de Boyacá*, pp. 296–303.
58. Juan Sámano to Minister of War, Cartagena, 26 September 1819, *La Batalla de Boyacá*, pp. 284–88. See also Miguel de la Torre to Juan Sámano, San Antonio de Cúcuta, 29 October 1819, AGI, PC, leg. 742;José María Ramírez to Juan Manuel Cajigal, Havana, 14 September 1819, AGI, PC, leg. 1945; and Pamphlets of Bishop Gregorio of Cartagena, 18 August 1819, 3 September 1819, AGI, PC, leg. 743.
59. Juan Sámano to Minister of War, Cartagena, 26 September 1819, *La Batalla de Boyacá*, pp. 284–88.
60. Juan Sámano to Juan Manuel Cajigal, Cartagena, 22 December 1819; and Juan Sámano to Pablo Morillo, Santa Fe, 8 August 1819; AGI, PC, leg. 742; Juan Sámano to Minister of War, Cartagena, 26 September 1819, 27 April 1820, AGI, PC, leg. 720A; and Díaz, *La reconquista española*, vol. 2, p. 375.
61. Pablo Morillo to Miguel de la Torre, Calabozo, 20 June 1819, and 12 July 1819, both in AHNM, Estado, leg. 8717, docs 245, 249.
62. Carlos Tolrá to Juan Sámano, Bambosa, 24 August 1819, AGI, PC, leg. 745.
63. Carlos Tolrá to Juan Sámano, 15 November 1819, AGI, PC. leg. 745.
64. Juan Sámano to Minister of War, Cartagena, 26 September 1819, *La Batalla de Boyacá*, pp. 284–88.
65. Gabriel de Torres to Ferdinand, Cartagena, 18 October 1819, *La Batalla de Boyacá*, pp. 296–303. See also Pablo Morillo to Ministry of War, Valencia, 29 March 1820, Rodríguez Villa, *Pablo Morillo*, vol. 4, pp. 165–72.
66. Gabriel de Torres to Ferdinand, Cartagena, 18 October 1819, AGI, ASF, leg. 748.

8: Armistice and Surrender

1. See Anna, *Spain and the Loss of America*, p. 115; and Josep Fontana, *La crisis del antiguo régimen, 1808–1833*, Editorial Crítica (Barcelona, 1988), pp. 141–53.
2. See Comellas, *Los primeros pronunciamientos*; and also Fontana, *La crisis del antiguo régimen*, pp. 127–40.
3. Raymond Carr, *Spain 1808–1939*, Oxford University Press (Oxford, 1975) p. 127; Fernández Almagro, *La emancipación de América*, pp. 97–98. See also Comellas, *Los primeros pronunciamientos*, pp. 303–9; and E. Christiansen, *The Origins of Military Power in Spain, 1800–1954*, Oxford University Press (Oxford, 1967), p. 19.
4. Comellas, *Los primeros pronunciamientos*, p. 304.
5. Juan Marchena Fernández, 'Militarismo y liberalismo en el Perú', unpublished conference paper delivered at the Primer Seminario Intensivo Erasmus de Historia Latinoamericana (Florence, 24 March 1994). The impact of the 1820 revolution in Spanish America is discussed in Rebecca Earle, 'The Spanish Political Crisis of 1820 and the Loss of New Granada', *Colonial Latin American Historical Review*, vol. 3:3 (1994).
6. Diario Extraordinario Constitutional del Gobierno de la Habana, 17 April 1820,

AGI, ASF, leg. 580. See also José María Ramírez to Juan Sámano, Havana, 19 April 1820, AGI, ASF, leg. 580.

7. Pedro Ruíz de Porras to Juan Sámano, Santa Marta, 15 May 1820, AGI, ASF, leg. 580.
8. The description of events in Cartagena is drawn, where not otherwise indicated, from the Resumen Documentado que manifiesta el origen y sucesos ocurridos en la Plaza de Cartagena de Indias desde el día 7 de Junio hasta el 5 de Julio últimos, con motivo del juramento de la constitución de la Monarquía Española by Gabriel de Torres, Cartagena, 1 August 1820, AGI, ASF, leg. 1011.
9. See Gabriel de Torres to Gabriel García Vallecilla, Cartagena, 23 March 1820, AGI, PC, leg. 742.
10. José Santa Cruz to José Cienfuegos, Portobelo, 29 June 1820, AGI, PC, leg. 1945.
11. See Resumen Documentado … by Gabriel de Torres, Cartagena, 1 August 1820, AGI, ASF, leg. 1011. The Bishop himself made no mention of this in his own report on events. See Bishop Gregorio José to the Ministry of Grace and Justice, Guanabacoa, 4 October 1820, AGI, ASF, leg. 748.
12. See Juan Sámano to Gabriel de Torres, Cartagena, 9 June 1820, printed in the Resumen Documentado … by Gabriel de Torres, Cartagena, 1 August 1820, AGI, ASF, leg. 1011 and also in AGI, PC, leg. 890B. See also Gabriel de Torres to Juan Sámano, Cartagena, 10 June 1820, AGI, PC, leg. 890B; and Anselmo Bierna y Maza to Juan Sámano, Cartagena, 12 June 1820, AGI, PC, leg. 890B.
13. Pablo Morillo to José María Barreiro, Barquisimeto, 20 July 1818, *Los Ejércitos del Rey*, vol. 1, pp. 25–28.
14. For Torres's (not unbiased) assessment of public opinion, see Gabriel de Torres to Ministry of Ultramar, Cartagena, 27 July 1820, AGI, ASF, leg. 748.
15. Report by the Cabildo, Cartagena, 31 December 1820, AGI, PC, leg. 716.
16. Gabriel de Torres to Juan Sámano, Cartagena, 29 June 1820, printed in the Resumen Documentado … by Gabriel de Torres, Cartagena, 1 August 1820, AGI, ASF, leg. 1011 and also in AGI, ASF, leg. 748.
17. See Morillo's letters to Miguel de la Torre in BRAH, Colección Morillo, Sig. 9/7664 (leg. 21), fols 104–57. See also Proclama de Pablo Morillo, Caracas, 8 June 1820, AGI, Indiferente General, leg. 1568; and Pablo Morillo to Antonio López de Mendoza, Valencia, 4 August 1820, AGI, PC, leg. 759B.
18. Pablo Morillo to Francisco Tomás Morales, Valencia, 29 April 1820, BRAH, signatura 9/7662 (leg. 19), fols 169–72. For further details of the splits in Venezuela resulting from the constitution, see Earle, 'The Spanish Political Crisis of 1820'.
19. Bando de Gabriel de Torres, Cartagena, 3 August 1820, AGI, PC, leg. 717.
20. Gabriel de Torres to the Secretary of State, Cartagena, 10 July 1820, AHNM, Estado, leg. 8725. Warleta left New Granada altogether, going first to Jamaica and thence to Spain. See Restrepo Saenz, *Gobernadores de Antioquia*, vol. 1, p. 304. Also see Francisco Warleta to Juan Sámano, Barranca, 9 June 1820, AGI, PC, leg. 713B. Colonel Antonio Cano also left his post, although the circumstances of his removal are not clear. See José Santa Cruz to José Cienfuegos, Portobelo, 29 June 1820, AGI, PC, leg. 1945.
21. Mariano Sixto to Pablo Morillo, Valencia, 11 December 1820, AHNM, Estado, leg. 8725. See also Gabriel de Torres to the Secretary of State, Cartagena, 10 July

1820, AHNM, Estado, leg. 8725.

22. Gabriel de Torres to Francisco Mosquera y Cabrera, Cartagena, 18 June 1820, AGI, PC, leg. 742.
23. For an eloquent discussion of the progressive loss of credit suffered by Spain, see Anna, *Spain and the Loss of America.*
24. Daniel Florencio O'Leary, *Memorias*, Editorial Santafé (Bogotá, 1952), vol. 3, p. 299.
25. Simón Bolívar to Gabriel de Torres, Turbaco, 28 August 1820, AGI, ASF, leg. 1017.
26. Anna, *Spain and the Loss of America*, p. 225.
27. See Heredia, *Planes españoles*, p. 19; and Francisco Montalvo to the Regency, Santa Marta, 27 June 1814, *Los últimos virreyes*, pp. 49–54.
28. Anna, *Spain and the Loss of America*, p. 225; and Delgado, *La independencia de América*, pp. 264–84, esp. p. 265. See also Pablo Morillo to Miguel de la Torre, Valencia, 19 August 1820, BRAH, Colección Morillo, sig. 9/7664 (leg. 21), ff. 181–83.
29. Declaration of the King to the Americas, Madrid, May, 1820, *Spain under the Bourbons*, p. 251–52. See also Anna, *Spain and the Loss of America*, pp. 225–27, 243, and Enciso Recio, *La opinión pública española*, pp. 150–51.
30. Anna, *Spain and the Loss of America*, p. 272.
31. Pablo Morillo to Minister of Overseas, Valencia, 26 July 1820, Rodríguez Villa, *Pablo Morillo*, vol. 4, pp. 204–9. See also Pablo Morillo to Francisco Tomás Morales, Valencia, 25 July 1820, BRAH, Colección Morillo, sig. 9/7662 (leg. 19), ff. 220–23; Pablo Morillo to Miguel de la Torre, Valencia, 19 August 1820, BRAH, sig. 9/7664 (leg. 21), ff. 181–83; Gabriel de Torres to the Ministry of Overseas, Cartagena, 22 September 1820, AGI, ASF, leg. 1017; Report by Celestino Bruguera, Paris, 12 July 1820, AGI, Indiferente General, leg. 1586, and Ramón Ayala to Gabriel de Torres, Turbaco, 23 December 1820, AGI, PC, leg. 709.
32. Pablo Morillo to Minister of War, Valencia, 6 August 1820, Rodríguez Villa, *Pablo Morillo*, vol. 4, pp. 214–17.
33. See the documents related to the selection of the commissioners in AGI, Indiferente General, leg. 1568. See especially Instrucciones reservadas para los comisionados que van ... a procurar la pacificación de los provincias disidentes de ultramar, [Palace, 15 April 1820], AGI, Indiferente General, leg. 1568; and Instrucciones reservadas, 9 June 1820, AGI, Indiferente General, leg. 1569.
34. Selection of commissioners, Cádiz, 17 May 1820, AGI, Indiferente General, leg. 1568.
35. Juan Jabat to Minister of Overseas, Palace, 22 June 1820, AGI, Indiferente General, leg. 1568; Ligeros apuntes en el expediente sobre ... los comisionados ..., n.d., AGI, Indiferente General, leg. 1569; Juan Barry to Antonio Porcel, Cádiz, 25 August 1820; AGI, ASF, leg. 668.
36. Juan Barry and Tomás de Urrechea to Antonio Porcel, Cádiz, 13 October 1820, AGI, ASF, leg. 668.
37. José Sartorio to Minister of Overseas, Caracas, 26 April 1821, AGI, Indiferente General, leg. 1571; Juan Barry to Minister of Overseas, Caracas, 26 April 1821, AGI, Indiferente General, leg. 1571; Juan Barry to Minister of Overseas, Puerto Cabello, 30 May 1821, AGI, Indiferente General, leg. 1569; Juan Barry to Minister

of Overseas, Puerto Cabello, 27 June 1821, AGI, Indiferente General, leg. 1569; and Juan Barry to Minister of Overseas, Puerto Cabello, 19 September 1821, AGI, ASF, leg. 668.

38. Juan Barry and Tomás to Urrechea to Simón Bolívar, Caracas, 25 December 1820, AGI, ASF, leg. 668; Tomás de Urrechea to Miguel de la Torre, Caracas, 23 February 1821, AHNM, Estado, leg. 8719, doc. 83; Tomás de Urrechea to Minister of Overseas, Seville, 23 June 1821, AGI, ASF, leg. 668; and Juan Barry to Minister of Overseas, Puerto Cabello, 27 July 1821, AGI, ASF, leg. 668. Espelius was permitted to return to Spain in 1821. José Sartorio to Minister of Overseas, Puerto Cabello, 19 November 1821, AGI, Indiferente General, leg. 1569 (also AGI, AC, leg. 55, doc. 26); and Juan Barry to Minister of Overseas, Puerto Cabello, 21 November 1821, AGI, AC, leg. 55, doc. 36.
39. Juan Barry to Minister of Overseas, Caracas, 17 March 1821, AGI, AC, leg. 55, doc. 14.
40. Dictamen de la comisión de Cortes, 1821, AGI, Indiferente General, leg. 1569.
41. José Sartorio to Miguel de la Torre, Puerto Cabello, 23 December 1821, AHNM, Estado, leg. 8719.
42. Order of Ferdinand, 26 January 1824, AGI, Indiferente General, leg. 1571; and William Spence Robertson, 'The Policy of Spain towards its Revolted Colonies, 1820–1823', *HAHR*, vol. 6 (1926), p. 45. The pathetic letters of Juan Barry and José Sartorio from 1822–1824 are in AGI, Indiferente General, leg. 1571.
43. The documents related to this announcement may be found in Rodríguez Villa, *Pablo Morillo*, vol. 4, pp. 258–68, 275–76. Duplicate documents may also be found in AHNM, Estado, leg. 8719, docs 1–7; and additional material is contained in AGI, Indiferente General, leg. 1568. Some of the acts of the Junta de Conciliación are located in AHNM, Estado, leg. 8733, doc. 24.
44. Pablo Morillo to Miguel de la Torre, Valencia, 27 July 1820, and 19 August 1820, BRAH, Colección Morillo, sig. 9/7664 (leg. 21), ff. 176–78, 181–83. See also Pablo Morillo to Minister of Overseas, Valencia, 26 July 1820, AGI, Indiferente General, leg. 1568.
45. Duque de Frías to Evaristo Pérez de Castro, London, 23 September 1820, AGI, Indiferente General, leg. 1568.
46. José Antonio Páez to Francisco Tomás Morales, San Juan de Payana, 13 July 1820; Fernando de Peñalver to Pablo Morillo, Palace of Soberano Congreso, Nueva Guayana, 13 July 1820; Pablo Morillo to Minister of Overseas, Valencia, 26 July 1820; Declaration of José Sánchez de Ron; and Pablo Morillo to Minister of Overseas, Valencia, 8 September 1820, all in AGI, Indiferente General, leg. 1568. See also O'Leary's account of the negotiations in O'Leary, *Bolívar and the War of Independence*, pp. 178–84.
47. Simón Bolívar to Pablo Morillo, San Cristóbal, 21 September 1820; Pablo Morillo to Simón Bolívar, San Carlos, 20 October 1820; Simón Bolívar to Pablo Morillo, Trujillo, 26 October 1820; and Poder de Simón Bolívar, Trujillo, 20 November 1820; all in Rodríguez Villa, *Pablo Morillo*, vol. 4, pp. 271–72, 278–80, 290–91. A helpful summary of the negotiations may be found in Manifiesto que de orden de la junta de conciliación hace don Josef Domingo Díaz ... sobre lo obrado hasta la conclusión de los tratados de armisticio y regularización de guerra, Caracas, 24

December 1820, AGI, ASF, leg. 668.

Bolívar also entered into negotiations with Miguel de la Torre over the proposed armistice. See the letters exchanged between Miguel de la Torre and Simón Bolívar, July 1820–April 1821, AHNM, Estado, leg. 8723, docs 4–24; and in AGI, Indiferente General, leg. 1568.

48. See Pablo Morillo to Minister of Overseas, Barquisimeto, 31 October 1820, AGI, Indiferente General, leg. 1568.

49. Pablo Morillo to Minister of Overseas, Barquisimeto, 31 October 1820, AGI, Indiferente General, ieg. 1568; and Madariaga, *Bolívar*, p. 380.

50. Many documents related to the negotiations may be found in Rodríguez Villa, *Pablo Morillo*, vol. 4, # 870, pp. 292–301, # 872, pp. 302–9. See also Francisco González de Linares to Pablo Morillo, Trujillo, 23 November 1820, Rodríguez Villa, *Pablo Morillo*, vol. 4, p. 310.

51. See Bases para el armisticio, Trujillo, 25 November 1820, Rodríguez Villa, *Pablo Morillo*, vol. 4, pp. 314–19.

52. In his private correspondence Morillo had been referring to the 'Gobierno de Colombia' for over five months. See, for example, Pablo Morillo to Vicente Sánchez Lima, Valencia, 22 June 1820, BRAH, Colección Morillo, sig. 9/7664 (leg. 21), ff. 5–6.

53. See Pablo Morillo to Minister of Overseas, Puerto Cabello, 16 December 1820, AGI, Indiferente General, leg. 1569.

54. See the copy of the armistice with the treaty regularizing the war printed in the *Gaceta de Caracas*, no. 19, 6 December 1820, AGI, Indiferente General, leg. 1568. (also in AHNM, Estado, leg. 8717, docs 5, 7.)

55. Simón Bolívar to Francisco de Paula Santander, Trujillo, 29 November 1820, *Selected Writings of Bolívar*, vol. 1, pp. 244–47. See also Francisco Zea to Viscount Castlereagh, London, 20 February 1821, *Britain and the Independence of Latin America*, vol. 1, pp. 375–76, for the views of a republican agent in Europe.

56. Morillo's description of his meeting with Bolívar, Rodríguez Villa, *Pablo Morillo*, vol. 4, pp. 320–23. Rodríguez Villa does not attribute this description to Morillo himself, but it is undoubtedly drawn for the autobiographical memoir begun by Morillo and preserved in the Biblioteca de la Real Academia de Historia in Madrid. See also Morillo's account of the meeting given in Groot, *Historia eclesiástica*, vol. 4, p. 134.

57. Simón Bolívar to Francisco de Paula Santander, Trujillo, 29 November 1820, in *Selected Writings of Bolívar*, vol. 1, pp. 244–47.

58. Compare José Antonio de Sucre to Simón Bolívar, Trujillo, 25 November 1820, in *Archivo de Sucre*, vol. 1: 1812–1821, Fundación Vicente Lecuna, Banco de la República (Caracas, 1973), pp. 218–19.

59. See Orden general del 14 de Agosto, AGI, PC, leg. 759B.

60. Pablo Morillo to Francisco Martínez de la Rosa, La Coruña, 24 March 1834, AGI, Estado, leg. 69, Doc. 60. See also O'Leary, *Bolívar and the War of Independence*, pp. xvi, 187.

61. For example, see Francisco Delgado to Pablo Morillo, Maracaibo, 6 December 1820, AHNM, Estado, leg. 8719, doc. 14.

62. See Simón Bolívar to Miguel de la Torre, Cúcuta, 19 February 1821, AHNM,

Estado, leg. 8723, doc. 18; and also Justo Briceño to Manuel Landa, Santa Marta, 22 December 1820, AHNM, Estado, leg. 8723, doc. 38, for similar problems in New Granada. See also Pablo Morillo to Minister of War, Caracas, 30 September 1820, Rodríguez Villa, *Pablo Morillo*, vol. 4, pp, 234–35.

63. Antonio Van-Halen to Miguel de la Torre, Caracas, March 1821, enclosed in Miguel de la Torre to Minister of Overseas, Caracas, 22 March 1821, AGI, AC, leg. 55, doc. 19.
64. See the negotiations between Miguel de la Torre and Simón Bolívar in AHNM, Estado, leg. 8723, docs 23, 24ff; and Actas de la Junta de Conciliación de Venezuela, 1821, AHNM, Estado, leg. 8733, doc. 24. See also Simón Bolívar to Fernando Peñalver, Barinas, 21 April 1821, *Selected Writings of Bolívar*, vol. 1, pp. 262–63.
65. Minister of War to Minister of Overseas, Palace, 9 September 1820, AGI, Indiferente General, leg. 1568; and Manuel de Urriola to Juan Sámano, Panama, 9 July 1820, AGI, PC, leg. 742.
66. Order by Ferdinand, San Lorenzo, 31 October 1820, AGI, PC, leg. 714A.
67. See Juan de la Cruz Mourgeon to Minister of Overseas, Puerto Cabello, 5 July 1821, AGI, AC, leg. 55; and Juan de la Cruz Mourgeon to Captain General of Cuba, Kingston, 7 August 1821, AGI, ASF, leg. 668.
68. Miguel de la Torre to Minister of Overseas, Puerto Rico, 16 September 1822, AGI, AC, leg. 55.
69. 'Saeta' or lampoon from Cartagena, 1820, AGI, Pasquines y Loas, leg. 9 (emphasis as in the original). See also Complaints about Manuel Cordero, Cartagena, 9 June 1821, AGI, PC, leg. 719B.
70. For the fall of Ríohacha, see Mariano Montilla to Francisco de Paula Santander, Ríohacha, 22 March 1820; and other related documents, all in AGI, PC, leg. 745; and also Pablo Morillo to Minister of War, Valencia, 29 March 1820, Rodríguez Villa, *Pablo Morillo*, vol. 4, pp. 165–72.
71. See First declaration of Gabriel de Torres, Proceso contra Gabriel de Torres, Havana, 2 November 1824, AGI, PC, leg. 2136A; Gabriel de Torres to Pedro Ruíz de Porras, Cartagena, 8 July 1820, AGI, PC, leg. 709; and Francisco Warleta to Juan Sámano, Barranca, 9 June 1820, AGI, PC, leg. 713B.
72. See Bando de Gabriel de Torres, Cartagena, 4 July 1820; Bando de Gabriel de Torres, Cartagena, 5 July 1820; and repeated order of 17 April 1821, all in AGI, PC, leg. 717; and various Bandos of Torres from July 1820 to April 1821, AGI, PC, leg. 2136C.
73. Francisco de Mosquera to Minister of State, Kingston, 15 August 1820, AGI, ASF, leg. 665.
74. See, for example, the documents about Cartagena's food supply in AGI, PC, leg. 715; Gabriel de Torres to Alejandro Ramírez, Cartagena, 19 August 1820; and Proclama de Gabriel de Torres, Cartagena, 13 September 1820; both in AGI, PC, leg. 714.
75. First declaration of Gabriel de Torres, Proceso contra Gabriel de Torres, Havana, 2 November 1824, AGI, PC, leg. 2136A.
76. See Miguel de la Torre to Minister of Overseas, Caracas, 21 December 1820, AGI, Indiferente General, leg. 1568; Vicente Sánchez Lima to Miguel José Gómez,

Arroyo Cardón, 23 November 1820; Vicente Sánchez Lima to Military commanders in Ríohacha, Moreno, 26 November 1820; Miguel José Gómez to Vicente Sánchez Lima, Arroyo Cardón, 29 November 1820; and Vicente Sánchez Lima to Pablo Morillo, Maracaibo, 8 December 1820; all in AGI, Indiferente General, leg. 1568. Also see AHNM, Estado, leg. 8722, docs 183–91.

77. See negotiations between Gabriel de Torres and Mariano Montilla, July 1820, AGI, ASF, leg. 1017.

78. Gabriel de Torres to Pablo Morillo, Cartagena, 18 August 1820, and 13 September 1820; both in AGI, PC, leg. 714; Gabriel de Torres to Minister of Overseas, Cartagena, 22 September 1820, AGI, ASF, leg. 1017; and Gabriel de Torres to Interim commander of Panama, Cartagena, 1 October 1820, AGI, PC, leg. 717.

79. See discussions about line of demarcation, December 1820, AHNM, Estado, leg. 8719, docs 9, 12; AHNM, Estado, leg. 8723, doc. 38; (for January–February 1821) AGI, PC, leg. 709; and Gabriel de Torres to Miguel de la Torre, Cartagena, 8 February 1821, AGI, PC, leg. 714.

80. Manuel Landa to Miguel de la Torre, Sasaria, 20 February 1821, AHNM, Estado, leg. 8719, doc. 21. See also the subsequent documents in the same leg., and also Manuel Landa to Miguel de la Torre, Caracas, 23 March 1821, AGI, AC, leg. 55, doc. 20.

81. Gabriel de Torres to Miguel de la Torre, Cartagena, 8 February 1821, AGI, PC, leg. 714.

82. Mariano Montilla to Gabriel de Torres, Turbaco, 29 May 1821, and 8 June 1821; Gabriel de Torres to Mariano Montilla, Cartagena, 23 June 1821; all in AGI, PC, leg. 709.

83. Gabriel de Torres to Minister of Overseas, Cartagena, 23 May 1821, AGI, ASF, leg. 668 (also AGI, Indiferente General, leg. 1568); and Surrender of the Castillo de Boca Chica, Turbaco, 7 July 1821, AGI, PC, leg. 709.

84. Gabriel de Torres to Luis de Rieux, Cartagena, 29 August 1821; and Luis de Rieux to Gabriel de Torres, Turbaco, 31 August 1821, both in AGI, PC, leg. 717. See the Proposals for the capitulation in AGI, PC, leg. 717. The details of the surrender negotiations are contained in AGI, PC, leg. 709.

85. Ortiz, *Agustín Agualongo y su tiempo*, p. 389.

86. Gerhard Masur, *Simón Bolívar*, University of New Mexico Press (Albuquerque, 1948), p. 455.

87. See, for example, José María Obando, *Apuntamientos para la historia*, Editorial ABC (Bogotá, 1945), vol. 1, p. 25; and Hamnett, 'Popular Insurrection and Royalist Reaction', p. 322.

88. Obando, *Apuntamientos*, vol. 1, p. 53; and José Rafael Sañudo, *Estudios sobre la vida de Bolívar*, Bolsilibro Bedout (Medellín, 1980), pp. 225–36.

89. See Simón Bolívar to José de San Martín, 22 June 1822, *Selected Writings of Bolívar*, vol. 1, p. 52; and Ortiz, *Agustín Agualongo*, pp. 438–40.

90. See Francisco José Zuluaga, *José María Obando: de soldado realista a caudillo republicano*, Banco Biblioteca Popular (Bogotá, 1985), p. 57; and Rebecca Earle, 'Regional Revolt and Local Politics in the Province of Pasto (Colombia), 1780–1850', unpublished M.A. dissertation, University of Warwick (Coventry, 1989), chapters 4 and 5.

91. See J.G. Pérez to Tomás Cipriano de Mosquera, 17 June 1822, José M. De-Mier (editor), *Historia de Colombia según sus protagonistas*, vol. 1, Colegio Máximo de la Américas de Colombia, Libreros Colombianos (Bogotá, 1987), p. 353; O'Leary, *Bolívar*, p. 227; and Sañudo, *Estudios sobre Bolívar*, p. 247.
92. Sañudo, *Estudios sobre Bolívar*, p. 248; Obando, *Apuntamientos*, vol. 1, pp. 58–59; and Restrepo, *Historia de la revolución*, vol. 4, p. 422.
93. See O'Leary, *Bolívar*, p. 223; and Simón Bolívar to José Antonio Sucre, 21 June 1823, in *Selected Writings of Bolívar*, vol. 1, p. 382. For details about Agualongo, see Ortiz, *Agustín Agualongo*.
94. Ezequiel Márquez, '¡Pasto!', *Boletín de Estudios Históricos*, vol. 5 (1934), p. 299.
95. Alberto Miramón, 'Agualongo, el guerrillero indomible', *BHA*, vol. 27 (1940), p. 974.
96. See Obando, *Apuntamientos*, vol. 1, pp. 63–73; Hamilton, *Travels through the Interior Provinces*, vol. 2, p. 58, and Report on Agualongo's execution, AHNC, Secretaría de Guerra y Marina, tomo 43, fols 679–72.
97. See Pérez, *Guerra irregular*, p. 337; Edgar Bastidas Urresty, *Las guerras de Pasto*, Ediciones Testimonio (Pasto, 1979), pp. 102–4; and Reports on Bandits, ACC, Independencia JI–15cr, sig. 6099.
98. See Obando, *Apuntamientos*, vol. 1, pp. 77–81; H.M. Wood to George Canning, Popayán, 30 June 1825; 12 August 1825; and 14 September 1825; all in PRO, F.O. 18/21, fols 86–91, 98–100, 101–2, respectively; Report on unrest in Pasto, Quito, 21 September 1824; and List of executed royalist *cabecillas*; both in AHNC, Secretaría de Guerra y Marina, tomo 47, fols 153, 155.
99. See Interrogation of Pedro Galíndez, September 1825, ACC, Independencia MI–3j, sig. 4202.
100. H.M. Wood to George Canning, Popayán, 12 August 1825, PRO, F.O. 18/21, fols 98–100.

Epilogue: Spain and the Loss of Colombia

1. The pre-1810 plans are discussed in McFarlane, *Colombia before Independence*, pp. 283–84.
2. The remarks which follow on the Congress of Cúcuta and Santander's government are drawn from Bushnell, *The Making of Modern Colombia*. Further information may be found in Bushnell, *The Santander Regime*.
3. For Páez, see John Lynch, *Caudillos in Spanish America, 1800–1850*, Clarendon Press (Oxford, 1992), pp. 275–315.
4. For Obando and López, see Zuluaga, *José María Obando*; Obando, *Apuntamientos*; and López, *Memorias*, vol. 1.
5. On the formation of Ecuador, see Mark J. van Aken, *King of the Night. Juan José Flores and Ecuador, 1824–1864*, University of California Press (Berkeley, 1989).
6. See McFarlane, 'The Transition from Colonialism in Colombia'; and Bushnell, *The Making of Modern Colombia*, pp. 48–55, and for cogent general remarks about the economic consequences of independence, Victor Bulmer Thomas, *The Economic History of Latin America since Independence*, Cambridge University Press (Cambridge, 1994), pp. 28–45. For comment on the impact of the war on gender relations, see

Earle, 'Rape and the Anxious Republic'. Growth in the printing and publishing, François-Xavier Guerra's prime bellwether of modernity, is discussed in David Bushnell, 'The Development of the Press in Great Colombia', *HAHR*, vol. 30 (1950); and Eduardo Posada-Carbó, 'The Role of Newspapers and Leaflets in Electoral Campaigns in Colombia, 1830–1930', unpublished conference paper, Twentieth International LASA Conference, 1995. Guerra's views on Spanish American modernity are set forth in *Modernidad e Independencias*.

7. Charles Stuart Cochrane, *Journal of a Residence and travels in Colombia during the Years 1823 and 1824* (1825), AMS Press (New York, 1971), vol. 1, p. 3.
8. See Delgado, *La independencia de América*, pp. 7–12, 315.
9. Fernández Almagro, *La emancipación de América*, pp. 7–14, 155–57; and Costeloe, *Response to Revolution*, pp. 1–3. A small poll conducted by the author suggests that Fernández Almagro's assertions continue to hold true.
10. For information on Spanish periodicals of the epoch, see Delgado, *La independencia de América*. Alberto Gil Novales lists many pamphlets and memoirs of the period which discuss the American question. See Alberto Gil Novales, 'La independencia de América en la conciencia española, 1820–1823', *Revista de Indias*, vol. 39 (1979), pp. 235–65.
11. The investigation against Torres filled four volumes of correspondence. See the Proceso contra Gabriel de Torres, AGI, PC, legs 2136A, 2136B, 2136C, 2136D.
12. See votes in Proceso contra Gabriel de Torres, AGI, PC, leg. 2136B.
13. The planned court-martial was motivated by the suspicion that Spanish officer had agreed to capitulate before the battle was begun. See Madariaga, *Bolívar*, pp. 487–490; Costeloe, *Response to Revolution*, p. 115, and Fernández Almagro, *La emancipación de América*, pp. 132–33, 163–64.
14. See González García, 'El aniquilamiento del ejército expedicionario', pp. 137–38.
15. Dictamen de la comisión de Cortes sobre la pacificación de América, 1821, AGI, Indiferente General, leg. 1569.
16. Fernández Almagro, *La emancipación de América*, pp. 131–32.
17. Fernández Almagro, *La emancipación de América*, pp. 148–49.
18. Lional Hervey to Marquis of Londonderry, Madrid, 27 May 1822, *Britain and the Independence of Latin America*, vol. 1, p. 386. See also Lional Hervey to Marquis of Londonderry, Madrid, 16 December 1821, *Britain and the Independence of Latin America*, vol. 1, p. 384; Costeloe, *Response to Revolution*, pp. 100, 220–21; and Anna, *Spain and the Loss of America*, pp. 272–74.
19. See Report by the Council of State, 6 June 1821, AGI, AC, leg. 55; Report by ambassador to United States, 1821, AGI, AC, leg. 55; Costeloe, *Response to Revolution*, pp. 93–99; and Fernández Almagro, *La emancipación de América*, pp. 129–57.
20. Costeloe, *Response to Revolution*, pp. 187–88, 197–98; and Anna, *Spain and the Loss of America*, pp. 277–78, 293–94.
21. A delightful account of the reception of the first Spanish ambassador in Mexico is provided in Francis Calderón de la Barca, *Life in Mexico during a Residence of Two Years in that Country* (1842), E.P. Dutton (New York, 1937).
22. For Spain's recognition of its former colonies, see Mark Van Aken, *Pan-Hispanism: its Origin and Development to 1866*, University of California Press (Berkeley, 1959);

William Spence Robertson, 'The Recognition of the Spanish Colonies by the Motherland', *HAHR*, vol. 1 (1918), pp. 70–91; and John Tate Lanning, 'Great Britain and Spanish Recognition of the Hispanic American States', *HAHR*, vol. 10 (1930), pp. 429–56.

23. For predictions of independence, see, for example, Francisco Silvestre, *Descripción del Reyno de Santa Fé de Bogotá*, Biblioteca Universitaria de Cultura Colombiana (1968), p. 116. The Abbé Raynal asserted that 'when these colonies have reached the degree of culture, enlightenment and population which is proper to them, will they not detach themselves from a country which has built its splendour on their prosperity?'. See Gerbi, *The Dispute of the New World*, p. 63. The economy of late eighteenth-century Spain is examined in John Lynch, *Bourbon Spain, 1700–1808*, Basil Blackwell (Oxford, 1993); and Miguel Artola, *Antiguo Régimen y revolución liberal*, Ariel (Barcelona, 1991).

24. Gabriel de Torres to Minister of Overseas, Cartagena, 22 September 1820, AGI, ASF, leg. 1017; and Report by Spanish Ambassador to United States, 1821, AGI, AC, leg. 55. See also Costeloe, *Response to Revolution*, pp. 167–68; and Fernández Almagro, *La emancipación de América*, pp. 149–51.

25. Spain's trade with both the former colonies and the rest of the world shrank drastically after the war. Josep Fontana has shown that, in 1827, Spain's total foreign trade had fallen by some seventy-five per cent from its level in 1792. (1792 was, admittedly, a year of unusually high commercial profit, and so is perhaps a misleading point for comparison. See Fisher, *Trade, War and Revolution*.) Certain American products, such as dye wood, vanished altogether from Spain's markets, and the American raw materials, such as cotton, needed for Spain's re-export trade ceased to be freely available. The effect was especially marked on Spain's great ports, particularly Cádiz. By 1824, only twenty of the city's three hundred shipowners remained in business, a third of the merchant companies had gone bankrupt, and the population had been reduced by nearly half. The other towns of Andalucía experienced proportional declines, while the fishing industry in Galicia 'languished for lack of trans-Atlantic demand'. Despite its lesser dependence on American trade, Catalonia, too, suffered economically after the war, although losses were perhaps partially compensated for by the reinvestment in Spain of capital withdrawn from the Americas. For Galicia, see Van Aken, *Pan-Hispanism*, pp. 22–23; for general comments on Spain's post-America syndrome, see Costeloe, *Response to Revolution*, pp. 150–70.

26. Costeloe, *Response to Revolution*, p. 167. The quotation is Costeloe's paraphrase. See also Fernández Almagro, *La emancipación de América*, pp. 95–97; Brading, *The First America*, p. 506; and Costeloe, *Response to Revolution*. Costeloe provides an excellent discussion of this topic. See especially pp. 2–4, 150–70.

Glossary of Spanish Terms

afrancesado Francophile, an admirer of the French Revolution.
aguardiente Sugar-cane brandy.
alcabala Sales tax levied on a variety of goods.
arroba A unit of weight equal to approximately 11 kilograms.
asesor/asesor general de gobierno Legal advisor. An *asesor general de gobierno* is a legal advisor to the viceroy.
audiencia High court, whose members, the *oidores*, also exercised some administrative and executive functions. The term also refers to the territory over which the audiencia has jurisdiction.
ayuntamiento Cabildo.
cabildo/cabildo abierto/cabildo extraordinario/cabildo pleno Town council. A *cabildo abierto* is a special meeting of the town council attended also by some members of the public. A *cabildo extraordinario* is a special, unscheduled meeting of the *cabildo*. A *cabildo pleno* is a plenary session of a *cabildo*.
cabo de sala Hospital orderly.
calentura Feverish illness.
camarilla Influential clique within government.
canario Native of Canary Islands.
castas Persons of mixed race.
caudillo Local political leader.
cédula Royal decree or order.
chapetón Spaniard.
consulado Association of merchants engaged in export trade.
contador de tabacos Accountant or auditor in charge of monitoring the accounts of the tobacco monopoly.
corregidor Magistrate or mayor.
Cortes Parliament.
curandero Folk healer.
desafectado Disaffected person.
desórdenes Disorders.
estanco/estanquillo State monopoly. An *estanquillo* is a local outlet or depository of the monopoly.

faccioso Troublemaker, armed rebel.
fanega In this context, a unit of volume roughly equal to fifty-five litres.
fuero In this context, special privileges that exempt an individuals from the jurisdiction of ordinary courts of law. Both priests and members of the military enjoyed special *fueros*.
gachupín Spaniard.
gente de color People of colour.
gente decente The gentry.
hacendado Owner of an estate, or *hacienda*.
hombres oscuros Conspirators.
indulto/indultado Official pardon. An *indultado* is someone who has been pardoned by the state.
infidencia/infidente Treason. An *infidente* is a traitor.
junta/junta extraordinaria Assembly or committee. A *junta extraordinaria* is a special, non-scheduled meeting.
libertador Liberator.
llanero/Llanos Cowboy dwelling in the vast prairie, or *Llanos*, between Colombia and Venezuela.
Madre Patria The fatherland, or, more precisely, the motherland.
oidor/oidor decano Judge on an *audiencia*. An *oidor decano* is the principal oidor.
olvido del pasado 'Forgetting of the past', hence, a pardon.
pardo Dark-skinned person, sometimes used synonymously with *mulatto*, a person of mixed white and black ancestry.
partido Political party.
patria The fatherland.
peso Silver coin divided into eight *reales de plata*, roughly equal to one dollar, indicated in this book by the dollar sign ($).
prócer Distinguished individual, in this context a 'founding father' of the Colombian state.
quinto Three per cent tax levied on gold before minting.
real A small coin, worth an eighth of a peso.
regidor Member of a *cabildo*.
resguardo Land set aside by the crown for use by Indian communities.
ruana Poncho.
trienio Period of three years, used to describe a term in office.
vecino A resident of a city entitled to participate in municipal politics.
zambo A person of mixed African and Indian ancestry, although the term might be applied to anyone of particularly dark skin.

Political Chronology 1808–1821

1808	
February	French troops invade Spain
2–3 May	Unsuccessful anti-French uprising in Madrid
5–8 May	Spanish monarchs surrender at Bayonne
May	Formation of patriotic juntas begins in Spain
19 July	Spanish victory at Battle of Bailén
19 August	News of French invasion reaches Santa Fe de Bogotá
5 September	Population of Santa Fe takes oath of loyalty to Ferdinand VII
25 September	Junta Central established
1809	
May–July	Elections held in New Granada for representatives to the Junta Central
10 August	First junta formed in Quito
1810	
29 January	Junta Central dissolves; Council of Regency formed in Cádiz
19 April	Caracas forms junta
14 June	Governor Montes deposed in Cartagena. Junta subsequently formed
3 July	Cali forms junta
4 July	Pamplona forms junta
9–10 July	Socorro forms junta
20 July	Santa Fe forms junta
21 July	Santa Fe swears loyalty to Regency
25 July	Viceroy and Vicereine placed under house arrest
26 July	Santa Fe revokes recognition of Regency. Crowd in Santa Fe frees prisoners from city's jails
27 July	Initial formation of revolutionary army in Santa Fe
6 August	Benito Pérez named Viceroy of New Granada
10 August	Santa Marta forms junta

13 August	Viceroy and Vicereine taken to prison
16 August	Viceroy and Vicereine sent to Cartagena
24 September	Spanish Cortes open in Cádiz
28 November	Troops from Caracas defeat royalist forces in Coro
8 December	Antonio Nariño returns to Santa Fe from prison
22 December	Congress opens in Santa Fe
1811	
21 March	Santa Fe sends troops against Mariquita
April	Second junta formed in Quito
25 May	State monopolies abolished in Santa Fe
11 June	Valencia rebels for royalists
5 July	Caracas declares independence
7 August	Instruments of torture burnt publicly in Santa Fe
September	Comisión de Reemplazos created
19 September	Nariño assumes command of government in Santa Fe
6 October	Santa Fe sends troops against Zipaquirá
5 November	Santa Fe sends troops against Chocontá
11 November	Cartagena declares independence
11 December	Quito declares independence
24 December	Nariño elected president in Santa Fe
1812	
19 March	Constitution of Cádiz approved in the Spanish Cortes
21 March	Audiencia de Santa Fe installed in Panama
26 March	Earthquake in Caracas
May	Domingo Monteverde's forces occupy Valencia and capture Caracas
25 July	Capitulation of San Marcos between Monteverde and Miranda
7 November	Toribio Montes captures Quito and begins to implement 1812 Constitution
November	War begins between federalists in Tunja and centralists in Santa Fe
1813	
1–9 January	Antonio Baraya mounts unsuccessful siege of Santa Fe
6 January	Insurgent forces capture Santa Marta
4–5 March	Insurgent forces expelled from Santa Marta
6 April	Santa Fe sends troops against Cúcuta

29 April	Liberty tree planted in Santa Fe
May	French forces abandon Madrid
10–11 May	Insurgent forces defeated at Santa Marta
1 June	Captain General Francisco de Montalvo arrives in Santa Marta
18 June	Simón Bolívar declares War to the Death
21 June	French forces defeated at Battle of Vitoria
30 June	Royalists capture Cali
5 July	Santa Fe declares independence from Spain
August	Bolívar's Campaña Admirable leads to capture of Caracas (7 August)
21 September	Insurgent forces led by Nariño depart for southern New Granada
10–11 December	Treaty of Valencay frees Spanish royal family

1814

January	Insurgents launch unsuccessful attack on Portobelo
14 January	Insurgent victory at Battle of Calibío
22 March	Ferdinand VII's triumphal re-entry to Spain
28 March	Royalist victory at Battle of Ciénaga Grande
6 April	Napoleon confined to Elba
10 April	Nariño's forces defeated in Pasto
4 May	Ferdinand VII annuls Constitution of Cádiz
13 May	Ferdinand VII arrives in Madrid
June–July	Forces of José Tomás Boves defeat Bolívar and capture Caracas (16 July)
17 September	Bolívar leaves Venezuela
5 December	Boves dies in battle
11–12 December	Bolívar's forces capture Santa Fe for Congress

1815

12 January	Congress returns to Santa Fe from Tunja
17 February	Expeditionary army leaves Cádiz
15 March	Expeditionary Army lands at Carúpano
April	Expeditionary Army conquers Margarita
24 April	Fire on the San Pedro Alcántara
12 May	Morillo establishes Permanent Courts-Martial in Caracas
15 May	Bolívar arrives in Jamaica
29 May	Jesuits allowed to return to New Granada
15 June	Santa Fe sends troops against Nare
22 July	Morillo arrives in Santa Marta

31 July	Ferdinand VII re-establishes Inquisition
2 August	Siege of Cartagena begins
9 September	Pedro Ruíz de Porras's troops arrive in Mompós
28 November	Royalists conquer Pamplona
6 December	Cartagena surrenders to Expeditionary Army
28 December	Royalists conquer Zaragosa

1816

16 February	Most of Expeditionary Army leaves Cartagena
18 February	Royalist victory at Battle of Los Remedios
by 19 February	Audiencia de Santa Fe moves to Cartagena
21–22 February	Royalist victory at Battle of Cachirí
24 February	Morillo establishes Permanent Courts-Martial in Cartagena
22 March	Royalist victory at Battle of Ceja Alta
7 April	Royalists capture Medellín
9 April	Montalvo issues pardon in Cartagena
23 April	Royalists capture Nare
28 April	New Granada is re-elevated to the status of Viceroyalty
30 April	Royalists capture Honda
May	Bolívar returns to Venezuela; republicans capture Margarita
5 May	Insurgent General Serviez captures Virgin of Chiquinquirá
6 May	Miguel de la Torre arrives in Santa Fe
16 May	Spanish troops recover Virgin of Chiquinquirá
26 May	Morillo enters Santa Fe
30 May	Royalist celebrations in Santa Fe. Morillo issues limited pardon. Council of Purification established in Santa Fe
6 June	Spanish begin to execute suspected insurgents
19 June-December	Executions continue in Santa Fe
29 June	Royalist victory at Battle of Cuchilla de Tambo
10 July	Royalist victory at Battle of La Plata
29 November	Morillo leaves Santa Fe for Venezuela
5 December	Archbishop returns to Santa Fe

1817

Throughout year	Activities of Third Division provoke unrest in southern New Granada
27 March	Audiencia de Santa Fe installed in Santa Fe

5 July	Juan Sámano authorized by Morillo to try cases of *infidencia*
17 July	Insurgent victory at Battle of Angostura
28 August	Sámano named Viceroy of New Granada
September	José García de León y Pizarro unveils plans for colonial reform
21 September	Ferdinand VII issues general pardon
10 November	Policarpa Salavarrieta executed in Santa Fe
1818	
12 February	Insurgent victory at Battle of Calabozo
16 March	Royalist victory at Battle of La Puerta
2 April	Royalist victory at Sabana de Onuto
1819	
15 February	Congress of Angostura opens
March	Insurgent forces gather in Cumaná. Royalist campaign in Llanos begins
10–11 July	Royalist victory at Battle of Puente de Gamesa
25 July	Battle of Pantano de Vargas
7 August	Insurgent victory at Battle of Boyacá
9 August	Insurgent forces occupy Santa Fe
September	Sámano settles in Cartagena
4 October	Insurgent forces capture Ríohacha
5 October	Royalists abandon Popayán
11 October	Royalists capture Ríohacha
10 November	Insurgent revolt in Ocaña
17 November	Insurgent revolt in Mompós
1820	
1 January	Liberal revolt begins in Spain
7–9 March	Ferdinand VII re-establishes Constitution of Cadiz
13 March	Insurgents occupy Ríohacha
16 April	Havana adopts Constitution of Cádiz
5 June	Insurgents burn, then abandon, Ríohacha
9 June	Sámano resigns as viceroy
10 June	Cartagena adopts Constitution of Cádiz
9 September	Alejandro Hore appointed Viceroy of New Granada
31 October	Juan de la Cruz Mourgeon appointed Viceroy of New Granada
11 November	Royalist special commissioners leave Cádiz. Insurgents capture Santa Marta

25–26 November	Armistice agreed between Bolívar and Morillo
December	Morillo returns to Spain. La Torre replaces him as commander of Expeditionary Army

1821

28 January	Maracaibo declares independence
6 May	Congress of Cúcuta opens
14 May	Insurgents capture Caracas
24 June	Insurgent victory at Battle of Carabobo
9–10 July	Insurgent siege of Cartagena begins
1 August	Sámano dies in Panama
4 August	La Torre replaced by Francisco Tomás Morales as commander of Expeditionary Army
10 October	Royalists evacuate Cartagena
10 November	Insurgents capture Puerto Cabello
11 November	Insurgents capture Santa Marta
November	Insurgents capture Panama

Bibliography

Unpublished Sources

ARCHIVES

Archivo Central del Cauca (Popayán, Colombia)
Independencia

Archivo General de Indias (Seville, Spain)
Audiencia de Caracas, Audiencia de Lima, Audiencia de Panama, Audiencia de Quito, Audiencia de Santa Fe, Correos, Diversos, Estado, Indiferente General, Mapas y Planos, Papeles de Cuba, Pasquines y Loas, Ultramar

Archivo General de Simancas (Simancas, Spain)
Estado

Archivo Histórico Nacional de Colombia (Santa Fe de Bogotá, Colombia)
Secretaría de Guerra y Marina, Secretaría de Guerra y Marina (Archivo Anexo), Visitas del Cauca

Archivo Histórico Nacional de Madrid (Madrid, Spain)
Estado (Archivo Torrepando)

Biblioteca de la Real Academia de Historia (Madrid, Spain)
Colección Morillo

British Library (London, England)
Egerton
Gayangos 15,740

Public Record Office (Kew, England)
Foreign Office Records

DISSERTATIONS AND UNPUBLISHED CONFERENCE PAPERS

Earle, Rebecca, 'Regional Revolt and Local Politics in the Province of Pasto (Colombia), 1780–1850', MA Dissertation, University of Warwick (Coventry, 1989)

Frías Núñez, Marcelo, 'Enfermedad y sociedad en la crisis colonial del antiguo régimen: Nueva Granada en el tránsito del siglo XVIII al XIX. Las epidemias de viruelas', Tesina de Licenciatura, Centro de Estudios Históricos (Madrid, 1991)

Guedea, Virginia, 'El pueblo de México y la política capitalina: 1808 y 1812', Seventeenth International LASA Congress, (1992)

Jaramillo U., Jaime; Meisal R., Adolfo; and Urrutia M., Miguel, 'Continuities and

Discontinuities in the Fiscal and Monetary Institutions of New Granada, 1783–1850', Buenos Aires preconference of the Twelfth International Economic History Congress (Seville, 1998)

Lomné, Georges, 'Las ciudades de la Nueva Granada: teatros y objetos de los conflictos de la memoria política (1810–1830)', Coloquio Internacional: Les Enjeux de la Mémoire (Paris, 1992)

Marchena Fernández, Juan, 'Militarismo y liberalismo en el Perú', Primer Seminario Intensivo Erasmus de Historia Latinoamericana (Florence, 1994)

Posada-Carbó, Eduardo, 'The Role of Newspapers and Leaflets in Electoral Campaigns in Colombia, 1830–1930', Twentieth International LASA Conference (1995)

Uribe Uran, Victor M., 'Rebellion of the Mandarins: Lawyers, Political Parties and the State in Colombia, 1780–1850', Doctoral Dissertation, University of Pittsburgh (Pittsburgh, 1993)

Vogel, Hans, 'The Wars of Independence in Northwest Argentina, 1810–1814', Fourth Spanish-Dutch Historical Colloquium (Avila, 1991)

Published Sources

Alamán, Lucas, *Historia de Méjico* (1849), 5 vols, Editorial Jus (Mexico City, 1969)

Albi, Julio, *Banderas olvidadas: el ejército realista en América*, Ediciones de Cultura Hispánica (Madrid, 1990)

Anna, Timothy, 'The Last Viceroys of New Spain and Peru: An appraisal', *American Historical Review*, vol. 81 (1976)

Anna, Timothy, *The Fall of the Royal Government in Mexico City*, University of Nebraska Press (Lincoln, 1978)

Anna, Timothy, *The Fall of the Royal Government in Peru*, University of Nebraska Press (Lincoln, 1979)

Anna, Timothy, *Spain and the Loss of America*, University of Nebraska Press (Lincoln, 1983)

Annino, Antonio, 'Pratiche creole e liberalismo nella crisis dello spazio urbano coloniale: il 29 novembre 1812 a Città del Messico', *Quaderni Storici: Notablili Elettori Elezioni*, no. 69 (1988)

Arámbarri, Francisco Xavier, *Hechos del General Pablo Morillo en América* (1821), Ediciones de la Embajada de Venezuela en España (Murcia, 1971)

Arboleda Llorente, José María (ed.), *Catálogo general detallado del Archivo Central del Cauca (época de la independencia)*, Universidad del Cauca (Popayán, 1975)

Archer, Christon, *The Army in Bourbon Mexico*, 1760–1810, University of New Mexico Press (Albuquerque, 1977)

Archer, Christon, '"La Causa Buena": The Counter-Insurgency Army of New Spain and the Ten Years War', in Jaime Rodríguez O. (ed.), *The Independence of Mexico and the Creation of the New Nation*, University of California Press (Los Angeles, 1989)

Archivo de Sucre, vol. 1: 1812–1821, Fundación Vicente Lecuna, Banco de la

República (Caracas, 1973)
Arrazola, Roberto (ed.), *Documentos para la Historia de Cartagena*, 2 vols, Edición Oficial (Cartagena, 1963)
Arrazola, Roberto, *Los mártires responden…* , Ediciones Hernández (Cartagena, 1973)
Artola, Miguel, *Antiguo régimen y revolución liberal*, Ariel (Barcelona, 1991)
Aymes, J.R., *La guerra de la independencia en España (1808–1814)*, Siglo Veintiuno (Madrid, 1990)
Barbier, Jacques, 'Peninsular Finance and Colonial Trade: the Dilemma of Charles IV's Spain', *JLAS*, vol. 12 (1980)
Bastidas Urresty, Edgar, *Las guerras de Pasto*, Ediciones Testimonio (Pasto, 1979)
Beaujón, Oscar, 'La medicina en la Campaña del Sur', *Boletín de la Academia Nacional de la Historia*, vol. 57 (Caracas, 1974)
Benson, Nettie Lee (ed.), *Mexico and the Spanish Cortes, 1810–1822*, Institute of Latin American Studies, University of Texas (Austin, 1968)
Bethell, Leslie, 'A Note on the Church and the Independence of Latin America', in Leslie Bethell (ed.), *The Independence of Latin America*, Cambridge University Press (Cambridge, 1987)
Blanchard, Peter, *Slavery and Abolition in Early Republican Peru*, SR Books (Wilmington, 1992)
Blosseville, Marqués Ernesto de and Morillo, Pablo, *Mémoires du Général Morillo, Comte de Carthagène, Marquis de la Puerta, rélátifs aux principaux événements de ses campagnes en Amèrique de 1815 à 1821, suivis de deux précis de Don José Domingo Díaz et du Général Don Miguel de la Torre*, P. Dufart (Paris, 1826)
Blossom, Thomas, *Nariño, Hero of Colombian Independence*, University of Arizona Press (Tucson, 1967)
Bolívar, Simón, *Escritos del Libertador*, 10+ vols, Sociedad Bolivariana de Venezuela (Caracas, 1973)
Bossa Herazo, Donaldo, *Cartagena independiente: tradición y desarrollo*, Ediciones Tercer Mundo (Bogotá, 1967)
Brading, David, *The First America, the Spanish Monarchy, Creole Patriots, and the Liberal State 1492–1867*, Cambridge University Press (Cambridge, 1991)
Buisson, Inge; Kahle, Günter; König, Hans-Joachim; and Pietschmann, Horst (eds), *Problemas de la formación del estado y de la nación en hispanoamérica*, Lateinamerikanische Forschung 13, Böhlau Verlag (Cologne, 1984)
Bulmer Thomas, Victor, *The Economic History of Latin America since Independence*, Cambridge University Press (Cambridge, 1994)
Burkholder, Mark, and Chandler, D.S., *From Impotence to Authority: The Spanish Crown and the American Audiencias, 1687–1808*, University of Missouri Press (Columbia, 1977)
Bushnell, David, 'The Development of the Press in Great Colombia', *HAHR*, vol. 30 (1950)
Bushnell, David, *The Santander Regime in Gran Colombia*, Greenwood Press

(Westport, 1970)
Bushnell, David, 'The Independence of Spanish South America', in Leslie Bethell (ed.), *The Independence of Latin America*, Cambridge University Press (Cambridge, 1987)
Bushnell, David, *The Making of Modern Colombia, a Nation in Spite of Itself*, University of California Press (Berkeley, 1993)
Bynum, William, 'Cullen and the Study of Fevers in Britain, 1760–1820', in Bynum, W.F., and Nutton, V. (eds), *Theories of Fever from Antiquity to the Enlightenment, Medical History*, Supplement no. 1 (London, 1981)
Bynum, W.F., and Porter, Roy (eds), *Companion Encyclopedia of the History of Medicine*, 2 Vols, Routledge (London, 1993)
Caballero, José María, *Diario*, Biblioteca de Bogotá, Editorial Villegas (Bogotá, 1990)
Cajigal, Juan Manuel de, *Memorias del Mariscal de Campo Don Juan Manuel de Cajigal sobre la revolución de Venezuela* (1819), Biblioteca Venezolana de Historia (Caracas, 1960)
Calderón de la Barca, Francis, *Life in Mexico during a Residence of Two Years in that Country* (1842), E.P. Dutton (New York, 1937)
Cárdenas Acosta, Pablo E., *El movimiento comunal de 1781 en el Nuevo Reino de Granada (Reivindicaciones Históricos)*, 2 vols, Tercer Mundo (Bogotá, 1980)
Carr, Raymond, *Spain: 1808–1975*, Clarendon Press (Oxford, 1982)
Carrera Damas, German, *Boves, aspectos socio-económicos*, Colección Vigilia (Caracas, 1968)
Cartas escritas desde Colombia durante un Viaje de Caracas a Bogotá y desde allí a Santa Marta en 1823, Archivo de la Economía Nacional, Banco de la República (Bogotá, 1975)
Cartas Santander-Bolívar, 1813–1820, vol. 1, Fundación para la Conmemoración del Bicentenario del Natalicio y del Sesquicentenario de la Muerte del General Francisco de Paula Santander, Biblioteca de la Presidencia de la República (Bogotá, 1988)
Cervera Pery, José, *La marina española en la emancipación de Hispanoamérica*, MAPFRE (Madrid, 1992)
Chastenet, Jacques, *Godoy, Master of Spain, 1792–1808*, Batchworth Press (London, 1953)
Christiansen, E., *The Origins of Military Power in Spain, 1800–1954*, Oxford University Press (Oxford, 1967)
Cochrane, Charles Stuart, *Journal of a Residence and Travels in Colombia during the Years 1823 and 1824* (1825), 2 vols, AMS Press (New York, 1971)
Colmenares, Germán, *Haciendas de los jesuítas en el Nuevo Reino de Granada, siglo XVIII*, Tercer Mundo (Bogotá, 1969)
Colmenares, Germán, 'La *historia de la revolución*' por José Manuel Restrepo: una prisión historiográfica' and 'Castas, patrones de poblamiento y conflictos sociales en las provincias del Cauca, 1810–1830', in Germán Colmenares *et al.*,

La independencia: ensayos de historia social, Instituto Colombiano de Cultura (Bogotá, 1986)

Comellas García Llera, José Luis, *Los primeros pronunciamientos en España, 1814–1820*, Consejo Superior de Investigaciones Científicas (Madrid, 1958)

Cooper, Donald, *Epidemic Disease in Mexico City, 1761–1813: an Administrative, Social and Medical Study*, University of Texas Press (Austin, 1965)

Cortés Vargas, Carlos (ed.), 'De la época del Terror', *BHA*, vol. 29:327 (1942)

Costeloe, Michael, 'Spain and the Spanish American Wars of Independence: the *Comisión de Reemplazos*, 1811–1820', *JLAS*, vol. 13 (1981)

Costeloe, Michael, *Response to Revolution: Imperial Spain and the Spanish American Revolutions, 1810–1840*, Cambridge University Press (Cambridge, 1986)

Curcio-Nagy, Linda A. (ed.), Special issue: 'Spectacle in Colonial Mexico', *The Americas*, vol. 52 (1996)

Dauxion Lavaysse, J.J., *Viaje a las Islas de Trinidad, Tobago, Margarita y a diversos partes de Venezuela en la América Meridional* (1813), Universidad Central de Venezuela (Caracas, 1967)

Dealy, Glen, 'Prolegomena on the Spanish American Political Tradition', *HAHR*, vol. 48 (1968)

Deas, Malcolm, 'The Fiscal Problems of Nineteenth-Century Colombia', *JLAS*, vol. 14 (1982)

Deas, Malcolm, 'Venezuela, Colombia and Ecuador', in Leslie Bethell (ed.), *Spanish America after Independence, c.1820–c.1870*, Cambridge University Press (1987)

Delgado, Jaime, *La independencia de América en la prensa española*, Seminario de Problemas Hispanoamericanos (Madrid, 1949)

Demélas, Marie-Danielle, and Saint-Geours, Yves, *Jerúsalen y Babilonia: Religión y política en el Ecuador, 1780–1880*, Biblioteca de Ciencias Sociales, vol. 21, Corporación Editorial Nacional (Quito, 1988)

De-Mier, José M. (ed.), *Historia de Colombia según sus protagonistas*, 3 vols, Colegio Máximo de la Américas de Colombia, Libreros Colombianos (Bogotá, 1987)

Díaz, Joseph Domingo, *Recuerdos sobre la revolución de Caracas*, Leon Amarita (Madrid, 1827)

Díaz Díaz, Oswaldo, *La reconquista española*, 2 vols, Historia Extensa de Colombia, vol. 6, Ediciones Lerner (Bogotá, 1967)

Díaz de Zuluaga, Zamira, 'La fuerza de trabajo en el Cauca Grande: 1810–1830', Germán Colmenares *et al.*, *La independencia: ensayos de historia social*, Instituto Colombiano de Cultura (Bogotá, 1986)

Díaz de Zuluaga, Zamira, 'El Cauca Grande en la independencia; estructura económico-social (1800–1830)', *Raices Históricas*, Academia Nariñense de Historia (Pasto, 1987)

Duffy, Christopher, *The Military Experience in the Age of Reason*, Routledge and Kegan Paul (London, 1987)

Duffy, Michael, *Soldiers, Sugar and Seapower: The British Expedition to the West Indies and the War against Revolutionary France*, Oxford University Press (Oxford, 1987)

Earle, Rebecca, 'Indian Rebellion and Bourbon Reform in New Granada: Riots in Pasto, 1780–1800', *HAHR*, vol. 73 (1993)

Earle, Rebecca, 'The Spanish Political Crisis of 1820 and the Loss of New Granada', *Colonial Latin American Historical Review*, vol. 3:3 (1994)

Earle, Rebecca, 'Information and Disinformation in Late Colonial New Granada', *The Americas*, vol. 54:2 (1997)

Earle, Rebecca, 'Rape and the Anxious Republic: Revolutionary Colombia, 1810–1830', in Dore, Elizabeth, and Molyneux, Maxine (eds), *Hidden Histories of Gender and the State in Latin America*, Duke University Press (Chapel Hill, 2000)

Enciso Recio, Luis Miguel, *La opinión pública española y la independencia hispanoamericana, 1819–1820*, Universidad de Valladolid (Valladolid, 1967)

Felstiner, Mary Lowenthal, 'Family Metaphors: the Language of an Independence Revolution', *Comparative Studies in Society and History*, vol. 25 (1983)

Fernández Almagro, Melchor, *La emancipación de América y su reflejo en la conciencia española*, Instituto de Estudios Políticos (Madrid, 1954)

Fisher, John, 'Royalism, Regionalism and Rebellion in Colonial Peru, 1808–1815', *HAHR*, vol. 59 (1979)

Fisher, John, *Trade, War and Revolution: Exports from Spain to Spanish America, 1797–1820*, Institute of Latin American Studies (University of Liverpool, 1992)

Fliegelman, Jay, *Prodigals and Pilgrims: the American Revolution against Patriarchal Authority, 1750–1800*, Cambridge University Press (Cambridge, 1982)

Flores Caballero, Romeo, *Counterrevolution: The Role of the Spaniards in the Independence of Mexico*, University of Nebraska Press (Lincoln, 1974)

Fontana, Josep, *La crisis del antiguo régimen, 1808–1833*, Editorial Crítica (Barcelona, 1979)

Fontana, Josep, *La quiebra de la monarquía absoluta, 1814–1820*, Editorial Ariel (Barcelona, 1987)

Franco, Jean, 'Un viaje poco romántico: viajeros británicos hacia Sudamérica, 1818–28', *Escritura*, vol. 7 (Caracas, 1979)

Friede, Juan (ed.), *La Batalla de Boyacá, 7 de agosto de 1819, a través de los archivos españoles*, Banco de la República (Bogotá, 1969)

Friede, Juan, *La otra verdad: la independencia americana vista por los españoles*, Tercer Mundo (Bogotá, 1972)

García Chuecos, Hector (ed.), *Causas de infidencia: Documentos inéditos relativos a la Revolución de la Independencia*, 2 vols, Imprenta Nacional (Caracas, 1952)

Garrido, Margarita, *Reclamos y representaciones: Variaciones sobre la política en el Nuevo Reino de Granada, 1750–1815*, Banco de la República (Bogotá, 1993)

Gerbi, Antonello, *The Dispute of the New World: The History of a Polemic, 1750–1900*, University of Pittsburgh Press (Pittsburgh, 1973)

Gil Novales, Alberto, 'La independencia de América en la conciencia española, 1820–1823', *Revista de Indias*, vol. 39 (1979)

Glick, Thomas, 'Science and Independence in Latin America (with special reference to New Granada)', *HAHR*, vol. 71 (1991)

Gómez, Thomas, 'La république des cuñados: Familles, pouvior et société à Santa Fé de Bogotá (XVIIIe siècle), *Caravelle*, special issue on 'L'expression des identités américaines a partir de 1492', vol. 62 (1994)

Gómez Hoyos, Rafael, *La independencia de Colombia*, MAPFRE (Madrid, 1992)

González García, Sebastián, 'El aniquilamiento del ejército expedicionario de Costa Firme (1815–1823)', *Revista de Indias*, vol. 22 (1962)

Grahn, Lance, 'An Irresoluble Dilemma: Smuggling in New Granada, 1713–1763', in Fisher, John, Kuethe, Allan J., and McFarlane, Anthony (eds), *Reform and Insurrection in Bourbon New Granada and Peru*, Louisiana State Press (Baton Rouge, 1990)

Grahn, Lance, *The Political Economy of Smuggling: Regional Informal Economies in Early Bourbon New Granada*, Westview Press (Boulder, 1997)

Griffin, Charles, *Los temas sociales y económicos en la época de la independencia*, Fundación John Boulton y Fundación Eugenio Mendoza (Caracas, 1962)

Groot, José Manuel, *Historia eclesiástica y civil de Nueva Granada*, 5 vols, Editorial M. Rivas (Bogotá, 1889–1893)

Groupe Interdisciplinaire de Recherche et de Documentation sur L'Amérique Latin, *L'Amérique Espagnole a l'Epoque des Lumieres: Tradition-Innovation-Representations*, Collection de la Maison des Pays Iberiques vol. 32 (Paris, 1987). Also published in Spanish by the Instituto de Cooperación Iberoamericana

Guerra, François-Xavier, *Modernidad e Independencias. Ensayos sobre las Revoluciones Hispánicas*, MAPFRE (Madrid, 1992)

Guerra, François-Xavier, 'La independencia de México y las revoluciones hispánicas', *Cuadernos de historia latinoamericana*: El liberalismo en Mexico, no. 1, (1993)

Guerra, François-Xavier and Quijada, Mónica (eds), *Imaginar la Nación*, AHILA (Hamburg, 1994)

Guerrero, Gustavo, *Documentos históricos para los hechos ocurridos en Pasto en la guerra de la independencia*, Imprenta del Departamento (1912)

Habermas, Jürgen, *The Structural Transformation of the Public Sphere: An Enquiry into a Category of Bourgeois Society*, MIT Press (Cambridge, 1991)

Hall, Francis, *Colombia: su estado actual* (1824), reprinted in David Sowell (ed.), *Santander y la opinión angloamericana*, Biblioteca de la Presidencia de la República (Bogotá, 1991)

Halperín Donghi, Tulio, 'Economy and Society', in Leslie Bethell (ed.), *Spanish America after Independence, c. 1820–1870*, Cambridge University Press (Cambridge, 1987)

Hamilton, J.P., *Travels through the Interior Provinces of Colombia*, 2 vols, John Murray

(London, 1827)

Hammerly, Michael, 'Selva Alegre, President of the Quiteña Junta of 1809: Traitor or Patriot?', *HAHR*, vol. 48 (1968)

Hamnett, Brian, 'The Counter Revolution of Morillo and the Insurgent Clerics of New Granada, 1815–1820', *The Americas*, vol. 32 (1976)

Hamnett, Brian, 'Mexico's Royalist Coalition: the Response to Revolution 1808–1821', *JLAS*, vol. 12 (1980)

Hamnett, Brian, 'Royalist Counterinsurgency and the Continuity of Rebellion: Guanajuato and Michoacán, 1813–1820', *HAHR*, vol. 62 (1982)

Hamnett, Brian, 'Popular Insurrection and Royalist Reaction: Colombian Regions, 1810–1823', in Fisher, John, Kuethe, Allan J., and McFarlane, Anthony (eds), *Reform and Insurrection in Bourbon New Granada and Peru*, Louisiana State Press (Baton Rouge, 1990)

Harding, Richard, *Amphibious Warfare in the Eighteenth Century: The British Expedition to the West Indies, 1740–1742*, The Royal Historical Society (Irthlingborough, 1991)

Hargreaves-Mawdsley, W.H. (ed.), *Spain under the Bourbons, 1700–1833*, University of South California Press (Columbia, 1973)

Heredia, Edmundo, 'El destino de la expedición de Morillo', *Anuario de Estudios Americanos*, vol. 29 (1972)

Heredia, Edmundo, *Planes españoles para reconquistar hispanoamerica, 1810/1818*, Editorial Universitaria de Buenos Aires (Buenos Aires, 1974)

Heredia, José Francisco, *Memorias del Regente Heredia (de las Reales Audiencia de Caracas y México)*, Editorial América (Madrid, n.d.)

Hernández de Alba, Guillermo, 'Recuerdos de la reconquista: el Consejo de Purificación', *BHA*, vol. 22 (1935)

Hernández de Alba, Guillermo (ed.), *Archivo Nariño 1812–1815*, vol. 5, Biblioteca de la Presidencia de la República (Bogotá, 1990)

Hernández y Dávalos, J.E. (ed.), *Colección de documentos para la Historia de la Guerra de Independencia de México de 1808 a 1821* (1878), 6 vols, Kraus Reprints (Nedeln, 1968)

Herrán Baquero, Mario, *El Virrey Don Antonio Amar y Borbón. La crisis del régimen colonial en la Nueva Granada*, Banco de la República (Bogotá, 1988)

Hunt, Lynn, *The Family Romance of the French Revolution*, University of California Press (Berkeley, 1993)

Izard, Miguel, *El miedo a la revolución: La lucha por la libertad en Venezuela, (1777–1830)*, Editorial Tecnos (Madrid, 1979)

Jackson, Robert, 'The Treatment or Mistreatment of Disease? Comments on Ronn Pineo's "Misery and Death in the Pearl of the Pacific: Health Care in Guayaquil, Ecuador, 1870–1925"', *HAHR*, vol. 72 (1991)

James, C.L.R., *The Black Jacobins. Toussaint L'Overture and the San Domingo Revolution*, Alison and Busby (London, 1984)

Jaramillo, Roberto, *El clero en la independencia*, Universidad de Antioquia (Medellín,

1946)
Jiménez Molinares, Gabriel, *Los mártires de Cartagena de 1816 ante el consejo de guerra y ante la historia*, 2 vols, Imprenta Departamental (Cartagena, 1948, 1950)
Juan, Jorge, and de Ulloa, Antonio, *Noticias Secretas de América*, Historia 16 (Madrid, 1990)
Kany, Charles, *Life and Manners in Madrid, 1750–1800*, AMS Press (New York, 1932)
Keegan, John, *A History of Warfare*, Hutchinson (London, 1993)
Kiple, Kenneth (ed.), *The Cambridge World History of Human Diseases*, Cambridge University Press (Cambridge, 1993)
König, Hans-Joachim, *En el Camino hacia la Nación: Nacionalismo en el proceso de formación del Estado y de la Nación de la Nueva Granada, 1750 à 1856*, Banco de la República (Bogotá, 1994)
Kuethe, Allan J., *Military Reform and Society in New Granada, 1773–1808*, University of Florida Press (Gainsville, 1978)
Kuethe, Allan J., 'The Early Reforms of Charles III in the Viceroyalty of New Granada, 1759–1776', in Fisher, John, Kuethe, Allan J., and McFarlane, Anthony (eds), *Reform and Insurrection in Bourbon New Granada and Peru*, Louisiana State Press (Baton Rouge, 1990)
Lambert, Eric, *Voluntarios británicos e irlandeses en la gesta bolivariana*, vol. 1, Edición de la Corporación Venezolana de Guayana (Caracas, 1981)
Lanning, John Tate, 'Great Britain and Spanish Recognition of the Hispanic American States', *HAHR*, vol. 10 (1930)
Lara, Jorge Salvador, *Quito*, MAPFRE (Madrid, 1992)
Leal, Ildefonso (ed.), *Documentos del Real Consulado de Caracas*, Universidad Central de Venezuela (Caracas, 1964)
Lecuna, Vicente (ed.), *Selected Writings of Bolívar*, 2 vols, The Colonial Press (New York, 1951)
Lee López, Alberto (ed.), *Los ejércitos del Rey, 1818–1819*, 2 vols, Biblioteca de la Presidencia de la República (Bogotá, 1989)
León Guerrero, Gerardo, '¿Por qué vinieron los quiteños? Dos invasiones al distrito de Pasto, 1809–1811', *Raices Historicas*, Academia Nariñense de Historia (Pasto, 1987)
Liévano Aguirre, Indalecio, *Los grandes conflictos sociales y económicos de nuestra historia*, 2 vols, Tercer Mundo (Bogotá, 1985)
López, José Hilario, *Memorias*, 2 vols, Editorial ABC (Bogotá, 1942)
López, Luis Horacio (ed.), *A los colombianos: Proclamas y discursos 1812–1840*, Biblioteca de la Presidencia de la República (Bogotá, 1988)
López Alvarez, Leopoldo, 'Campaña del sur y destrucción del ejército patriota', *Boletín de Estudios Históricos*, vol. 2, (Pasto, 1929)
Lovett, Gabriel, *Napoleon and the Birth of Modern Spain*, 2 vols, New York University Press (New York, 1965)
Lynch, John, *The Spanish American Revolutions, 1808–1826*, W.W. Norton (New

York, 1986)

Lynch, John, 'The Origins of Spanish American Independence', in Leslie Bethell (ed.), *The Independence of Latin America*, Cambridge University Press (Cambridge, 1987)

Lynch, John, *Caudillos in Spanish America, 1800–1850*, Clarendon Press (Oxford, 1992)

Lynch, John, *Bourbon Spain, 1700–1818*, Basil Blackwell (Oxford, 1993)

Mackesy, Piers, *The War for America, 1775–1783*, Longmans (London, 1964)

Madariaga, Salvador de, *Bolívar*, Hollis and Carter (London, 1952)

Marchena Fernández, Juan, *Oficiales y soldados en el Ejército de America*, Escuela de Estudios Hispano-Americanos (Seville, 1983)

Marchena Fernández, Juan, *Ejércitos y milicias en el mundo colonial americano*, MAPFRE (Madrid, 1992)

Márquez, Ezequiel, '¡Pasto!', *Boletín de Estudios Históricos*, vol. 5 (Pasto, 1934)

Martínez Delgado, Luis, and Ortiz, Sergio Elias (eds), *El periodismo en la Nueva Granada, 1810–1811*, Biblioteca Eduardo Santos, vol. 22, Editorial Kelly (Bogotá, 1960)

Martínez Riaza, Ascensión, 'Las diputaciones provinciales americanas en el sistema liberal español', *Revista de Indias*, vol. 52 (1992)

Marx, Karl, and Engels, Frederick, Despatches for the *New York Daily Tribune* (1854), reprinted in *Revolution in Spain*, Greenwood Press (Westport, 1975)

Masur, Gerhard, *Simón Bolívar*, University of New Mexico Press (Albuquerque, 1948)

Mathias, Peter, 'Swords and Ploughshares: The Armed Forces, Medicine and Public Health in the Late Eighteenth Century', in Winter, J.M. (ed.), *War and Economic Development*, Cambridge University Press (Cambridge, 1975)

McFarlane, Anthony, 'Civil Disorders and Popular Protests in Late Colonial New Granada', *HAHR*, vol. 30 (1984)

McFarlane, Anthony, 'The Transition from Colonialism in Colombia, 1819–1875', in Abel, Christopher and Lewis, Colin (eds), *Latin America: Economic Imperialism and the State: The Political Economy of the External Connection from Independence to the Present*, The Athlone Press (London, 1985)

McFarlane, Anthony, '"The Rebellion of the Barrios': Urban Insurrection in Bourbon Quito', in Fisher, John, Kuethe, Allan J., and McFarlane, Anthony (eds), *Reform and Insurrection in Bourbon New Granada and Peru*, Louisiana State Press (Baton Rouge, 1990)

McFarlane, Anthony, *Colombia before Independence: Economy, Society, and Politics under Bourbon Rule*, Cambridge University Press (Cambridge, 1993)

McFarlane, Anthony, 'Identity, Enlightenment and Political Dissent in Late Colonial Spanish America', *Transactions of the Royal Historical Society*, Sixth series, vol. 8 (1998)

Mejía Mejía, J.C., 'El clero de Pasto y la insurrección del 28 de octubre de 1822', *Boletín de Estudios Históricos*, vol. 4 (1932)

Mercado, Jorge, *Campaña de invasión del Teniente General Don Pablo Morillo, 1815–1816*, Ejército de Colombia, Estado Mayor General (Bogotá, 1919)

Minchom, Martin, *The People of Quito, 1690–1810: Change and Unrest in the Underclass*, Westview Press (Boulder, 1994)

Miramón, Alberto, 'Agualongo, el guerrillero indomible', *BHA*, vol. 27 (1940)

Monsalve, José Dolores, *Mujeres de la Independencia*, Academia Colombiana de Historia, Biblioteca de Historia Nacional, vol. 38 (Bogotá, 1926)

Mora de Tovar, Gilma Lucía, *Aguardiente y conflictos sociales en la Nueva Granada durante el siglo XVIII*, Universidad Nacional de Colombia (Bogotá, 1988)

Nariño, Antonio, *Escritos políticos*, El Ancora (Bogotá, 1982)

Obando, José María, *Apuntamientos para la historia*, 2 vols, Editorial ABC (Bogotá, 1945)

O'Leary, Daniel Florencio, *Memorias*, 3 vols, Editorial Santafé (Bogotá, 1952)

O'Leary, Daniel Florencio, *Bolívar and the War of Independence*, University of Texas Press (Austin and London, 1970)

O'Phelen Godoy, Scarlett, 'Por el rey, religión y la patria: Las juntas de gobierno de 1809 en La Paz y Quito', *Bulletin de l'Institut Français d'Etùdes Andines*, vol. 17 (1988)

Ortiz, Sergio Elías, *Agustín Agualongo y su tiempo*, Editorial ABC (Bogotá, 1958)

Ortiz, Sergio Elías, *Génesis de la revolución del 20 de julio de 1810*, Biblioteca Eduardo Santos, vol. 19, Editorial Kelly (Bogotá, 1960)

Ortiz, Sergio Elías, *Franceses en la independencia de la Gran Colombia*, Biblioteca Eduardo Santos, vol. 1, Editorial ABC (Bogotá, 1971)

Ots y Capdequi, José María, *Las instituciones del Nuevo Reino de Granada al tiempo de la independencia*, Consejo Superior de Investigaciones Científicas (Madrid, 1958)

Pagden, Anthony, 'Identity Formation in Spanish America', in Canny, Nicolas and Pagden, Anthony (eds), *Colonial Identity in the Atlantic World*, Princeton University Press (Princeton, 1987)

Pagden, Anthony, *European Encounters with the New World*, Yale University Press (New Haven, 1993)

Pérez, Eduardo, *Guerra irregular en la independencia de la Nueva Granada y Venezuela, 1810–1830*, Publicaciones de la Universidad Pedagógica y Tecnológica de Colombia (Tunja, 1982)

Pike, Frederick, *Hispanismo, 1898–1936*, University of Notre Dame Press (Notre Dame, 1971)

Pombo, Manuel Antonio and Guerra, José Joaquín (eds), *Constituciones de Colombia*, Biblioteca Popular de Cultura Colombiana (Bogotá, 1951)

Porras Troconis, Gabriel, *La magna epopeya de Cartagena: el sitio del año 1815*, Editorial Temis (Bogotá, 1965)

Porter, Roy, *Disease, Medicine and Society in England, 1550–1860*, The Economic History Society (London, 1993)

Posada, Eduardo, 'Las Memorias de Morillo', *BHA*, vol. 1 (1903)

Posada, Eduardo and Ibáñez, P.M. (eds), *Los últimos virreyes de Nueva Granada, Relación de Mando del Virrey Don Francisco Montalvo y noticias del Virrey Sámano sobre la pérdida del reino (1813–1819)*, Biblioteca de la Juventud Hispano-Americana, Editorial América (Madrid, n.d.)

Posada, Eduardo and Ibáñez, P.M. (eds), *Relaciones de Mando. Memorias presentadas por los gobernantes del Nuevo Reino de Granada*, Imprenta Nacional (Bogotá, 1910)

Pratt, Mary Louise, *Imperial Eyes: Travel Writing and Transculturation*, Routledge (London, 1992)

Ramos, Demetrio, 'Las Cortes de Cádiz y América', *Revista de Estudios Políticos*, vol. 126 (1962)

Rausch, Jane, *A Tropical Plains Frontier: the Llanos of Colombia, 1531–1831*, University of New Mexico Press (Albuquerque, 1984)

Restrepo, José Manuel, *Autobiographia, con apuntamientos sobre la emigración que hice en 1816 de la provincia de Antioquia a la de Popayán*, Biblioteca de la Presidencia de Colombia, vol. 30 (Bogotá, 1957)

Restrepo, José Manuel, *Historia de la revolución de Colombia* (1827), 6 vols, Editorial Bedout (Medellín, 1969)

Restrepo Canal, Carlos (ed.), *Nariño Periodista*, Academia Colombiana de Historia, vol. 20, Editorial Kelly (Bogotá, 1960)

Restrepo Saenz, José María, *Gobernadores de Antioquia, 1571–1819*, vol. 1, Imprenta Nacional (Bogotá, 1932)

Restrepo Saenz, José María, *Gobernadores y próceres de Neiva*, Biblioteca de Historia Nacional, vol. 63 (Bogotá, 1941)

Restrepo Saenz, José María, *Biografías de los mandatarios y ministros de la real Audiencia (1671–1819)*, Biblioteca de Historia Nacional, vol. 84, Editorial Cromos (Bogotá, 1952)

Restrepo Tirado, Ernesto, *Historia de la Provincia de Santa Marta*, 2 vols, Ministerio de Educación Nacional (Bogotá, 1953)

Riaño, Camilo, *La campaña libertadora de 1819*, Editorial Andes (Bogotá, 1969)

Riaño Camilo, *Historia Militar: La independencia, 1810–1815*, Historia Extensa de Colombia, vol. 18, Editorial Lerner (Bogotá, 1971)

Rieu-Millan, Marie Laure, *Los diputados americanos en las Cortes de Cádiz (igualdad o independencia)*, Consejo Superior de Investigaciones Científicas (Madrid, 1990)

Rieu-Millan, Marie-Laure, 'Les Cortès de Cadix face à la dissidence américaine: les raisons d'un échec (1810–1814)', *Caravelle*, no. 68 (1997)

Robertson, William Spence, 'The Recognition of the Spanish Colonies by the Motherland', *HAHR*, vol. 1 (1918)

Robertson, William Spence, 'The Policy of Spain towards its Revolted Colonies, 1820–1823', *HAHR*, vol. 6 (1926)

Rodríguez, Mario, *The Cádiz Experiment in Central America, 1808 to 1826*, University of California Press (Berkeley, 1978)

Rodríguez Guerrero, Ignacio, 'Repercusiones de la revolución quiteña de 10 de agosto de 1809, en la Nueva Granada', *Revista de Historia*, vol. 7 (Pasto, 1967)

Rodríguez O., Jaime, *The Independence of Spanish America*, Cambridge University Press (Cambridge, 1998)
Rodríguez Plata, Horacio, *La antigua provincia del Socorro y la independencia*, Biblioteca de Historia Nacional, vol. 98 (Bogotá, 1963)
Rodríguez Villa, Antonio, *El Teniente General Don Pablo Morillo, Primer Conde de Cartagena, Marqués de la Puerta (1778–1837)*, 4 vols, Real Academia de Historia (Madrid, 1908–1910)
Rodríguez Villa, Antonio, *El Teniente General Don Pablo Morillo, Primer Conde de Cartagena, Marqués de la Puerta (1778–1837)*, 2 vols, Editorial América (Madrid, 1920)
Rudé, George, *Revolutionary Europe, 1783–1815*, Fontana Press (London, 1964)
Rydjord, John, 'British Mediation between Spain and her Colonies, 1811–1813', *HAHR*, vol. 21 (1941)
Sañudo, José Rafael, *Estudios sobre la vida de Bolívar*, Editorial Bedout (Medellín, 1980)
Sevilla, Rafael, *Memorias de un oficial del ejército español, campañas contra Bolívar y los separatistas de América*, Editorial América (Madrid, 1916)
Silva, Renan, *Prensa y revolución a finales del siglo XVIII. Contribución a un análisis de la formación de la ideología de independencia nacional*, Banco de la República (Bogotá, 1989)
Silvestre, Francisco, *Descripción del Reyno de Santa Fé de Bogotá*, Biblioteca Universitaria de Cultura Colombiana, Universidad Nacional de Colombia (1968)
Soto Arango, Diana, Puig-Samper, Miguel Angel, and Arboleda, Luis Carlos (eds), *La Ilustración en América Colonial*, Consejo Superior de Investigaciones Científicas (Paracuellos de Jarama, 1995)
Stoan, Stephen, *Pablo Morillo and Venezuela, 1815–1820*, Ohio State University Press (Columbus, 1974)
Taylor, William, *Drinking, Homicide and Rebellion in Colonial Mexican Villages*, Stanford University Press (Stanford, 1979)
Thomas, Hugh, *Cuba, or the Pursuit of Freedom*, Eyre and Spottiswoode (London, 1971)
Thompson, J.M. (ed.), *Napoleon's Letters*, Everyman's Library (London, 1964)
Torres Bautista, Mariano E., 'De la fiesta monárquica a la fiesta cívica: El tránsito del poder en Puebla, 1821–1822', *Historia Mexicana*, vol. 45:2 (1995)
Torres y Peña, José Antonio de, *Memorias sobre la revolución y sucesos de Santafé de Bogotá, en el transtorno de la Nueva Granada y Venezuela* (1814), reprinted in Hernández de Alba, Guillermo (ed.) *Memorias del Presbítero José Antonio de Torres y Peña*, Biblioteca de Historia Nacional, vol. 92, Editorial Kelly (Bogotá, 1960)
Tovar, Hermes, 'Guerras de opinión y represión en Colombia durante la independencia (1810–1820)', *Anuario Colombiano de Historia Social y de la Cultura*, no. 11 (1983)
Tovar, Hermes, 'La lenta ruptura con el pasado colonial (1810–1850)' in

Ocampo, José Antonio (ed.), *Historia económica de Colombia*, Siglo Veintiuno (Bogotá, 1987)

Twinam, Ann, *Miners, Merchants, and Farmers in Colonial Colombia*, University of Texas Press (Austin, 1982)

Ullrick, Laura, 'Morillo's Attempt to Pacify Venezuela', *HAHR*, vol. 3 (1920)

Uribe, Victor, 'Kill all the Lawyers!: Lawyers and the Independence Movement in New Granada, 1809–1820', *The Americas*, vol. 52:2 (1995)

Van Aken, Mark, *Pan-Hispanism: its Origin and Development to 1866*, University of California Press (Berkeley, 1959)

Van Aken, Mark J., *King of the Night. Juan José Flores and Ecuador, 1824–1864*, University of California Press (Berkeley, 1989)

Van Allen, Mark, 'The Lingering Death of the Indian Tribute in Ecuador', *HAHR*, vol. 61 (1981)

Van Young, Eric, 'Quetzalcóatl, King Ferdinand, and Ignacio Allende Go to the Seashore; or Messianism and Mystical Kingship in Mexico, 1800–1821', in Rodríguez O., Jaime (ed.), *The Independence of Mexico and the Creation of the New Nation*, University of New Mexico Press (Los Angeles, 1989)

Van Young, Eric, 'The Messiah and the Masked Man: Popular Ideology in Mexico, 1810–1821', in Kaplan, Steven (ed.), *Indigenous Responses to Western Christianity*, New York University Press (New York, 1995)

Vidales, Carlos, 'El agente diplomático sueco Severin Lorich y su misión en la Gran Colombia (1823)', Informes de Investigación, Instituto de Estudios Latinoamericanos (Stockholm, 1991)

Voltes, Pedro, *Fernando VII, vida y reinado*, Editorial Juventud (Barcelona, 1985)

Waddell, D.A.G., 'British Neutrality and Spanish-American Independence: the Problem of Foreign Enlistment', *JLAS*, vol. 19 (1987)

Waddell, D.A.G., 'Anglo-Spanish Relations and the "Pacification of America" during the "Constitutional triennium" 1820–1823', *Anuario de Estudios Americanos*, vol. 44 (1989)

Webster, C.K. (ed.), *Britain and the Independence of Latin America, 1812–1830*, 2 vols, Octagon Books (New York, 1970)

Woodward, Margaret, 'The Spanish Army and the Loss of America, 1810–1824', *HAHR*, vol. 48 (1968)

Zavala, Iris, *Masones, comuneros y carbonarios*, Siglo XXI (Madrid, 1971)

Zuluaga, Francisco *José María Obando: de soldado realista a caudillo republicano*, Biblioteca Banco Popular (Bogotá, 1985)

Zuluaga, Francisco, 'Clientelismo y guerrillas en el Valle del Patía, 1536–1811', in Germán Comenares *et al.*, *La independencia, ensayos de historia social*, Instituto Colombiano de Cultura, (Bogotá, 1986)

Index